MASTER THE CIVIL SERVICE EXAMS

5th Edition

Shannon R. Turlington

PETERSON'S
Publishing

About Peterson's Publishing

Peterson's Publishing provides the accurate, dependable, high-quality education content and guidance you need to succeed. No matter where you are on your academic or professional path, you can rely on Peterson's print and digital publications for the most up-to-date education exploration data, expert test-prep tools, and top-notch career success resources—everything you need to achieve your goals.

For more information, contact Peterson's Publishing, 3 Columbia Circle, Suite 205, Albany, NY 12203-5158; 800-338-3282 Ext. 54229; or find us online at www.petersonspublishing.com.

Certified Chain of Custody

60% Certified Fiber Sourcing and
40% Post-Consumer Recycled

www.sfiprogram.org

*This label applies to the text stock.

OUR PROMISE
SCORE HIGHER. GUARANTEED.

Peterson's Publishing, a Nelnet company, focuses on providing individuals and schools with the best test-prep products—books and electronic components that are complete, accurate, and up-to-date. In fact, we're so sure this book will help you improve your score on this test that we're guaranteeing you'll get a higher score. If you feel your score hasn't improved as a result of using this book, we'll refund the price you paid.

Guarantee Details:

If you don't think this book helped you get a higher score, just return the book with your original sales receipt for a full refund of the purchase price (excluding taxes or shipping costs or any other charges). Please underline the book price and title on the sales receipt. Be sure to include your name and mailing address. This offer is restricted to U.S. residents and to purchases made in U.S. dollars. All requests for refunds must be received by Peterson's within 120 days of the purchase date. Refunds are restricted to one book per person and one book per address.

Send to:
Peterson's Publishing, a Nelnet company
Customer Service
3 Columbia Circle, Suite 205
Albany, NY 12203-5158

This guarantee gives you the limited right to have your purchase price refunded only if you are not satisfied that this book has improved your ability to score higher on the applicable test. If you are not satisfied, your sole remedy is to return this book to us with your sales receipt (within 120 days) so that we may refund the amount you paid for the book. Your refund is limited to the manufacturer's suggested retail price listed on the back of the book. This offer is void where restricted or prohibited.

Contents

Contents

Before You Begin

Master the Civil Service Exams gives you a structured, step-by-step tutorial program that can help you master all the basics. It covers all the key points and gives you the practice you need to score high on your civil service exam.

WHO SHOULD USE THIS BOOK?

Master the Civil Service Exams is written for civil service candidates who want to prepare for their exam in the smartest way possible but whose study time is limited. This book is for you if you can answer yes to the following statements:

- You know that you'll get the most out of a structured, step-by-step tutorial program that takes the guesswork out of test preparation.

- You want to prepare on your own time and at your own pace, but you don't have time for a preparation program that takes weeks to complete.

- You want a guide that covers all the key points you need to know but doesn't waste time on topics you don't absolutely have to know for the exam.

- You want to avoid taking risks with this all-important exam by relying on "beat the system" guides that are long on promises but short on substance.

HOW THIS BOOK IS ORGANIZED

- **Part I** gives you a quick overview of important facts you need to know about the civil service job market and whether you must take an entry-level exam to qualify. You'll learn where to get job information; how to apply for federal, state, and municipal positions; and what to expect on a civil service exam. You'll also get some general test-taking tips that will help you score higher on test day.

- **Part II** offers a Diagnostic Test to help you identify your areas of strength and those areas where you will need to spend more time in your review sessions.

- **Part III** focuses on the concepts and strategies you'll need to know for the verbal sections of most civil service exams. You'll cover grammar and usage, spelling, synonyms, sentence completions, verbal analogies, and effective expression as they are assessed on civil service exams. You'll also learn the fundamentals of reading comprehension, judgment, observation and memory, and mechanical aptitude skills. At the end of each chapter, you'll apply what you learned to civil service–type practice exercises.

- **Part IV** teaches you the ins and outs of alphabetizing and filing, clerical speed and accuracy, and typing and stenography. Here, too, you'll find skill-building practice exercises.

- **Part V** focuses on the arithmetic covered on most civil service exams. You'll review fractions and decimals, percents, ratio and proportion, graphs and tables, and arithmetic reasoning in preparation for your test. You'll learn strategies for solving each question type, and you'll sharpen your skills by working through practice exercises.

- **Part VI** contains four full-length practice tests that are as close as you can get to the real thing. Take them under timed conditions and you'll experience just how it feels to take an actual civil service exam. Two of the practice tests give you a great opportunity to gauge your progress and focus your study in key areas, including English grammar and usage; spelling; synonyms; sentence completions; verbal analogies; reading comprehension; judgment, communication, and memory; and mechanical aptitude. Two additional practice tests will help you prepare for the Municipal Office Aide and Senior Office Typist exams. As you finish each exam, check your answers against the answer key and read the explanation for each question you missed. Actually, it's a good idea to read all the Answer Explanations.

- The **Appendixes** provide additional information that we hope will be helpful as your begin your search for a civil service job. In Appendix A, you'll find a listing of occupations available in the federal government—professional occupations and trade, craft, or labor occupations. Appendix B offers a sample of jobs typically available in state and municipal governments. If you are a veteran looking for a civil service job, you'll find essential information in Appendix C. Appendix D provides helpful details on government hiring of individuals with disabilities.

Once you have read and worked through this intensive, focused preparation program, you'll be more than ready to score high on your civil service exam, and you will be a more attractive applicant for the position you're seeking.

SPECIAL STUDY FEATURES

Master the Civil Service Exams is designed to be as user-friendly as it is complete. To this end, it includes several features to make your preparation more efficient.

Overview

Each chapter begins with a bulleted overview listing the topics covered in the chapter. This will allow you to quickly target the areas in which you are most interested.

Bonus Information

As you work your way through the book, check the margins to find bonus information and advice. You'll find the following kinds of information:

Note

Notes highlight need-to-know information about the civil service exams, whether it's details about applying for a position, how scores are tallied, or the structure of a question type.

Tip

Tips provide valuable strategies and insider information to help you score your best on the civil service exams.

Alert!

Alerts do just what they say—alert you to common pitfalls and misconceptions you might face or hear regarding the civil service exams.

YOU'RE WELL ON YOUR WAY TO SUCCESS

You've made the decision to work for the federal government or for your state or local government and have taken a very important step in that process. *Master the Civil Service Exams* will help you score high and prepare you for everything you'll need to know on the day of your exam and beyond it. Good luck!

GIVE US YOUR FEEDBACK

Peterson's publishes a full line of books— test prep, career preparation, education exploration, and financial aid. Peterson's publications can be found at high school guidance offices, college libraries and career centers, and your local bookstore and library. Peterson's books are now also available as eBooks.

We welcome any comments or suggestions you may have about this publication. Your feedback will help us make educational dreams possible for you—and others like you.

PART I

START WITH THE BASICS

Civil Service Jobs

OVERVIEW

- Federal employment
- State and local government employment
- Obtaining job information
- How to apply
- Summing it up

FEDERAL EMPLOYMENT

The federal government is the nation's largest employer. It employs more than 2.8 million civilian workers in the United States and an additional 100,000 civilian workers—one-half of whom are U.S. citizens—in U.S. territories and other countries. Government occupations other than military service represent nearly every kind of job in private employment, as well as some jobs unique to the federal government, including regulatory inspectors, foreign service officers, and Internal Revenue Service (IRS) agents. Many civilian federal employees are employed through the legislative branch (Congress, the General Accountability Office, the Government Printing Office, and the Library of Congress) and the judicial branch (the Supreme Court and the U.S. Court system). By far the greatest number of federal civilian employees work for the executive branch—over 2.7 million. The General Services Administration (GSA), an independent agency of the executive branch, oversees $500 billion in federal spending a year. It supplies federal purchasing agents with cost-effective products and services from suppliers as well as develops policies covering travel by federal employees and the management of government property. It's responsible for the construction of new federal buildings and greening older buildings.

Categories of Federal Jobs

Nearly every occupation in the private sector is also represented in the federal civil service. If you are seeking a career in government service, you will probably be able to put to use the skills you've already acquired. Here's a quick look at the major categories of federal positions:

- **Professional.** These positions require knowledge in a specialized field, usually acquired through college-level or postgraduate education. Among those filling these positions are engineers, accountants, attorneys, biologists, physicists, and chemists.

- **Administrative and managerial.** Employees in these positions are responsible for overseeing contracts with the private sector and purchasing goods and services for the government. Positions include contract specialists, budget analysts, purchasing officers, claims examiners, product control specialists, administrative assistants, personnel officers, and IRS officers.

- **Investigative and law enforcement.** Several government agencies employ police officers and investigators in positions ranging from guarding property and patrolling borders to involvement in highly technical intelligence operations. These agencies include the Department of Justice, the State Department, the Treasury Department, the U.S. Postal Service, the Customs Bureau, the Federal Bureau of Investigation (FBI), and the Department of Homeland Security.

- **Technical.** These positions typically employ workers involved in support work in nonroutine professional or administrative fields, such as computer technology and electronic technology.

- **Clerical.** This broad field includes hundreds of different positions: Nearly one-half of the jobs in federal civil service are clerical. Positions include secretaries, administrative assistants, court reporters, mail clerks, information clerks, and workers in computer and related occupations.

- **Labor and mechanical.** Most people do not realize that the U.S. government is the largest employer of mechanical and manual workers and laborers in the country. Positions include mobile equipment operators, mechanics, machine tool and metal workers, maintenance and repair workers, and food preparation and service workers.

- **Unskilled.** Thousands of positions in federal government service are open to people with few skills or with only a small amount of training. These include housekeeping aides, janitors, laundry workers, and mess attendants.

Pathways for Students and Recent Graduates to Federal Careers

The Pathways program was established under President Barack Obama to attract students and recent graduates to jobs in the Federal government. There are three aspects to the program as described by the following:

- **Internship program.** This program is designed to provide students enrolled in a wide variety of educational institutions, from high school to graduate level, with opportunities to work in agencies and explore federal government careers while still in school. Internships are paid work experience, either part-time or full-time. Each hiring agency primarily administers its own Internship Program. Positions are related to the intern's academic career goals or field of study. The website usajobs.com provides information on specific internship openings.

- **Recent graduates program.** This program affords developmental experiences in the federal government to promote possible careers in the civil service for recent graduates with associate, bachelor's, master's, professional, doctoral, vocational, or technical degrees or certificates. The program is primarily administered by the hiring agency. The program is one year in length and includes a minimum of 40 hours of formal, interactive training. Information about openings is available at usajobs.com.

- **The Presidential Management Fellows Program.** This two-year leadership program provides entry-level positions for candidates with masters or professional degrees. The goal is to develop a cadre of potential federal government leaders. Finalists are selected based on an evaluation of candidates' experience and accomplishments and a rigorous assessment process. OPM directs the process and works with agencies wishing to hire fellows. For information, check the Presidential Management Fellows Program in the Office of Personnel Management (OPM) at pmf.gov.

Candidates who successfully complete their program may be eligible for conversion to a permanent federal government position.

To assist potential candidates for the Pathways program, the Office of Personnel Management hosts www.usajobs.gov/StudentJobs. The site lists Federal jobs by college major along with an index of Federal agencies. Each entry in the index describes the work of the agency and provides contact information for job seekers. Job openings are posted on the www.usajobs.gov website as they become available.

Summer Jobs and Volunteering for the Federal Government

Limited summer, or seasonal, employment is available throughout the federal government. Most jobs are in metropolitan areas, although jobs may also be available in National Parks and at National Historic Sites or similar locations that have high numbers of seasonal visitors. Applications are accepted typically from December through April 15, and the jobs tend to run from mid-May through September 30. You can find information on summer jobs at www.usajobs.com.

Unpaid volunteer assignments are another avenue for gaining work experience in the Federal government. The departments that typically have accepted the largest number of student volunteers have been the Departments of Defense, Commerce, Health and Human Services, Interior, Justice, State, Treasury, and Veterans Affairs. These volunteer assignments offer training opportunities to high school and college students that are separate from the Internship Program, which pays students.

The volunteer opportunities should be related to a student's academic program so that the student can explore career options while developing personal and professional skills. Assignments typically last for three to four months and are performed during the school year and/or during summer or school vacations. Check your telephone directory blue pages under "U.S. Government" for the phone number of the Federal agency that you're interested in volunteering for and ask for the Human Resources person. You can also visit your school's guidance, career counseling, placement, or internship office for additional information.

NOTE: Other than student volunteers, the Federal law prohibits Federal departments from accepting volunteers. There are a few exceptions such as emergency situations, assistance to employees with disabilities, and the use of unpaid experts and consultants. The National Park Service and the Forest Service also have some volunteer opportunities. If you're interested in volunteering for a specific agency and are not a student, contact the Federal agency directly.

Job Arrangements

Flex-time, telecommuting, job sharing, and nontraditional configurations of the workday and work week such as four 10-hour days per week are options for some positions in the federal government. Arrangements such as these must be worked out at the time of hiring.

Part-time positions from 16 to 32 hours a week are also available throughout the federal government. Check www.usajobs.com for information on open part-time positions by region and/or agency.

Qualifications and Requirements

Jobs in the federal government appear in the General Schedule (GS), which assigns grades to jobs according to the difficulty of duties and responsibilities and the knowledge, experience, and skills required. Selection requirements are based on studies of the training, experience, and skills required for successful job performance at different grade levels.

Job applicants must meet the education and/or experience requirements, show evidence of having the required skills, and pass a job-related written test. Generally, a high school diploma or previous job experience is all you need to qualify for a job at the entry-level grade. As you gain experience, you become eligible for promotion to higher-level, more specialized jobs. You can also enter the federal government at higher grade levels if you already have the appropriate specialized experience or additional education required.

For most positions, you must have either six months or one year of experience at a comparable level to that of the next-lower grade level to qualify for experience for any grade higher than the entry level. For some positions at GS-11 and lower, you must have obtained experience at two levels below that of the job. Each job announcement provides specific information about the level of experience you need to qualify for the position.

The following educational and experience requirements are typical for various categories of civil service positions:

- **Professional.** Require highly specialized knowledge. Typically, you must have a bachelor's degree or higher in a specific field.

- **Administrative and managerial.** Usually do not require specialized knowledge. A bachelor's degree and/or responsible job experience, however, is required. In general, you must begin at the trainee level and learn the duties of the job after being hired.

- **Investigative and law enforcement.** Requirements vary greatly depending on the job. In general, these positions require a bachelor's degree, specialized training, good physical condition, and/or previous relevant experience.

- **Technical and clerical.** Entry-level positions in these fields usually require a high school diploma or equivalent, although junior college or technical school training may enable you to enter a field at a higher level. No additional experience or training may be necessary.

- **Labor and mechanical.** These positions, particularly those requiring a skilled trade, often require relevant experience. Apprenticeships for those with no previous training, however, may be available for some positions.

- **Unskilled.** Many positions require little or no prior training or experience. These positions include that of janitor, maintenance worker, and messenger.

Age

In addition to education, experience, and skill requirements, you must meet general age and physical requirements for joining the civil service. The government sets no maximum age limit for federal employment. The usual minimum age is 18, but high school graduates as young as 16 may apply for many jobs. If you are younger than 18 and you are out of school, but are not a high school graduate, you may be hired only if you have successfully completed a formal vocational training program or school authorities have signed a form approving your preference for work instead of additional schooling. The agency that wants to hire you will provide the form. Also, if you are at least 16 years of age and are in high school, you may work during school vacations or during the year on a formal student employment program.

Physical Requirements

You must be physically able to perform the duties of the position in which you're interested, and you must be emotionally and mentally stable. This does not mean that a physical disability will disqualify you, as long as you can perform the work efficiently and without posing a hazard to yourself or others. Of course, there are some positions—such as border patrol agent, firefighter, and criminal investigator—that can be filled only by applicants who are in top-notch physical condition. Whenever this is the case, the physical requirements are described in detail in the job announcement.

The federal government is the world's largest employer of the physically disabled and has a strong program aimed at employing those who are disabled. If you have a physical disability, contact the Selective Placement Coordinator at the agency in which you're interested for special placement assistance. State the nature of your disability on your application, so that special testing arrangements can be made to accommodate your needs.

TIP

Some positions, particularly those in law enforcement and firefighting, have specific age limits, generally between 34 and 37 years of age, because of the nature of the work. Be sure to check job announcements carefully before applying.

Working Conditions and Benefits

More than one-half of federal civilian employees are paid according to the General Schedule (GS), a pay scale for those in professional, administrative, technical, and clerical jobs and for workers such as guards and messengers. Salaries under the GS are set to correspond to pay levels in similar occupations in the private sector. GS pay rates are uniform throughout most of the country, although they are adjusted upward in areas with very high cost-of-living indexes, such as New York City, Los Angeles, and San Francisco. In areas with low cost-of-living indexes, GS pay scale amounts may exceed those of most private-sector workers.

High school graduates with no related work experience usually begin in GS-2 jobs, but some who have special skills begin at grade GS-3. Graduates of two-year colleges and technical schools typically begin at the GS-4 level. Professional and administrative employees with bachelor's degrees can enter at grades GS-5 or GS-7, depending on experience and academic record, and those with a master's degree or Ph.D. or equivalent experience may enter at the GS-9 or GS-11 level.

Advancement to a higher pay grade generally depends on one's level of ability and work performance, as well as on the availability of jobs at higher-grade levels. Most agencies fill vacancies by promoting their own employees whenever possible. Promotions are based on increases in responsibility and the demonstration of increased experience and skill.

It's not always necessary to move to a new job to advance in pay grade. Sometimes an employee's work assignments change a great deal in the ordinary course of business—in other words, the job "grows," or expands, in responsibility. When that happens, a position classifier determines whether the position should be reclassified to a higher grade because of increased difficulty or responsibility.

Most employees receive within-grade pay increases at one-, two-, or three-year intervals if their work is acceptable or better. However, in poor economic times, the government—federal, state, and local—may declare a pay freeze, ending pay increases for a period of time. (Some managers and supervisors receive increases based on job performance rather than on time in a specific grade.) Within-grade increases may also be awarded to recognize high-quality service.

Federal jobs offer many benefits in addition to pay, including health and life insurance, retirement benefits, and holidays.

SALARY TABLE 2012-GS
RATES FROZEN AT 2010 LEVELS

EFFECTIVE JANUARY 2012

Annual Rates by Grade and Step

Grade	Step 1	Step 2	Step 3	Step 4	Step 5	Step 6	Step 7	Step 8	Step 9	Step 10	WITHIN GRADE AMOUNTS
1	$ 17,803	$ 18,398	$ 18,990	$ 19,579	$ 20,171	$ 20,519	$ 21,104	$ 21,694	$ 21,717	$ 22,269	VARIES
2	20,017	20,493	21,155	21,717	21,961	22,607	23,253	23,899	24,545	25,191	VARIES
3	21,840	22,568	23,296	24,024	24,752	25,480	26,208	26,936	27,664	28,392	728
4	24,518	25,335	26,152	26,959	27,786	28,603	29,420	30,237	31,054	31,871	817
5	27,431	28,345	29,259	30,173	31,087	32,001	32,915	33,829	34,743	35,657	914
6	30,577	31,596	32,615	33,634	34,653	35,672	36,691	37,710	38,729	39,748	1019
7	33,979	35,112	36,245	37,378	38,511	39,644	40,777	41,910	43,043	44,176	1133
8	37,631	38,885	40,139	41,393	42,647	43,901	45,155	46,409	47,663	48,917	1254
9	41,563	42,948	44,333	45,718	47,103	48,488	49,873	51,258	52,643	54,028	1385
10	45,771	47,297	48,823	50,349	51,875	53,401	54,927	56,453	57,979	59,505	1526
11	50,287	51,963	53,639	55,315	56,991	58,667	60,343	62,019	63,695	65,371	1676
12	60,274	62,283	64,292	66,301	68,310	70,319	72,328	74,337	76,346	78,355	2009
13	71,674	74,063	76,452	78,841	81,230	83,619	86,008	88,397	90,786	93,175	2389
14	84,697	87,520	90,343	93,156	95,989	98,812	101,635	104,458	107,281	110,104	2823
15	99,628	102,949	106,270	109,591	112,912	116,233	119,554	122,875	126,196	129,517	3321

SALARY TABLE 2012-GS
RATES FROZEN AT 2010 LEVELS

EFFECTIVE JANUARY 2012

Hourly Basic (B) Rates by Grade and Step
Hourly Overtime (O) Rates by Grade and Step

Grade	B/O	Step 1	Step 2	Step 3	Step 4	Step 5	Step 6	Step 7	Step 8	Step 9	Step 10
1	B	$ 8.53	$ 8.82	$ 9.10	$ 9.38	$ 9.67	$ 9.83	$ 10.11	$ 10.39	$ 10.41	$ 10.67
	O	12.80	13.23	13.65	14.07	14.51	14.75	15.17	15.59	15.62	16.01
2	B	9.59	9.82	10.14	10.41	10.52	10.83	11.14	11.45	11.76	12.07
	O	14.39	14.73	15.21	15.62	15.78	16.25	16.71	17.18	17.64	18.11
3	B	10.46	10.81	11.16	11.51	11.86	12.21	12.56	12.91	13.26	13.60
	O	15.69	16.22	16.74	17.27	17.79	18.32	18.84	19.37	19.89	20.40
4	B	11.75	12.14	12.53	12.92	13.31	13.71	14.10	14.49	14.88	15.27
	O	17.63	18.21	18.80	19.38	19.97	20.57	21.15	21.74	22.32	22.91
5	B	13.14	13.58	14.02	14.46	14.90	15.33	15.77	16.21	16.65	17.09
	O	19.71	20.37	21.03	21.69	22.35	23.00	23.66	24.32	24.98	25.64
6	B	14.65	15.14	15.63	16.12	16.60	17.09	17.58	18.07	18.56	19.05
	O	21.98	22.71	23.45	24.18	24.90	25.64	26.37	27.11	27.84	28.58
7	B	16.28	16.82	17.37	17.91	18.45	19.00	19.54	20.08	20.62	21.17
	O	24.42	25.23	26.06	26.87	27.68	28.50	29.31	30.12	30.93	31.76
8	B	18.03	18.63	19.23	19.83	20.43	21.04	21.64	22.24	22.84	23.44
	O	27.05	27.95	28.85	29.75	30.65	31.56	32.46	32.90	32.90	32.90
9	B	19.92	20.58	21.24	21.91	22.57	23.23	23.90	24.56	25.22	25.89
	O	29.88	30.87	31.86	32.87	32.90	32.90	32.90	32.90	32.90	32.90
10	B	21.93	22.66	23.39	24.13	24.86	25.59	26.32	27.05	27.78	28.51
	O	32.90	32.90	32.90	32.90	32.90	32.90	32.90	32.90	32.90	32.90
11	B	24.10	24.90	25.70	26.50	27.31	28.11	28.91	29.72	30.52	31.32
	O	32.90	32.90	32.90	32.90	32.90	32.90	32.90	32.90	32.90	32.90
12	B	28.88	29.84	30.81	31.77	32.73	33.69	34.66	35.62	36.58	37.54
	O	32.90	32.90	32.90	32.90	32.90	33.69	34.66	35.62	36.58	37.54
13	B	34.34	35.49	36.63	37.78	38.92	40.07	41.21	42.36	43.50	44.65
	O	34.34	35.49	36.63	37.78	38.92	40.07	41.21	42.36	43.50	44.65
14	B	40.58	41.94	43.29	44.64	45.99	47.35	48.70	50.05	51.40	52.76
	O	40.58	41.94	43.29	44.64	45.99	47.35	48.70	50.05	51.40	52.76
15	B	47.74	49.33	50.92	52.51	54.10	55.69	57.29	58.88	60.47	62.06
	O	47.74	49.33	50.92	52.51	54.10	55.69	57.29	58.88	60.47	62.06

Work Hours

The usual government work week is 40 hours. Most government employees work 8 hours per day, Monday through Friday. In some cases, the nature of the work may call for a different work week, and as in many other businesses, employees sometimes have to work overtime. If you are required to work overtime, you will either be paid for the extra time or given time off as compensation.

Training

Training for increased responsibility in a government position is often provided on the job, and employees are encouraged to continue their own training and education. You may participate in individual career development programs and receive job-related training in your own agency, in other agencies, or outside the government (in industrial plants and universities, for example). In addition, the government sponsors formal training courses and may pay for outside training that is directly related to improving job performance.

Benefits

Employees are regularly rated on job performance. In most agencies, the ratings are "outstanding," "satisfactory," and "unsatisfactory." Employees with "outstanding" ratings receive extra credit toward retention in case of layoffs. An employee whose rating is "unsatisfactory" may be dismissed or assigned to another position.

INCENTIVE AWARDS

Government agencies encourage employees to suggest better, simpler, or more economical ways to perform their work. A suggestion or invention that results in savings or improved service may result in a cash award for you, or you may be rewarded for outstanding job performance or other acts deserving recognition.

VACATION AND SICK LEAVE

Most federal employees earn annual leave for vacation and other purposes according to the number of years they've been in the federal service. Vacation benefits begin at thirteen working days a year for most new full-time employees and increase with length of employment. Most full-time employees also earn thirteen days of sick leave with pay each year, regardless of length of service.

INJURY COMPENSATION

The government provides generous compensation benefits, including medical care, for employees who suffer injuries in the performance of their official duties. Death benefits are provided to survivors should such injuries result in death.

GROUP LIFE INSURANCE

As a federal employee, you receive low-cost basic term life insurance and also accidental death and dismemberment. The government pays part of the premium, and the employee pays the rest. Employees may also upgrade to an optional policy with better benefits.

HEALTH CARE

The government sponsors a voluntary health insurance program for federal employees. The program offers a variety of plans to meet individual needs, including basic coverage and major medical protection against costly illnesses. The government contributes part of the premium and the employee pays the balance through payroll deductions.

RETIREMENT PROGRAM

Under the Federal Employees Retirement System (FERS), federal employees are covered under a combined Social Security and supplemental retirement program of Basic Benefits and a Thrift Savings Plan. The Social Security system is the same one that most U.S. workers contribute to. Federal employees also contribute to a Basic Benefits Plan, which is an annuity. The Thrift Savings Plan is similar to a 401(k) plan that workers on their own or through their employer may contribute to. The federal government matches employee contributions up to a certain percentage, set by law. The earnings grow tax-free.

PAID HOLIDAYS

Government workers are entitled to the following ten regular paid holidays each year:

1. New Year's Day (January 1)
2. Martin Luther King, Jr.'s Birthday (third Monday in January)
3. Presidents' Day (third Monday in February)
4. Memorial Day (last Monday in May)
5. Independence Day (July 4)
6. Labor Day (first Monday in September)
7. Columbus Day (second Monday in October)
8. Veterans Day (November 11)
9. Thanksgiving Day (fourth Thursday in November)
10. Christmas Day (December 25)

STATE AND LOCAL GOVERNMENT EMPLOYMENT

State and local governments provide a large and expanding source of job opportunities in a variety of fields. More than 19 million people work for state and local agencies throughout the United States; about three-fourths of these employees work in local government, such as county, municipality, town, and school district governments.

As with federal employment, nearly every kind of job available in the private sector is also available in state and local employment. However, some positions are unique to state and local government, including the following:

- **Public education.** Educational services comprise the majority of jobs in state and local government—10.9 million. School systems, colleges, and universities employ not only teachers but also administrative personnel, librarians, guidance counselors, nurses, dieticians, clerks, and maintenance workers.

- **Health services.** Over 1.5 million people are employed in health and hospital work, including physicians, nurses, medical laboratory technicians, and hospital attendants.

- **Highway work.** More than 500,000 people work in highway construction and maintenance. Positions include civil engineers, surveyors, equipment operators, truck drivers, concrete finishers, carpenters, and construction workers.

- **Governmental control and finance.** These positions account for about 1.3 million employees, including those in the justice system, tax enforcement, and general administration. Specific positions include city managers, property assessors, and budget analysts, as well as clerks and database managers.

- **Law enforcement and firefighting.** More than 1.7 million people work in law enforcement. This includes not only police officers and detectives, but also administrative, clerical, and custodial workers. Local governments employ 383,000 non-volunteer firefighters, many of whom work part-time.

You can find other state and local government work in these fields:

- Corrections
- Housing and urban renewal
- Libraries
- Local utilities
- Natural resources
- Parks and recreation
- Public transportation
- Public welfare
- Sanitation
- Sewage disposal

These types of positions require people with diverse experiences, such as economists, electrical engineers, electricians, pipe fitters, clerks, foresters, and bus drivers.

State and local government job requirements, salary scales, and benefits vary from state to state and from one municipality to another, but in general they're comparable to those of federal government employment. As with federal jobs, applicants must meet certain educational and/or experience requirements, show evidence of having the required skills, and pass a job-related written test.

The official employment website of the U.S. federal government is USAJOBS: www.usajobs.gov.

OBTAINING JOB INFORMATION

When government agencies need to fill positions, they publish job announcements or examination announcements (see Figure 1.1). Such an announcement lists nearly all you need to know about the job, including work requirements, salary, duties, and location. It also tells you when and where to file for the exam, which application forms you must complete, and where you can find the forms.

Most job announcements also provide a deadline for filing your application. No application mailed past the deadline date is considered. If you are required to apply online, you are no longer able to do so once the deadline has passed. If the top of the first page of the announcement says "No Closing Date," this means that no deadline has been set and that applications are accepted until all open positions are filled.

Study the job announcement carefully. It will answer many of your questions and help you decide whether you want the position and are qualified for it. The precise duties of the position are outlined in detail, usually under the heading "Description of Work." Before you apply, make sure that your experience and ability match the range of duties listed, and that you meet all the educational, experience, and special requirements.

The job announcement also describes the type of test, if any, you will need to take to be considered for the position—so pay close attention to this section of the announcement. It tells you what areas are covered in the written test and lists the specific subjects on which questions will be asked. Sometimes an announcement will also provide sample questions or describe the method of rating the exam. This is invaluable information when you're preparing to take the exam. In some cases, you will not be required to take an exam; instead, you'll be considered based on your education, experience, and achievements. You may need to answer questions about yourself, however. They may be in the form of what is known as a KSA essay for knowledge, skills, and abilities, or they may be a series of assessment questions that ask about your experience, skills, and abilities. Both measure how well you fit the requirements of the job you're applying for.

FIGURE 1.1

Problem Solver Maryland.gov Online Services State Agencies Phone Directory

Search 🔍

Home > Job Seekers > Maryland State Job Openings

Powered by JobAps.

ADMINISTRATOR II

Recruitment #13-002587-003

DATE OPENED	1/23/2013 6:00:00 AM
FILING DEADLINE	2/7/2013 11:59:00 PM
SALARY	$44,600.00 - $71,399.00/year
EMPLOYMENT TYPE	Full-Time
HR ANALYST	Jane Smith
WORK LOCATION	Baltimore County

Introduction

This is a position specific recruitment for an Administrator II. This recruitment will be used to fill current and future vacancies for this position/function only. The resulting eligible list will be maintained for one year. Persons interested in future vacancies within this classification must re-apply.

GRADE

17

LOCATION OF POSITION

Maryland Emergency Management Agency

Camp Fretterd Military Reservation

5401 Rue Saint Lo Drive

Reisterstown, MD 21136

Main Purpose of Job

Support the implementation and execution of the Maryland Emergency Management Agency, Active Learning and Exercising Branch Strategic Plan. Develop, implement and execute the State Training and Exercise Plan (TEP). Throughout the State, support the design, development, conduct, evaluation, after action reporting, improvement planning, and corrective action process of all-hazard, HSEEP-guided exercises. Throughout, lead the identification of training needs, and address identified training needs through the delivery of training. Support the development of event and incident after action reports/improvement plans and lead the corrective action process.

MINIMUM EDUCATION OR GENERAL REQUIREMENTS

Education: A Bachelor's degree from an accredited college or university.

2. Additional graduate level education at an accredited college or university may be substituted at the rate of 30 semester credit hours on a year to year basis for the required general experience.

SELECTIVE QUALIFICATIONS

Two (2) years of experience leading and supporting the delivery of Emergency Management and Homeland Security related training and Homeland Security Exercise and Evaluation Program (HSEEP)-guided exercises

LICENSES, REGISTRATIONS AND CERTIFICATIONS

Employees in this classification may be assigned duties which require the operation of a motor vehicle. Employees assigned such duties will be required to possess a motor vehicle operator's license valid in the State of Maryland.

SELECTION PROCESS

Please make sure that you provide sufficient information on your application (and on separate pages, if necessary) to show that you meet the qualifications for this recruitment. All information concerning your qualifications must be submitted by the closing date. We will not consider information submitted after this date. Successful candidates will be ranked as Best Qualified, Better Qualified, or Qualified and placed on the employment (eligible) list for at least one year.

EXAMINATION PROCESS

Your application is part of the examination process. The examination will consist of a rating of your education, training and experience related to the requirements of this position. The rating will be based on the information provided on your State application. Therefore, it is important that you provide all the experience and education that is related to this position completely and accurately.

FURTHER INSTRUCTIONS

If you **_cannot_** apply online, then you must complete a blank Maryland Application for State Employment by clicking on "Apply via paper application." Please annotate the position title and job number on the top of the application. All questions must be answered **completely** on the application. Resumes will not be considered.

Upon completion, please mail your application to:

Maryland Emergency Management Agency

Camp Fretterd Military Reservation

5401 Rue Saint Lo Drive

Reisterstown, MD 21136

ATTN: HUMAN RESOURCES

TTY Users: call via Maryland Relay

As an equal opportunity employer Maryland is committed to recruiting, retaining and promoting employees who are reflective of the State's diversity.

Click on a link below to apply for this position:

Fill out the Application NOW using the Internet.	Apply Online
Apply via Paper Application.	You may also download and complete the Paper Application here.

Follow us on:

Contact the Office | Accessibility | Privacy Notice

Toll Free: 877.634.6361

Learning About Federal Jobs

Federal government job openings across most parts of the federal government and in all areas of the country are listed on www.usajobs.gov. The USAJOBS website is operated by the Office of Personnel Management (OPM) and lists thousands of vacancies for federal positions. As many as 20,000 job openings may be posted on the site at any one time. However, some agencies post jobs only on their own websites. If you're looking for a job at a specific agency, do a search of their employment sections and employment information pages. Jobs in the federal judiciary, for example, are not listed on www.usajobs.gov.

USAJOBS is the portal for applying for most federal jobs. You can register and create an account where you can develop multiple versions of your resume to suit different job descriptions, set up job search agents, and upload and save documents such as transcripts. Once you have an account, you can begin your search for job openings that fit your career goals. You can fill out all the forms and answer all the questions required to apply for a job as well as submit them and your supporting documents online for most jobs. However, some agencies will accept applications by mail or fax. You need to read the job announcement carefully to see what the agency will accept.

Applying online or by mail or fax may seem very impersonal, but if you have questions, job announcements generally contain the name and contact information for the hiring representative in the agency posting the job.

If you do not have a computer, you can find information about federal jobs at your state's American Job Centers/One-Stop Career Centers or by using the computers at your local public library. Area newspapers may also list available federal jobs in their classified job sections either in print or online. College and university placement offices and professional contacts can also be good sources of information.

Learning About State and Municipal Jobs

State and municipal governments make job opportunities known in various ways. Check the following places for job announcements:

- **American Jobs Centers.** The American Job Centers, formerly called One-Stop Career Centers, are administered by the state where they are located, with the financial assistance of the federal government. Almost 2,000 of them are scattered throughout the country. You'll find the address of the one nearest you in your local telephone directory, or online at www.servicelocator.org/onestopcenter.asp.

- **State Civil Service Commission** (located in your state's capital city).

- **Civil Service Commission.** Some cities—particularly large ones—have Civil Service Commissions, which sometimes go by another name such as the Department of Personnel. You should be able to find the address and phone number in your local telephone directory under "City Departments."

TIP

The Office of Personnel Management Web site (http://www.opm.gov) also offers valuable information for job seekers including links to information on veterans preference points, government diversity and inclusion policies, training and development programs, and similar information on policies and programs for federal government employees.

- **City and statewide publications** devoted to civil service employees. These publications, such as the *Chief-Leader* (for New York City), often list many job openings. Local newspapers may also run a regular section on regional civil service news.

- **School boards and boards of education.** These groups employ the greatest proportions of state and local personnel. Ask directly for information about job openings. In addition to teachers and teachers' aides, school districts employ media center directors, maintenance people, and bus drivers.

- **City and state municipal buildings.** These offices usually post job openings available in your municipality. You can also check to see whether your local township has a website where job opportunities are posted.

- **Local libraries.** Check bulletin boards and other areas of public posting at your local library to see whether government jobs are listed.

- **Local college or university placement offices.** These departments can provide a wealth of information on civil service jobs.

If you have Internet access, visit your state's official website. Many include announcements of job openings in state government, and some enable you to apply electronically. In addition, some state sites also connect to county or city sites within the state. You should easily be able to locate your state's website via a search engine such as www.google.com.

HOW TO APPLY

The job announcement specifies which application form you should use and where to get it. Civil service application forms differ little from state to state or from one locality to another. The questions, which have been formulated through years of experimentation, are simple and direct and designed to elicit as much relevant information as possible. Many applications are now submitted online.

Applying for a Federal Job

The process of applying for a federal job is straightforward, but it will take time. The first step is to go online to www.usajobs.com and create an account. This is the key to your application process. When you click on the "Create an Account" page, you will see a list of activities that you will be able to do once you have created your account:

- Build and store up to five different resumes

- Save and automate job searches

- Save and apply for jobs

- Search by Agency, Occupation, and Location for job openings

- Find special hiring programs

- Discover the jobs in high demand

TIP

Some resume-writing tips include the following: Don't be vague; be descriptive, but succinct. Don't be fancy; use plain English.

To create your account, you will need to enter basic information about yourself such as name, address, contact number, social security number, and e-mail. You may then create a resume or upload one that you already have. You can also come back to your account and create up to four more resumes that you tailor to specific jobs.

Once you have your account and resume, you can start your job search by going back to the USAJOBS home page and searching by keywords; job title; agency; skills; control number, if have one; or by location. You will then be sent to a listing of jobs that you can scroll through. A search for any federal jobs in Philadelphia, Pennsylvania located 141 results across a variety of departments and agencies and grades. The listing provides a way to refine results by agency, grade, salary, work schedule, work type, and posting date.

Once you find a job you're interested in, click on the job title and the full job posting will appear. The posting describes the following:

- Salary range

- Open period (the length of the posting)

- Series and grade (in the civil service system)

- Position information (basic information such as full-time or part-time)

- Promotion potential

- Duty locations (cities where this type of job is open if the job announcement is not for a specific position at a specific location)

- Who may apply (note that almost all jobs are open only to U.S. citizens)

- Job summary: Description of the job

- Key requirements

- Duties

- Qualifications required

- How you will be evaluated

- Benefits

- Other information

- Instructions on how to apply

- Required documents

- Agency contact information

- What to expect next

Once you find a job that interests you, carefully review the "Qualifications and Evaluations" to ensure that you are qualified for the job. The evaluation section also lists what your application must include. The first item is your resume, which should include detailed information to support your qualifications for the specific job. That's why you can create or upload up to five different resumes. One general resume won't necessarily highlight the experience, skills, and abilities required for a specific job.

Today, most government jobs require some form of self-assessment as part of the application. This is the second part of your application. You will be able to preview these assessment or occupational questions, which are specific to the job for which you are applying, in the evaluation section before beginning any applications. This saves you from applying for jobs that don't really match your experience, skills, and abilities.

The documentation listed under Required Documents make up the third part of your application. Depending on the job announcement, you may need to include a cover letter, or it may be optional.

Sample Assessment Questionnaire

The following is a sample assessment questionnaire for a job as a clerical employee. As you can see the questions are meant to measure a prospective employee's experience, skill, and abilities.

NOTE

The hiring agency may provide links on its site to pages offering tips on preparing resumes or writing a cover letter. Be sure to read the information, which can help you better tailor your answers to the agency's needs.

GRADE: 05

GS-5 Choose one answer that best describes your education and experience as described in the vacancy announcement.

1. I possess at least one year of specialized experience equivalent to at least the GS-4 level in the Federal service as described in the vacancy announcement.
2. I have successfully completed four full years of education above high school level.
3. I possess a combination of post-high school education and specialized experience.
4. I do not meet any of the requirements as described.

GRADE: 06

GS-6 Choose one answer that best describes your education and experience as described in the vacancy announcement.

1. I possess at least one year of specialized experience equivalent to at least the GS-5 level in the Federal service as described in the vacancy announcement.
2. I possess ½ year of appropriate graduate level education (9 semester hours of 13.5 quarter hours or equivalent) in a field of study directly related to the work of this position.
3. I possess a combination of appropriate specialized experience and graduate level education.
4. I do not meet any of the requirements as described.

GRADE: ALL GRADES

Please be aware that this vacancy announcement is only open to United States Citizens.

1. Are you a United States Citizen? ___ Yes ___ No

2. I certify, to the best of my knowledge that all the information in my application is true, and that I have truthfully and accurately represented my work experience, knowledge, skills, abilities and education. I understand that providing false or fraudulent information may be grounds for not hiring me or for firing me after I begin work. I also certify that I have read the entire vacancy announcement; that I have reviewed my answers to the eligibility questions for accuracy; and that I understand what supporting documentation, if any, is required for submission and when it's due. ___ Yes ___ No

3. Do you possess a typing skill of at least 40 wpm? ___ Yes ___ No

4. From the choices below, please select the software application(s) that you are proficient in (proficient means you understand and utilize a major part of the system's functionality/capabilities). (Select all that apply)

    ___ Microsoft Word

    ___ Other word processing software such as WordPerfect, WordPro, etc

    ___ Microsoft Power Point

    ___ Other presentation software such as CorelDraw, Freelance Graphic, etc

    ___ E-mail (i.e. Lotus Notes, GroupWise, Microsoft Outlook, etc.)

    ___ Microsoft Access

    ___ Microsoft Excel

    ___ Other data management/spreadsheet software such as Lotus 1-2-3, Lotus Approach, Peachtree, etc

    ___ Other Applications including Government systems and commercial off-the-shelf (COTS) systems

    ___ None of the above.

5. Describe your level of skill/experience with Microsoft Word.

    ___ I am a beginner and am learning to use this software now.

    ___ I have used standard formatting features in Microsoft Word including headers/footers/styles/page numbers and symbols.

    ___ In addition to skills listed in #2, I have developed and formatted complex documents with multiple columns, chapters, and/or sections with different formats.

    ___ In addition to skills listed in #2 and #3, I have created and edited documents containing references with footnotes, bibliography or indexes.

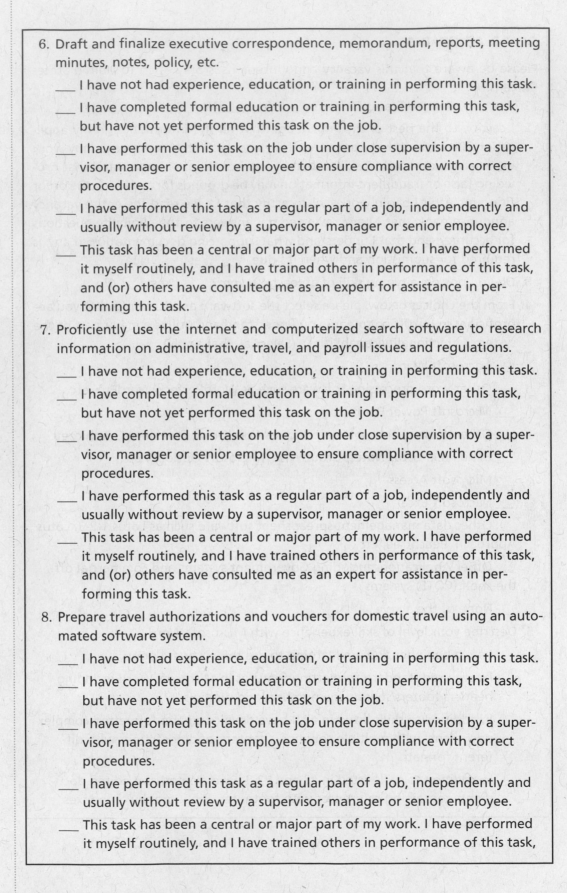

6. Draft and finalize executive correspondence, memorandum, reports, meeting minutes, notes, policy, etc.

___ I have not had experience, education, or training in performing this task.

___ I have completed formal education or training in performing this task, but have not yet performed this task on the job.

___ I have performed this task on the job under close supervision by a supervisor, manager or senior employee to ensure compliance with correct procedures.

___ I have performed this task as a regular part of a job, independently and usually without review by a supervisor, manager or senior employee.

___ This task has been a central or major part of my work. I have performed it myself routinely, and I have trained others in performance of this task, and (or) others have consulted me as an expert for assistance in performing this task.

7. Proficiently use the internet and computerized search software to research information on administrative, travel, and payroll issues and regulations.

___ I have not had experience, education, or training in performing this task.

___ I have completed formal education or training in performing this task, but have not yet performed this task on the job.

___ I have performed this task on the job under close supervision by a supervisor, manager or senior employee to ensure compliance with correct procedures.

___ I have performed this task as a regular part of a job, independently and usually without review by a supervisor, manager or senior employee.

___ This task has been a central or major part of my work. I have performed it myself routinely, and I have trained others in performance of this task, and (or) others have consulted me as an expert for assistance in performing this task.

8. Prepare travel authorizations and vouchers for domestic travel using an automated software system.

___ I have not had experience, education, or training in performing this task.

___ I have completed formal education or training in performing this task, but have not yet performed this task on the job.

___ I have performed this task on the job under close supervision by a supervisor, manager or senior employee to ensure compliance with correct procedures.

___ I have performed this task as a regular part of a job, independently and usually without review by a supervisor, manager or senior employee.

___ This task has been a central or major part of my work. I have performed it myself routinely, and I have trained others in performance of this task, and (or) others have consulted me as an expert for assistance in performing this task.

9. Prepare requisitions for the procurement of basic services and supplies, ensuring necessary justification and approvals are obtained.

___ I have not had experience, education, or training in performing this task.

___ I have completed formal education or training in performing this task, but have not yet performed this task on the job.

___ I have performed this task on the job under close supervision by a supervisor, manager or senior employee to ensure compliance with correct procedures.

___ I have performed this task as a regular part of a job, independently and usually without review by a supervisor, manager or senior employee.

___ This task has been a central or major part of my work. I have performed it myself routinely, and I have trained others in performance of this task, and (or) others have consulted me as an expert for assistance in performing this task.

10. Process and maintain property management records.

___ I have not had experience, education, or training in performing this task.

___ I have completed formal education or training in performing this task, but have not yet performed this task on the job.

___ I have performed this task on the job under close supervision by a supervisor, manager or senior employee to ensure compliance with correct procedures.

___ I have performed this task as a regular part of a job, independently and usually without review by a supervisor, manager or senior employee.

___ This task has been a central or major part of my work. I have performed it myself routinely, and I have trained others in performance of this task, and (or) others have consulted me as an expert for assistance in performing this task.

11. Experience using a computerized financial system for entering and maintaining data.

___ I have not had experience, education, or training in performing this task.

___ I have completed formal education or training in performing this task, but have not yet performed this task on the job.

___ I have performed this task on the job under close supervision by a supervisor, manager or senior employee to ensure compliance with correct procedures.

___ I have performed this task as a regular part of a job, independently and usually without review by a supervisor, manager or senior employee.

___ This task has been a central or major part of my work. I have performed it myself routinely, and I have trained others in performance of this task, and (or) others have consulted me as an expert for assistance in performing this task.

12. Describe your level of skill/experience with Microsoft Excel.

___ I have not had experience, education, or training in performing this task.

___ I have basic user experience with this software, including formatting options, sort and filter, and styles.

___ I have developed formulas using standard Excel functions.

___ In addition to developing formulas using standard Excel functions and I have imported and exported data from/to sources like Access or Word.

___ In addition to developing formulas using standard Excel functions and importing and exporting data from/to sources like Access or Word, I have created and used pivot tables to summarize data.

13. Maintain office files/records for retrieval/reference/storage in compliance with files maintenance and disposition schedules.

___ I have not had experience, education, or training in performing this task.

___ I have completed formal education or training in performing this task, but have not yet performed this task on the job.

___ I have performed this task on the job under close supervision by a supervisor, manager or senior employee to ensure compliance with correct procedures.

___ I have performed this task as a regular part of a job, independently and usually without review by a supervisor, manager or senior employee.

___ This task has been a central or major part of my work. I have performed it myself routinely, and I have trained others in performance of this task, and (or) others have consulted me as an expert for assistance in performing this task.

14. Establish and maintain a variety of paper and computer files and record keeping systems.

___ I have not had experience, education, or training in performing this task.

___ I have completed formal education or training in performing this task, but have not yet performed this task on the job.

___ I have performed this task on the job under close supervision by a supervisor, manager or senior employee to ensure compliance with correct procedures.

___ I have performed this task as a regular part of a job, independently and usually without review by a supervisor, manager or senior employee.

___ This task has been a central or major part of my work. I have performed it myself routinely, and I have trained others in performance of this task, and (or) others have consulted me as an expert for assistance in performing this task.

15. Do you have experience compiling information for events such as meetings, briefings, and workshops? ___ Yes ___ No

16. Search files, documents or other sources for informational materials to prepare responses to inquiries, briefing packages or background for meetings or conferences.

    ___ I have not had experience, education, or training in performing this task.

    ___ I have completed formal education or training in performing this task, but have not yet performed this task on the job.

    ___ I have performed this task on the job under close supervision by a supervisor, manager or senior employee to ensure compliance with correct procedures.

    ___ I have performed this task as a regular part of a job, independently and usually without review by a supervisor, manager or senior employee.

    ___ This task has been a central or major part of my work. I have performed it myself routinely, and I have trained others in performance of this task, and (or) others have consulted me as an expert for assistance in performing this task.

17. Participate in meetings to record, author and publish accurate minutes, and to independently track progress of identified action items.

    ___ I have not had experience, education, or training in performing this task.

    ___ I have completed formal education or training in performing this task, but have not yet performed this task on the job.

    ___ I have performed this task on the job under close supervision by a supervisor, manager or senior employee to ensure compliance with correct procedures.

    ___ I have performed this task as a regular part of a job, independently and usually without review by a supervisor, manager or senior employee.

    ___ This task has been a central or major part of my work. I have performed it myself routinely, and I have trained others in performance of this task, and (or) others have consulted me as an expert for assistance in performing this task.

18. Coordinate information and prepare folders of material to be used to discuss with members at meetings, forums, work groups, etc.

    ___ I have not had experience, education, or training in performing this task.

    ___ I have completed formal education or training in performing this task, but have not yet performed this task on the job.

___ I have performed this task on the job under close supervision by a supervisor, manager or senior employee to ensure compliance with correct procedures.

___ I have performed this task as a regular part of a job, independently and usually without review by a supervisor, manager or senior employee.

___ This task has been a central or major part of my work. I have performed it myself routinely, and I have trained others in performance of this task, and (or) others have consulted me as an expert for assistance in performing this task.

19. Review and edit technical and/or nontechnical materials, identifying inadequacies in format, grammar, or construction in accordance with accepted standards

___ I have not had experience, education, or training in performing this task.

___ I have completed formal education or training in performing this task, but have not yet performed this task on the job.

___ I have performed this task on the job under close supervision by a supervisor, manager or senior employee to ensure compliance with correct procedures.

___ I have performed this task as a regular part of a job, independently and usually without review by a supervisor, manager or senior employee.

___ This task has been a central or major part of my work. I have performed it myself routinely, and I have trained others in performance of this task, and (or) others have consulted me as an expert for assistance in performing this task.

20. Read, comprehend, interpret and act on a variety of incoming and outgoing materials including official correspondence, technical and administrative reports.

___ I have not had experience, education, or training in performing this task.

___ I have completed formal education or training in performing this task, but have not yet performed this task on the job.

___ I have performed this task on the job under close supervision by a supervisor, manager or senior employee to ensure compliance with correct procedures.

___ I have performed this task as a regular part of a job, independently and usually without review by a supervisor, manager or senior employee.

___ This task has been a central or major part of my work. I have performed it myself routinely, and I have trained others in performance of this task, and (or) others have consulted me as an expert for assistance in performing this task.

21. Communicate both orally and in writing to receive, give or clarify information needed to complete work assignments.

___ I have not had experience, education, or training in performing this task.

___ I have completed formal education or training in performing this task, but have not yet performed this task on the job.

___ I have performed this task on the job under close supervision by a supervisor, manager or senior employee to ensure compliance with correct procedures.

___ I have performed this task as a regular part of a job, independently and usually without review by a supervisor, manager or senior employee.

___ This task has been a central or major part of my work. I have performed it myself routinely, and I have trained others in performance of this task, and (or) others have consulted me as an expert for assistance in performing this task.

Using the Online Application Process

The OPM recommends that you download the job posting so that you can easily refer to it as you complete your application. The application process itself has five steps:

1. Create or upload a resume on www.usajobs.gov.
2. Apply online.
3. Answer the online questions and submit your online application.
4. Review and confirm your submission, which you will then be able to track through USAJOBS.
5. Submit required documents, online or by fax or mail.

Depending on the agency and whether you are applying online or by fax, you may need to complete OPM Form 1203-FX. A sample form is provided in Figure 1.2 on the upcoming pages. Be sure to double-check your application before you submit it to be sure that you have responded to each of the questions. Here is some information on items you will need to provide.

Social Security Number

Enter your Social Security Number in the space indicated. Your Social Security Number (SSN) is requested under the authority of Executive Order 9397 to uniquely identify your records and distinguish them from those of other applicants who may have the same or a similar name. As allowed by law or presidential directive, your SSN is used by employers, schools, banks, and other people or entities who may know you to seek information about you. Providing your SSN is voluntary; however, most listing agencies cannot process your application without it.

NOTE

You will be asked on your application whether someone may contact your present employer. If you say no, it will not affect your employment opportunities—but try to provide some form of evaluation or letter of recommendation to compensate.

Vacancy Identification Number

Enter the Vacancy Identification Number of the job for which you are applying. The number is listed on the position announcement.

Numbered Items

Complete all twenty-five numbered items as indicated below:

1. **Title of job.** Enter the name of the position for which you are applying.

2. **Biographic data.** Enter your contact information. All biographic information is required except for your telephone number (I) and the contact time (J).

3. **E-mail address.** Provide a current e-mail address. Indicate whether you wish to be contacted by e-mail.

4. **Work information.** Provide contact information regarding your current employment, if applicable.

5. **Employment availability.** Enter information regarding your employment preferences.

6. **Citizenship.** Indicate whether you are currently a U.S. citizen.

7. **Background information.** Provide background information as requested by the vacancy announcement.

8. **Other information.** Indicate your gender (A) and date of birth (B).

9. **Languages.** Complete this section as instructed in the vacancy announcement.

10. **Lowest grade.** Enter the lowest pay grade level that you will accept for this position.

11. **Miscellaneous information.** Leave this section blank unless otherwise instructed in the vacancy announcement.

12. **Special knowledge.** Leave this section blank unless otherwise instructed in the vacancy announcement.

13. **Test location.** Leave this section blank unless otherwise instructed in the vacancy announcement.

14. **Veterans' preference claim.** If you are not entitled to claim veterans' preference, mark "No preference claimed." Except for disabled veterans, (1) those who entered active duty on or after October 15, 1976, and before September 8, 1980, must have an authorized campaign badge; OR, (2) those who enlisted after September 7, 1980, or entered active duty (through means other than enlistment) on or after October 14, 1982, must have (a) completed at least twenty-four months of continuous active duty service AND have served in a campaign or expedition for which a campaign medal has been authorized; OR (b) have served at least one day during the period for which a campaign medal has been authorized; OR (c) have served at least one day during the period of August 2, 1990 through January 2, 1992 AND have twenty-four months of continuous, active duty service, or been a reservist activated during that period; OR (d) have served 180 or more consecutive days, any part of which occurred during the period beginning September 11, 2001 and ending on

a future date prescribed by Presidential proclamation or law as the last date of Operation Iraqi Freedom. Those who returned from military service at the rank of major, lieutenant commander, or higher are not entitled to veteran preference except as disabled veterans.

(15) **Dates of active duty—military service.** If you served or are serving in the military, enter your dates of active duty, unless you have claimed derived preference (i.e., widows, spouses, and so on). Use this date format: (mm/dd/yyyy).

(16) **Availability date.** Leave this section blank unless otherwise instructed in the vacancy announcement.

(17) **Service computation date.** Leave this section blank unless otherwise instructed in the vacancy announcement.

(18) **Other date.** Leave this section blank unless otherwise instructed in the vacancy announcement.

(19) **Job preference.** Leave this section blank unless otherwise instructed in the vacancy announcement.

(20) **Occupational specialties.** Select/enter at least one occupational specialty. The specialty code for a specific position will be provided.

(21) **Geographic availability.** Select/enter at least one geographic location in which you are interested and will accept employment. The location code for a specific position will be provided.

(22) **Consideration for Transition Assistance Plan.** In this section, indicate if you are a surplus or displaced federal employee requesting special priority consideration under the Career Transition Assistance Plan (CTAP) or the Interagency Career Transition Assistance Plan (ICTAP). Note: To receive consideration for CTAP or ICTAP, you must submit the necessary supporting documentation.

(23) **Job related experience.** Leave this section blank unless otherwise instructed in the vacancy announcement.

(24) **Personal background information.** Leave this section blank unless otherwise instructed in the vacancy announcement.

(25) **Occupational questions.** Leave this section blank unless otherwise instructed in the vacancy announcement.

FIGURE 1.2

U.S. Office of Personnel Management
Occupational Questionnaire - OPM Form 1203-FX

Form Approved
OMB No. 3206-0040

51562

Please fill in the following items on each page of this application form. To review the Privacy Act and Public Burden Statements, please refer to the cover page of this form. If this information is not included, we cannot process your application. You must return pages 1 through 6.

Social security number

☐☐☐ - ☐☐ - ☐☐☐☐

Vacancy identification number

☐☐☐☐☐☐☐☐☐

Follow the instructions on the vacancy announcement.
- For optimum accuracy, it is recommended that characters be written block style following the examples below.
- Do not write on or outside the boxes.
- Do not use special characters. Use only the characters shown.
- PRINT your responses in the boxes and/or blacken in the appropriate ovals.
- Use black ink. Do not staple this form.
- You may obtain an electronic copy of this form at http://www.opm.gov/forms.

| A | B | C | D | E | F | G | H | I | J | K | L | M | N | O | P | Q | R | S | T | U | V | W | X | Y | Z |

| 0 | 1 | 2 | 3 | 4 | 5 | 6 | 7 | 8 | 9 |

Shade circle like this: ●
Not like this: ⊗ ✓

1. Print title of job applying for _____

2. Biographic data

    A. First name
☐☐☐☐☐☐☐☐☐☐☐☐☐☐☐

    B. Middle initial
☐

C. Last name
☐☐☐☐☐☐☐☐☐☐☐☐☐☐☐☐

D. Street address (house number, street, apartment number, where you want to receive mail)
☐☐☐☐☐☐☐☐☐☐☐☐☐☐☐☐☐☐☐☐☐☐
☐☐☐☐☐☐☐☐☐☐☐☐☐☐☐☐☐☐☐☐☐☐
☐☐☐☐☐☐☐☐☐☐☐☐☐☐☐☐☐☐☐☐☐☐

E. City
☐☐☐☐☐☐☐☐☐☐☐☐☐

F. State Use Standard State Postal Codes (abbreviations). If outside the United States of America, and you do not have a military address, print "OV" in State and fill in Country, leaving Zip Code blank.
☐☐

G. Zip code
☐☐☐☐☐

+ 4 (optional)
- ☐☐☐☐

H. Country
☐☐☐☐☐☐☐☐☐☐☐☐☐☐☐

I. Telephone number
☐☐☐☐☐☐☐☐☐☐☐

J. Contact time
○ Day   ○ Night   ○ Either

Use numbers only - no punctuation or spaces. Include area code if within the United States of America.

3. E-Mail address (print your complete e-mail address)
    A. Notify me by e-mail:
    ○ Yes   ○ No   B. _____

U.S. Office of Personnel Management
Previous Edition Usable

Page 1 of 6

OPM Form 1203-FX
Revised August 2002

51562

Please fill in the following items on each page of this application form. To review the Privacy Act and Public Burden Statements, please refer to the cover page of this form. If this information is not included, we cannot process your application. You must return pages 1 through 6.

Social security number

Vacancy identification number

4. Work information (if applicable)

A. Place of employment

B. Work address

C. Work city

D. Work state
Use Standard State Postal Codes (abbreviations). If outside the United States of America, and you do not have a military address, print "OV" in State and fill in Country, leaving Zip Code blank.

E. Work zip code   + 4 (optional)

F. Work country

G. Work telephone number

Extension (if applicable)

Use numbers only - no punctuation or spaces. Include area code if within the United States of America.

5. Employment availability - Are you available for

A. Full-time employment   Y N
  - 40 hours per week? ○ ○
B. Part-time employment of
  - 16 or fewer hrs/week? ○ ○
  - 17 to 24 hrs/week? ○ ○
  - 25 to 32 hrs/week? ○ ○
C. Temporary employment lasting
  - less than 1 month? ○ ○
  - 1 to 4 months? ○ ○
  - 5 to 12 months? ○ ○
D. Jobs requiring travel away from home for
  - 1 to 5 nights/month? ○ ○
  - 6 to 10 nights/month? ○ ○
  - 11 plus nights/month? ○ ○
E. Other employment questions (see instructions)
         Y N   Y N
  Question 1. ○ ○   Question 4. ○ ○
  Question 2. ○ ○   Question 5. ○ ○
  Question 3. ○ ○   Question 6. ○ ○

6. Citizenship
Are you a citizen of the United States of America?
  ○ Yes   ○ No

7. Background information
(see vacancy announcement instructions)
         Y N   Y N
  Question 1. ○ ○   Question 4. ○ ○
  Question 2. ○ ○   Question 5. ○ ○
  Question 3. ○ ○   Question 6. ○ ○

8. Other information
(see vacancy announcement instructions)

A. Gender   ○ Male   ○ Female

B.   Date of birth (mm/dd/yyyy)

51562

Please fill in the following items on each page of this application form. To review the Privacy Act and Public Burden Statements, please refer to the cover page of this form. If this information is not included, we cannot process your application. You must return pages 1 through 6.

Social security number   Vacancy identification number

9. Languages (see vacancy announcement instructions)   10. Lowest grade

11. Miscellaneous information

12. Special knowledge   13. Test location

14. Veterans' preference

○ No Preference Claimed

○ 5 Points Preference Claimed

10 Point Preference - You must submit a completed Standard Form 15, Application for 10-Point Veterans' Preference.

○ 10 Points Preference Claimed

   (award of a Purple Heart or service-connected disability of less than 10%)

○ 10 Points Compensable Disability Preference Claimed

   (disability rating of at least 10% and less than 30%)

○ 10 Points Other

   (spouse, widow, widower, mother preference claimed)

○ 10 Points Compensable Disability Preference Claimed

   (disability rating of 30% or more)

When entering dates in the following fields, please use the format: mm/dd/yyyy

15. Dates of active duty - military service
   (skip if no veterans' preference is claimed in block 14)

From: /   /

To: /   /

16. Availability date
   /   /

17. Service computation date
   /   /

18. Other date
   /   /

19. Job preference (see vacancy announcement instructions)

1○	6○	11○	16○	21○	26○	31○	36○	41○	46○	51○	56○	61○	66○
2○	7○	12○	17○	22○	27○	32○	37○	42○	47○	52○	57○	62○	67○
3○	8○	13○	18○	23○	28○	33○	38○	43○	48○	53○	58○	63○	68○
4○	9○	14○	19○	24○	29○	34○	39○	44○	49○	54○	59○	64○	69○
5○	10○	15○	20○	25○	30○	35○	40○	45○	50○	55○	60○	65○	70○

51562

Please fill in the following items on each page of this application form. To review the Privacy Act and Public Burden Statements, please refer to the cover page of this form. If this information is not included, we cannot process your application. You must return pages 1 through 6.

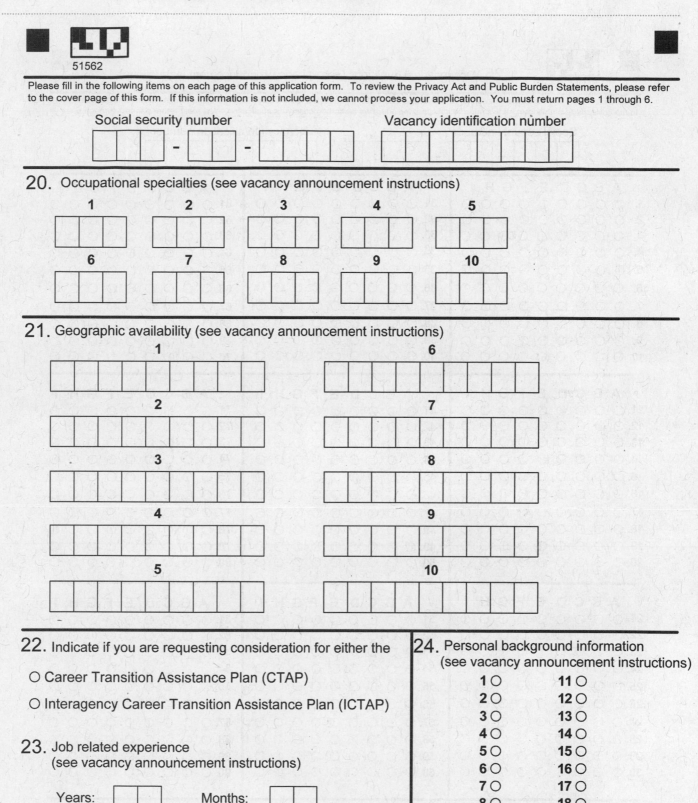

Social security number

☐☐☐ – ☐☐ – ☐☐☐☐

Vacancy identification number

☐☐☐☐☐☐☐☐☐

20. Occupational specialties (see vacancy announcement instructions)

1 ☐☐☐   2 ☐☐☐   3 ☐☐☐   4 ☐☐☐   5 ☐☐☐

6 ☐☐☐   7 ☐☐☐   8 ☐☐☐   9 ☐☐☐   10 ☐☐☐

21. Geographic availability (see vacancy announcement instructions)

1 ☐☐☐☐☐☐☐☐☐   6 ☐☐☐☐☐☐☐☐☐

2 ☐☐☐☐☐☐☐☐☐   7 ☐☐☐☐☐☐☐☐☐

3 ☐☐☐☐☐☐☐☐☐   8 ☐☐☐☐☐☐☐☐☐

4 ☐☐☐☐☐☐☐☐☐   9 ☐☐☐☐☐☐☐☐☐

5 ☐☐☐☐☐☐☐☐☐   10 ☐☐☐☐☐☐☐☐☐

22. Indicate if you are requesting consideration for either the

○ Career Transition Assistance Plan (CTAP)

○ Interagency Career Transition Assistance Plan (ICTAP)

23. Job related experience
(see vacancy announcement instructions)

Years: ☐☐   Months: ☐☐

24. Personal background information
(see vacancy announcement instructions)

1 ○   11 ○
2 ○   12 ○
3 ○   13 ○
4 ○   14 ○
5 ○   15 ○
6 ○   16 ○
7 ○   17 ○
8 ○   18 ○
9 ○   19 ○
10 ○   20 ○

U.S. Office of Personnel Management   Page 4 of 6   OPM Form 1203-FX
Revised August 2002
facebook.com/petersonspublishing

51562

25. Occupational questions (see vacancy announcement instructions)

Please fill in the following items on each page of this application form. To review the Privacy Act and Public Burden Statements, please refer to the cover page of this form. If this information is not included, we cannot process your application. You must return pages 1 through 6.

Social security number

☐☐☐ - ☐☐ - ☐☐☐☐

Vacancy identification number

☐☐☐☐☐☐☐☐☐☐

	A B C D E F G H I
1.	○ ○ ○ ○ ○ ○ ○ ○ ○
2.	○ ○ ○ ○ ○ ○ ○ ○ ○
3.	○ ○ ○ ○ ○ ○ ○ ○ ○
4.	○ ○ ○ ○ ○ ○ ○ ○ ○
5.	○ ○ ○ ○ ○ ○ ○ ○ ○
6.	○ ○ ○ ○ ○ ○ ○ ○ ○
7.	○ ○ ○ ○ ○ ○ ○ ○ ○
8.	○ ○ ○ ○ ○ ○ ○ ○ ○
9.	○ ○ ○ ○ ○ ○ ○ ○ ○
10.	○ ○ ○ ○ ○ ○ ○ ○ ○

	A B C D E F G H I
31.	○ ○ ○ ○ ○ ○ ○ ○ ○
32.	○ ○ ○ ○ ○ ○ ○ ○ ○
33.	○ ○ ○ ○ ○ ○ ○ ○ ○
34.	○ ○ ○ ○ ○ ○ ○ ○ ○
35.	○ ○ ○ ○ ○ ○ ○ ○ ○
36.	○ ○ ○ ○ ○ ○ ○ ○ ○
37.	○ ○ ○ ○ ○ ○ ○ ○ ○
38.	○ ○ ○ ○ ○ ○ ○ ○ ○
39.	○ ○ ○ ○ ○ ○ ○ ○ ○
40.	○ ○ ○ ○ ○ ○ ○ ○ ○

	A B C D E F G H I
61.	○ ○ ○ ○ ○ ○ ○ ○ ○
62.	○ ○ ○ ○ ○ ○ ○ ○ ○
63.	○ ○ ○ ○ ○ ○ ○ ○ ○
64.	○ ○ ○ ○ ○ ○ ○ ○ ○
65.	○ ○ ○ ○ ○ ○ ○ ○ ○
66.	○ ○ ○ ○ ○ ○ ○ ○ ○
67.	○ ○ ○ ○ ○ ○ ○ ○ ○
68.	○ ○ ○ ○ ○ ○ ○ ○ ○
69.	○ ○ ○ ○ ○ ○ ○ ○ ○
70.	○ ○ ○ ○ ○ ○ ○ ○ ○

	A B C D E F G H I
11.	○ ○ ○ ○ ○ ○ ○ ○ ○
12.	○ ○ ○ ○ ○ ○ ○ ○ ○
13.	○ ○ ○ ○ ○ ○ ○ ○ ○
14.	○ ○ ○ ○ ○ ○ ○ ○ ○
15.	○ ○ ○ ○ ○ ○ ○ ○ ○
16.	○ ○ ○ ○ ○ ○ ○ ○ ○
17.	○ ○ ○ ○ ○ ○ ○ ○ ○
18.	○ ○ ○ ○ ○ ○ ○ ○ ○
19.	○ ○ ○ ○ ○ ○ ○ ○ ○
20.	○ ○ ○ ○ ○ ○ ○ ○ ○

	A B C D E F G H I
41.	○ ○ ○ ○ ○ ○ ○ ○ ○
42.	○ ○ ○ ○ ○ ○ ○ ○ ○
43.	○ ○ ○ ○ ○ ○ ○ ○ ○
44.	○ ○ ○ ○ ○ ○ ○ ○ ○
45.	○ ○ ○ ○ ○ ○ ○ ○ ○
46.	○ ○ ○ ○ ○ ○ ○ ○ ○
47.	○ ○ ○ ○ ○ ○ ○ ○ ○
48.	○ ○ ○ ○ ○ ○ ○ ○ ○
49.	○ ○ ○ ○ ○ ○ ○ ○ ○
50.	○ ○ ○ ○ ○ ○ ○ ○ ○

	A B C D E F G H I
71.	○ ○ ○ ○ ○ ○ ○ ○ ○
72.	○ ○ ○ ○ ○ ○ ○ ○ ○
73.	○ ○ ○ ○ ○ ○ ○ ○ ○
74.	○ ○ ○ ○ ○ ○ ○ ○ ○
75.	○ ○ ○ ○ ○ ○ ○ ○ ○
76.	○ ○ ○ ○ ○ ○ ○ ○ ○
77.	○ ○ ○ ○ ○ ○ ○ ○ ○
78.	○ ○ ○ ○ ○ ○ ○ ○ ○
79.	○ ○ ○ ○ ○ ○ ○ ○ ○
80.	○ ○ ○ ○ ○ ○ ○ ○ ○

	A B C D E F G H I
21.	○ ○ ○ ○ ○ ○ ○ ○ ○
22.	○ ○ ○ ○ ○ ○ ○ ○ ○
23.	○ ○ ○ ○ ○ ○ ○ ○ ○
24.	○ ○ ○ ○ ○ ○ ○ ○ ○
25.	○ ○ ○ ○ ○ ○ ○ ○ ○
26.	○ ○ ○ ○ ○ ○ ○ ○ ○
27.	○ ○ ○ ○ ○ ○ ○ ○ ○
28.	○ ○ ○ ○ ○ ○ ○ ○ ○
29.	○ ○ ○ ○ ○ ○ ○ ○ ○
30.	○ ○ ○ ○ ○ ○ ○ ○ ○

	A B C D E F G H I
51.	○ ○ ○ ○ ○ ○ ○ ○ ○
52.	○ ○ ○ ○ ○ ○ ○ ○ ○
53.	○ ○ ○ ○ ○ ○ ○ ○ ○
54.	○ ○ ○ ○ ○ ○ ○ ○ ○
55.	○ ○ ○ ○ ○ ○ ○ ○ ○
56.	○ ○ ○ ○ ○ ○ ○ ○ ○
57.	○ ○ ○ ○ ○ ○ ○ ○ ○
58.	○ ○ ○ ○ ○ ○ ○ ○ ○
59.	○ ○ ○ ○ ○ ○ ○ ○ ○
60.	○ ○ ○ ○ ○ ○ ○ ○ ○

	A B C D E F G H I
81.	○ ○ ○ ○ ○ ○ ○ ○ ○
82.	○ ○ ○ ○ ○ ○ ○ ○ ○
83.	○ ○ ○ ○ ○ ○ ○ ○ ○
84.	○ ○ ○ ○ ○ ○ ○ ○ ○
85.	○ ○ ○ ○ ○ ○ ○ ○ ○
86.	○ ○ ○ ○ ○ ○ ○ ○ ○
87.	○ ○ ○ ○ ○ ○ ○ ○ ○
88.	○ ○ ○ ○ ○ ○ ○ ○ ○
89.	○ ○ ○ ○ ○ ○ ○ ○ ○
90.	○ ○ ○ ○ ○ ○ ○ ○ ○

U.S. Office of Personnel Management   Page 5 of 6   OPM Form 1203-FX
Revised August 2002

51562

25. Occupational questions (continued)

Please fill in the following items on each page of this application form. To review the Privacy Act and Public Burden Statements, please refer to the cover page of this form. If this information is not included, we cannot process your application. You must return pages 1 through 6.

Social security number   Vacancy identification number

☐☐☐ - ☐☐ - ☐☐☐☐   ☐☐☐☐☐☐☐☐☐

	A B C D E F G H I		A B C D E F G H I		A B C D E F G H I
91.	○ ○ ○ ○ ○ ○ ○ ○ ○	121.	○ ○ ○ ○ ○ ○ ○ ○ ○	151.	○ ○ ○ ○ ○ ○ ○ ○ ○
92.	○ ○ ○ ○ ○ ○ ○ ○ ○	122.	○ ○ ○ ○ ○ ○ ○ ○ ○	152.	○ ○ ○ ○ ○ ○ ○ ○ ○
93.	○ ○ ○ ○ ○ ○ ○ ○ ○	123.	○ ○ ○ ○ ○ ○ ○ ○ ○	153.	○ ○ ○ ○ ○ ○ ○ ○ ○
94.	○ ○ ○ ○ ○ ○ ○ ○ ○	124.	○ ○ ○ ○ ○ ○ ○ ○ ○	154.	○ ○ ○ ○ ○ ○ ○ ○ ○
95.	○ ○ ○ ○ ○ ○ ○ ○ ○	125.	○ ○ ○ ○ ○ ○ ○ ○ ○	155.	○ ○ ○ ○ ○ ○ ○ ○ ○
96.	○ ○ ○ ○ ○ ○ ○ ○ ○	126.	○ ○ ○ ○ ○ ○ ○ ○ ○	156.	○ ○ ○ ○ ○ ○ ○ ○ ○
97.	○ ○ ○ ○ ○ ○ ○ ○ ○	127.	○ ○ ○ ○ ○ ○ ○ ○ ○	157.	○ ○ ○ ○ ○ ○ ○ ○ ○
98.	○ ○ ○ ○ ○ ○ ○ ○ ○	128.	○ ○ ○ ○ ○ ○ ○ ○ ○	158.	○ ○ ○ ○ ○ ○ ○ ○ ○
99.	○ ○ ○ ○ ○ ○ ○ ○ ○	129.	○ ○ ○ ○ ○ ○ ○ ○ ○	159.	○ ○ ○ ○ ○ ○ ○ ○ ○
100.	○ ○ ○ ○ ○ ○ ○ ○ ○	130.	○ ○ ○ ○ ○ ○ ○ ○ ○	160.	○ ○ ○ ○ ○ ○ ○ ○ ○

	A B C D E F G H I		A B C D E F G H I		A B C D E F G H I
101.	○ ○ ○ ○ ○ ○ ○ ○ ○	131.	○ ○ ○ ○ ○ ○ ○ ○ ○	161.	○ ○ ○ ○ ○ ○ ○ ○ ○
102.	○ ○ ○ ○ ○ ○ ○ ○ ○	132.	○ ○ ○ ○ ○ ○ ○ ○ ○	162.	○ ○ ○ ○ ○ ○ ○ ○ ○
103.	○ ○ ○ ○ ○ ○ ○ ○ ○	133.	○ ○ ○ ○ ○ ○ ○ ○ ○	163.	○ ○ ○ ○ ○ ○ ○ ○ ○
104.	○ ○ ○ ○ ○ ○ ○ ○ ○	134.	○ ○ ○ ○ ○ ○ ○ ○ ○	164.	○ ○ ○ ○ ○ ○ ○ ○ ○
105.	○ ○ ○ ○ ○ ○ ○ ○ ○	135.	○ ○ ○ ○ ○ ○ ○ ○ ○	165.	○ ○ ○ ○ ○ ○ ○ ○ ○
106.	○ ○ ○ ○ ○ ○ ○ ○ ○	136.	○ ○ ○ ○ ○ ○ ○ ○ ○	166.	○ ○ ○ ○ ○ ○ ○ ○ ○
107.	○ ○ ○ ○ ○ ○ ○ ○ ○	137.	○ ○ ○ ○ ○ ○ ○ ○ ○	167.	○ ○ ○ ○ ○ ○ ○ ○ ○
108.	○ ○ ○ ○ ○ ○ ○ ○ ○	138.	○ ○ ○ ○ ○ ○ ○ ○ ○	168.	○ ○ ○ ○ ○ ○ ○ ○ ○
109.	○ ○ ○ ○ ○ ○ ○ ○ ○	139.	○ ○ ○ ○ ○ ○ ○ ○ ○	169.	○ ○ ○ ○ ○ ○ ○ ○ ○
110.	○ ○ ○ ○ ○ ○ ○ ○ ○	140.	○ ○ ○ ○ ○ ○ ○ ○ ○	170.	○ ○ ○ ○ ○ ○ ○ ○ ○

	A B C D E F G H I		A B C D E F G H I		A B C D E F G H I
111.	○ ○ ○ ○ ○ ○ ○ ○ ○	141.	○ ○ ○ ○ ○ ○ ○ ○ ○	171.	○ ○ ○ ○ ○ ○ ○ ○ ○
112.	○ ○ ○ ○ ○ ○ ○ ○ ○	142.	○ ○ ○ ○ ○ ○ ○ ○ ○	172.	○ ○ ○ ○ ○ ○ ○ ○ ○
113.	○ ○ ○ ○ ○ ○ ○ ○ ○	143.	○ ○ ○ ○ ○ ○ ○ ○ ○	173.	○ ○ ○ ○ ○ ○ ○ ○ ○
114.	○ ○ ○ ○ ○ ○ ○ ○ ○	144.	○ ○ ○ ○ ○ ○ ○ ○ ○	174.	○ ○ ○ ○ ○ ○ ○ ○ ○
115.	○ ○ ○ ○ ○ ○ ○ ○ ○	145.	○ ○ ○ ○ ○ ○ ○ ○ ○	175.	○ ○ ○ ○ ○ ○ ○ ○ ○
116.	○ ○ ○ ○ ○ ○ ○ ○ ○	146.	○ ○ ○ ○ ○ ○ ○ ○ ○	176.	○ ○ ○ ○ ○ ○ ○ ○ ○
117.	○ ○ ○ ○ ○ ○ ○ ○ ○	147.	○ ○ ○ ○ ○ ○ ○ ○ ○	177.	○ ○ ○ ○ ○ ○ ○ ○ ○
118.	○ ○ ○ ○ ○ ○ ○ ○ ○	148.	○ ○ ○ ○ ○ ○ ○ ○ ○	178.	○ ○ ○ ○ ○ ○ ○ ○ ○
119.	○ ○ ○ ○ ○ ○ ○ ○ ○	149.	○ ○ ○ ○ ○ ○ ○ ○ ○	179.	○ ○ ○ ○ ○ ○ ○ ○ ○
120.	○ ○ ○ ○ ○ ○ ○ ○ ○	150.	○ ○ ○ ○ ○ ○ ○ ○ ○	180.	○ ○ ○ ○ ○ ○ ○ ○ ○

You have now completed the OPM Form 1203-FX. When submitting, **do not** include the cover page. Only submit pages numbered 1 through 6.

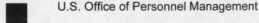

facebook.com/petersonspublishing

The following Privacy Act and Public Reporting Burden statements are for informational purposes only. Please do not return this page with your application package.

Privacy Act

The Office of Personnel Management is authorized to rate applicants for Federal jobs under sections 1302, 3301, and 3304 of title 5 of the U.S. Code. Section 1104 of title 5 allows the Office of Personnel Management to authorize other Federal Agencies to rate applicants for Federal jobs. We need the information you put on this form to see how well your education and work skills qualify you for a Federal job. We also need information on matters such as citizenship and military service to see whether you are affected by laws we must follow in deciding who may be employed by the Federal Government.

We must have your Social Security Number (SSN) to identify your records because other people may have the same name and birthdate. The Office of Personnel Management may also use your SSN to make requests for information about you from employers, schools, banks, and others who know you, but only as allowed by law or Presidential directive. The information we collect by using your SSN will be used for employment purposes and also for studies and statistics that will not identify you.

Information we have about you may also be given to Federal, State and local agencies for checking on law violations or for other lawful purposes. We may send your name and address to State and local Government agencies, Congressional and other public offices, and public international organizations, if they request names of people to consider for employment. We may also notify your school placement office if you are selected for a Federal job.

Giving us your SSN or any of the other information is voluntary. However, we cannot process your application, which is the first step toward getting a job, if you do not give us the information we request.

Public Reporting Burden

The public reporting burden of information is estimated to vary from 20 minutes to 45 minutes to complete this form including time for reviewing instructions, gathering the data needed, and completing and reviewing entries. The average time to complete this form is 30 minutes. Send comments regarding the burden estimate or any other aspect of this collection of information, including suggestions for reducing this burden to: U.S. Office of Personnel Management, Office of the Chief Information Officer, 1900 E Street, NW, CHP 500, Washington, DC 20415; and to the Office of Information and Regulatory Affairs, Office of Management and Budget, Paperwork Reduction Project 3206-0040, Washington, DC 20503.

SUBMITTING A CIVIL SERVICE JOB APPLICATION

Taking an exam is now much less common than submitting a resume, an assessment or occupational questionnaire, and an application form for state and municipal government jobs as well as for federal positions. However, about 20 percent of civil service positions still involve exams. These include clerical and technology jobs that often require tests of speed, accuracy, and judgment. The remaining positions are filled based on competitive evaluation of applicants' experience, skills, abilities, and education.

The following pages offer examples of three cover letters and resumes tailored to three hypothetical civil service positions at the state level.

FIGURE 1.3

James Johnson
123 Main Street
Dallas, Texas 53132
Phone: 555.222.1212

August 20, 2013

Human Resources Office
New York State Banking Department
One State Street
New York, NY 10004-1417

Re: Bank Examiner Trainee I (Exam 20-598); OC-APP-3 #20598 (4/07)

To Whom It May Concern:

I am responding to your position listing for Bank Examiner Trainee I, dated August 12, 2013.
The application, my resume, and three (3) letters of reference are attached. For the past year, I have
provided consulting and management training services, but I am now eager to continue with a career in
banking. I would be honored to make a strong contribution to your team's efforts in this position.

After having carefully reviewed the requirements of this position, I am confident that my skills, abilities,
and experience effectively match your requirements for this position. I have nearly 10 years' experience
in banking and the financial industry, both in the private sector and in the government arena.

Throughout my career in banking, I have derived great satisfaction from serving clients well. I enjoy
working with dynamic teams. I also enjoy working with the public, demonstrating banking services. I
believe I would contribute to your professional environment because I find the banking industry to be
both challenging and rewarding.

May I arrange an interview to further discuss my qualifications? I am available to meet with you at a
mutually convenient time.

Thank you for your consideration of my application.

Sincerely,

James Johnson

Encl.

123 Main St., Dallas, TX 53132   Phone: 555.222.1212

James Johnson

Objective

To work in banking as a loan officer or a bank examiner

Experience

2012–Present   Progressive Bank   Dallas, TX
Consultant and Trainer

- Conduct on-site regulatory compliance reviews and in-house training programs for bank employees, including both deposit and lending-related statutes

- Responsibilities include defining standards for project preparation, business blueprint, realization, and testing phases.

2010–2012   Progressive Bank   Dallas, TX
Bank Teller

- Served customers from diverse backgrounds in the Dallas metropolitan area

- Worked with bank officers to ensure efficient delivery of services

- Suggested new methods to increase retention of customers

2008–2009   Friendly Bank of Dallas   Dallas, TX
Bank Teller Assistant

- Helped assess the level of customer service and methods to increase delivery of great customer service

- Supervised interns in developing customer satisfaction surveys

2007–2008   Duffy Vineyards   Dallas, TX
Junior Sales Associate

- Worked with team to market local vineyard products

2006–2007   Lit Ware, Inc.   Dallas, TX
Sales Representative

- Worked in direct sales of plastic containers for home use

- Received company's highest sales award in 2007

- Helped develop training course in sales

Education

2002-2006   South Ridge State University   Dallas, TX

- Course of study: Finance and accounting; B.S. degree attained.

Interests

Running, golf, tennis, computers

FIGURE 1.4

Jane A. Smith
4 New Street
Chicago, Illinois 60601
Phone: 555.234.5678

—————

August 20, 2013

H.S. Smith
Room 541
Bureau of Personnel Management
2300 S. Dirksen Parkway
Springfield, IL 62744

Re: Developmental Aide Trainee; OC-APP #4 10-010 / 10-011 (2-07L)

To Whom It May Concern:

I am responding to your listing for the Developmental Aide Trainee position, dated August 10, 2013. The application, my resume, and three letters of reference are attached. After having carefully reviewed the requirements of this position, I am confident that my skills, abilities, and experience well match your requirements for this position.

For the past year, I have served as a Developmental Aide with Kinder Kids. Prior to that, I worked as a Developmental Aide with the Institute for Childhood Development in Chicago and as an assistant at a local daycare center. All of my previous positions have provided the opportunity to deepen my understanding of child development and teaching strategies.

I would be grateful for an opportunity to work for the State of Illinois as a Developmental Aide Trainee. Such an experience would be valuable to me as I pursue a career that utilizes my skills in a learning environment. I can assure you that I will devote my strong work ethic to serving your agency in this capacity.

May I arrange an interview to further discuss my qualifications? I am available for an interview at a mutually convenient time. Please feel free to contact me at the telephone number above.

Thank you for your time and consideration.

Sincerely,

Jane A. Smith

Encl.

4 New Street, Chicago, IL 60601   P: 555.234.5678

Jane A. Smith

Objective

To contribute to the understanding of early childhood development through study and application of innovative methods in education and testing

Experience

2009–Present   Kinder Kids   Chicago, IL
Developmental Aide

- Emphasized learning for children 4 to 6 years of age
- Worked with children to help them understand the role of preschool in preparing them for elementary school
- Suggested new methods to increase retention of new reading skills

2007–2009   The Institute for Childhood Development Chicago, IL
Developmental Aide

- Helped assess the level of preparedness of children 6 to 8 years old for foreign language education
- Supervised interns in early childhood development

2005–2007   Bright Eyes Daycare, Inc.   Chicago, IL
Teacher Assistant

- Worked as assistant in the two-year-old class
- Helped youngsters during all activities, including meals
- Helped plan weekly activities with head teacher

Education

2001-2005   Chicago State University   Chicago, IL

- Course of study: Early Childhood Development

Interests

Running, nutrition, reading

References

Available upon request

FIGURE 1.5

Maria E. Jones
123 Street Avenue
Apt. 2B
Sacramento, California 94203

Phone: 555.333.4444

August 20, 2013

Personnel Office
Attn: Mrs. Sylvia Smith
P.O. Box 9992
Sacramento, CA 94203

Re: Food Service Worker I; OMRDD, DOH, OC-APP #4 20-484

To Whom It May Concern:

I am responding to your position listing for Food Service Worker I, dated August 10, 2013. The application and my resume are attached. I am happy to provide letters of references upon request. After having carefully reviewed the requirements of this position, I am confident that my skills, abilities, and experience qualify me to serve as a Food Service Worker I for your organization.

For the past year, I have worked as a Food Service Technician in the cafeteria at a local hospital in Walnut Creek. I have an undergraduate degree in psychology, and I am very interested in the way that nutrition affects a person's physical well being. I would appreciate the chance to increase my knowledge and skills through hands-on experience working for the State of California. I am a dedicated, reliable employee, and I bring enthusiasm to a team environment.

May I arrange an interview to further discuss my qualifications? I am available for an interview at a mutually convenient time. Please feel free to contact me at the telephone number above.

Thank you for your consideration of my application. I look forward to hearing from you.

Sincerely,

Maria E. Jones

123 Street Avenue, Apt. 2B   P: 555.333.4444
Sacramento, California 94203

Maria E. Jones

Objective   To work as a physical therapist in a progressive hospital

Experience   2010–Present   Arbor Hospital   Walnut Creek, CA
Food Service Technician

- Emphasized efficient, safe delivery of food to patients
- Learned to keep food and food delivery costs to a minimum without sacrificing quality
- Suggested new food products that increased efficiency and nutrition

2008–2010   Broadmoor Physical Therapy Institute   Capitola, CA
Food Service Technician

- Served staff and clients during breakfast and lunch
- Supervised interns learning food service trade

2007–2008   New Meadow Vineyard   Sacramento, CA
Junior Sales Associate

- Worked with team to market local vineyard products
- Created brochures featuring product nutritional information

2006–2007   ABC Nursing Home   Sacramento, CA
Activities Assistant

- Assisted patients in all daily activities
- Responsible for compiling weekly reports for state
- Developed new reading program for patients

Education   2002–2006   Prescott College   Prescott, AZ

- Course of study: Psychology

Interests   Nutrition, gardening, running, reading

References   Available upon request

TIP

Experience you acquired more than fifteen years ago may be summarized in one block if it is not applicable to the type of position for which you are applying.

Tips for Completing Your Job Application

Give every job application serious attention. It is the first important step toward getting the position you want. Consider the following tips:

- **Make a first draft.** This is especially important when you're writing your employment history and recording other types of experience. Rewrite the draft as many times as you need to until you've produced a comprehensive, well-written account. Review your background and make a list of specific on-the-job duties, outside activities, knowledge, and experiences that may enhance your qualifications for the position.

- **Use a computer or typewriter to fill out the application form.** If this isn't possible, complete the application neatly and clearly using blue or black ink.

- **Provide a complete employment history.** Use all the lines allotted to each job description. If you need more space, use plain white paper to continue. Do not summarize; explain fully, but succinctly. Be sure that you label every attachment with the appropriate job announcement number, your birthdate, your name, and the item number. Be specific about what tasks you performed in each job you've had.

- **Provide a complete educational history.** Include the names of all the schools you've attended going as far back as high school. Include school locations, the dates you attended, the subjects you studied, the total number of classroom or credit hours you earned, the diplomas or degrees you received, and any other pertinent data. Include the cities or towns, the dates you attended, your major if you have an associate or a bachelor's degree, the diplomas or degrees you received, and any other pertinent data. Also list military training, leadership orientation, career specialty training, and the like.

- **List honors and awards.** Many people are modest about awards. This is not the time to be modest. Honors and awards do not have to be earthshakingly important to be included. For example, cite scholarships and elections to any honor society and other groups if you're a recent graduate. Cite awards and honors related to your career and also any community awards if they are relevant. Recent awards are usually the most important, but if you've received only a few awards, list those that are relevant to your work even if you received them some years ago.

- **List special qualifications, experiences, and skills.** Be honest in evaluating your abilities. Even if they do not seem directly related to the position, be sure to mention any familiarity with a foreign language, software programs, typing skills, licenses and certificates you have earned, experience with equipment or machines, membership in professional and nonprofit organizations, material you have written, examples of public speaking events, and relevant hobbies. For example, cite scholarships and elections to an honor society if you're a recent graduate. Cite awards and honors related to your career and also community awards if they are relevant. Recent awards are usually the most important, and the USAJOBS tips for resume-building says to list only awards and honors received in the last five years.

- **List available professional references.** Ask people who know you and who know your work to provide a reference. Make sure that they can be easily reached, and include their phone numbers or other contact information. Do not list people who are out of the country, have no phone, or whose whereabouts are unknown to you. Be sure to ask your references for permission to use their names.

- **Put the job announcement number on all application materials.** The number appears on the front of the job announcement. Also list your name, birthdate, and the position for which you're applying on all materials, in case parts of your application become separated.

- **Never embellish or falsify information.** Your application will be examined closely and facts will be checked. If you were ever fired, say so. It is better to state this openly than to have an examiner find out from a former employer.

- **Don't put employment history or other material into one long paragraph.** Aim for a clear, well-organized presentation. This is especially important if you use more space than what is provided on the application. Break up long descriptions into short sentences and paragraphs, and use headings. Also, use action verbs and avoid abbreviating or using the passive voice.

- **Consider your options carefully.** Most of the questions on the application form are straightforward. Be sure, however, to put some extra thought into answering the following:

    o *Locations where you're willing to work.* Sometimes vacancies are available in several locations. Would you accept employment in any location or do you want to work in a specific place? Either way, list all the places where you're willing to work.

    o *Lowest grade or pay you will accept.* You will not be considered for a job that pays less than the amount you provide. Although the position salary is clearly stated in the announcement, it's possible that an earlier opening in the same occupation carries less responsibility and thus pays a lower entrance-level salary.

    o *Temporary or part-time employment.* Temporary positions arise frequently, and part-time positions occasionally open up as well. Willingness to accept a temporary assignment or part-time position may be good ways of getting in the door. Both could lead to a full-time job.

TIP

Include a college transcript only if the job announcement requests one.

SUMMING IT UP

- Major categories of federal positions include: professional, administrative, investigative and law enforcement, technical, clerical, labor and mechanical, and unskilled. Each of these categories (except unskilled) requires certain educational and experience requirements.

- Some federal positions may be attained through special government programs, in which applicants do not require experience to qualify but may have to take a test to indicate aptitude for the position. These programs include part-time and summer employment, student work-study programs and student temporary employment, and the PMF program (Presidential Management Fellows Program).

- Jobs in the federal government appear in the General Schedule (GS), which assigns grades to jobs according to the difficulty of duties and responsibilities and the knowledge, experience, and skills required.

- Generally, a high school diploma or previous job experience qualifies you for an entry-level job. With experience, federal employees are eligible for promotion to higher-level, more specialized jobs. You may also begin employment with the federal government at a higher grade level if you already have specialized experience or additional education.

- If you are a U.S. Armed Forces veteran, you may be eligible for Veteran Preference points, which enable you to increase your exam score by either 5 or 10 points. If you're eligible, be sure to indicate the fact on your application or resume.

- Employment with the federal government comes with a number of benefits, including job training, generous vacation and sick time allowances, life and health insurance, and retirement benefits.

- As with federal employment, nearly every kind of job available in the private sector is also available in state and local employment. Fields that are unique to state and local government include public education, highway work, governmental control and finance, and law enforcement and firefighting.

- State and local government job requirements, salary scales, and benefits are generally comparable to those of federal government employment. As with federal jobs, applicants must meet educational and/or experience requirements and show evidence of having the required skills, and they may have to pass a job-related written test.

- Government agencies fill positions through job announcements or exam announcements. Study the announcements carefully, and be sure that you meet all the educational, experience, and special requirements before applying for a position.

- The official employment website of the U.S. federal government is USAJOBS: www.usajobs.gov. The Office of Personnel Management website also provides information for job seekers, including job announcements, veteran preferences, online applications, and locations of Federal Job Information Centers. Check out www.opm.gov.

- For information on state and local government jobs, contact your American Jobs Center, the State Civil Service Commission, the nearest big city's Civil Service Commission, city and statewide civil service publications, school boards and boards of education, and city and state municipal offices. You might also check your local library or nearby college and university placement offices.

Exam Essentials

chapter 2

OVERVIEW

- What to expect on the federal civil service exam
- What to expect on state and municipal exams
- Biographical and achievement inventory
- Preparing for a civil service exam
- How the exam is administered
- Exam ratings
- Test-taking strategies
- Summing it up

WHAT TO EXPECT ON THE FEDERAL CIVIL SERVICE EXAM

Congress passed the Civil Service Act to ensure that federal employees are hired based on individual merit and fitness. The Civil Service Act provides for competitive exams and the selection of new employees from among the most qualified applicants. Any U.S. citizen may take civil service exams. For most jobs, the agency doing the hiring rates exams to determine which applicants are eligible for the jobs to be filled. Some federal jobs are exempt from civil service requirements. Most of these positions, however, are covered by separate merit systems of other agencies, such as the State Department, the Federal Bureau of Investigation, the Nuclear Regulatory Commission, or the Tennessee Valley Authority.

There are two main types of civil service exams: competitive and noncompetitive. In a competitive exam, all applicants for a position compete with each other. The better your score, the better your chance of being appointed. In a noncompetitive exam, each applicant is tested solely to determine qualifications for a given position. You need only pass to become eligible for the job.

The purpose of civil service exams is to identify candidates who have the aptitude and ability to learn the job easily and to do it well. The subjects tested on the exam are closely related to the duties of the position. The written tests for federal occupations measure verbal, clerical, arithmetic, and any other skills needed for the job. On many clerical exams, for instance, the exam consists of two tests: one measuring verbal ability, and another measuring clerical ability. Test requirements vary depending on the agency and the type of position.

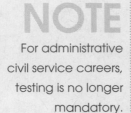

NOTE

For administrative
civil service careers,
testing is no longer
mandatory.

Check the job announcement to confirm the test battery that you will have to take. If the announcement indicates that a written test will be given, you will receive a notice in the mail telling you when and where to report for the test.

Pay special attention to the section of the job announcement describing the kind of exam given for the open position. It explains what areas are covered in the written test and lists the specific subjects on which questions will be asked. Sometimes, sample questions are given.

Testing Verbal Ability

Most civil service exams include a section to test verbal ability. The verbal portion of the exam tests you in the following areas:

- Spelling, meaning, and relationship of words
- Recognition of sentences that are grammatically correct
- Reading, understanding, and using written material

These test tasks relate to a variety of job tasks, such as proofreading and correcting typed copy, using instruction manuals, organizing new files of related materials, and carrying out written instructions.

Testing Clerical Ability

The clerical portion of the exam is a test of speed and accuracy on different clerical tasks. Because speed is being measured, this portion of the exam is more closely timed than other portions. Also, because accuracy is being measured, there is often a penalty for wrong answers, unlike other portions of the exam. You may be tested on any or all of the following areas: alphabetic filing, name and number checking, and typing. Some clerical tests also include a stenography or coding portion.

Testing Arithmetic Ability

Not all exams include an arithmetic section—it depends on the job you are applying for. Many clerical jobs, cashiers, and positions in the manual trades do require some level of arithmetic ability. You may be tested on any of the following:

- Fractions, decimals, and percentages
- Graphs and tables
- Ratio and proportion
- Reasoning problems, including work, distance, taxation, and payroll problems

Other Exam Topics

Depending on the job that you are applying for, you may be tested on other topics. These include general aptitude questions for qualities necessary for the job, and questions testing specific abilities not covered in the clerical portion of the exam. For example, general aptitude questions may measure judgment and communication skills, which are necessary for many jobs. Other subjects are more specific: observation and memory for police officers, firefighters, corrections officers, court officers, and similar positions; and mechanical ability for firefighters, custodians, and mechanical workers in many trades.

WHAT TO EXPECT ON STATE AND MUNICIPAL EXAMS

Following the lead of the federal government, every state has instituted some form of merit-based hiring procedure. In matters of internal hiring, each state has complete autonomy. No higher authority tells a state which positions must be filled by examination or which exam to use. In the interests of efficiency and fairness in hiring, nearly all states fill positions through civil service exams.

Many states offer their testing services to counties and municipalities as well. Thus, if you qualify on a state-administered exam, you may have your name and ranking listed on any number of eligibility rosters in counties or towns in which you are willing to work. In other states, state testing is only for state positions, and counties and municipalities have their own independent systems.

As testing arrangements vary from state to state, so do procedures and the tests themselves. Because of the differences in state exams, it is not possible to give you the precise information you need for the exam in your state. But many state and municipal exams follow the lead of the federal civil service exam style, measuring verbal, clerical, arithmetic, and mechanical abilities, as well as other skills, depending on the job.

BIOGRAPHICAL AND ACHIEVEMENT INVENTORY

Many federal and state civil service exams conclude with a self-descriptive inventory. This inventory is set up to look like a multiple-choice test and is timed like a test, but it is not a test at all. There are no right or wrong answers. Rather, the examiners are looking for a pattern of achievements, interests, and personality traits that they can compare to the profile of currently active, successful people in the same occupation.

Aside from high school and college–related questions, you are asked about your likes and dislikes and about the impression that you make on others. There are questions about how you rank yourself in relation to other people, about what your friends think of you, and about the opinions of supervisors or teachers. Do not try to second-guess the testers to give the "right" answer on the biographical and achievement inventory. Internal checks for consistency and honesty are built into the questions. Your best bet is to answer quickly and candidly. Dwelling over the questions is not likely to help.

You cannot really study for this inventory. The only possible preparation is searching old school records to refresh your memory about subjects you studied and your attendance,

NOTE

Exam subjects and formats vary the most among law enforcement and corrections exams. By contrast, clerical exams are more limited to the nature of clerical work itself and are more universal.

grades, and extracurricular activities. If you cannot find your records, just answer to the best of your ability.

PREPARING FOR A CIVIL SERVICE EXAM

Obviously, some education is necessary to answer questions in reading, spelling, grammar, English usage, and arithmetic. But they demand less schooling than most other subjects employed in testing candidates for particular jobs. Government agencies favor these general test subjects, because they probe a candidate's native intelligence and aptitude for learning how to do a job and succeed in it. The agency does not want to handicap candidates who have been deprived of a full education.

Ability questions, such as those testing clerical and mechanical ability, are designed to assess the effects of a specific course of training. These tests assume that applicants have had a specific course of instruction, job apprenticeship, or other relatively uniform experience.

Because aptitude and ability tests overlap, you will clearly benefit from studying the subject matter and learning how to achieve the highest scores on general questions. Experience has shown that it is possible to improve your score and, thus, to better demonstrate your aptitude for the job. With the great variety in exams, especially among state and municipal exams, the best preparation is thorough grounding in basic skills and practice with many kinds of exam questions.

The test questions and review materials in this book are based on the requirements of a variety of job announcements, as well as on questions that have appeared on actual tests. It will be worth your time to try your hand at all the practice questions and sample exams, even if you do not think they will appear on your exam. You want to prepare yourself for whatever type of question you may encounter. In a field of competent applicants, familiarity with different question styles and strategies can give you the competitive edge, a higher score, and an offer of employment.

Any test-taking practice will help in preparation for the exam. In addition, knowing what to expect and familiarity with techniques of effective test-taking should give you the confidence you need to do your best. The following list will help you prepare for a civil service exam, or any exam for that matter:

- **Prepare for the exam.** Do not make the test harder than it has to be by not preparing yourself. You are taking a very important step by reading this book and taking the sample tests. This will help you become familiar with the test and the kinds of questions that you will have to answer. Make a study schedule and stick to it. Regular, daily study is important.

- **Answer all the practice questions.** Read the sample questions and directions for taking the test carefully. When you take the sample tests, time yourself as you will be timed in the real test. Do not be satisfied with merely the correct answer to each question. Do research on the other choices to see why they were incorrect. You will broaden your background and be more adequately prepared for the actual exam.

- **Don't look at the correct answers before answering the practice questions on your own.** This can fool you into thinking that you understand a question when you really do not. Try the question on your own first, and then compare your answer with the one given. In a sample test, you are your own grader; you do not gain anything by pretending to understand something that you really do not. Study answer explanations whenever they are supplied, because they may give you extra insights—even into the questions that you answered correctly.

- **Review what you have learned.** Once you have studied something thoroughly, review it the next day so that the information will be firmly fixed in your mind.

- **Tailor your study to the subject matter.** Do not study everything in the same manner. Give special attention to your areas of weakness and to areas that are more likely to be covered on your exam.

- **Study where you won't be interrupted or distracted.** You will concentrate better if you work away from distractions such as phone calls from friends, chit-chat from family, television shows, and so on. Choose a comfortable, well-lit study spot that's as far as possible from the distractions of daily life. That might mean going to the public library.

- **Stay physically fit.** You cannot retain information well when you are uncomfortable, have headaches, or are tense. Try to get some exercise even if it's getting off the bus or subway a stop or two early and walking the rest of the way to where you're going.

- **Don't try to learn too much in one study period.** If your mind starts to wander, take a short break and then return to your work.

HOW THE EXAM IS ADMINISTERED

Civil service exams are generally made up of multiple-choice questions. Most multiple-choice tests consist of a question booklet and a separate answer sheet. The question booklet begins with general instructions for taking the test, including the rules and regulations governing your exam, the number of questions, how the exam is timed, and signals used when time is up. Specific directions for different types of questions are explained in the section of the question booklet before each new type of question. Some federal agencies, states, and localities use computer-based tests. Typically, candidates can take a tutorial to ensure they understand the functions of the software and how to use the computer for the specific test. An examiner will be in the room during the test should a problem arise. The time is shown on the screen, and the program will time out automatically. Directions are explained directly for each type of question on the screen.

In the test room, the examiner will hand out forms for you to fill out, or will direct you to screens to complete, and will give you the instructions that you must follow in taking the exam. The examiner will tell you how to fill in the grids on the forms and will explain time limits and timing signals. If you do not understand any of the

TIP

When you go to your exam, be sure to bring a pen, three No. 2 pencils, an eraser, and any forms you received when you registered for the exam.

instructions, ask questions. Do not score less than your best because the examiner did not explain something fully, or you didn't understand.

Follow the examiner's instructions exactly. Fill in the grids on the forms carefully and accurately. Do not begin until you are told to begin, and stop as soon as the examiner tells you to stop. Do not turn pages until you are told to do so or go back to parts that you have already completed. If you are taking the test on a computer, you will only be able to go back within the section you are working in. Any infraction of the rules is considered cheating: Your test paper will not be scored, and you will not be eligible for appointment.

Multiple-choice questions have four or five answer choices lettered (A) through (D) or (E). Each question has one best answer. You must read the question carefully, think, choose the best answer, and blacken the matching lettered circle on the separate answer sheet, or click on the correct answer. If you mark your answer neatly, there is no room for scoring errors in marking a multiple-choice answer sheet. You can be sure of accuracy and objectivity.

EXAM RATINGS

Applicants who meet the minimum experience and education requirements and skill levels for the job are given numerical ratings based on their written test scores. You will be notified of your rating by mail. If you pass the exam, you will receive an eligible rating—that is, your name will be placed on a list for appointment, with the highest test scores at the top of the list. Eligible applicants who are not selected for the position are restored to the list for consideration for other openings. If you fail the exam, you can usually take it again as long as applications are being accepted. If you pass but want to improve your score, you can usually retake the test after a year has passed, if the announcement is open at that time.

Once you achieve a rating on a standardized exam, such as a clerical exam, you do not have to take the test again to apply for similar jobs. You also do not have to reestablish that you meet the minimum experience and education requirements or have the required skills. Your rating will expire after a certain period, as indicated on the rating form. Be sure to notify the agency that gave you a rating of address, name, or availability changes. When writing, give your full name, your Social Security number, the title of the job announcement, and the rating you received.

How the Exam Is Scored

The method of rating on all civil service exams is on a scale of 100, with 70 as the usual passing mark. Written tests are most frequently rated by machine. In some written exams, and for rating experience and training, two examiners work independently. In case of a protest about the rating, a third examiner is assigned to rate the exam again. Thus, the chances of error, arbitrary grading, or bias are almost completely eliminated.

On most exams, you get one point for each correct answer. You get no credit for a wrong answer or for a question that you did not answer. Most importantly, you do not lose any credit for a wrong answer. A wrong answer is simply not a right answer. You get no credit, but the wrong answer itself does not work against you.

A few exams or portions of exams do not follow this scoring rule, especially clerical exams that measure accuracy under time pressure. A part of the federal clerical exam penalizes wrong answers, for instance. In some cases, the number of wrong answers is subtracted from the number of right answers. More often, a portion of the wrong answers—usually one fourth—is subtracted from the number of correct answers.

Not many exams consist of exactly 100 questions. Some contain only 80, others 140 or more. All scores are finally reported on the basis of 100. What this means is that while you get one point for each correct answer, that answer may not be adding exactly one point to your score. The examiners create a confidential formula that converts raw scores (the number you got right) to the final, scaled rating, which determines your ranking on the eligibility list. When an announcement specifies "70 percent required," it refers to the score that is reported after the conversion (and before the addition of veterans' credit).

Rating Nontested Positions

If you applied for a job that did not require a written test, your rating is based on the experience and training you described in your application and on any required supporting evidence. When all this information has been gathered, you will be rated, and the agency will tell you how your qualifications look to the examiners. That is all there is to it, until you are called to the job.

Veteran Preference Points

If you are a veteran of the U.S. Armed Forces, you may be eligible for Veteran Preference points that will give you an edge in the civil service hiring process. Veterans Preference points enable you to increase your exam score by either 5 or 10 points, depending on your eligibility. They may also allow you to submit certain job applications after the closing date for the exam.

To qualify for Veteran Preference in general, you must meet the following three criteria:

1 You must have received an honorable or general discharge.

2 If you are a retiree, your rank must be lower than major or lieutenant commander, unless you are a disabled veteran.

3 You must not be in the National Guard or Reserve active duty for training purposes.

TIP

If you're eligible to claim Veteran Preference, be sure to indicate the fact on your application or resume. To claim a 10-point preference, you must complete form SF-15, Application for 10-Point Veteran Preference.

5-Point Preference

If you meet the general criteria outlined above and you have passed your civil service exam, an additional 5 points may be added to your exam score. To gain the 5 points, you must have served during any of these periods:

- Any time between 12/07/1941 and 07/01/1955
- For more than 180 consecutive days during the period 01/31/1955 through 10/15/1976
- From 08/02/1990 through 01/02/1992 during the Gulf War
- During the period beginning September 11, 2001 and ending on a future date prescribed by Presidential proclamation or law as the last date of Operation Iraqi Freedom.
- In a military campaign for which a campaign medal has been authorized

10-Point Preference

You may have 10 points added to your passing exam score if you qualify as any of the following:

- A veteran with a service-connected disability
- A veteran receiving compensation, disability benefits, or a pension from the military
- A veteran who has received a Purple Heart (this qualifies you as a disabled veteran)
- The unmarried spouse of a veteran who is deceased (certain restrictions apply)
- The spouse of a veteran who cannot work because of a service-related disability
- The mother of a veteran who died during service
- The mother of a permanently and totally disabled veteran

TIP

For more information about Veteran Preference points and your eligibility, contact the Veterans Employment Coordinator of the agency where you are seeking employment.

TEST-TAKING STRATEGIES

When taking the exam, you can employ a number of strategies that will help you complete the test more accurately and quickly and will boost your overall score. For example:

- **Read every word of the instructions.** Aside from actually knowing the answer, careful reading is what most influences your choosing the right answer. Misreading directions causes the greatest problems. For example, if the directions ask you to choose the word that means the opposite of the underlined word, and you choose the word that means the same as the underlined word, you will mark wrong answers for a whole series of questions and do poorly on the exam. If you have time, reread any complicated instructions after you do the first few questions to check that you really do understand them. Whenever you are allowed to, ask the examiner to clarify anything you do not understand.
- **Read every word of every question.** Careful reading must extend beyond the reading of directions to the reading of each individual question. Qualifying words like *most, least, only, best, probably, definitely, not, all, every*, and *except* make a big difference in determining the correct answer to a specific question. Since reading

is key to success with multiple-choice questions, your preparation should include a lot of attention to reading and reading-based questions. Once you have mastered the techniques of dealing with reading-based questions, you will be well-equipped to tackle all aspects of the civil service exam.

- **Make notes on scratch paper or the question booklet.** Usually, you are allowed to write in the question booklet. You can put a question mark next to the number of a question at which you took a guess, calculate the answers to math questions, cross out eliminated answer choices, or underline key words. If you are not permitted to write in the question booklet, you will be issued scratch paper for figuring and writing notes to yourself. When using scratch paper or the question booklet for taking notes, do not forget to mark the final answer on the answer sheet. Only the answer sheet is scored; all other notes are disregarded.

- **Mark answers neatly and carefully.** The separate answer sheet is the only record of answers that is scored. Blacken your answer space firmly and completely. A correct answer response looks like this:

  The following are incorrectly marked responses:

  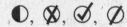

  The scoring machine might not notice these marks. If the scoring machine does not register your answer, you will not get any credit for it. If you are taking the test on computer, be sure you click the answer circle, and, if necessary, click "submit."

- **Manage your time.** Before you begin, take a moment to plan your progress through the test. Although you are not usually expected to finish all the questions, you should at least get an idea of how much time you need to spend on each question in order to answer them all. For example, if there are 60 questions to answer and you have 30 minutes, you will have about 30 seconds to spend on each question.

- **Check your answers.** If you finish any part before time is up, use the remaining time to check that each question is answered in the right space and that you marked only one answer for each question. Return to the difficult questions and rethink them. But keep in mind that second guessing yourself about your answers is not usually a good idea. Your first answer is often the right answer. You do not get a bonus for leaving early, so if you finish before time is up, stay until the end of the exam. If you cannot finish any exam part before time is up, do not worry. If you are accurate, you can do well even without finishing. It is even possible to earn a rating of 100 without entirely finishing an exam part if you are very accurate. At any rate, do not let your performance on any one part affect your performance on any other part.

- **Guess when wrong answers do not count against you.** In most portions of the exam, wrong answers do not take points off your score, so a guess cannot hurt you. The best guess is the educated guess. If you are not sure of the right answer, try to eliminate the obviously wrong answers. If you can narrow the field and guess from among fewer choices, you will raise the odds of guessing right. But even if you

TIP

Before testing begins, ask what scoring method will be used on your particular exam. You can then guide your guessing procedure accordingly.

have no idea at all, a guess still gives you a chance of getting the question right. Not answering at all ensures that the question will be counted wrong. If you are about to run out of time, mark all the remaining blanks with the same letter. According to the law of averages, you should get some portion of those questions right.

- **Don't guess when wrong answers do count against you.** On some tests, a correct answer gives you one point, a skipped space gives you nothing at all but costs you nothing, and a wrong answer costs you 1/4 point. On this type of test, do not randomly guess—you could hurt your score. (Be sure to keep careful track of skipped questions so you do not mark the wrong lines on your answer sheet.) Although you should not make random guesses, an educated guess can still help you on this type of test. Do not rush to fill answer spaces randomly at the end. Instead, work as quickly as possible while concentrating on accuracy until time is called. Then, stop and leave the remaining answers blank.

- **Don't mark more than one answer for each question.** If more than one circle for any question is blackened, even if one of the answers is correct, the scoring machine will give no credit for that question. You may change your mind and your answer. When you change an answer, be careful to fully and cleanly erase the first answer. You do not want the machine to misread your choice. Never cross out an answer in favor of a new choice. You must erase, or the machine will read both old and new answers and give you no credit.

- **Be careful in marking answers.** If you mark an answer in the wrong place, it will be scored as wrong. If you notice that you have slipped out of line, you must erase all answers from the point of the error and redo all those questions. Most civil service exams allow sufficient time to finish, but you do not have the time to waste erasing and reanswering large blocks of questions. Therefore, do not skip any questions or jump around looking for easy questions to answer first. Do not omit a question even if you have no idea of the correct answer. If you are forced to guess so as to answer every question in order, then do so. If you answer every question in order, there should be no chance to slip. (The exception to this rule, of course, is when wrong answers count against you.)

- **Don't spend too much time on any one question.** If you get stuck, do not take the puzzler as a personal challenge. Either guess and mark the question in the question booklet, or skip it entirely, marking the question as a skip and taking care to skip the answer space on the answer sheet. If there is time at the end of the exam portion, you can return and give marked questions another try.

TIP

Check often to be sure that the question number matches the answer space and that you have not skipped a space by mistake.

SUMMING IT UP

- Any U.S. citizen may take civil service exams. In most cases, the agency seeking new employees rates these exams to determine which applicants are eligible for open positions.

- Civil service exams may be competitive or noncompetitive. With competitive exams, all applicants for a position compete with one another, so the higher your score, the better your chance of being hired. With noncompetitive exams, each applicant is tested to determine his or her qualifications for a given position and you do not compete with other applicants.

- Most federal civil service exams include a section that assesses your verbal ability. This type of section includes questions about spelling, meaning, and relationship of words; recognition of grammatically correct sentences; and reading, understanding, and using written material.

- Clerical sections of federal civil service exams test your speed and accuracy in performing various clerical tasks, including alphabetical filing, name and number checking, and typing. Some clerical exams also include a stenography or coding section.

- Some federal civil service exams include an arithmetic section. You may be tested on fractions, decimals, and percentages; graphs and tables; ratio and proportion; and reasoning problems of various sorts, including work, distance, taxation, and payroll.

- In addition to verbal ability, clerical ability, and arithmetic, some federal civil service exam questions may measure your judgment and communication skills; observation and memory skills; or mechanical ability.

- Each state has a merit-based hiring procedure and has complete autonomy over internal hiring for state civil service positions. Nearly all state governments fill positions through civil service exams, and as with the federal government, most include sections measuring verbal, clerical, arithmetic, and mechanical abilities.

- A self-descriptive inventory may also be a part of your civil service exam. This is a timed, multiple-choice test, but there are no right or wrong answers and you cannot study for these questions. Examiners are looking for a pattern of achievements, interests, and personality traits that they can compare to those of current employees in similar or related positions. Don't second-guess the questions; answering all questions quickly and honestly is the best way to proceed.

- The most useful way to prepare for taking a civil service exam is to be sure you've polished up your basic skills, and to practice with many types of exam questions. Review the test tips in this chapter and take the Practice Tests for experience with the kinds of test questions you're likely to see on your civil service exam.

- Applicants meeting minimum experience and education requirements and skill levels for a job are rated numerically based on their written test scores. You'll be notified by mail of your rating. If you've passed your civil service exam, you'll receive an eligible rating and your name is placed on a list for appointment. If you are not selected for the position, your name is restored to the list for consideration for other positions.

- All civil service exams are scored on a scale of 100, with 70 being the usual passing score (even if the test does not contain 100 questions). Written tests are almost always machine-scored; on most exams, you receive one point for each correct answer and no credit for a wrong or unanswered question. Exceptions to this type of scoring include clerical exams that measure accuracy under time constraints. For positions that do not require taking a written test, your rating is based on the experience and training you described in your application and on any required supporting information.

- If you're a U.S. Armed Forces veteran, remember to indicate that fact on your application or resume. You may be eligible for Veteran Preference points that increase your exam score by either 5 or 10 points, depending on your eligibility level.

- Follow the test-taking strategies outlined in this chapter to help you complete your test more accurately and quickly and boost your overall civil service exam score.

PART II

DIAGNOSING YOUR STRENGTHS AND WEAKNESSES

Practice Test 1: Diagnostic Test

ANSWER SHEET PRACTICE TEST 1: DIAGNOSTIC

1. Ⓐ Ⓑ Ⓒ Ⓓ   11. Ⓐ Ⓑ Ⓒ Ⓓ   21. Ⓐ Ⓑ Ⓒ Ⓓ   31. Ⓐ Ⓑ Ⓒ Ⓓ Ⓔ

2. Ⓐ Ⓑ Ⓒ Ⓓ   12. Ⓐ Ⓑ Ⓒ Ⓓ   22. Ⓐ Ⓑ Ⓒ Ⓓ   32. Ⓐ Ⓑ Ⓒ Ⓓ Ⓔ

3. Ⓐ Ⓑ Ⓒ Ⓓ   13. Ⓐ Ⓑ Ⓒ Ⓓ   23. Ⓐ Ⓑ Ⓒ Ⓓ Ⓔ   33. Ⓐ Ⓑ Ⓒ Ⓓ Ⓔ

4. Ⓐ Ⓑ Ⓒ Ⓓ   14. Ⓐ Ⓑ Ⓒ Ⓓ   24. Ⓐ Ⓑ Ⓒ Ⓓ Ⓔ   34. Ⓐ Ⓑ Ⓒ Ⓓ Ⓔ

5. Ⓐ Ⓑ Ⓒ Ⓓ   15. Ⓐ Ⓑ Ⓒ Ⓓ   25. Ⓐ Ⓑ Ⓒ Ⓓ Ⓔ   35. Ⓐ Ⓑ Ⓒ Ⓓ Ⓔ

6. Ⓐ Ⓑ Ⓒ Ⓓ   16. Ⓐ Ⓑ Ⓒ Ⓓ   26. Ⓐ Ⓑ Ⓒ Ⓓ Ⓔ   36. Ⓐ Ⓑ Ⓒ Ⓓ Ⓔ

7. Ⓐ Ⓑ Ⓒ Ⓓ   17. Ⓐ Ⓑ Ⓒ Ⓓ   27. Ⓐ Ⓑ Ⓒ Ⓓ Ⓔ   37. Ⓐ Ⓑ Ⓒ Ⓓ Ⓔ

8. Ⓐ Ⓑ Ⓒ Ⓓ   18. Ⓐ Ⓑ Ⓒ Ⓓ   28. Ⓐ Ⓑ Ⓒ Ⓓ Ⓔ   38. Ⓐ Ⓑ Ⓒ Ⓓ Ⓔ

9. Ⓐ Ⓑ Ⓒ Ⓓ   19. Ⓐ Ⓑ Ⓒ Ⓓ   29. Ⓐ Ⓑ Ⓒ Ⓓ Ⓔ   39. Ⓐ Ⓑ Ⓒ Ⓓ Ⓔ

10. Ⓐ Ⓑ Ⓒ Ⓓ   20. Ⓐ Ⓑ Ⓒ Ⓓ   30. Ⓐ Ⓑ Ⓒ Ⓓ Ⓔ   40. Ⓐ Ⓑ Ⓒ Ⓓ Ⓔ

Practice Test 1: Diagnostic Test

40 Questions • 30 Minutes

Directions: Read each question carefully. Select the best answer and darken the proper space on the answer grid.

1. *Mentor* means most nearly
   (A) advisor
   (B) leader
   (C) authority
   (D) supervisor

2. *Tribute* means most nearly
   (A) evidence
   (B) applause
   (C) honor
   (D) criticism

3. *Renown* means most nearly
   (A) difference
   (B) honorable
   (C) fortunate
   (D) fame

4. The **itinerary** for the four days in New York City was packed with things to do.
   Itinerary means most nearly
   (A) agenda
   (B) route
   (C) timeframe
   (D) travel plan

5. My **impression** of her was unfavorable when I first met her.
   Impression most nearly means
   (A) opinion
   (B) image
   (C) appearance
   (D) effect

Directions: In questions 6–10, decide which sentence is the best with respect to grammar and usage suitable for a formal letter or report.

6. (A) Clerks perform a vareity of administrative and clerical duties necessary to operating state and local government.
   (B) Clerical people do a lot of jobs in administrative and clerical fields to run state and local governments.
   (C) Jobs at the clerk level is vital to running state and local governments effectively.
   (D) Clerks perform a number of administrative and clerical duties that are necessary if state and local governments are to run smoothly.

65

NOTE

The directions are stated as if you are taking the exam in a paper-and-pencil format. If you will be taking the exam on computer, each section will have directions specific to how to answer questions on computer.

7. **(A)** Clerk-typists perform keyboarding and clerical duties, they may write short letters and memos, sort mail, filing forms, and check materials.

(B) Clerk-typists perform keyboarding and clerical duties that may include writing short letters and memos, sorting mail, filing forms, and checking materials.

(C) Clerk-typists perform keyboarding and clerical duties that may include writing short letters, memos, sorting mail, filing forms, and checking materials.

(D) Clerk-typists perform keyboarding, clerical duties, writing short letters, memos, sort mail file forms, and check materials.

8. **(A)** An applicant typically must meet age and medical requirements, have a high school diploma or have served in the military, and have a personality suited to police work.

(B) Applicants typically must meet age and medical requirements and have a high school diploma or have served in the military they also need a personality suited to police work.

(C) Typically, applicants for police work has to meet age and medical requirements and a high school diploma or military service and a good personality to be a police officer.

(D) Applicants have to meet certain requirements: age and health, have a high school diploma or military service, and a personality suited to police work.

9. **(A)** Him and me were looking into computer-related jobs in state government, but we needed more experience with certain types of software.

(B) Computer-related jobs appeal to him and I, but we need more experience.

(C) They were interested in computer-related jobs, but they believe they need more experience in certain software programs.

(D) State government jobs in computers pay good and interest he and I.

10. **(A)** Social workers in the area of planning and policy propose ways to bring about needed change in institutions.

(B) Planing and policy initatives are important specilties in some social work positions.

(C) A social worker may have responsibilities in areas in which they have little training such as developing policy.

(D) Social work is an interesting field people which are interested in helping others go into this field.

Directions: In questions 11–14, find the correct spelling of the word, and darken the proper answer space. If no suggested spelling is correct, darken space **(D)**.

11. **(A)** relible
    (B) relyable
    (C) reliable
    (D) None of the above

12. **(A)** restaurant
    (B) restorent
    (C) restorant
    (D) None of the above

13. **(A)** receivership
    (B) recievership
    (C) recievurship
    (D) None of the above

14. **(A)** simultaineously
    (B) simultainiously
    (C) similtaineously
    (D) None of the above

Directions: For questions 15–22, read each paragraph and answer the question that follows it by darkening the letter of the correct answer on your answer sheet. Answer each question in the answer space with the corresponding number.

15. Keyboarding may be the most important skill that students can learn today. Considering the prevalence of desktop and laptop computers, touchscreen keyboards on smart phones and tablets, and Blu-ray keyboards for tablets, people in the future may never have to manually write anything ever again. Some schools have stopped teaching cursive and teach only printing because students find handwriting too difficult. On the other hand, schools must begin to teach keyboarding in primary grades or we'll become a nation of hunt-and-peck typists.

The paragraph best supports the statement that technology

    (A) has created a nation of hunt-and-peck typists.
    (B) is making the ability to communicate by typing a necessary skill.
    (C) will affect how students learn manual dexterity skills in the future.
    (D) has made cursive obsolete.

16. Assume that your duties include purchasing office equipment. You must buy 9 new copiers. The subtotal comes to $1,799.91.

How much is the total price when a 6 percent sales tax is added?

    (A) $1,907.90
    (B) $1,990.95
    (C) $2,107.99
    (D) $2,229.90

17. Smoking is one of the major causes of fires in the home. We all know about not smoking in bed, but there is another danger that many people don't think about: tossing an improperly extinguished cigarette in a wastebasket. A person may think the cigarette is out, but it doesn't take much to start a fire in a wastebasket with paper in it or even crumpled tissues.

The paragraph best supports the statement that fires can start

(A) where we least expect them to.

(B) because someone hasn't put out a cigarette completely.

(C) because we are not aware of certain hazards.

(D) because of careless smokers.

18. Assume that you are asked to lead a team on a project. One of the other people named to the team is someone you don't like, and the feeling is mutual. The best action for you to take is to

(A) tell your supervisor that you and the other employee don't get along, and ask for the person to be removed from the team.

(B) ignore the person and any contributions the person makes at meetings.

(C) meet with the person before the first meeting and discuss how you two can work together on the project.

(D) meet with the person before the first meeting and tell him/her to leave the team voluntarily or you will tell your supervisor why you don't want him/her on the team.

19. If a key punch operator can complete 318 cards in one hour, how many key punch operators are needed to complete 4,770 cards?

(A) 11

(B) 15

(C) 21

(D) 26

20. Assume your job duties include counting and recording school fees for the middle school. At the beginning of the school year, students presented you with cash and 60 checks. The checks were divided as follows: 18 checks for $75 each, 31 checks for $140, 10 checks for $130, and one check for $200 as a donation toward fees for any child who couldn't afford to pay. In addition, you received two $50 bills, two $20 bills, seven $10 bills, and three $5 bills. How much did you collect in school fees?

(A) $6,395

(B) $7,415

(C) $7,650

(D) $8,555

21. The Milford Police Force wrote the following number of tickets involving vehicles:

Type of Ticket	Monday	Tuesday	Wednesday	Thursday	Friday
Parking	5	14	16	31	42
Moving	0	0	3	1	4
Expired registration	0	0	0	1	0

What percentage of the total number of tickets written were moving violations?

(A) 6.8%

(B) 10%

(C) 12.4%

(D) 14.6%

22. Assume that your job is to check employee expense accounts before submitting them to the department head for approval. You have noticed over time that one employee appears to be overcharging for meals while on business trips. Some receipts appear to be altered. The best action for you to take would be to

(A) report the employee to your department head.

(B) ask the employee about the apparent overages, and give her a chance to change them.

(C) report the employee to the auditing department.

(D) confront the employee yourself about the apparent overages.

Directions: Perform the computation as indicated in the question, and find the answer among the list of alternative responses. If the correct answer is not given among the choices, mark choice (E).

23. Add: 39 + 14

(A) 42

(B) 49

(C) 51

(D) 53

(E) None of the above

24. Subtract: 107 – 88

(A) 9

(B) 11

(C) 19

(D) 29

(E) None of the above

25. Multiply: 24 × 32

(A) 678

(B) 766

(C) 768

(D) 867

(E) None of the above

26. Divide: 546 ÷ 14

(A) 34

(B) 39

(C) 42

(D) 46

(E) None of the above

27. Multiply: 12.46×0.52

(A) 5.0032

(B) 5.092

(C) 6.48

(D) 6.68

(E) None of the above

28. Add: $\dfrac{7}{14} + \dfrac{5}{42}$

(A) $\dfrac{7+5}{56}$

(B) $\dfrac{3}{10}$

(C) $\dfrac{7}{8}$

(D) $\dfrac{35}{56}$

(E) None of the above

29. Divide: $\dfrac{4}{7} \div \dfrac{11}{7}$

(A) $\dfrac{4}{11}$

(B) 44

(C) $\dfrac{7}{4}$

(D) $\dfrac{44}{49}$

(E) None of the above

Directions: In each line across the page are three names, addresses, or codes that are very much alike. Compare the three and decide which ones are EXACTLY alike. On your answer sheet, mark:

(A) if ALL THREE names, addresses, or codes are exactly ALIKE.

(B) if only the FIRST and SECOND names, addresses, or codes are exactly ALIKE.

(C) if only the FIRST and THIRD names, addresses, or codes are exactly ALIKE.

(D) if only the SECOND and THIRD names, addresses, or codes are exactly ALIKE.

(E) if ALL THREE names, addresses, or codes are DIFFERENT.

30. Bridget Herron	Brigette Herron	Brigetta Heron
31. 6937621	6937261	6937261
32. 1401 Azalea Court	4011 Azalea Court	1401 Azalea Court
33. S. Peter Eisner	Peter S. Essner	S. Peter Eisner
34. 1068280	1068280	1068280
35. Marielle Johnson	Marielle Johnson	Marielle Johanson
36. Alexa Tsiskaridze	Alexa Tsiskaridze	Alexa Tsikaridsi

Directions: In questions 37–40, find the correct place for the given name.

37. Tanaka, Hari

  (A) –

    Tanaka, Harold

  (B) –

    Tanaka, Howard

  (C) –

    Tanna, George

  (D) –

    Tanner, Michael

  (E) –

38. Wong, Vivienne

  (A) –

    Wang, V. W.

  (B) –

    Wang, Vivian

  (C) –

    Wonder, R.V. William

  (D) –

    Wong, Vernon

  (E) –

39. d'Orsey, Eugene

(A) –

D'Anton, Raymond

(B) –

D'Orcy, F. W.

(C) –

D'Orsay, Leonard

(D) –

D'Orsi, Edw.

(E) –

40. Blaskett, Thomas A.

(A) –

Blankenship, Victor

(B) –

Blankenstein, T.Victor

(C) –

Blochner, H.A.

(D) –

Block, Marian

(E) –

ANSWER KEY AND EXPLANATIONS

1. A	11. C	21. A	31. D
2. C	12. A	22. A	32. C
3. D	13. A	23. D	33. C
4. D	14. D	24. C	34. A
5. A	15. B	25. C	35. B
6. D	16. A	26. B	36. B
7. B	17. C	27. C	37. A
8. A	18. C	28. E	38. E
9. C	19. B	29. A	39. D
10. A	20. B	30. E	40. C

1. **The correct answer is (A).** A *mentor* helps and advises someone with less experience who is typically younger. A supervisor may be a mentor, but not necessarily.

2. **The correct answer is (C).** A *tribute* is an honor, which may include applause, but that's not the meaning of *tribute*.

3. **The correct answer is (D).** *Renown* means "fame."

4. **The correct answer is (D).** An *itinerary* is a travel plan or schedule, but it is not the same as an *agenda,* which is a list or outline of things to be considered or done.

5. **The correct answer is (A).** An impression may be an image, but not in this sentence, where it most closely means *opinion.*

6. **The correct answer is (D).** Choice (A) is incorrect because *variety* is misspelled; remember "*i*" before "*e*" except after "*c*" or sounding like "*a*" in *neighbor and weigh.* Choice (B) uses the colloquial expression "a lot of," which should not be used in formal communication, that is, job situations. Choice (C) is incorrect because *jobs* is plural so its predicate should be plural. Don't be confused by any phrase that comes between the subject and verb.

7. **The correct answer is (B).** Choice (A) is incorrect because it is a run-on sentence. Two stand-alone thoughts (clauses) are joined by a comma. You need either a period at the end of the first thought, a conjunction such as *and* or *that,* or a semicolon. Also, the series of duties is not parallel; *filing* should be *file.* Choice (C) is incorrect because *memos* is part of the thought "writing short letters and memos." Choice (D) has the same problem and a similar problem: the "and" between "keyboarding" and "clerical duties" is missing. The comma between "sort mail" and "file forms" is missing, and the series of duties is not parallel.

8. **The correct answer is (A).** Choice (B) is incorrect because it's a run-on sentence. A punctuation mark or con-

junction is needed between "military" and "they." Choice (C) lets a phrase between the subject and verb interfere with using the correct form of the verb; *has* should be *have*. Also, a "good personality" is not the same as a "personality suited to police work." Choice (D) has several problems. The colon could work here if the elements were parallel. You need to add verbs to "age and health" and "a personality suited to police work," or remove *have* from "have a high diploma or military service."

9. **The correct answer is (C).** Choice (A) is incorrect because *him* and *me* are the object forms of the personal pronouns, and the subject forms are needed in the sentence; the pronouns are the subject of the sentence. Choice (B) is incorrect because although *him* is correct, *I* is not. The object form *me* is needed for the word is the object of the preposition *to*. Choice (D) is incorrect because *good,* an adjective, should be *well,* the adverb, because it modifies the verb *pay*. Also, *he* and *I* should be the object forms *him* and *me*. They are the object of the predicate *interest*.

10. **The correct answer is (A).** *Planning, initiatives,* and *specialties* are misspelled so eliminate Choice (B). Choice (C) is incorrect because *they* should be *he (or he or she)* to agree with its antecedent "a social worker." Choice (D) is incorrect because it is a run-on sentence. There should be a punctuation mark or conjunction between "field" and "people." Also, *which* should be *who*.

11. **The correct answer is (C).** The correct spelling is *reliable*.

12. **The correct answer is (A).** The correct spelling is *restaurant*.

13. **The correct answer is (A).** The correct spelling is *receivership*.

14. **The correct answer is (D).** The correct spelling is *simultaneously*.

15. **The correct answer is (B).** Only choice (B) accurately identifies the main idea of the paragraph. Choice (A) is incorrect because the paragraph says that the nation *will become,* not *has become* a nation of hunt-and-peck typists. There is nothing in the paragraph about manual dexterity skills so you can eliminate choice (C). Choice (D) is incorrect because although the paragraph mentions cursive, it does not say that all schools have stopped teaching it, thus implying that cursive is not yet obsolete.

16. **The correct answer is (A).** You don't need to know how many copiers were bought to figure out the sales tax because you already know the subtotal before the sales tax is calculated and the amount of the sales tax:

    $1,799.91 \times 1.06 = $1,907.9046$.

    Rounded to the nearest tenth = $1,907.90.

    This is the short way to figure out the answer. You could also multiply the total price of the 9 copiers ($1,799.91) by the percentage of sales tax (0.06), and add that to the total price, but it's one step more.

17. **The correct answer is (C).** The main idea of the paragraph is that fires can happen because of a lack of awareness of the possibility of a fire hazard. Choice (A) is close to the main idea, but it is not quite it. Choices (B) and (D) are mentioned in the paragraph either explicitly or implicitly as causes of fires, but they are not what the paragraph is mainly about.

18. **The correct answer is (C).** The best idea is to meet with the person before the first meeting and discuss how you can work together on the

project. Threatening a team member or trying to coerce the person, choice (D), is never a good idea. It's better to be straightforward with the person. Choice (A) is the last resort if the person obstructs the team's work or undermines the team leader's authority. Choice (B), ignoring the person and any contributions he or she makes at meetings, is never a good idea.

19. **The correct answer is (B).** You know the total and the amount completed in one hour by one person. To find how many more workers are needed: 4,770 ÷ 318 = 15.

20. **The correct answer is (B).** To find the total, first multiply the number of checks by the amount on each check, determine the amount of cash, and then add it all together:

    (18 × 75) + (31 × 140) + (10 × 130) + 200 + (2 × 50) + (2 × 20) + (7 × 10) + (3 × 5) =

    1,350 + 4,340 + 1,300 + 200 + 100 + 40 + 70 + 15 = $7,415.

21. **The correct answer is (A).** Add the total number of tickets written and divide by the number of moving violation tickets:

    5 + 14 + 16 + 31 + 42 + 3 + 1 + 4 + 1 = 117.

    8 ÷ 117 × 100 = 6.8%

22. **The correct answer is (A).** The correct action to take is to report the employee to your department head. You don't want to get mixed up in expense account cheating so you don't want to select choices (B) or (D). Reporting the employee to the auditing department, choice (C), goes over your supervisor's head, and that is not a good idea.

23. **The correct answer is (D).** 53

24. **The correct answer is (C).** 19

25. **The correct answer is (C).** 768

26. **The correct answer is (B).** 39

27. **The correct answer is (C).** 6.48

28. **The correct answer is (E).** None of the above.

29. **The correct answer is (A).** $\frac{4}{11}$

30. **The correct answer is (E).** All three names are different.

31. **The correct answer is (D).** The second and third numbers are alike.

32. **The correct answer is (C).** The first and third numbers are alike.

33. **The correct answer is (C).** The first and third numbers are alike.

34. **The correct answer is (A).** All three numbers are the same.

35. **The correct answer is (B).** The first and second names are the same.

36. **The correct answer is (B).** The first and second names are the same.

37. **The correct answer is (A).** Tanka, Hari; Tanaka, Harold

38. **The correct answer is (E).** Wong, Vernon, Wong, Vivienne

39. **The correct answer is (D).** D'Orsay, Leonard; d'Orsey, Eugene; D'Orsi, Edw.

40. **The correct answer is (C).** Blankenstein, T. Victor; Blaskett, Thomas A.; Blochner, H.A.

SELF-EVALUATION

Since there is only a single exam score, your performance on any single question type does not matter. In order to earn a high score, however, you must do well on all parts of the exam. Using the following self-evaluation chart, check how many of each question type and content area you missed to gauge your performance on that question type and for that content area. For the purposes of this Diagnostic Test, it doesn't matter if your particular test will not have a question type given here, chances are that the content/skill area—math, accuracy, grammar, reasoning, comprehension—will be on your exam. Concentrate your efforts on improving the areas that your score shows you had the most difficulty with. The following chart indicates which chapters you should review as you study this book.

SELF-EVALUATION CHART

Question Type	Question Numbers	Chapter(s) to Review
Judgment	18, 22	11
Grammar and Usage	1–5, 6–10	4, 6–9
Spelling	11–14	5
Clerical Speed and Accuracy	30–36	14
Reading Comprehension	15, 17	10
Alphabetizing and Filing	37–40	13
Computation	23–29	16–19
Work Problems	16, 19, 20, 21	19

PART III
VERBAL ABILITY

English Grammar and Usage

chapter 4

OVERVIEW

- The parts of speech
- Rules of sentence structure
- Rules of agreement
- Avoiding common errors
- Other rules you must know
- Summing it up

THE PARTS OF SPEECH

A strong grasp of the basic rules of English grammar is essential for scoring well on this part of the exam. All of the following rules should be review for you. Study these rules until you are sure you understand them, so that recognizing errors in the questions on the exam will come naturally to you.

Review the basic parts of speech:

- A **noun** is a person, place, thing, or idea: *teacher, city, desk, democracy.*
- **Pronouns** substitute for nouns: *he, they, ours, those.*
- An **adjective** describes a noun: *warm, quick, tall, blue.*
- A **verb** expresses action or state of being: *yell, interpret, feel, are.*
- An **adverb** modifies a verb, adjective, or another adverb: *slowly, well, busily.*
- **Conjunctions** join words, sentences, and phrases: *and, but, or.*
- A **preposition** shows position in time or space: *in, during, after, behind.*

It's also important to know what phrases are. A phrase is any group of related words that has no subject or predicate and that is used as a single part of speech. Phrases may be built around prepositions, articles, gerunds, or infinitives, but they cannot stand by themselves as sentences.

Nouns and Pronouns

The antecedent of the pronoun is the noun to which a pronoun refers. A pronoun must agree with its antecedent in gender, person, and number. The pronoun generally refers to the nearest noun. Make certain that the grammatical antecedent is indeed the intended antecedent. Consider this sentence: "Since the mouth of the cave was masked by underbrush, it provided an excellent hiding place." This is incorrect, because "it" refers to underbrush, not the intended antecedent "cave." You may find that the most effective way to clear up an ambiguity is to revise the sentence so the pronoun is not used.

Both pronouns and nouns have three cases:

❶ **Subjective:** The subject, noun/pronoun of address, or predicate noun/pronoun. Examples of subjective pronouns include *I, he, she, we,* and *they.*

❷ **Objective:** The direct object, indirect object, or object of a preposition. Examples of objective pronouns include *me, him, her, us,* and *them.*

❸ **Possessive:** The form that shows possession. Examples of possessive pronouns include *mine, his, hers, ours,* and *theirs.*

There are several rules relating to noun and pronoun case that you should know:

- The subject of a verb is in the subjective case even if the verb is understood and not expressed. Example: They are as old as *we.* (Check your answer by silently finishing off the sentence: *as we are.*)

- Nouns or pronouns connected by a form of the verb "to be" are always in the nominative case. Example: It is *I.* (Not *me.*)

- *Who* and *whoever* are in the nominative case; *whom* and *whomever* are in the objective case. Examples: The trapeze artist *who* ran away with the clown broke the lion tamer's heart. (*Who* is the subject of the verb *ran.*) Invite *whomever* you wish to accompany you. (*Whomever* is the object of the verb *invite.*)

- The object of a preposition or transitive verb takes a pronoun in the objective case. Example: It would be impossible for *me* to do that job alone. (*Me* is the object of the preposition *for.*)

- A noun or pronoun modifying a gerund should be in the possessive case. Example: Is there any criticism of *Arthur's* going? (*Going* is the gerund.)

Verbs

You can't have a sentence without a verb. Verbs indicate action, or condition (state) of being.

- A verb that expresses action is an **action verb** such as *drive, make, take, bring, eat.*
- There are also **helping verbs** and **linking verbs.**
  - Helping verbs combine with the main verb to form a verb phrase, such as *is going* or *has worked.* The main helping verbs are *do, does, did; have, has, had; will, would, could, should; can, may; must.*
  - Linking verbs connect the subject with a word that describes or identifies it, for example, <u>Charlene is</u> a good <u>worker</u>. The main linking verb is the verb *to be* and its forms: *am, are, is, was, were, been.*
  - Other linking verbs are *appear, become, continue, feel, grow, look, remain, seen, smell, sound, taste,* and *turn.*

TIP

Be careful using the different forms of the personal pronouns. *Jack and me are going* is incorrect because *me* is the objective form of the first person pronoun, and you need a subject. *They invited Jack and I to go* is also incorrect. You need the objective form here.

Verbs have four principal parts:

1 Present (bake)

2 Present participle (baking)

3 Past (baked)

4 Past participle (baked)

The *–ing* and *–ed* endings you see here are the usual way of forming present and past participles, but some verbs have irregular past and past participles, for example, *slept / slept, ate / eaten, knew / known, sat / sat.*

Verbs may be in the active or passive voice.

- When a verb is in the active voice, the subject is the doer of the action: *Sheena opened the door.*

- When the verb is in the passive voice, the subject is not the doer: *The door was opened by Sheena.* Passive voice uses a form of the main verb and a form of the verb *to be.*

When you are writing, it is always better to use active voice than passive voice.

Verbs have six tenses. Tense tells when something is or is done.

1 **Present tense:** It is happening now *(eat, drive, make).*

2 **Past tense:** It happened before *(ate, drove, made).*

3 **Future tense:** It is going to happen *(will eat, will drive, will make).*

4 **Present perfect:** It began in the past and continues into the present *(has eaten, have driven, have made).*

5 **Past perfect:** It happened in the past before another action happened *(had eaten, had driven, had made).*

6 **Future perfect:** It will take place in the future before another action happens *(will have eaten, will have driven, will have made).*

Verbs may be singular or plural depending on the subject. Regardless of the voice or tense, the verb must agree in person and number with the subject. If the subject is in the third person, singular number *(he, she, it)*, the form of the linking or helping verb must be *is* or *has, does.*

Adjectives and Adverbs

Often, it is unclear whether you should use an adjective or an adverb. Remember that adjectives modify nouns and pronouns, and adverbs modify verbs, adjectives, and other adverbs. Sometimes, context must determine which is used. Consider this sentence: "The old man looked angry." In this case, you must use an adjective because you are describing a noun, *the old man*. Consider this sentence: "The old man looked *angrily* out the window." Now, you must use an adverb because you are describing a verb, *looked*.

Adjectives answer the questions "Which one?" "What kind?" and "How many?" Adverbs answer the questions "Why?" "How?" "Where?" "When?" and "To what degree?"

Place adverbs, clauses, and phrases near the words they modify to prevent confusion. For example, "The man was willing to sell only one horse" is better than "the man was *only* willing to sell one horse," because the adverb *only* modifies the adjective *one*, rather than the verb *was willing*.

Whenever you use a modifier, it must modify something. For example, the sentence "While away on vacation, the pipes burst" is incorrect. The pipes were not on vacation, so the phrase does not modify anything. A better way to say it is "While we were on vacation, the pipes burst."

Conjunctions and Prepositions

Conjunctions connect words, phrases, and clauses. There are three general types of conjunctions:

- **Coordinate:** Placed next to the words and ideas it connects. Examples of coordinate conjunctions include *and* and *but*.

- **Subordinate:** Connects a dependent idea in a sentence with the main thought. Subordinate conjunctions are used to indicate concession (*although, even if, though*), to show cause (*now that, because, as, since*), to describe a condition (*provided that, if only, except that, unless*), to indicate purpose (*in order to, so that*), or to fix a time (*as long as, ever since, until, after, when, now*).

- **Correlative:** Used in pairs and usually placed next to the words they connect. Examples of correlative conjunction pairs are: *neither / nor, either / or*, and *not only / but also*.

Prepositions are connecting words that show a noun or pronoun's relationship to other words in the sentence. They're almost always combined with other words in constructions known as prepositional phrases.

A prepositional phrase acts as an adjective or adverb to locate something in time and space, to modify a noun, or to describe where or under what conditions something occurred. Examples of common prepositions include: *about, above, across, after, against, along, among, around, at, before, behind, below, beneath, beside, between, by, down, during, except, for, from, in, in front of, inside, instead of, into, near, off, on, on top of, onto, out of, outside, over, past, through, to, toward, under, until, up, upon, with, within,* and *without.*

In day-to-day speech, people often use prepositions where they aren't needed. Review the examples below and be sure you know where to eliminate or replace extraneous prepositions.

- He met ~~up with~~ the new president yesterday.
- The boy fell off ~~of~~ the bicycle.

TIP

The best test for the placement of modifiers is to read the sentence literally. If the sentence does not make sense, it is wrong. The meaning of the sentence should be clear to any reader.

NOTE

Hardly, scarcely, barely, only, and *but* (when it means only) are negative words. Do not use another negative in combination with any of these words. Incorrect: I can't hardly read the small print.

- She threw the ball out ~~of~~ the window.
- My parents wouldn't let the dog inside ~~of~~ the house. (or use *in* in place of *inside of*)
- Where did Harry go ~~to~~?
- Park your car ~~in back of~~ the office building. (use *behind* instead)
- Where is your house ~~at~~?

RULES OF SENTENCE STRUCTURE

You should know the following basic rules of good sentence structure:

- Every sentence must contain a verb. A group of words without a verb is a sentence fragment, not a sentence.
- Every sentence must have a subject. The subject may be a noun, pronoun, phrase, or clause functioning as a noun. In commands, however, the subject is usually not expressed but is understood to be *you*.
- A subordinate clause must never stand alone. It is not a complete sentence, despite the fact that it has a subject and a verb. Subordinate clauses may act as adverbs, adjectives, or nouns. A subordinate adverbial clause is usually introduced by a subordinating conjunction, such as *when, while, because, as soon as, if, after, although, as before, since, than, though, until,* and *unless*. Subordinate adjective and noun clauses may be introduced by the pronouns *who, which,* and *that*.

RULES OF AGREEMENT

The following are sometimes tricky rules of subject-verb agreement and verb tense that you must know:

- A verb should agree in number with the subject of the sentence. Example: Poor study *habits are* the leading cause of unsatisfactory achievement in school.
- A verb should not be made to agree with a noun that is part of a phrase following the subject. Example: *Mount Snow,* one of my favorite ski areas, *is* in Vermont.
- A subject consisting of two or more nouns joined by a coordinating conjunction takes a plural verb. Example: Paul *and* Sue *were* the last to arrive.
- When the conjunctions *or, either/or,* and *neither/nor* are used, the number of the verb agrees with the last subject. Example: Either the cat or the *mice take* charge in the barn.
- The number of the verb is not affected when words introduced by *with, together with, no less than, as well as,* etc., modify the subject. Example: The *captain,* together with the rest of the team, *was delighted* by the victory celebration.
- In sentences beginning with *there is* and *there are,* the verb agrees with the noun that follows it. Example: There *is not* an unbroken *bone* in her body.
- Statements equally true in the past and the present are usually expressed in the present tense. Example: He said that Venus *is* a planet. (Although he made the statement in the past, the fact remains that Venus is a planet.)

NOTE

Each, either, neither, anyone, anybody, somebody, someone, every, everyone, one, no one, and *nobody* are singular pronouns. Each of these words takes a singular verb and a singular pronoun. Example: Neither Mike nor Joe likes to admit he is wrong.

- When expressing a condition contrary to fact or a wish, use the subjunctive form *were*. Example: I wish I *were* a movie star.

AVOIDING COMMON ERRORS

The following are common but subtle errors. Train yourself to concentrate on each sentence so that you can recognize errors.

- Comparisons must be logical and complete. Incorrect: Wilmington is larger than any city in Delaware. Correct: Wilmington is larger than any *other* city in Delaware. (Wilmington cannot be larger than itself.)

- Comparisons and other groups must be parallel. Incorrect: She spends all her time eating, asleep, and on her studies. Correct: She spends all her time eating, *sleeping,* and *studying.* (All three present participle forms are used as nouns.)

- Avoid needless shifts in point-of-view—a change within the sentence from one verb tense to another, from one subject to another, or from one person or number to another. Incorrect: Mary especially likes math, but history is also enjoyed by her. (The subject shifts from Mary to history, and the voice shifts from active to passive.) Correct: Mary especially likes math, but she also enjoys history.

- Avoid the *is when* and *is where* constructions. Incorrect: A limerick *is when* a short poem has a catchy rhyme. Correct: A limerick is a short poem with a catchy rhyme.

OTHER RULES YOU MUST KNOW

The following list of rules is far from comprehensive. In fact, it is purposely kept brief so that you can learn every rule and every hint. You will find these rules invaluable for all your writing.

Capitalization Rules

- Capitalize the first word of a sentence.
- Capitalize all proper names.
- Capitalize days of the week, months of the year, and holidays.
- Do not capitalize the seasons.
- Capitalize the first and all other important words in a title including the forms of the verb *to be.* Example: *The Art of Promotion* or *The Winner Is a Major Shock to Fans.*
- Capitalize common nouns only when they are used as part of proper names. Example: Yesterday I visited *Uncle Charles*, my favorite *uncle*.
- Capitalize the points of the compass only when referring to a specific place or area. Example: Many retired persons spend the winter in the *South*.
- Do not capitalize the points of the compass when referring to a direction. Example: Many birds fly *south* in the winter.

- Capitalize languages and specific place names used as modifiers, but do not capitalize any other school subjects. Example: Next year I will study *French,* biology, and *English* literature.

- Capitalize the first word of a direct quotation. Example: Alexander Pope wrote, "*A* little learning is a dangerous thing."

- Do not capitalize the first word within quotation marks if it does not begin a complete sentence, as when a direct quotation is broken. Example: "I tore my stocking," she told us, "because the drawer was left open."

Punctuation Rules

Using the Apostrophe

Use an apostrophe in the following situations:

- To indicate possession. When indicating possession, the apostrophe means "belonging to everything to the left of the apostrophe." Use this rule to test for correct placement. For example, childrens' or "belonging to the childrens" is obviously incorrect, while children's or "belonging to the children" is correct. This placement rule applies at all times, even with compound nouns and with entities made up of two or more names. For example, father-in-law's means "belonging to a father-in-law," and Brown and Sons' delivery truck means "delivery truck belonging to Brown and Sons."

- In a contraction in place of the omitted letter or letters. Examples: haven't, we're, class of '85, '90s.

- To form plurals of numbers, letters, and phrases referred to as words. Example: The Japanese child pronounced his *l*'s as *r*'s.

Using the Colon

Use a colon in the following situations:

- After a salutation in a business letter. Example: Dear Board Member:
- To separate hours from minutes. Example: The eclipse occurred at 10:36 a.m.
- Use of the colon is optional in the following cases:
  o To introduce a list, especially after expressions like *as follows* or *the following*.
  o To introduce a long quotation.
  o To introduce a question, such as "My question is this: Are you willing to punch a time clock?"

Using the Comma

Use a comma in the following situations:

- After the salutation of a personal letter. Example: Dear Mary,
- After the complimentary close of a letter. Example: Cordially yours,

- To set off a noun in direct address. Example: When you finish your homework, Jeff, take out the garbage.
- To set off an appositive—a phrase that follows a noun or pronoun and means the same thing. Example: Mr. Burke, our lawyer, gave us some good advice.
- To set off parenthetical expressions—words or phrases that interrupt the flow of the sentence—such as *however, though, for instance,* and *by the way.* Examples: We could not, however, get him to agree. Test for placement of commas in a parenthetical expression by reading aloud. If you pause before and after the expression, set it off with commas.
- Between two or more adjectives that equally modify a noun. Example: The jolly, fat, ruddy man laughed.
- To separate words, phrases, or clauses in a series. Example: Place coats, umbrellas, and boots in the closet.
- To separate a direct quotation from the speaker. Example: She said, "I must leave work on time today."
- After an introductory phrase of five or more words. Example: Because the prisoner had a history of attempted jailbreaks, he was guarded heavily.
- After a short introductory phrase whenever the comma would aid clarity. Example: To Dan, Phil was a friend as well as brother.
- Before a coordinating conjunction unless the two clauses are very short. Example: The boy wanted to borrow a book from the library, but the librarian would not allow him to take it until he had paid his fines.
- To set off a nonrestrictive adjective phrase or clause—one that can be omitted without changing the meaning of the sentence. Example: Our new sailboat, which has bright orange sails, is very seaworthy. A restrictive phrase or clause is vital to the meaning of a sentence and cannot be omitted. Do not set it off with commas. Example: A sailboat that has no sails is useless.
- If the sentence might be subject to different interpretations without a comma. Examples: My brother Bill is getting married. (This implies that I have more than one brother.) My brother, Bill, is getting married. (In this case, Bill is an appositive and presumably the only brother.)
- If a pause would make the sentence clearer and easier to read. Incorrect: After all crime must be punished. Correct: After all, crime must be punished.

Using the Dash

Use a dash in the following situations:

- For emphasis or to set off an explanatory group of words. Example: The tools of his trade—probe, mirror, cotton swabs—were neatly arranged on the dentist's tray. Unless the set-off expression ends a sentence, dashes, like parentheses, must be used in pairs.

- To break up a thought. Example: There are five—remember I said five—good reasons to refuse their demands.

Using the Hyphen

Use a hyphen in the following situations:

- To divide a word at the end of a line. Always divide words between syllables.

- In numbers from twenty-one to ninety-nine.

- To join two words serving together as a single adjective before a noun. Example: We left the highway and proceeded on a well-paved road.

- With the prefixes *ex-, self-,* and *all-,* and with the suffix *-elect.* Examples: ex-Senator, self-appointed, all-state, Governor-elect.

- To avoid ambiguity. Example: After the custodian recovered use of his right arm, he re-covered the office chairs.

- To avoid an awkward union of letters. Examples: self-independent, shell-like.

Using the Semicolon

Use a semicolon in the following situations:

- To separate a series of phrases or clauses, each of which contains commas. Example: The old gentleman's heirs were Margaret Whitlock, his half-sister; William Frame, companion to his late cousin, Robert Bone; and his favorite charity, the Salvation Army.

- To avoid confusion with numbers. Example: Add the following: $1.25; $7.50; and $12.89.

- Two main clauses must be separated by a conjunction or by a semicolon, or they must be written as two sentences. A semicolon never precedes a coordinating conjunction. The same two clauses may be written in any one of three ways:

  o   Autumn had come and the trees were almost bare.

  o   Autumn had come; the trees were almost bare.

  o   Autumn had come. The trees were almost bare.

Using the Period, Question Mark, and Exclamation Point

- Use a period at the end of a sentence that makes a statement, gives a command, or makes a "polite request" in the form of a question that does not require an answer.

- Use a period after an abbreviation and after the initial in a person's name. Example: Gen. Robert E. Lee.

- Use a question mark after a request for information.

- Use an exclamation point to express strong feeling or emotion, or to imply urgency. Example: Congratulations! You broke the record.

TIP

If you are uncertain about how to use the semicolon to connect independent clauses, write two sentences instead.

Using Quotation Marks

Use quotation marks in the following situations:

- To enclose all directly quoted material. Words not quoted must remain outside the quotation marks. Example: "If it's hot on Sunday," she said, "we'll go to the beach." Do not enclose an indirect quote in quotation marks. Example: She said that we might go to the beach on Sunday.

- Around words used in an unusual way. Example: A surfer who "hangs ten" is performing a maneuver on a surfboard, not staging a mass execution.

- To enclose the title of a short story, essay, short poem, song, or article. Example: Robert Louis Stevenson wrote a plaintive poem called "Bed in Summer." Titles of books and plays are not enclosed in quotation marks. They are printed in italics. In handwritten or typed manuscript, underscore titles of books and plays. Examples: The song "Tradition" is from *Fiddler on the Roof*. The song "Tradition" is from <u>Fiddler on the Roof</u>. (if handwritten)

Remember these rules for placing quotation marks correctly:

- Periods and commas always go inside quotation marks. Example: Pornography is sold under the euphemism "adult books."

- Question marks and exclamation points go inside quotation marks if they are part of the quotation. If the whole sentence containing the quotation is a question or exclamation, the punctuation goes outside the quotation marks. Example: What did you really mean when you said "I do"?

- Colons and semicolons always go outside the quotation marks. Example: He said, "War is destructive"; she added, "Peace is constructive."

- When a multiple-paragraph passage is quoted, each paragraph of the quotation must begin with quotation marks, but ending quotation marks are used only at the end of the last quoted paragraph.

- Direct quotations are bound by all the rules of sentence structure. Beware of run-on sentences in divided quotations. Incorrect: "Your total is wrong," he said, "add the column again." Correct: "Your total is wrong," he said. "Add the column again." In the correct example, the two independent clauses form two separate sentences.

EXERCISE

Directions: In each of the following questions, there are four sentences. Choose the grammatically incorrect sentence. When you are finished, check your answers in the section immediately following the questions.

1. **(A)** Everyone at camp must have his medical certificate on file before participating in competitive sports.
   (B) A crate of oranges were sent from Florida for all the children in cabin six.
   (C) John and Danny's room looks as if they were prepared for inspection.
   (D) Three miles is too far for a young child to walk.

2. **(A)** Being tired, I stretched out on a grassy knoll.
   (B) While we were rowing on the lake, a sudden squall almost capsized the boat.
   (C) Entering the room, a strange mark on the floor attracted my attention.
   (D) Mounting the curb, the empty car crossed the sidewalk and came to rest against a building.

3. **(A)** Not one in a thousand readers take the matter seriously.
   (B) He was able partially to accomplish his purpose.
   (C) You are not as tall as he.
   (D) The people began to realize how much she had done.

4. **(A)** In the case of members who are absent, a special letter will be sent.
   (B) The visitors were all ready to see it.
   (C) I like Burns's poem "To a Mountain Daisy."
   (D) John said that he was sure he seen it.

5. **(A)** Neither the critics nor the author were right about the reaction of the public.
   (B) The senator depended upon whoever was willing to assist him.
   (C) I don't recall any time when Edgar has broken his word.
   (D) Every one of the campers but John and me is going on the hike.

6. **(A)** B. Nelson & Co. has a sale on sport shirts today.
   (B) Venetian blinds—called that although they probably did not originate in Venice—are no longer used as extensively as they were at one time.
   (C) He determined to be guided by the opinion of whoever spoke first.
   (D) There was often disagreement as to whom was the better Shakespearean actor, Evans or Gielgud.

7. **(A)** Never before have I seen anyone who has the skill John has when he repairs engines.
   (B) If anyone can be wholly just in his decisions, it is he.
   (C) Because of his friendliness, the new neighbor was immediately accepted by the community.
   (D) Imagine our embarrassment when us girls saw Miss Maltinge sitting with her beau in the front row.

8. **(A)** The general regarded whomever the colonel honored with disdain.

   (B) Everyone who reads this book will think themselves knights errant on missions of heroism.

   (C) The reason why the new leader was so unsuccessful was that he had fewer responsibilities.

   (D) All the new mechanical devices we have today have made our daily living a great deal simpler, it is said.

9. **(A)** I can but do my best.

   (B) I cannot help comparing him with his predecessor.

   (C) I wish that I was in Florida now.

   (D) I like this kind of grapes better than any other.

10. **(A)** Neither Tom nor John was present for the rehearsal.

    (B) The happiness or misery of men's lives depends on their early training.

    (C) Honor as well as profit are to be gained by these studies.

    (D) The egg business is only incidental to the regular business of the general store.

11. **(A)** The Board of Directors has prepared a manual for their own use.

    (B) The company has announced its new policy of advertising.

    (C) The jury was out about thirty minutes when it returned a verdict.

    (D) The flock of geese creates a health hazard for visitors with allergies.

12. **(A)** Two thirds of the building are finished.

    (B) Where are Mr. Keene and Mr. Herbert?

    (C) Neither the salespeople nor the manager want to work overtime.

    (D) The committee was agreed.

13. **(A)** The coming of peace effected a change in her way of life.

    (B) Spain is as weak as, if not more weaker than, it was in 1900.

    (C) In regard to that, I am not certain what my attitude will be.

    (D) That unfortunate family faces the problem of adjusting itself to a new way of life.

14. **(A)** I wondered why it was that the mayor objected to the governor's reference to the new tax law.

    (B) I have never read *Les Miserables,* but I plan to read it this summer.

    (C) After much talk and haranguing, the workers received an increase in wages.

    (D) Charles Dole, who is a member of the committee, was asked to confer with commissioner Wilson.

15. **(A)** Most employees, and he is no exception do not like to work overtime.

    (B) The doctor had carelessly left all the instruments on the operating table.

    (C) Despite all the power he has, I should still hate to be in his shoes.

    (D) I feel bad because I gave such a poor performance in the play tonight.

16. **(A)** Of London and Paris, the former is the wealthier.

    (B) Of the two cities visited, White Plains is the cleanest.

    (C) Chicago is larger than any other city in Illinois.

    (D) The United States is the wealthiest nation, and, of all others, China is the most populous.

17. **(A)** It was superior in every way to the book previously used.

    (B) His testimony today is different from that of yesterday.

    (C) The letter will be sent to the United States senate this week.

    (D) The flowers smelled so sweet that the whole house was perfumed.

18. **(A)** When either or both habits become fixed, the student improves.

    (B) When the supervisor entered the room, he noticed that the book was laying on the desk.

    (C) Neither his words nor his action was justifiable.

    (D) A calm almost always comes before a storm.

19. **(A)** Who did they say won?

    (B) Send in the candidate, Ann.

    (C) The question of who should be leader arose.

    (D) All the clerks including those who have been appointed recently are required to work on the new assignment.

20. **(A)** Mrs. Black the supervisor of the unit has many important duties.

    (B) This is the woman whom I saw.

    (C) She could solve even this problem.

    (D) She divided the money among the three of us.

21. **(A)** He felt deep despair (and who has not?) at the evidence of man's inhumanity to people.

    (B) You will be glad, I am sure, to give the book to whoever among your young friends has displayed an interest in animals.

    (C) When independence day falls on a Sunday, it is officially celebrated on Monday.

    (D) Being a stranger in town myself, I know how you feel.

22. **(A)** The task of filing these cards is to be divided equally between you and he.

    (B) A series of authentic records of Native American people is being published.

    (C) The Smokies is the home of the descendants of this brave tribe.

    (D) Five dollars is really not too much to pay for a book of this type.

23. **(A)** The game over, the spectators rushed out on the field and tore down the goalposts.

    (B) The situation was aggravated by disputes over the captaincy of the team.

    (C) Yesterday they lay their uniforms aside with the usual end-of-the-season regret.

    (D) It is sometimes thought that politics is not for the high-minded.

24. **(A)** Consider that the person which is always idle can never be happy.

    (B) Because a man understands a woman does not mean they are necessarily compatible.

    (C) He said that accuracy and speed are both essential.

    (D) "Is it possible that the better of the two coats is less expensive?" asked Raoul.

25. **(A)** Everyone entered promptly but her.

    (B) Each of the messengers were busily occupied.

    (C) At which exit did you leave him?

    (D) The work was not done well.

ANSWER KEY AND EXPLANATIONS

1. B	6. D	11. A	16. B	21. C
2. C	7. D	12. C	17. C	22. A
3. A	8. B	13. B	18. B	23. C
4. D	9. C	14. D	19. D	24. A
5. A	10. C	15. A	20. A	25. B

1. **The correct answer is (B).** The subject of the sentence is *crate*, which takes a singular verb. Correct: A crate of oranges *was* sent from Florida for all the children in cabin six.

2. **The correct answer is (C).** The sentence literally reads as if the strange mark entered the room. A better way to write it would be: *When I entered the room, a strange mark on the floor attracted my attention.*

3. **The correct answer is (A).** The subject of the sentence is *one*, which takes a singular verb. Correct: Not one in a thousand readers *takes* the matter seriously.

4. **The correct answer is (D).** The verb is missing its helping verb had. You can't use a participle form alone as a verb. Correct: John said that he was sure he *had seen* it.

5. **The correct answer is (A).** When two nouns (or pronouns) are joined by the correlative conjunction *neither/nor*, the verb agrees with the last subject. Correct: Neither the critics nor the author *was* right about the reaction of the public.

6. **The correct answer is (D).** *Who* is the subject of the verb following it, *was*. Correct: There was often disagreement as to *who* was the better Shakespearean actor, Evans or Gielgud.

7. **The correct answer is (D).** As the subject of the verb *saw*, the correct word is *we*, not *us*. Correct: Imagine our embarrassment when we girls saw Miss Maltinge sitting with her beau in the front row.

8. **The correct answer is (B).** The sentence switches number in the middle. Correct: Everyone who reads this book will think *himself a knight errant on a mission of heroism.*

9. **The correct answer is (C).** Use the subjunctive, *were*, when stating a wish. Correct: I *wish* that I *were* in Florida now.

10. **The correct answer is (C).** The phrase *as well as profit* does not add to the number of the subject, so the verb should be singular. Correct: Honor as well as profit *is* to be gained by these studies.

11. **The correct answer is (A).** The sentence switches number in the middle (Board of Directors is singular). Correct: The Board of Directors has prepared a manual for *its* own use.

12. **The correct answer is (C).** Because *neither/nor* is a correlative conjunction, the verb must agree with the nearest noun. Correct: Neither the salespeople nor the manager *wants* to work overtime.

13. **The correct answer is (B).** You don't need both the comparative ending *–er* and the word *more* to create the comparative form. Correct: Spain is as weak as, if not weaker than, it was in 1900.

14. **The correct answer is (D).** *Commissioner Wilson* is a specific commissioner, so the C must be capitalized. Correct: Charles Dole, who is a

member of the committee, was asked to confer with *Commissioner* Wilson.

15. **The correct answer is (A).** Parenthetical expressions must always be enclosed in commas. Correct: Most employees, *and he is no exception,* do not like to work overtime.

16. **The correct answer is (B).** The comparative *-er* is used when only two items are being compared; *-est* requires three or more items. Correct: Of the two cities visited, White Plains is the *cleaner*.

17. **The correct answer is (C).** The specific noun *senate* must be capitalized. Correct: The letter will be sent to the United States *Senate* this week.

18. **The correct answer is (B).** The verb *to lay* should be used only when it can be replaced with *to put*; at all other times use a form of the verb *to lie*. Correct: When the supervisor entered the room, he noticed that the book was *lying* on the desk.

19. **The correct answer is (D).** Omitting the clause does not change the meaning of the remaining words, so it is nonrestrictive and should be set off by commas. Correct: All the clerks, *including those who have been appointed recently,* are required to work on the new assignment.

20. **The correct answer is (A).** Appositives should be set off by commas. Correct: Mrs. Black, *the supervisor of the unit,* has many important duties.

21. **The correct answer is (C).** Holidays are always capitalized. Correct: When *Independence Day* falls on a Sunday, it is officially celebrated on Monday.

22. **The correct answer is (A).** Pronouns that are objects of prepositions should be in the objective case. Correct: The task of filing these cards is to be divided equally between you and *him*.

23. **The correct answer is (C).** Because the sentence occurred in the past (*yesterday*), the verb should be in the past tense. Correct: Yesterday they *laid* their uniforms aside with the usual end-of-the-season regret.

24. **The correct answer is (A).** Use *who* when referring to people and *which* when referring to objects. Correct: Consider that the person *who* is always idle can never be happy.

25. **The correct answer is (B).** *Each* is singular. Correct: Each of the messengers *was* busily occupied.

SUMMING IT UP

- A strong grasp of basic English grammar is essential for scoring well on the civil service exams. Study the rules until you're sure you understand them, so that you can easily recognize errors in the questions that appear on your exam.

- The basic parts of speech are: noun, pronoun, adjective, verb, adverb, conjunction, and preposition. A phrase is any group of related words that has no subject or predicate and is used as a single part of speech.

- Pronouns and nouns have three cases: subjective, objective, and possessive. Make sure you know the rules relating to these cases by studying the section in this chapter devoted to nouns and pronouns.

- Verbs indicate action or condition of being. Verbs may also serve as helping or linking verbs. Verbs have six tenses and may be in the active or passive voice. Regardless of the voice or tense, verbs must agree in person and number with their subjects.

- Telling adjectives from adverbs is sometimes difficult. Remember that adjectives modify nouns and adverbs modify verbs, adjectives, and other adverbs. Adjectives answer the questions "Which one?" "What kind?" and "How many?" Adverbs answer the questions "Why?" "How?" "When?" and "To what degree?"

- To do well on the civil service exam, review the basic rules of good sentence structure, subject-verb agreement, and verb tense.

- It pays to be sure you know the rules of capitalization and punctuation. You will see questions relating to these rules on your civil service exam.

Spelling

OVERVIEW

- **Essential spelling rules**
- **Strategies for answering common spelling questions**
- **Summing it up**

ESSENTIAL SPELLING RULES

The rules outlined in this section will see you through almost any spelling question that you may face. Study these rules and their most common exceptions. Memorize as many as you can.

1 i before e except after c or when sounding like ay as in *neighbor* or *weigh*. Exceptions: *neither, leisure, foreign, seize, weird, height.*

2 If a word ends in y preceded by a vowel, keep the y when adding a suffix. Examples: *day, days; attorney, attorneys.*

3 If a word ends in y preceded by a consonant, change the y to i before adding a suffix. Examples: *try, tried; lady, ladies.* To avoid double i, retain the y before the suffixes -*ing* and -*ish*. Examples: *fly, flying; baby, babyish.*

4 A silent e at the end of a word is usually dropped before a suffix beginning with a vowel. Examples: dine + ing = dining; locate + ion = location; use + able = usable; offense + ive = offensive. Words ending in ce and ge retain e before the suffixes -*able* and -*ous* in order to retain the soft sounds of e and g. Examples: peace + able = peaceable; courage + ous = courageous.

5 A silent e is usually kept before a suffix beginning with a consonant. Examples: care + less = careless; late + ly = lately; one + ness = oneness; game + ster = gamester. Some exceptions must simply be memorized.

6 Exceptions to rules 4 and 5 are: *truly, duly, awful, argument, wholly, ninth, mileage, dyeing, acreage,* and *canoeing.*

7 A one-syllable word that ends in a *single* consonant preceded by a *single* vowel doubles the final consonant before a suffix beginning with a vowel or y. Examples: *hit, hitting; drop, dropped; big, biggest; mud, muddy.* But *help* becomes *helping* because *help* ends in two consonants, and *need* becomes *needing* because the final consonant is preceded by two vowels.

8 A word with more than one syllable (that accents the *last* syllable and ends in a *single* consonant preceded by a single vowel) doubles the final consonant when adding a suffix beginning with a vowel. Examples: *begin, beginner*; *admit, admitted*. But *enter* becomes *entered* because the accent is not on the last syllable.

9 A word ending in <u>er</u> or <u>ur</u> doubles the <u>r</u> in the past tense if the word is accented on the *last* syllable. Examples: *occur, occurred*; *prefer, preferred*; *transfer, transferred*.

10 A word ending in <u>er</u> does not double the <u>r</u> in the past tense if the accent does *not* fall on the last syllable. Examples: *answer, answered*; *offer, offered*; *differ, differed*.

11 When -full is added to the end of a noun to form an adjective, the final <u>l</u> is dropped. Examples: *cheerful, cupful, hopeful*.

12 All words beginning with *over* are one word. Examples: *overcast, overcharge, overhear*.

13 All words with the prefix *self* are hyphenated. Examples: *self-control, self-defense, self-evident*.

14 *Percent* is never hyphenated.

15 The letter <u>q</u> is always followed by <u>u</u>. Examples: *quiz, bouquet, acquire*.

16 *Welcome* is one word with one <u>l</u>.

17 *All right* is always two words; there is no such word as *alright*.

18 *Already* means prior to some specified time; *all ready* means completely ready. Example: By the time I was *all ready* to go to the play, the bus had *already* left.

19 *Altogether* means entirely; *all together* means in sum or collectively. Example: There are *altogether* too many people to seat in this room when we are *all together*.

20 *Their* is the possessive of "they"; *they're* is the contraction for "they are"; and *there* is "that place." Example: *They're* going to put *their* books over *there*.

21 *Your* is the possessive of "you"; *you're* is the contraction for "you are." Example: *You're* certainly planning to leave *your* muddy boots outside.

22 *Whose* is the possessive of "who"; *who's* is the contraction for "who is." Example: Do you know *who's* ringing the doorbell or *whose* car is in the street?

23 *Its* is the possessive of "it"; *it's* is the contraction for "it is." Example: *It's* I who put *its* stamp on the letter.

Develop a personal program for improving your spelling. Think of your own private "devils"—the words that you must look up every time. Everyone has such words. Make a list of these words, correctly spelled. Keep adding to the list right up to exam day, including those words that you miss on the practice exercises. Each day that you have extra study time, type through the list three times. By typing your troublesome words correctly, your hands and fingers will get used to the "feel" of the correct spelling, and your eye will become accustomed to seeing the words correctly spelled. Frequent repetition will embed the correct spellings in your mind.

STRATEGIES FOR ANSWERING COMMON SPELLING QUESTIONS

The following exercises illustrate the three most common types of spelling questions found on civil service exams. By studying these examples, you can easily tackle the spelling questions on the actual exam.

One common variety of spelling question looks like this:

Directions: In each group of four words, one word is misspelled. Find the misspelled word and mark its letter on your answer sheet.

1. **(A)** business
    (B) manufacturer
    (C) possibly
    (D) recieved

In this case, you would mark (D) on your answer sheet because *recieved* is spelled incorrectly. Refer back to rule 1 in the previous section if you are unsure why choice (D) is incorrect.

A second common spelling question looks like this:

Directions: In each group of three words, one word may be misspelled. If you find one word that is incorrectly spelled, mark its letter on your answer sheet. If all the words are spelled correctly, mark (D).

1. **(A)** foreign
    (B) acreage
    (C) occurred
    (D) none of these

In this case, all three words are spelled correctly, so the answer is (D). If you thought one of these words was spelled incorrectly, refer back to spelling rule 1, the exceptions to rule 4, and rule 8 in the previous section.

Or you might run into spelling questions with somewhat more complicated instructions, like this:

Directions: Each question consists of three words, any or all of which may be spelled incorrectly. On your answer sheet:

      Mark (A) if *ONLY ONE* word is misspelled.
      Mark (B) if *TWO WORDS* are misspelled.
      Mark (C) if *ALL THREE* words are misspelled.
      Mark (D) if *NO WORDS* are misspelled.

    1.   offered   hopefull   usable

For this question, you would mark (B), because two words are misspelled—the first two. The correct spellings are *offered* (see rule 9) and *hopeful* (see rule 10). If you are unsure why *usable* is correct, refer back to rule 4.

Try another question:

    2.   acquire   welcome   per-cent

For this question, you should mark (A) as your answer, because only one word, *percent,* is misspelled (see rule 13). Look back at rules 14 and 15 to learn why the other two words are spelled correctly. If you find this third type of spelling question on your exam, you must be very careful to mark the letters of your answers as indicated in the directions. Refer to the directions frequently to refresh your memory on which letter goes with which answer.

The following spelling exercises will give you practice spotting words that are spelled incorrectly. The three most common types of spelling questions are included—one in each set of practice exercises. You will find the correct answer in the "Answer Key" section following the practice exercises. Sometimes it helps to answer spelling questions by looking away from the given choices and writing the word on the margin of your question booklet or on your scratch paper. Then, check to see if the spelling you believe is correct is given as one of the choices.

EXERCISE 1

Directions: In each group of four words, one is misspelled. Mark the letter of the misspelled word.

1. (A) hyphen
   (B) index
   (C) office
   (D) diferent

2. (A) corporation
   (B) handel
   (C) foreign
   (D) material

3. (A) adress
   (B) exactly
   (C) research
   (D) vertical

4. (A) occupation
   (B) accross
   (C) authority
   (D) invoice

5. (A) guardian
   (B) certified
   (C) voucher
   (D) mispelled

6. (A) trustee
   (B) multipal
   (C) promissory
   (D) valuable

7. (A) traveler
   (B) pamphlet
   (C) agencys
   (D) permit

8. (A) automatic
   (B) proportion
   (C) announcement
   (D) municiple

9. (A) recruitment
   (B) mentioned
   (C) optional
   (D) commision

10. (A) responsibility
    (B) disabled
    (C) vetran
    (D) misleading

11. (A) competetive
    (B) review
    (C) erroneous
    (D) license

12. (A) familiarity
    (B) accredited
    (C) payment
    (D) distributer

13. (A) localities
    (B) servise
    (C) central
    (D) occupation

14. (A) offerred
    (B) jogging
    (C) threaten
    (D) advertise

15. (A) vending
    (B) tomorrow
    (C) strangly
    (D) barometer

16. (A) anounce
    (B) local
    (C) grasshopper
    (D) farmer

17. (A) historical
    (B) dustey
    (C) kindly
    (D) anniversary

18. (A) current
    (B) comunity
    (C) cement
    (D) calves

19. (A) changeing
    (B) explained
    (C) diameter
    (D) consent

20. (A) sword
    (B) selfassured
    (C) signed
    (D) taste

EXERCISE 2

Directions: In each question, one of the words may be spelled incorrectly, or all three may be spelled correctly. If one of the words is spelled incorrectly, mark the letter of this word. If all three words are spelled correctly, mark (D).

1. (A) gratful
   (B) census
   (C) analysis
   (D) none of these

2. (A) installment
   (B) retreive
   (C) concede
   (D) none of these

3. (A) dismissal
   (B) conscientious
   (C) indelible
   (D) none of these

4. (A) percieve
   (B) anticipate
   (C) acquire
   (D) none of these

5. (A) facility
   (B) reimburse
   (C) assortment
   (D) none of these

6. (A) plentifull
   (B) advantageous
   (C) similar
   (D) none of these

7. (A) guarantee
   (B) repel
   (C) ommission
   (D) none of these

8. (A) maintenance
   (B) liable
   (C) announcement
   (D) none of these

9. (A) exaggerate
   (B) seize
   (C) condenm
   (D) none of these

10. (A) pospone
    (B) altogether
    (C) grievance
    (D) none of these

11. (A) argument
    (B) reciept
    (C) complain
    (D) none of these

12. (A) sufficient
    (B) declaim
    (C) visible
    (D) none of these

13. (A) expirience
    (B) dissatisfy
    (C) alternate
    (D) none of these

14. (A) occurred
    (B) noticable
    (C) appendix
    (D) none of these

15. **(A)** anxious
    (B) warranty
    (C) calender
    (D) none of these

16. **(A)** fundamental
    (B) dissapear
    (C) accidentally
    (D) none of these

17. **(A)** guidance
    (B) across
    (C) carreer
    (D) none of these

18. **(A)** pamphlet
    (B) always
    (C) commit
    (D) none of these

19. **(A)** excessive
    (B) permited
    (C) appointment
    (D) none of these

20. **(A)** personnel
    (B) resource
    (C) colledge
    (D) none of these

EXERCISE 3

Directions: Each question consists of three words, any or all of which may be spelled incorrectly. Beside each question:

  Mark (A) if *ONLY ONE* word is misspelled.
  Mark (B) if *TWO WORDS* are misspelled.
  Mark (C) if *ALL THREE* words are misspelled.
  Mark (D) if *NO WORDS* are misspelled.

1. professor   satisfactorally   weight
2. sabbatical   accomplishment   occasionally
3. associate   bookeeping   carefuly
4. dictater   beforhand   deceit
5. accidently   supervisor   efficiently
6. bureau   manifest   scheduling
7. auxilary   machinary   distorsion
8. synthesis   harrassment   exemplify
9. receiveable   bankrupcy   chronological
10. facsimile   requisition   liability
11. proxey   pollish   courtesy
12. negotiable   acknowledgment   notarary
13. confidential   typograpfical   memmoranda
14. pertainent   codify   ellimination
15. corrective   performence   clogging

exercises

ANSWER KEY

Exercise 1

1. D	5. D	9. D	13. B	17. B
2. B	6. B	10. C	14. A	18. B
3. A	7. C	11. A	15. C	19. A
4. B	8. D	12. D	16. A	20. B

Exercise 2

1. A	5. D	9. C	13. A	17. C
2. B	6. A	10. A	14. B	18. D
3. D	7. C	11. B	15. C	19. B
4. A	8. D	12. D	16. B	20. C

Exercise 3

1. A	4. B	7. C	10. D	13. B
2. D	5. A	8. A	11. B	14. B
3. B	6. D	9. B	12. A	15. A

SUMMING IT UP

- A thorough knowledge of basic English spelling rules is essential for scoring well on the civil service exams. Study these rules and their most common exceptions and try to memorize as many as possible, so that you can easily recognize errors in the questions that appear on your exam.

- You will see three common types of spelling questions on your civil service exam: One type asks you to find the misspelled word among the answer choices; a second type asks you to determine whether any of the answer choices are misspelled (they may not be); and a third and somewhat more complicated type will ask you to choose whether one, two, three, or no words are misspelled among the answer choices. Be sure to read the directions very carefully so that you know what you are being asked.

Synonyms

OVERVIEW

- What are synonyms?
- Strategies for answering synonym questions
- Summing it up

WHAT ARE SYNONYMS?

Two words are *synonyms* if they mean the same thing. In a synonym question, you must pick the word or phrase closest in meaning to the given word. Remember that you are looking for the best match among the choices given, not necessarily a perfect match. You may encounter another type of vocabulary question—antonym questions. *Antonyms* are two words that have opposite meanings. In an antonym question, you must choose the word or phrase that most nearly means the opposite of the given word. The strategies for tackling antonym questions are similar to those for answering synonym questions, keeping in mind that you are looking for an answer that means the opposite, rather than the closest match.

Synonym questions are more commonly found on civil service exams, however, which is why this chapter focuses on them. When dealing with vocabulary questions, you must read the directions carefully to determine whether you should choose the opposite of the given word—its antonym—or its closest match—its synonym. Not paying close attention to the directions could result in answering an entire section of the exam incorrectly.

When you are faced with a synonym question, follow these three steps to answer the question:

1 Read the question carefully.

2 If you know right away that some of the answer choices are wrong, eliminate them.

3 From the remaining answer choices, select the one that most closely means the same as the given word, even if it is a word that you yourself do not normally use. The correct answer may not be a perfect synonym, but of the choices offered, it is the best fit.

chapter 6

Here is an example of a typical synonym question:

1. FACSIMILE means most nearly
    (A) summary
    (B) exact copy
    (C) list
    (D) artist's sketch

The correct answer is (B). This is a straightforward vocabulary question. The given word is rather difficult, but the choices are not tricky. A *facsimile* is a copy that looks exactly like the original—a photocopy, for instance. The word contains the root *simile*, meaning "like." Choice (C), *list*, has no connection with facsimile. Choices (A), *summary*, and (D), *artist's sketch*, are in a sense copies of something else, but not exact copies.

Here is another example:

2. FRAUDULENT means most nearly
    (A) suspicious
    (B) deceptive
    (C) unfair
    (D) despicable

The correct answer is (B). The word *fraudulent* means "characterized by deceit or trickery, especially deliberate misrepresentation." Therefore, *deceptive* is the best synonym. Choice (A), *suspicious*, "sensing that something is wrong without definite proof," could describe a person's reaction to a fraudulent situation. Choices (C), *unfair*, and (D), *despicable*, could both be used to describe a fraudulent act. The basic meanings of these three words, however, are completely different from the meaning of *fraudulent*.

Some tests phrase synonym questions as a sentence. You must then make sure that your answer makes sense in the given sentence and does not change the sentence's meaning. The following is an example of this kind of synonym question:

3. We had to *terminate* the meeting because a fire broke out in the hall. *Terminate* most nearly means
    (A) continue
    (B) postpone
    (C) end
    (D) extinguish

The correct answer is (C). Even if you do not know what *terminate* means, you can eliminate choice (A) because it does not make much sense to say, "We had to *continue* the meeting because a fire broke out in the hall." Choice (B), *postpone*, means "to put off until another time." It makes sense in the given sentence, but it also changes the meaning of the sentence. Choice (D), *extinguish*, is similar in meaning to *terminate* but not as close as *end*. One can extinguish, or "put an end to," a fire but not a meeting.

STRATEGIES FOR ANSWERING SYNONYM QUESTIONS

Answering synonym questions depends largely upon your knowledge of vocabulary. You can apply the following strategies to arrive at the correct answer, if you do not recognize it immediately:

- If you have a general idea about what the word means but are having trouble choosing an answer, try using the word in a short sentence. Then substitute each of the answer choices in the same sentence to see which one seems to fit the sentence best without changing its meaning.

- Try to break the given word into parts to see if the suffix (ending) or the prefix (beginning) gives a clue about its meaning. For example, if you are asked to find the synonym for *previous*, you may remember that the prefix *pre-* usually means "before." You could use that as a clue to help you choose the correct answer.

You must watch out for traps of logic, though. Study the following example:

1. PERTINENT means most nearly
    (A) relevant
    (B) prudent
    (C) true
    (D) respectful

The correct answer is (A). *Pertinent* means "having some bearing on or relevance to." In the sentence "Her testimony was pertinent to the investigation," you could put *relevant* in the place of *pertinent* without changing the meaning. Choice (B), *prudent*, means "careful" or "wise." Although it sounds somewhat like *pertinent*, its meaning is different. Choice (C) may seem possible because something that is *pertinent* should also be *true*. But watch out. Not everything that is true is pertinent.

Choice (D), *respectful*, is misleading. Its opposite, *disrespectful*, is a synonym for the word *impertinent*. You might logically guess, then, that *respectful* is a synonym for *pertinent*. The best way to avoid a trap like this is to remember how you have seen or heard the word used. You never see *pertinent* used to mean *respectful*.

EXERCISE 1

Directions: Select the word or phrase closest in meaning to the given word.

1. RETAIN means most nearly
   (A) pay out
   (B) play
   (C) keep
   (D) inquire

2. ENDORSE means most nearly
   (A) sign up for
   (B) announce support for
   (C) lobby for
   (D) renounce

3. INTRACTABLE means most nearly
   (A) confused
   (B) misleading
   (C) instinctive
   (D) unruly

4. CORRESPONDENCE means most nearly
   (A) letters
   (B) files
   (C) testimony
   (D) response

5. OBLITERATE means most nearly
   (A) praise
   (B) doubt
   (C) erase
   (D) reprove

6. LEGITIMATE means most nearly
   (A) democratic
   (B) legal
   (C) genealogical
   (D) underworld

7. DEDUCT means most nearly
   (A) conceal
   (B) withstand
   (C) subtract
   (D) terminate

8. MUTILATE means most nearly
   (A) paint
   (B) damage
   (C) alter
   (D) rebel

9. EGRESS means most nearly
   (A) extreme
   (B) extra supply
   (C) exit
   (D) high price

10. HORIZONTAL means most nearly
    (A) marginal
    (B) in a circle
    (C) left and right
    (D) up and down

11. CONTROVERSY means most nearly
    (A) publicity
    (B) debate
    (C) revolution
    (D) revocation

12. PREEMPT means most nearly
    (A) steal
    (B) empty
    (C) preview
    (D) appropriate

13. CATEGORY means most nearly
    (A) class
    (B) adherence
    (C) simplicity
    (D) cataract

14. APATHY means most nearly
    (A) sorrow
    (B) indifference
    (C) aptness
    (D) sickness

15. TENTATIVE means most nearly
    (A) persistent
    (B) permanent
    (C) thoughtful
    (D) provisional

16. PER CAPITA means most nearly
    (A) for an entire population
    (B) by income
    (C) for each person
    (D) for every adult

17. DEFICIENT means most nearly
    (A) sufficient
    (B) outstanding
    (C) inadequate
    (D) bizarre

18. INSPECT means most nearly
    (A) disregard
    (B) look at
    (C) annoy
    (D) criticize

19. OPTIONAL means most nearly
    (A) not required
    (B) infrequent
    (C) choosy
    (D) for sale

20. IMPLIED means most nearly
    (A) acknowledged
    (B) stated
    (C) predicted
    (D) hinted

exercises

EXERCISE 2

Directions: Select the word or phrase closest in meaning to the given word.

1. PRESUMABLY means most nearly
   - (A) positively
   - (B) helplessly
   - (C) recklessly
   - (D) supposedly

2. TEXTILE means most nearly
   - (A) linen
   - (B) cloth
   - (C) page
   - (D) garment

3. FISCAL means most nearly
   - (A) critical
   - (B) basic
   - (C) personal
   - (D) financial

4. STRINGENT means most nearly
   - (A) demanding
   - (B) loud
   - (C) flexible
   - (D) clear

5. PROCEED means most nearly
   - (A) go forward
   - (B) parade
   - (C) refrain
   - (D) resume

6. BROCHURE means most nearly
   - (A) ornament
   - (B) flowery statement
   - (C) breakage
   - (D) pamphlet

7. PERMEABLE means most nearly
   - (A) penetrable
   - (B) durable
   - (C) unending
   - (D) allowable

8. LIMIT means most nearly
   - (A) budget
   - (B) sky
   - (C) point
   - (D) boundary

9. SCRUPULOUS means most nearly
   - (A) conscientious
   - (B) unprincipled
   - (C) intricate
   - (D) neurotic

10. STALEMATE means most nearly
    - (A) pillar
    - (B) deadlock
    - (C) maneuver
    - (D) work slowdown

11. COMPETENT means most nearly
    - (A) inept
    - (B) informed
    - (C) capable
    - (D) caring

12. SOMATIC means most nearly
    - (A) painful
    - (B) drowsy
    - (C) indefinite
    - (D) physical

13. OBSTACLE means most nearly
    (A) imprisonment
    (B) hindrance
    (C) retaining wall
    (D) leap

14. REDUNDANT means most nearly
    (A) concise
    (B) reappearing
    (C) superfluous
    (D) lying down

15. SUPPLANT means most nearly
    (A) prune
    (B) conquer
    (C) uproot
    (D) replace

16. HAPHAZARD means most nearly
    (A) devious
    (B) without order
    (C) aberrant
    (D) risky

17. COMMENSURATE means most nearly
    (A) identical
    (B) of the same age
    (C) proportionate
    (D) measurable

18. ACCELERATE means most nearly
    (A) drive fast
    (B) reroute
    (C) decline rapidly
    (D) speed up

19. PURCHASED means most nearly
    (A) charged
    (B) bought
    (C) ordered
    (D) supplied

20. ZENITH means most nearly
    (A) depths
    (B) astronomical system
    (C) peak
    (D) solar system

exercises

ANSWER KEY

Exercise 1

1. C	5. C	9. C	13. A	17. C
2. B	6. B	10. C	14. B	18. B
3. D	7. C	11. B	15. D	19. A
4. A	8. B	12. D	16. C	20. D

Exercise 2

1. D	5. A	9. A	13. B	17. C
2. B	6. D	10. B	14. C	18. D
3. D	7. A	11. C	15. D	19. B
4. A	8. D	12. D	16. B	20. C

SUMMING IT UP

- The civil service exam will present questions about synonyms, which are two words that have the same or similar meanings. In these questions, you must choose the answer choice that most closely matches the given word. Remember that you are looking for the *best* match, not necessarily a perfect match.

- You may also encounter antonym questions on your exam: words with opposite or nearly opposite meanings. The strategy for tackling antonym questions is much like that of answering synonym questions—but keep in mind that you are looking for the *opposite* in meaning rather than the closest match, so read the directions very carefully.

- Take these steps to successfully choose the correct answers to synonym questions: Read the question carefully, eliminate any answer choices that you know for certain are wrong, and then select the remaining answer choice that most nearly means the same as the given word, even if it is not a word that you normally use.

Sentence Completions

OVERVIEW

- What are sentence completions?
- Strategies for answering sentence completion questions
- Summing it up

WHAT ARE SENTENCE COMPLETIONS?

In a sentence completion question, you are given a sentence or long passage in which something has been left blank. A number of words or phrases are suggested to fill that blank. You must select the word or phrase that will best complete the meaning of the passage as a whole. Although more than one answer may make sense, the best choice will be the one that is most exact, appropriate, or likely, considering the information given in the sentence or passage.

Follow these four steps to answer a sentence completion question:

1 Read the question carefully, looking at all the answer choices.

2 Eliminate any answer choices that are obviously wrong.

3 Of the remaining choices, select the one that best completes the meaning of the sentence or passage given.

4 To check yourself, read the sentence or passage through again, putting your answer in the blank.

STRATEGIES FOR ANSWERING SENTENCE COMPLETION QUESTIONS

The following example shows you how to follow these steps in answering a sentence completion question:

1. Trespassing on private property is _____ by law.
   (A) proscribed
   (B) warranted
   (C) prescribed
   (D) eliminated

First, eliminate any choices that are obviously wrong. Choice (B), *warranted*, may remind you of a warrant for arrest, which might be the result of trespassing; *warranted*, however, means "justified," which would make the given sentence

chapter 7

TIP

Watch out for words that look alike but have different meanings, such as *proscribed* and *prescribed* in the first example. Read each answer choice carefully so that you will not fall for this trap.

obviously untrue. Choice (C), *prescribed*, means "recommended"; like *warranted*, it makes no sense in the given sentence.

Now, select the best answer from the remaining choices and insert it into the blank to be sure that it makes sense in the given sentence. Choice (D), *eliminated*, is a likely choice, but it doesn't fit the sentence; the law may be intended to eliminate trespassing, but it can never be completely successful in doing so. Therefore, the most likely and thus the correct answer is choice (A), *proscribed*.

Try another example question:

2. Despite the harsh tone of her comments, she did not mean to _____ any criticism of you personally.
   (A) infer

   (B) aim

   (C) comply

   (D) imply

You can eliminate choice (C), *comply*, which means "obey" and makes no sense in the context. Choice (B), *aim*, is more likely, but it doesn't work in the sentence as given. You might say, "She did not mean to aim any criticism *at* you," but you would not normally say, "She did not mean to aim any criticism *of* you."

Be careful of choice (A), *infer*; this word is often confused with *imply*. *Infer* means "conclude from reasoning or implication." A speaker implies, whereas a listener infers. **The correct answer is (D)**, *imply*, which means "suggest indirectly."

Sentence completion questions often contain clue words that help you determine the missing word:

* **Contrast words** tell you that the missing word should contrast with another idea stated in the sentence: *although; despite; though; but; however; rather than; not; yet; instead of.*

* **Support words** tell you that the missing word is supported by another part of the sentence: *and; for; furthermore; also; because; so.*

* **Summary words** tell you that the missing word summarizes an idea already stated in the sentence: *as a result; finally; in conclusion; on the whole.*

* **Cause-and-effect words** tell you that the missing word is an effect of a cause stated in the sentence, or vice versa: *consequently; so that; thus; since; if; therefore; accordingly.*

Try the following question:

3. The department's _____ does not allow for unlimited copying by all the instructors in the program. Each instructor can be reimbursed for copying expenses only up to ten dollars.

   (A) paperwork

   (B) staff

   (C) organization

   (D) budget

The correct answer is (D), *budget,* since the concern here is with money. A budget puts limits on spending. Choices (A), *paperwork,* and (B), *staff,* aren't appropriate to the meaning of the passage. Choice (C), *organization,* is barely possible, but only because it is so vague. *Budget* both makes sense and is much more exact.

Tackle one more example question:

4. If the company offered a settlement commensurate with the damages sustained, the couple would _____ their right to a hearing.

   (A) cancel

   (B) ensue

   (C) waive

   (D) assert

The correct answer is (C), *waive,* which means "forego" or "give up." One *waives* something to which one is entitled, such as a right. Choice (A), *cancel,* is similar in meaning but is not used in this way. One can cancel a hearing, but not a right. Choice (B), *ensue,* may mislead you by its similarity to *sue.* The sentence does imply that the couple is suing or planning to sue the company for damages of some sort. However, *ensue* simply means "follow as a result" and so makes no sense in this context. Choice (D), *assert,* here means the opposite of *waive.* One can assert a right, but the meaning of the first part of the sentence makes this choice unlikely.

TIP

If you are having trouble finding the correct answer, look for clues in the overall subject of the sentence. In the third example, the sentence is primarily about money, so you can assume that the answer is a word that relates to money—budget.

EXERCISE

Directions: Each of the following sentences or passages contains a blank. Select the word or phrase that will best complete the meaning of the sentence or passage as a whole.

1. He was the chief _____ of his uncle's will. After taxes he was left with an inheritance worth close to twenty thousand dollars.
   - **(A)** exemption
   - **(B)** pensioner
   - **(C)** beneficiary
   - **(D)** contestant

2. In view of the extenuating circumstances and the defendant's youth, the judge recommended _____.
   - **(A)** conviction
   - **(B)** a defense
   - **(C)** a mistrial
   - **(D)** leniency

3. The basic concept of civil service is that where a public job exists, all those who possess the _____ shall have an opportunity to compete for it.
   - **(A)** potential
   - **(B)** contacts
   - **(C)** qualifications
   - **(D)** credits

4. They would prefer to hire someone fluent in Spanish since the neighborhood in which the clinic is located is _____ Hispanic.
   - **(A)** imponderably
   - **(B)** sparsely
   - **(C)** consistently
   - **(D)** predominantly

5. The lover of democracy has an _____ toward totalitarianism.
   - **(A)** antipathy
   - **(B)** attitude
   - **(C)** empathy
   - **(D)** idolatry

6. The candidate's _____ was carefully planned; she traveled to six cities and spoke at nine rallies.
   - **(A)** pogrom
   - **(B)** itinerary
   - **(C)** adjournment
   - **(D)** apparition

7. _____ recommendations are generally more constructive than vague complaints or blanket praise.
   - **(A)** Justified
   - **(B)** Nebulous
   - **(C)** Sweeping
   - **(D)** Specific

8. In the face of an uncooperative Congress, the Chief Executive may find himself _____ to accomplish the political program to which he is committed.
   - **(A)** impotent
   - **(B)** equipped
   - **(C)** neutral
   - **(D)** contingent

9. The authorities declared an _____ on incoming freight because of the trucking strike.

   (A) impression

   (B) immolation

   (C) embargo

   (D) opprobrium

10. The information we have available on that question is _____: The form, scope, and reliability of the documents vary tremendously so it is difficult to determine its validity.

    (A) essential

    (B) lacking

    (C) questionable

    (D) minimal

11. The _____ on the letter indicated that it had been mailed in Minnesota three weeks previously.

    (A) address

    (B) stamp

    (C) postmark

    (D) envelope

12. The television ads _____ an unprecedented public response. Sales skyrocketed and within a few months the brand name had become a household word.

    (A) boosted

    (B) promised

    (C) elicited

    (D) favored

13. The chairman submitted a _____ for the new equipment, but it will not be delivered for two weeks.

    (A) requisition

    (B) reason

    (C) proposal

    (D) plea

14. With all his courtroom experience, the attorney was able to pry very little information out of the _____ witness.

    (A) cooperative

    (B) recalcitrant

    (C) reactionary

    (D) testifying

15. Although for years substantial resources had been devoted to alleviating the problem, a satisfactory solution remained _____.

    (A) costly

    (B) probable

    (C) elusive

    (D) esoteric

16. The local police department will not accept for _____ a report of a person missing from his residence if such residence is located outside of the city.

    (A) foreclosure

    (B) convenience

    (C) investigation

    (D) control

17. The consumer group is optimistic about the _____ of the new regulations on the industry's safety standards.

    (A) incision

    (B) effect

    (C) affectation

    (D) input

18. The mayor sent a letter _____ our invitation and commending us on our work; she regrets that she will be unable to attend the opening ceremonies due to a prior commitment.

    (A) rebuffing

    (B) reconsidering

    (C) returning

    (D) acknowledging

19. His wealth of practical experience and his psychological acuity more than _____ his lack of formal academic training.

(A) concede to

(B) comprise

(C) compensate for

(D) educate for

20. Suffering from hay fever, he was _____ to spend his time indoors.

(A) coerced

(B) forced

(C) strengthened

(D) pushed

21. The treaty cannot go into _____ until it has been ratified by the Senate.

(A) distribution

(B) limit

(C) effect

(D) check

22. You will have to speak to the head of the agency; I am not _____ to give out that information.

(A) willing

(B) authorized

(C) programmed

(D) happy

23. When new individuals have proved their capability and reliability, they ought to achieve journeyman status in the company _____.

(A) intrinsically

(B) permanently

(C) automatically

(D) decisively

24. The object may be _____ but the plan as presented is far from practicable.

(A) compensatory

(B) laudable

(C) precarious

(D) subversive

25. You must _____ a copy of your latest federal income tax return before your loan application can be considered.

(A) surrender

(B) replicate

(C) supplement

(D) submit

ANSWER KEY AND EXPLANATIONS

1. C	6. B	11. C	16. C	21. C
2. D	7. D	12. C	17. B	22. B
3. C	8. A	13. A	18. D	23. C
4. D	9. C	14. B	19. C	24. B
5. A	10. C	15. C	20. B	25. D

1. **The correct answer is (C).** Because the subject received a benefit from his uncle's will, *beneficiary* fits the sentence best.

2. **The correct answer is (D).** The words "extenuating circumstances" and "youth" should tip you off that the judge will be merciful, or recommend *leniency*.

3. **The correct answer is (C).** As you learned earlier in this book, you must have the *qualifications* for the job.

4. **The correct answer is (D).** The cause-and-effect clue "since" tells you that the second part of the sentence is the cause of the first part. If the neighborhood is *predominantly*, or "mostly," Hispanic, then clinic workers there would need to speak Spanish.

5. **The correct answer is (A).** Totalitarianism is the opposite of democracy, so someone who loves democracy would naturally feel *antipathy*, or a strong feeling of "distaste," toward totalitarianism.

6. **The correct answer is (B).** The words "planned" and "traveled" suggest that the best answer is *itinerary*, which means "a planned route on a journey."

7. **The correct answer is (D).** The word "than" contrasts the last part of the sentence with the first part; therefore, you should choose an answer that means the opposite of vague—*specific*.

8. **The correct answer is (A).** In this case, *impotent* means "powerless"; if Congress is uncooperative, the President is probably powerless.

9. **The correct answer is (C).** The words "because of" are a cause-and-effect clue. If truckers are on strike, then there is no one to bring in the freight, so there must be an *embargo*, or "prohibition," of it.

10. **The correct answer is (C).** None of the choices fit the sentence as well as *heterogeneous*.

11. **The correct answer is (C).** The only thing that can indicate when and where a letter was mailed is the *postmark*.

12. **The correct answer is (C).** *Elicited* means "brought out" or "provoked"; the ads brought out an unprecedented response, as indicated by the following sentence.

13. **The correct answer is (A).** In a business context, the correct term is *requisition*, or "a formal request for."

14. **The correct answer is (B).** Since the witness gave very little information, he is obviously *recalcitrant*, or "stubbornly resistant to authority."

15. **The correct answer is (C).** The word "although" contrasts the two parts of the sentence; therefore, the best answer is *elusive*—the solution to the problem evaded all the attempts to find it.

16. **The correct answer is (C).** Since the sentence is about the police, *investigation* is the best choice.

17. **The correct answer is (B).** The best choice is *effect*, or "result." Be careful of *affectation*, which looks like *effect* but actually means "artificial behavior designed to impress others."

18. **The correct answer is (D).** The mayor did *acknowledge*, or "recognize," the invitation. Since she politely declined, she did not *rebuff*, *return*, or *reconsider* the invitation.

19. **The correct answer is (C).** *Compensate for*, or "make up for," best fits the sentence.

20. **The correct answer is (B).** A person who has hay fever may need to stay indoors, but it would be something the person would want to do. No one would make him do so, which is the definition of *coerce*. *Strengthened* and *pushed* don't make sense in the context of this sentence either.

21. **The correct answer is (C).** Once the Senate ratifies a treaty, it goes into effect. *Distribution* might seem like a good answer, but is not the best choice.

22. **The correct answer is (B).** The best answer is *authorized*—"permitted" or "allowed"; the speaker may be *willing* or *happy* to give out the information, but still cannot because he's not allowed by his superior, the head of the agency.

23. **The correct answer is (C).** The word "when" implies that the second part of the sentence—the effect—should happen as soon as the first part—the cause—occurs; in other words, it should happen *automatically*.

24. **The correct answer is (B).** The word "but" contrasts the first part of the sentence with the second part; the best fit is *laudable*, or "deserving praise."

25. **The correct answer is (D).** *Submit*, or "give," best fits the meaning of the sentence.

SUMMING IT UP

- In a sentence completion question, you're presented with a sentence or passage in which some part has been left blank. Your answer choices consist of several words or phrases that may fit grammatically in the blank, and you are to choose the word or phrase that best completes the meaning of the sentence or passage as a whole.

- Follow these steps to successfully choose the correct answers to sentence completion questions: Read the question carefully, eliminate any answer choices that you know for certain are wrong, and then select the remaining answer choice that most nearly means the same as the given word, even if it is not a word that you normally use. As a double-check, read the passage again, putting your answer in the blank.

- Be on the lookout for words that look alike but have different meanings. Read each answer choice carefully so that you will not fall into this common "trap."

Verbal Analogies

chapter 8

OVERVIEW

- What are verbal analogy questions?
- Strategies for answering verbal analogy questions
- Summing it up

WHAT ARE VERBAL ANALOGY QUESTIONS?

A verbal analogy question has four terms in two pairs. You are given the first complete pair, which establishes the relationship. You must then choose a pair of words whose relationship is *most* similar to the relationship in the given pair.

One type of verbal analogy question gives the first pair of words and the first half of the second pair, followed by a list of possible matches. This kind of question looks like this:

CLOCK is to TIME as THERMOMETER is to

The four answer choices are all single words. You must choose the one pair that completes a relationship with thermometer that is analogous to the relationship between clock and time.

Or you may just be given the first pair of words, and then a selection of paired terms from which you must find the one that implies the same relationship as the given pair. This kind of question looks like this:

CLOCK : TIME ::

The four answer choices are all pairs of words. You must choose the pair that has an analogous relationship to the relationship between clock and time.

STRATEGIES FOR ANSWERING VERBAL ANALOGY QUESTIONS

To answer these questions, look at the given pair of words and decide what the relationship between the words is. Then choose the answer that has the most similar relationship to the given pair of words. Follow these four steps:

1 Read each question carefully.

2 Establish what the correct relationship is between the two terms in the given pair.

3 Study the selection of possible answers carefully and eliminate any that do not share the same relationship as the given pair.

4 Read the remaining choices through again, this time substituting the key relationship word from the sample pair (CLOCK measures TIME, THERMOMETER measures TEMPERATURE).

Try this question:

1. SPEEDOMETER is to POINTER as WATCH is to
    (A) case
    (B) hands
    (C) dial
    (D) numerals

The correct answer is (B). First consider what a *pointer* is used for on a *speedometer*. It indicates speed at a particular moment. A *watch* uses *hands* (choice B) for the same general function, that is, to indicate something at a particular moment. In this case, the hands indicate time. Choice (A), *case*, is incorrect because the watch case has nothing to do with this function. Choices (C), *dial*, and (D), *numerals*, are wrong because although the dial and the numbers have to do with indicating time, they don't perform the specific function of indicating something at any one particular moment.

Try another sample question:

2. WINTER is to SUMMER as COLD is to
    (A) wet
    (B) future
    (C) warm
    (D) freezing

The correct answer is (C). *Winter* and *summer* are opposites, so you should look for an answer choice that means the opposite of *cold*.

Now, try the other kind of verbal analogy:

3. SPELLING : PUNCTUATION ::
    (A) pajamas : fatigue
    (B) powder : shaving
    (C) bandage : cut
    (D) biology : physics

The correct answer is (D). *Spelling* and *punctuation* are parts of the mechanics of English. Biology and physics are parts of the field of science. Therefore, the pair of words with the most analogous relationship to the given pair is answer choice (D). In this type of question, it may help to substitute the colons for words when you read the question in your head. You would read the third example like this: "Spelling is to punctuation as _____ is to _____."

EXERCISE 1

Directions: In each question, the first two words have a certain relationship to each other. Select the letter of the word that is related to the third word in the same way that the first two words are related.

1. ORATION is to CHAT as BANQUET is to
   - (A) festival
   - (B) party
   - (C) wedding
   - (D) snack

2. INCLEMENT is to CLEAR as PERTINENT is to
   - (A) pert
   - (B) cloudy
   - (C) irrelevant
   - (D) perceptive

3. WHEAT is to FLOUR as GRAPE is to
   - (A) vintage
   - (B) vine
   - (C) wine
   - (D) fruit

4. COMMON is to IRON as RARE is to
   - (A) steak
   - (B) crowd
   - (C) humor
   - (D) diamond

5. VICTORY is to CONTEST as KNOWLEDGE is to
   - (A) professor
   - (B) test
   - (C) degree
   - (D) study

6. DIAGNOSIS is to ANALYSIS as THESIS is to
   - (A) antithesis
   - (B) research
   - (C) paper
   - (D) college

7. MARE is to FILLY as KING is to
   - (A) throne
   - (B) prince
   - (C) queen
   - (D) kingdom

8. ARMY is to RECRUIT as RELIGION is to
   - (A) priest
   - (B) worshipper
   - (C) convert
   - (D) acolyte

9. OPULENCE is to LUXURY as POVERTY is to
   - (A) penury
   - (B) misery
   - (C) charity
   - (D) hunger

10. WILL is to CODICIL as CONSTITUTION is to
    - (A) preamble
    - (B) amendment
    - (C) law
    - (D) independence

EXERCISE 2

Directions: In each question, the two capitalized words have a certain relationship to each other. Select the letter of the pair of words that are related in the same way as the two capitalized words.

1. INTIMIDATE : FEAR ::
   - **(A)** maintain : satisfaction
   - **(B)** astonish : wonder
   - **(C)** soothe : concern
   - **(D)** feed : hunger

2. STOVE : KITCHEN ::
   - **(A)** window : bedroom
   - **(B)** sink : bathroom
   - **(C)** television : living room
   - **(D)** trunk : attic

3. CELEBRATE : MARRIAGE ::
   - **(A)** announce : birthday
   - **(B)** report : injury
   - **(C)** lament : bereavement
   - **(D)** face : penalty

4. MARGARINE : BUTTER ::
   - **(A)** cream : milk
   - **(B)** lace : cotton
   - **(C)** nylon : silk
   - **(D)** egg : chicken

5. NEGLIGENT : REQUIREMENT ::
   - **(A)** careful : position
   - **(B)** remiss : duty
   - **(C)** cautious : injury
   - **(D)** cogent : task

6. GAZELLE : SWIFT ::
   - **(A)** horse : slow
   - **(B)** wolf : hungry
   - **(C)** swan : graceful
   - **(D)** elephant : gray

7. IGNOMINY : DISLOYALTY ::
   - **(A)** fame : heroism
   - **(B)** castigation : praise
   - **(C)** death : victory
   - **(D)** approbation : consecration

8. SATURNINE : MERCURIAL ::
   - **(A)** Saturn : Venus
   - **(B)** Apennines : Alps
   - **(C)** redundant : wordy
   - **(D)** crucial : trivial

9. ORANGES : MARMALADE ::
   - **(A)** potatoes : vegetable
   - **(B)** jelly : jam
   - **(C)** tomatoes : ketchup
   - **(D)** cake : picnic

10. BANISH : APOSTATE ::
    - **(A)** reward : traitor
    - **(B)** welcome : ally
    - **(C)** remove : result
    - **(D)** avoid : truce

11. CIRCLE : SPHERE ::
    - **(A)** square : cube
    - **(B)** balloon : jet plane
    - **(C)** heaven : hell
    - **(D)** wheel : orange

12. OPEN : SECRETIVE ::
    - **(A)** mystery : detective
    - **(B)** tunnel : toll
    - **(C)** forthright : dishonest
    - **(D)** better : best

13. AFFIRM : HINT ::
   (A) say : deny
   (B) assert : convince
   (C) confirm : reject
   (D) charge : insinuate

14. THROW : BALL ::
   (A) kill : bullet
   (B) shoot : gun
   (C) question : answer
   (D) hit : run

15. SPEEDY : GREYHOUND ::
   (A) innocent : lamb
   (B) animate : animal
   (C) voracious : tiger
   (D) sluggish : sloth

16. TRIANGLE : PYRAMID ::
   (A) cone : circle
   (B) corner : angle
   (C) square : box
   (D) pentagon : quadrilateral

17. IMPEACH : DISMISS ::
   (A) arraign : convict
   (B) exonerate : charge
   (C) imprison : jail
   (D) plant : reap

18. EMULATE : MIMIC ::
   (A) slander : defame
   (B) praise : flatter
   (C) aggravate : promote
   (D) complain : condemn

19. HAND : NAIL ::
   (A) paw : claw
   (B) foot : toe
   (C) head : hair
   (D) ear : nose

20. SQUARE : DIAMOND ::
   (A) cube : sugar
   (B) circle : ellipse
   (C) innocence : jewelry
   (D) pentangle : square

ANSWER KEY AND EXPLANATIONS

Exercise 1

1. D	3. C	5. D	7. B	9. A
2. C	4. D	6. B	8. C	10. B

1. **The correct answer is (D).** An *oration* is a far more elaborate form of speech than a chat; a *banquet* is a far more elaborate form of meal than a *snack*.

2. **The correct answer is (C).** *Inclement* is the opposite of *clear*; *pertinent* is the opposite of *irrelevant*.

3. **The correct answer is (C).** *Flour* comes from *wheat*; *wine* comes from *grapes*.

4. **The correct answer is (D).** A characteristic of *iron* is that it is *common*; a characteristic of a *diamond* is that it is *rare*.

5. **The correct answer is (D).** A *contest* results in *victory*; *study* results in *knowledge*.

6. **The correct answer is (B).** *Diagnosis* comes after careful *analysis*; a *thesis* comes after thorough *research*.

7. **The correct answer is (B).** The *mare* is a parent of a *filly*; the *king* is a parent of a *prince*.

8. **The correct answer is (C).** A *recruit* is new to the *army*; a *convert* is new to a *religion*.

9. **The correct answer is (A).** *Opulence* is the same as *luxury*; *poverty* is the same as *penury*.

10. **The correct answer is (B).** The purpose of a *codicil* is to change a *will*; the purpose of an *amendment* is to change the *constitution*.

Exercise 2

1. B	5. B	9. C	13. D	17. A
2. B	6. C	10. B	14. B	18. B
3. C	7. A	11. D	15. D	19. A
4. C	8. D	12. C	16. C	20. B

1. **The correct answer is (B).** To *intimidate* is to inspire *fear*; to *astonish* is to inspire *wonder*.

2. **The correct answer is (B).** A *stove* is often part of a *kitchen*; a *sink* is often part of a *bathroom*.

3. **The correct answer is (C).** You happily *celebrate* a *marriage*; you sorrowfully *lament* a *bereavement*.

4. **The correct answer is (C).** *Margarine* is a manufactured substitute for *butter*; *nylon* is a manufactured substitute for *silk*.

5. **The correct answer is (B).** A person may be *negligent* in meeting a *requirement*; he may similarly be *remiss* in performing his *duty*.

6. **The correct answer is (C).** A *gazelle* is known to be *swift*; a *swan* is known to be *graceful*.

7. **The correct answer is (A).** One falls into *ignominy* if one shows *disloyalty*; one gains *fame* if one shows *heroism*.

8. **The correct answer is (D).** *Saturnine* and *mercurial* are antonyms; so are *crucial* and *trivial*.

9. **The correct answer is (C).** *Marmalade* is made from *oranges*; *ketchup* is made from *tomatoes*.

10. **The correct answer is (B).** An *apostate* is *banished*; an *ally* is *welcomed*.

11. **The correct answer is (D).** All four—*circle, sphere, wheel*, and *orange*—are round.

12. **The correct answer is (C).** *Open* is the opposite of *secretive*; *forthright* is the opposite of *dishonest*.

13. **The correct answer is (D).** When you *affirm*, you are direct; when you *hint*, you are indirect. When you *charge*, you are direct; when you *insinuate*, you are indirect.

14. **The correct answer is (B).** One *throws* a *ball*; one *shoots* a *gun*.

15. **The correct answer is (D).** A *greyhound* is proverbially *speedy*; a *sloth* is proverbially *sluggish*.

16. **The correct answer is (C).** A *triangle* is a three-sided plane figure; a *pyramid* is a three-sided solid figure. A *square* is a four-sided plane figure; a *box* is a four-sided solid figure.

17. **The correct answer is (A).** To *impeach* is to charge or challenge; if the impeachment proceedings are successful, the charged person is *dismissed*. To *arraign* is to call into court as a result of accusation; if the accusation is proven, the arraigned person is *convicted*.

18. **The correct answer is (B).** To *emulate* is to imitate another person's good points; to *mimic* is to imitate another person. To *praise* is to speak well of another person; to *flatter* is to praise another person.

19. **The correct answer is (A).** For people, the thin substance at the end of a *hand* is called a *nail*; for animals, the horny sheath at the end of a *paw* is called a *claw*.

20. **The correct answer is (B).** A *diamond* is a partially compressed *square*; an *ellipse* is a partially compressed *circle*.

SUMMING IT UP

- A verbal analogy question presents four terms in two pairs. The first pair presents a relationship between the words; you are to choose a pair of words whose relationship is most similar to the relationship presented in the given pair.

- One type of verbal analogy question gives you a pair of words and the first half of a second pair, and asks you to choose the word that completes a relationship that is analogous to the relationship between the first pair. Another type presents the first pair of words and then a selection of paired terms as answer choices. You are to choose the set that most nearly matches the relationship between the presented pair.

- Follow these steps to answer verbal analogy questions successfully: Read each question carefully; establish the relationship between the terms in the given pair; study the answer choices carefully and eliminate any that you know are incorrect; and read the remaining choices again, substituting the key relationship word from the sample pair.

Effective Expression

OVERVIEW

- **What is being tested?**
- **Strategies for answering effective expression questions**
- **Summing it up**

WHAT IS BEING TESTED?

Effective expression questions test the entire range of grammatical skills, including knowledge of correct grammar, spelling, word usage, and sentence formation. They also test reading comprehension and writing skills. Everything that you have learned so far will come into play when answering these questions. Even if you do not find effective expression questions on your civil service exam, studying the questions in this chapter will be a great help in preparing for the entire verbal ability portion of the exam.

Before answering any of the practice questions, it will be helpful to turn back to Chapter 4 and review the rules of grammar. If you have time, quickly review the spelling rules listed in Chapter 5 as well.

STRATEGIES FOR ANSWERING EFFECTIVE EXPRESSION QUESTIONS

In the effective expression portion of the exam, you are presented with a long passage. Some portions of the passage are underlined and numbered. Corresponding to each numbered portion are three different ways of saying the same thing, and choice (A), which is always "NO CHANGE." You must choose the answer that is the best way to phrase the expression, which may be to leave it as it is stated.

Follow these four steps to answer an effective expression question:

1 Read through the passage quickly to determine the sense of the passage.

2 Return to the first underlined portion.

3 Choose the best answer from the following criteria:

- If you feel that there is an error in grammar, sentence structure, punctuation, or word usage in the underlined portion, mark the correct choice from the answers given.

- If the underlined portion appears to be correct, but you believe that one of the alternatives would be more effective, mark that choice.

chapter 9

- If you feel that the underlined portion is correct and the most effective choice, mark answer choice (A), NO CHANGE.

4 After answering quickly and to the best of your knowledge, go on to the next underlined portion.

Try a sample question:

If a <u>person were to try</u> stripping the disguises from actors while they play
1
a scene upon the stage, showing to the audience <u>there real looks</u> and the
2
faces they were <u>born with. Would</u> not such a one spoil the whole play?
3
Destroy the illusion and <u>any play was ruined.</u>
4

1. **(A)** NO CHANGE
   (B) Person were to try
   (C) Person was to try
   (D) person was to try

2. **(A)** NO CHANGE
   (B) their real looks
   (C) there Real Looks
   (D) they're "real looks"

3. **(A)** NO CHANGE
   (B) born to—would
   (C) born. Would
   (D) born with, would

4. **(A)** NO CHANGE
   (B) any Play was ruined
   (C) any play is ruined?
   (D) any play is ruined.

In this example:

1. **The correct answer is (A).** The passage is correct as shown; therefore, NO CHANGE is the best selection.
2. **The correct answer is (B).** The possessive pronoun is spelled *their*.
3. **The correct answer is (D).** The comma corrects the sentence fragment.
4. **The correct answer is (D).** The present tense *is* is consistent with the present tense *destroy*.

Remember to look for the best, most effective answer. Even if the underlined portion of the passage is technically correct, it may not be the best way to phrase the expression.

EXERCISE

Directions: In each of the following passages, some portions are underlined and numbered. Corresponding to each numbered portion are three different ways of saying the same thing. If you feel that an underlined portion is correct and is stated as well as possible, mark choice (A), NO CHANGE. If you feel that there is an error in the underlined portion or if one of the alternatives would be more effective, choose the correct answer.

PASSAGE 1

The standardized educational or psychological <u>tests, that are</u> widely used to aid in
1
selecting, classifying, assigning, or <u>promoting students</u>, employees, and military
2
personnel have been the target of recent attacks in books, magazines, and

<u>newspapers that are printed every day</u>. The target is wrong, for in attacking the tests,
3
critics <u>revert attention from</u> the fault that <u>lays with illinformed</u> or incompetent users.
4   5
The tests themselves are merely <u>tools; with</u> characteristics that can be
6
<u>assessed reasonably precise</u> under specified conditions. Whether the results will be
7
valuable, meaningless, or even misleading <u>are dependent partly upon</u> the tool itself
8
but largely upon the user.

1. **(A)** NO CHANGE
   (B) tests that are
   (C) tests: which are
   (D) tests; which are

2. **(A)** NO CHANGE
   (B) promoting of students
   (C) promotion of students
   (D) promotion for students

3. **(A)** NO CHANGE
   (B) the daily press
   (C) newspapers that are published daily
   (D) the daily newspaper press

4. **(A)** NO CHANGE
   (B) revert attention to
   (C) divert attention from
   (D) avert attention from

5. **(A)** NO CHANGE
   (B) lies with poorly-informed
   (C) lays with poor-informed
   (D) lies with ill-informed

6. **(A)** NO CHANGE
   (B) tools with
   (C) tools, possessed of
   (D) tools; whose

7. **(A)** NO CHANGE
   (B) assessed as to its reasonable precision
   (C) assessed reasonably and with precision
   (D) assessed with reasonable precision

8. **(A)** NO CHANGE
   (B) is dependent partly upon
   (C) depend partly upon
   (D) depends partly upon

PASSAGE 2

The forces that generate conditions conducive to crime and <u>riots, are stronger</u> in urban
                                                                                9

communities <u>then in rural areas</u>. Urban living is more anonymous <u>living, it</u> often
              10   11

releases the individual from community restraints more common in
<u>tradition, oriented societies</u>. <u>But</u> more freedom from constraints and controls also
         12   13

provides greater freedom to deviate from the law. In the more impersonalized,
<u>formally, controlled</u> urban society regulatory orders of conduct are often directed
         14

by distant bureaucrats. The police are strangers <u>which execute</u> these prescriptions
                                                    15

on, at worst, an alien sub-community and, at best, an <u>anonymous and unknown</u> set of
                                                         16

subjects. Minor offensives in a small town or village are often handled
<u>without resort to</u> official police action. As disputable as such action may seem to be,
      17

<u>you will find it results</u> in fewer recorded violations of the law compared to the city.
          18

9. **(A)** NO CHANGE
   (B) rioting, are stronger
   (C) riots are more strong
   (D) riots are stronger

10. **(A)** NO CHANGE
    (B) then in rural communities
    (C) than in rural areas
    (D) then they are in the country

11. **(A)** NO CHANGE
    (B) living. It
    (C) living; which
    (D) living. Because it

12. **(A)** NO CHANGE
    (B) traditional oriented societies
    (C) traditionally, oriented societies
    (D) tradition-oriented societies

13. **(A)** NO CHANGE
    (B) Moreover
    (C) Therefore
    (D) Besides

14. **(A)** NO CHANGE
    (B) formally controlled
    (C) formalized controlled
    (D) formally-controlled

15. **(A)** NO CHANGE
    (B) they execute
    (C) executing
    (D) who conduct executions of

16. **(A)** NO CHANGE
    (B) anonymously unknown
    (C) anonymous
    (D) anonymous, unknown

17. **(A)** NO CHANGE
    (B) without their having to resort to
    (C) without needing
    (D) outside the limits of

18. **(A)** NO CHANGE
    (B) they say it results
    (C) you will say, "It results
    (D) it nonetheless results

PASSAGE 3

Human beings are born with a desire to <u>communicate with</u> other human <u>beings, they</u>
                                                           19   20

satisfy this desire in many ways. A smile communicates <u>a friendly feeling,</u> a clenched
                                                                              21

<u>fist anger;</u> tears, sorrow. From the first days of life, <u>pain and hunger are expressed by baby's</u>
22   23

by cries and actions. Gradually they add expressions of pleasure and <u>smiling</u> for a familiar
                                                                                                       24

face. Soon they begin to reach out <u>for picking up.</u> <u>Those people who are human beings</u> also
                                                        25   26

use words to communicate. Babies eventually learn the language of <u>there</u> parents. If the
                                                                                            27

parents speak English, the baby will learn to speak English. If the parents speak Spanish,
<u>a Spanish-speaking baby will result.</u> An <u>American baby</u> who is taken from his natural
                  28   29

parents and brought up by foster parents who speak Chinese, Urdu, Swahili, or any
other language <u>will talk</u> the language of the people around him instead of English.
                          30

19. (A) NO CHANGE

    (B) communicate to

    (C) communicate about

    (D) communicate

20. (A) NO CHANGE

    (B) beings. They

    (C) beings; and they

    (D) beings—who

21. (A) NO CHANGE

    (B) a friendly, feeling;

    (C) friendship,

    (D) a friendly feeling;

22. (A) NO CHANGE

    (B) fist an angry feeling,

    (C) fist, anger;

    (D) fist, angriness,

23. (A) NO CHANGE

    (B) babies express pain or hunger

    (C) a baby's pain or hunger are expressed

    (D) pain and hunger is expressed by babies

24. (A) NO CHANGE

    (B) smiled

    (C) smiles

    (D) he may smile

25. (A) NO CHANGE

    (B) to pick up

    (C) and pick up

    (D) to be picked up

26. (A) NO CHANGE

    (B) (BEGIN new paragraph) Those people who are human beings

    (C) (BEGIN new paragraph) Human being babies

    (D) (BEGIN new paragraph) Human beings

27. (A) NO CHANGE

    (B) their

    (C) they're

    (D) OMIT

28. **(A)** NO CHANGE
    (B) their baby will speak Spanish.
    (C) the baby will learn spanish.
    (D) there baby will speak Spanish.

29. **(A)** NO CHANGE
    (B) American Baby
    (C) american baby
    (D) american-born baby

30. **(A)** NO CHANGE
    (B) will be speaking
    (C) will speak
    (D) will talk of

ANSWER KEY AND EXPLANATIONS

1. B	7. D	13. A	19. A	25. D
2. A	8. D	14. B	20. B	26. D
3. B	9. D	15. C	21. D	27. B
4. C	10. C	16. C	22. C	28. B
5. D	11. B	17. A	23. B	29. A
6. B	12. D	18. D	24. C	30. C

1. **The correct answer is (B).** The phrase following *tests* is an essential part of this sentence and should not be set off by commas.

2. **The correct answer is (A).** This is correct.

3. **The correct answer is (B).** The three words *the daily press* say everything that is said by the other, more wordy choices.

4. **The correct answer is (C).** *Divert*, meaning "to turn from one course to another," is the most appropriate choice. *Revert* means "to return" and *avert* means "to turn away or prevent."

5. **The correct answer is (D).** The present tense of the verb *to lie*, meaning "belonging to," is required here. Also, choice (B) can't be correct because you don't use a hyphen to combine a word ending in *-ly (poorly-informed)* with the words it modifies.

6. **The correct answer is (B).** It is not necessary to separate the prepositional phrase from the rest of the sentence.

7. **The correct answer is (D).** This is the clearest and least-awkward choice.

8. **The correct answer is (D).** The clause "Whether the results will be valuable, meaningless, or even misleading" is the subject of the predicate, so the verb must be singular.

9. **The correct answer is (D).** Do not use a comma to separate a subject and a verb (except when the subject contains a nonessential clause, an appositive, or another phrase that is set off by two commas).

10. **The correct answer is (C).** *Than*, a conjunction, is used after the comparative degree of an adjective or adverb. *Then*, an adverb, means "at that time" or "next."

11. **The correct answer is (B).** To correct this run-on sentence, it is necessary to add a period after *living*. Beginning the next sentence with *Because* creates a sentence fragment rather than a complete sentence.

12. **The correct answer is (D).** Use a hyphen in unit modifiers immediately preceding the word or words modified. *Tradition-oriented* is a unit modifier.

13. **The correct answer is (A).** *But* is correct to indicate a contrasting idea. *Moreover* and *besides* mean "in addition to what has been said." *Therefore* means "for that reason."

14. **The correct answer is (B).** Do not use a comma to divide an adverb from the word it modifies. In this case, *formally* modifies the adjective *controlled*. Remember that adverbs can modify verbs, adjectives, and other adverbs. The *-ly* ending is a giveaway that *formally* is an adverb.

15. **The correct answer is (C).** The participle *executing*—meaning "carrying out," not "putting to death"—is the correct word for this sentence. *Which* refers to things, not to people. Choice (B) creates a run-on sentence.

16. **The correct answer is (C).** *Anonymous* means "unknown."

17. **The correct answer is (A).** This is the most concise and correct way to make this statement.

18. **The correct answer is (D).** As written, this sentence illustrates a needless shift in subject (from *action* to *you*), which results in a dangling modifier.

19. **The correct answer is (A).** This is correct.

20. **The correct answer is (B).** As written, this is a run-on sentence. To correct it, add a period after *beings* and start a new sentence with *They*.

21. **The correct answer is (D).** Use a semicolon to separate sentence parts of equal rank if one or more of these parts is subdivided by commas.

22. **The correct answer is (C).** Use a comma to indicate the omission of a word or words. This phrase actually means "a clenched fist (communicates) anger."

23. **The correct answer is (B).** Avoid the shift from the active to the passive voice. The possessive *baby's* is incorrectly substituted for the plural *babies*.

24. **The correct answer is (C).** *And* is used to connect similar grammatical elements, in this case the noun *expressions* and the noun *smiles*.

25. **The correct answer is (D).** The present infinitive is correct, because the action of the infinitive is present or future in relation to the action of the finite verb *begin*.

26. **The correct answer is (D).** The introduction of a new topic—the use of words to communicate—indicates the need for a new paragraph. *Human beings* are people, and so the phrase *Those people who are* is unnecessary.

27. **The correct answer is (B).** The possessive pronoun needed here is *their*. *There* refers to place, and *they're* is a contraction for "they are."

28. **The correct answer is (B).** A comparison is being drawn between English- and Spanish-speaking families. The two sentences that form the comparison should be parallel in structure. *Spanish* is a proper noun and must begin with a capital letter.

29. **The correct answer is (A).** *American* is a proper noun and should be capitalized; *baby* is merely a noun and needs no capital letter.

30. **The correct answer is (C).** *Speak the language* is idiomatically correct.

SUMMING IT UP

- Effective expression questions test your entire range of grammatical skills, including your knowledge of grammar, spelling, word usage, and sentence formation. To practice for these questions, it may be helpful to turn back to Chapters 3 and 4 in this book and review the rules of grammar and spelling.

- In effective expression questions, you are presented with a long passage in which some portions are underlined and numbered. Corresponding to each numbered part are three different ways of saying the same thing, or NO CHANGE. You must choose the answer that presents the best way to phrase the expression.

- Follow these steps to answer effective expression questions successfully: Read through the passage quickly to determine its sense; return to the first underlined portion; choose the best answer based on criteria outlined in this chapter; and after answering, go on to the next underlined portion and do the same.

Reading Comprehension

chapter 10

OVERVIEW
- Types of reading comprehension questions
- Strategies for answering reading comprehension questions
- Summing it up

TYPES OF READING COMPREHENSION QUESTIONS

Some exams present classic reading comprehension questions that provide a passage and then ask questions on the details of the passage and, perhaps, on its meaning. Other exams require candidates to indicate proper behavior based on their reading of printed procedures and regulations. Still another type of reading-based question requires candidates to reason and choose the next steps based on information presented in a passage. There are nearly as many variations of the reading-based question as there are test-makers.

In the past few years, the federal government has introduced a new style of reading comprehension question into many of its exams. The reading selection itself is very short, and it is followed by only one question. At first glance, the task is deceptively simple. However, the paragraph is often dense with information and difficult to absorb. The question may be phrased in a circular, oblique, or negative fashion. Total concentration is needed for answering this type of reading question. You will get the opportunity to practice both this type of reading-based question and the classic reading comprehension question at the end of this chapter.

Most often, you will be given a reading passage and then asked to answer a series of questions based on the passage. The following are the most common kinds of questions asked:

- **Question of fact or detail.** You may have to mentally rephrase or rearrange informaton, but you should find the answer stated in the body of the passage.

- **Best title or main idea.** The answer may be obvious, but the incorrect choices to the "main idea" question are often half-truths that are easily confused with the main idea. They may misstate the idea, omit part of the idea, or even offer a supporting idea quoted directly from the text. The correct answer is the one that covers the largest part of the selection.

- **Interpretation.** This type of question asks you what the selection means, not just what it says. On police examples, questions based on definitions of crimes fall into this category, for example.

- **Vocabulary.** Some civil service reading passages directly or indirectly ask the meanings of certain words used in the passage.
- **Inference.** This is the most difficult type of reading comprehension question. It asks you to go beyond what the passage says and predict what might happen next. Your answer must be based on the information in the passage and your own common sense, but not on any other information that you may have about the subject.

Don't worry if you're unfamiliar with the subject discussed in the reading selection. You don't need to have any knowledge about the subject of the passage because the answer to the question is always given in the passage itself.

STRATEGIES FOR ANSWERING READING COMPREHENSION QUESTIONS

Before you begin to devote attention to strategies for dealing with reading-based questions, give some thought to your reading habits and skills. How well do you read? Do you concentrate? Do you get the point on your first reading? Do you notice details?

Between now and test day, resolve to improve your reading concentration and comprehension. A daily newspaper—print or online—provides excellent material for you to practice reading comprehension skills. Here are some tips for using news articles, columns, opinion pieces, and news blogs to improve your reading comprehension:

- Make a point of reading all the way through any article that you begin. Don't be satisfied with the first paragraph or two.
- Notice points of view, arguments, and supporting information. If you're reading a print newspaper, underline details and ideas that seem to be crucial to the meaning. If you're reading an online version, use a pencil and paper to make notes.
- When you finish your reading, summarize the piece for yourself. Do you know what the main idea is? The purpose of the article? The attitude of the writer if it's a blog, column, or opinion piece? The points of view in any controversy? Did you find that you wanted to know more details?
- Skim your notes or parts you underlined. Did you focus on important words and ideas? Did you understand what you read?

Success with reading-based questions depends on more than reading comprehension. You must also know how to draw the answers from the reading selection and be able to distinguish the best answer from a number of answers that all seem to be good ones, or from a number of answers that all seem to be wrong.

To answer a reading comprehension question, follow these nine steps:

1 Read the questions—not the answer choices, just the questions themselves—before you read the passage. The questions will alert you to look for certain details, ideas, and points of view in the passage. If you are taking a paper-and-pencil test, underline key words in the questions to help direct your attention as you read.

2 Skim the passage rapidly to get an idea of its subject matter, its organization, and the point being made. If key words or ideas pop out at you, underline them. Don't consciously search out details at this point.

3 Now read the selection again carefully with comprehension as your main goal. Give attention to details and point of view.

4 Return to the questions and read the first question carefully. Determine exactly what is being asked.

5 Read all the answer choices. Don't rush to choose the first answer that might be correct.

6 Eliminate choices that clearly conflict with the paragraph.

7 If you still have two or more choices left, look for the specific section of the passage that covers the information given in each of the choices.

8 Compare the facts carefully until you can eliminate the remaining incorrect choices.

9 Don't spend too much time on any one question. If looking back at the passage doesn't help you find the answer, choose from among the remaining answers and move on to the next question.

Be alert for hints as to what the author of the passage thinks is important. Phrases such as "note that," "it is important that," and "do not overlook" give clues to what the writer is stressing.

A major cause of error on reading comprehension questions is misreading questions, so read each question carefully and be sure that you understand what it's asking. Watch for negative or all-inclusive words that can greatly affect your answer, like "always," "never," "all," "only," "every," "absolutely," "completely," "none," "entirely," and "no." Be careful of these words in answer choices. Often, these qualifiers make an answer incorrect.

TIP

Avoid inserting your judgments into your answers. Even if you disagree with the author or even if you spot a factual error in the passage, you must answer based on what is stated or implied in the passage.

EXERCISE

Directions: Answer each question on the basis of the information stated or implied in the accompanying reading passage.

PASSAGE 1

The recipient gains an impression of a business letter before beginning to read the message. Facts that give a good first impression include margins
(5) and spacings that are visually pleasing, formal parts of the letter that are correctly placed according to the style of the letter, copy that is free of errors, and transcript that is even
(10) and clear. The problem for the typist is how to produce that first, positive impression of her work.

There are several general rules that a typist can follow when she wishes
(15) to prepare a properly spaced letter on a sheet of letterhead. The width of a letter should ordinarily not be less than four inches, nor more than six inches. The side margins should
(20) also have a proportionate relation to the bottom margin, as well as the space between the letterhead and the body of the letter. Usually the most appealing arrangement is when the
(25) side margins are even, and the bottom margin is slightly wider than the side margins. In some offices, however, a standard line length is used for all business letters, and the typist then
(30) varies the spacing between the date line and the inside address according to the length of the letter.

1. The best title for the preceding paragraph is
   (A) "Writing Office Letters."
   (B) "Making Good First Impressions."
   (C) "Judging Well-Typed Letters."
   (D) "Proper Spacing for Office Letters."

2. Which of the following might be considered the way that people quickly judge the quality of a business letter?
   (A) by measuring the margins to see if they are correct
   (B) by looking at the placement of elements in the letter for overall visual appeal
   (C) by scanning the body of the letter for meaning
   (D) by checking for misspelled names in the letter

3. What would definitely be undesirable as the average line length of a typed letter?
   (A) Four inches
   (B) Five inches
   (C) Six inches
   (D) Seven inches

4. When the line length is kept standard, the person typing
   (A) does not have to vary the spacing at all because this also is standard.
   (B) adjusts the spacing between the date line and inside address for different lengths of letters.
   (C) uses the longest line as a guideline for spacing between the date line and inside address.
   (D) varies the number of spaces between the lines.

PASSAGE 2

Cotton fabrics treated with XYZ Process have features that make them far superior to any previously known flame-retardant-treated cot-
(5) ton fabrics. XYX Process-treated fabrics endure repeated laundering and dry cleaning; they are glow-resistant as well as flame-resistant; when exposed to flames or intense heat they
(10) form tough, pliable, and protective chars; they are inert physiologically to persons handling or exposed to the fabric; they are only slightly heavier than untreated fabrics and
(15) are susceptible to further wet and dry finishing treatments. In addition, the treated fabrics exhibit little or no adverse change in feel, texture, and appearance and are shrink-, rot-, and
(20) mildew-resistant. The treatment reduces strength only slightly. Finished fabrics have "easy care" properties in that they are wrinkle-resistant and dry rapidly.

5. It is most accurate to state that the author in the preceding selection presents

(A) facts but reaches no conclusion concerning the value of the process.

(B) a conclusion concerning the value of the process and facts to support that conclusion.

(C) a conclusion concerning the value of the process unsupported by facts.

(D) neither facts nor conclusions, but merely describes the process.

6. Of the following articles, which is the XYZ Process most suitable for?

(A) Nylon stockings

(B) Woolen shirt

(C) Silk tie

(D) Cotton bedsheet

7. Of the following aspects of the XYZ Process, which is NOT discussed in the preceding selection?

(A) Costs

(B) Washability

(C) Wearability

(D) The human body

8. The main reason for treating a fabric with XYZ Process is to

(A) prepare the fabric for other wet and dry finishing treatment.

(B) render it shrink-, rot-, and mildew-resistant.

(C) increase its weight and strength.

(D) reduce the chance that it will catch fire.

9. Which of the following would be considered a minor drawback of the XYZ Process?

(A) It forms chars when exposed to flame.

(B) It makes fabrics mildew-resistant.

(C) It adds to the weight of fabrics.

(D) It is compatible with other finishing treatments.

PASSAGE 3

Language performs an essentially social function. It helps us communicate and achieve a great measure of concerted action. Words are signs
(5) that have significance by convention, and the people who do not adopt the conventions simply fail to communicate. They do not "get along," and a social force arises that encourages
(10) them to achieve the correct associations. By "correct" we mean as used by other members of the social group. Some of the vital points about language are brought home to an English
(15) visitor to the United States, and vice versa, because our vocabularies are nearly the same, but not quite.

10. As defined in the preceding selection, usage of a word is "correct" when it is
   (A) defined in standard dictionaries.
   (B) used by the majority of persons throughout the world who speak the same language.
   (C) used by a majority of educated persons who speak the same language.
   (D) used by other persons with whom we are associating.

11. The author is concerned primarily with the
   (A) meaning of words.
   (B) pronunciation of words.
   (C) structure of sentences.
   (D) origin and development of language.

12. The main language problem of an English visitor to the United States stems from the fact that an English person
   (A) uses some words that have different meanings for Americans.
   (B) has different social values than the Americans.
   (C) has had more exposure to non-English speaking persons than Americans have had.
   (D) pronounces words differently from the way Americans do.

PASSAGE 4

In applying for a job with the federal government, you will more than likely need to complete a self-assessment of your experience, skills, and
(5) abilities. This approach to hiring is part of a reform of the way that the federal government recruits, hires, and retains workers that was started under President Barack Obama in
(10) 2010. The purpose is to make hiring more efficient and result in more qualified employees.

The self-assessment tool is also called an occupational questionnaire
(15) or a job-specific questionnaire. What exactly is it? According to the OPM, "an occupational questionnaire is an assessment method used to screen and rate job applicants." It is com-
(20) posed of a series of questions tailored to the requirements for each specific job. The questionnaire is normally administered online and submitted as part of a candidate's application.
(25) The result is a self-rating of the person's training and experience.

The question formats are similar from job to job and department to department within the government.
(30) Questions are typically multiple choice or yes/no and cover a variety of competencies related to the particular position. Typically, a questionnaire will have five to ten items for
(35) each competency that is to be measured for the position. Because of the format, occupational questionnaires are a quick and inexpensive way to screen for minimum qualifications
(40) while determining the most qualified candidate.

In addition, occupational questionnaires can assess a wide variety of knowledge, skills, abilities, and
(45) competencies—once the subject of arduous and time-consuming essays. They are easy to automate, and, unlike traditional civil services exams, test security is not an issue. It doesn't
(50) matter who knows what the ques-

tions are because there are no right or wrong answers. The concept of measuring training and experience is a familiar one to government agencies
(55) that routinely use performance as a measure of employee competence.

13. The best title for the preceding selection is

(A) "How to Complete an Occupational Questionnaire."

(B) "How to Write an Occupational Questionnaire."

(C) "Occupational Questionnaires: Their Use and Format."

(D) "Occupational Questionnaires

14. The federal government switched to the use of occupational questionnaires

(A) to make hiring more efficient and to identify more qualified employees.

(B) to save money.

(C) to screen more candidates more quickly.

(D) because occupational questionnaires are more valid.

15. Implicit in the selection is the idea that

(A) secure testing is too costly.

(B) candidates screened in the past were not always the best candidates.

(C) the government cares more about saving money than taking time to screen candidates.

(D) competencies are more important today than in the past.

16. It is important to revise a general resume to match your self-assessment for a specific job so that

(A) your self-assessment is supported by your experience and education.

(B) your self-assessment and your resume are correlated.

(C) you don't seem to be lying.

(D) you show that you understand the importance of your education and experience in qualifying for a job.

17. Keeping occupational questionnaires secure is unnecessary because they

(A) are administered online.

(B) can be downloaded and printed by candidates to review ahead of completing them.

(C) are not difficult to answer.

(D) are not tests.

18. *Competency* in the sense used in the passage (line 35) means

(A) suitableness.

(B) condition.

(C) adequateness.

(D) ability.

PASSAGE 5

The modern conception of the economic role of the public sector (government), as distinct from the private sector, is that every level of (5) government is a link in the economic process. Government's contribution to political and economic welfare must, however, be evaluated not merely in terms of its technical ef- (10) ficiency, but also in the light of its acceptability to a particular society at a particular state of political and economic development. Even in a dictatorship, this principle is formally (15) observed, although the authorities usually destroy the substance by presuming to interpret to the public its collective desires.

19. The paragraph best supports the statement that

(A) it is not true that some levels of government are not links in the economic process.

(B) all dictatorships observe the same economic principles as other governments.

(C) all links in the economic process are levels of government.

(D) the contributions of some levels of government do not need to be evaluated for technical efficiency and acceptability to society.

(E) no links in the economic process are institutions other than levels of government.

PASSAGE 6

All property is classified as either personal property or real property, but not both. In general, if something is classified as personal property, it (5) is transient and transportable in nature, while real property is not. Things such as leaseholds, animals, money, and intangible and other moveable goods are examples of per- (10) sonal property. Permanent buildings and land, on the other hand, are fixed in nature and are not transportable.

20. The paragraph best supports the statement that

(A) if something is classified as personal property, it is not transient and transportable in nature.

(B) some forms of property are considered to be both personal property and real property.

(C) permanent buildings and land are real property.

(D) permanent buildings and land are personal property.

(E) tangible goods are considered to be real property.

ANSWER KEY AND EXPLANATIONS

1. D	5. B	9. C	13. C	17. D
2. B	6. D	10. D	14. A	18. D
3. D	7. A	11. A	15. B	19. A
4. B	8. D	12. A	16. A	20. C

1. **The correct answer is (D).** The best title for any selection is the one that takes in all the ideas presented without being too broad or too narrow. Choice (D) provides the most inclusive title for this passage. A look at the other choices shows you why. Choice (A) can be eliminated because the passage discusses typing a letter, not writing one. Although the first paragraph states that a letter should make a good first impression, the passage is clearly devoted to the letter, not the first impression, so choice (B) can be eliminated. Choice (C) puts the emphasis on the wrong aspect of the word-processed letter. The passage concerns how to prepare a properly spaced letter, not how to judge one.

2. **The correct answer is (B).** Both placement of elements and visual appeal are mentioned in the first paragraph as ways to judge the quality of a typed letter. The first paragraph states that the margins should be "visually pleasing" in relation to the body of the letter, but that doesn't imply margins of a particular measure, so choice (A) is incorrect.

3. **The correct answer is (D).** This answer comes from the information provided in the second paragraph, that the width of a letter "should not be less than four inches, nor more than six inches." According to this rule, seven inches is an undesirable line length.

4. **The correct answer is (B).** The answer to this question is stated in the last sentence of the passage. When a standard line length is used, the typist "varies the spacing between the date line and the inside address according to the length of the letter." The passage offers no support for any other choice.

5. **The correct answer is (B).** This is a combination main idea and interpretation question. If you cannot answer this question readily, reread the passage. The author clearly thinks that the XYZ Process is terrific and says so in the first sentence. The rest of the selection presents a wealth of facts to support the initial claim.

6. **The correct answer is (D).** At first glance, you might think that this is an inference question requiring you to make a judgment based upon the few drawbacks of the process. Closer reading, however, shows you that there is no contest for the correct answer here. This is a simple question of fact. The XYZ Process is a treatment for cotton fabrics.

7. **The correct answer is (A).** Cost is not mentioned; all other aspects of the XYZ Process are. If you are having trouble finding mention of the effect of the XYZ Process on the human body, look up *inert* and *physiologically* in the dictionary.

8. **The correct answer is (D).** This is a main idea question. You must dis-

tinguish between the main idea and the supporting and incidental facts.

9. **The correct answer is (C).** Obviously, a drawback is a negative feature. The selection mentions only two negative features. The treatment reduces strength slightly, and it makes fabrics slightly heavier than untreated fabrics. Only one of these negative features is offered among the answer choices.

10. **The correct answer is (D).** The answer to this question is stated in the next-to-last sentence of the passage.

11. **The correct answer is (A).** This main idea question is an easy one to answer. You should have readily eliminated all the wrong choices.

12. **The correct answer is (A).** This is a question of fact. The phrasing of the question is quite different from the phrasing of the last sentence, but the meaning is the same. You may have found this reading selection more difficult to absorb than some of the others, but you should have had no difficulty answering this question by eliminating the wrong answers.

13. **The correct answer is (C).** Questions that ask about the best title are really asking for the main idea. Choice (A) can't be correct because the selection has no information about how to complete the questionnaire. Choice (B) is incorrect because there is no information about how to write a questionnaire. Choice (D) might work, but choice (C) is more specific about the content of the selection, so it's a better choice.

14. **The correct answer is (A).** This answer is found in the last sentence in paragraph 1. The purpose of the occupational questionnaires is to make hiring more efficient and result in more qualified employees.

15. **The correct answer is (B).** This is the only answer that can be implied from the content. The inexpensiveness of the occupational questionnaire is mentioned as a benefit, but there is no indication that secure testing, choice (A), was used prior to the introduction of occupational questionnaires. There is no evidence to support choice (C); it is mentioned that occupational questionnaires can be completed quickly, but there is no connection to saving money. There is also no mention of past practices in evaluating candidates, choice (D). This doesn't mean that candidates weren't evaluated, only that the topic was not discussed in this selection about the new practice.

16. **The correct answer is (A).** All the answers appear to be true, but choice (A)—that your self-assessment is supported by your experience and education—is the best answer because it encompasses the other answers. It is the most complete.

17. **The correct answer is (D).** Occupational questionnaires are not tests; they are more like an inventory of one's abilities.

18. **The correct answer is (D).** A *competency* is the *ability* of an individual to do a job properly.

19. **The correct answer is (A).** This answer can be inferred from the first sentence of the paragraph, which states that "every level of government is a link in the economic process." It can be deduced that its contradictory statement, "some levels of government are not links in the economic process," cannot be true.

Choice (B) isn't supported by the paragraph because it goes beyond the information given. The third sentence of the paragraph states that a dictatorship observes (at least formally) one of the same principles as other governments. It cannot be concluded from this that dictatorships observe more than this one principle in common with other governments.

Choices (C) and (E) represent incorrect interpretations of the information given in the first sentence, which states that "every level of government is a link in the economic process." You can't infer from this statement that "all links in the economic process are levels of government," only that some are. We know that the category "all levels of government" is contained in the category "links in the economic process," but we don't know if links in the economic process exist that are not levels of government. In regard to choice (E), it cannot be inferred that "no links in the economic process are institutions other than levels of government," because that would be the same as saying that all links in the economic process are levels of government.

Choice (D) isn't supported by the passage because the second sentence implies that the contributions of *all* levels of government must be evaluated for technical efficiency and acceptability to society. There is nothing to suggest that the contributions of some levels of society do *not* need to be evaluated.

Note that in this question, the correct answer follows from one sentence in the paragraph, the first sentence. The rest of the paragraph presents additional information about the public sector and its effects on society that is relevant to the discussion but not necessary to make the inference. Part of your task is to understand what you read and then to discern which conclusions follow logically from statements in the passage. Consequently, you will find some questions necessitate the use of all or most of the statements presented in the paragraph, while others require only one statement to infer the correct answer.

20. **The correct answer is (C).** The answer can be inferred from information contained in the first, second, and fourth sentences. The first sentence is a disjunction; that is, it presents two mutually exclusive alternatives—"all property is classified as either personal property or real property, but not both." The second sentence states that "if something is classified as personal property, it is transient and transportable in nature." The fourth sentence states that "permanent buildings and land…are fixed in nature and are not transportable." You can conclude that, since permanent buildings and land are not transient and transportable in nature, they are not personal property. In view of the disjunction in the first sentence, it can be seen that they must be real property.

Choice (A) is incorrect because it contradicts the information presented in the second sentence. Choice (B) is incorrect because it contradicts the first sentence, which states that "all property is classified as either personal property or real property, but not both."

Choice (D) contradicts the information presented in the second and fourth sentences. The second sentence states that "if something is classified as personal property, it is transient and transportable in nature." The fourth sentence indicates that permanent buildings and land don't have these qualities. Therefore, you can conclude that they are not personal property.

Choice (E) seems to be derived from the third sentence, which says that intangible goods are examples of personal property. However, you can't conclude from this statement that tangible goods are real property. In fact, the third sentence gives examples of tangible goods that are personal property.

SUMMING IT UP

- Reading comprehension questions vary depending on which civil service exam you are taking. Some present classic reading comprehension questions, in which a passage is provided and you are asked questions on the details of the passage. Another type requires you to indicate proper behavior based on your reading of procedures and regulations. A third type asks you to reason and then choose the next steps based on information presented in the passage.

- A newer reading comprehension question type presents a very short passage and then asks you a single question about it. This type of question can seem deceptively easy, but the passage is usually dense and filled with complex information that is not always presented directly.

- The most common types of reading comprehension questions include: questions of fact or detail, questions asking you to choose the best title or main idea for a passage, questions asking you to interpret information presented, questions that directly or indirectly ask the meaning of certain words used in the passage, and questions that ask you to go beyond what the passage actually says and predict what might happen next.

- Don't be concerned if you're unfamiliar with the subjects presented in the reading selections. You are not expected to have any knowledge about the subject because the answer is always presented somewhere and in some way in the passage itself.

- Before you take your exam, you can practice strategies for dealing with reading-based questions. Resolve to improve your reading comprehension and concentration skills. Make a point of reading all the way through any article you begin. Read with a pencil handy to mark details and ideas that seem most important, or make notes if you're reading online. Summarize articles after you've finished reading them. Skim your underlinings or notes and determine whether you focused on the main ideas.

Judgment,
Communication,
and Memory

OVERVIEW

- Strategies for answering judgment questions
- Strategies for answering communication skill questions
- Strategies for answering observation and memory questions
- Summing it up

STRATEGIES FOR ANSWERING JUDGMENT QUESTIONS

Good judgment is a necessary skill for many positions in federal, state, and local government. Even the entry-level employee who works under close supervision has occasions when he or she must rely on his or her own good judgment in dealing with an emergency situation—or in choosing priorities when there is no supervisor to consult. Almost all multiple-choice civil service exams include some questions designed to measure judgment, either directly or indirectly. For test-taking purposes, judgment is defined as a process of combining knowledge and understanding with common sense. Even though judgment questions resemble reading comprehension questions, they are different in that you must choose the best answer based on your accumulated knowledge and common sense. The answer will not necessarily be given in the reading selection. Clues to the correct answer, however, may be found in the reading passage, so reading comprehension will play a large part in answering judgment questions correctly.

To recognize judgment questions and understand how to answer them, try the following practice exercises. You must read the passage and choose the best answer for the question asked. The correct answers and explanations of those answers follow the exercise.

chapter 11

EXERCISE: JUDGMENT

1. Decisions about handcuffing or restraining inmates are often up to the corrections officers involved. An officer is legally responsible for exercising good judgment and for taking necessary precautions to prevent harm both to the inmate involved and to others. In which one of the following situations is handcuffing or other physical restraint most likely to be needed?

   (A) An inmate seems to have lost control of his senses and is banging his fists repeatedly against the bars of his cell.

   (B) During the past two weeks, an inmate has deliberately tried to start three fights with other inmates.

   (C) An inmate claims to be sick and refuses to leave his cell for a scheduled meal.

   (D) During the night, an inmate begins to shout and sing, disturbing the sleep of other inmates.

2. While you are working on a routine assignment, a coworker asks you to help her for a few minutes so that she can complete an assignment that has top priority and must be completed immediately. Of the following, the best action for you to take should be to

   (A) tell her to find somebody else who does not look busy and ask that person for help.

   (B) tell her you will help her as soon as you complete your own work.

   (C) help her to complete her assignment and then go back to your work.

   (D) tell her that your work is as important to you as her work is to her, and continue to work on your own assignment.

3. A police officer stationed along the route of a parade has been ordered not to allow cars to cross the route while the parade is in progress. An ambulance driver on an emergency run attempts to drive an ambulance across the route while the parade is passing. Under these circumstances, the officer should

   (A) ask the driver to wait while the officer calls headquarters and obtains a decision.

   (B) stop the parade long enough to permit the ambulance to cross the street.

   (C) direct the ambulance driver to the shortest detour available, which will add at least ten minutes to the run.

   (D) hold up the ambulance in accordance with the order.

4. An office worker frequently complains to the building custodian that her office is poorly lighted. The best action for the building custodian to follow is to

   (A) ignore the complaints because they come from a habitual crank.

   (B) inform the worker that illumination is a fixed item built into the building originally and evidently is the result of faulty planning by the architect.

   (C) request a licensed electrician to install additional ceiling lights.

   (D) investigate for faulty illumination features in the room, such as dirty lamp globes and incorrect lamp wattage.

5. Suppose that one of your neighbors walks into the police precinct where you are an administrative aide and asks you to make 100 photocopies of a flyer he intends to distribute in the neighborhood. Of the following, what action should you take in this situation?

   (A) Pretend that you do not know the person and order him to leave the building.

   (B) Call a police officer and report the person for attempting to make illegal use of police equipment.

   (C) Tell the person that you will make the copies when you are off duty.

   (D) Explain that you cannot use police equipment for non-police work.

6. A police officer, walking a beat at 3 a.m., notices heavy smoke coming out of a top-floor window of a large apartment building. Out of the following, the action the officer should take first is to

   (A) make certain that there really is a fire.

   (B) enter the building and warn all the occupants of the apartment building.

   (C) attempt to extinguish the fire before it gets out of control.

   (D) call the fire department.

7. An elevator inspector on routine inspection for the Building Department notices a number of dangerous situations in the basement of the building she is in. Of the following conditions that she notices, which is the most dangerous and should be reported immediately?

   (A) Gas is leaking from a broken pipe.

   (B) The sewer pipe is broken.

   (C) Water is seeping into the basement.

   (D) The basement is unlighted.

8. There are times when an employee of one city department should notify and seek assistance from employees of another department. A parking enforcement agent is checking meters on a busy one-way street. Of the following situations he notices, which should he report immediately?

   (A) A rat runs out of a building and into the storm sewer across the street.

   (B) A wire is dangling over the sidewalk, giving off sparks.

   (C) A car is parked directly in front of a hydrant.

   (D) Two men are sitting on the front steps of a building sharing a marijuana joint.

ANSWER KEY AND EXPLANATIONS

1. A	3. B	5. D	7. A
2. C	4. D	6. D	8. B

1. **The correct answer is (A).** The inmate who repeatedly bangs his fists against the bars of his cell is in immediate danger of causing himself bodily harm. The inmate must be restrained. The other inmates require attention, and their situations must be dealt with, but they do not require physical restraint.

2. **The correct answer is (C).** There are a number of points to take into consideration: Your own task is described as routine; the coworker's assignment is described as one that has top priority; and the coworker has asked for only a few minutes of your time. If you were involved in "rush" work yourself, you might refuse to help until you had finished your own task, but under these circumstances, help get the priority work done. A side benefit to be considered here is maintaining a good relationship with the coworker, so that you, too, may request assistance at some time when your job demands it.

3. **The correct answer is (B).** Without any knowledge of police rules, common sense dictates that saving lives is the number one priority. An ambulance on an emergency run is on a mission to save a life. Lifesaving takes precedence over the desire for an uninterrupted parade, despite the officer's prior orders.

4. **The correct answer is (D).** The repeated complaints may be quite legitimate if the lighting problem has not been corrected. Do not dismiss the office worker as a "crank."

The custodian should check out the fixtures personally before calling in an electrician. Costs can be held down by having house staff perform those tasks for which they are qualified.

5. **The correct answer is (D).** Where calm, reasoned explanation is offered as an answer choice, it is nearly always the correct answer. There is no need to be impolite or hostile to the neighbor. He may not even realize that he is asking you to do something that is not permitted. He will respect you for obeying the rules.

6. **The correct answer is (D).** A police officer is a police officer and not a firefighter. Eliminate choices (A) and (C) at once. It is the job of the firefighters to ascertain whether or not there really is a fire and to put it out. Since the building is a large one and fires spread rapidly, the practical move is to call the fire department immediately rather than running through the building alone trying to rouse all the occupants. Firefighters will have greater manpower to do this efficiently and are trained in nighttime rousing procedures.

7. **The correct answer is (A).** Leaking gas can ignite, causing a fire. If a large amount of gas collects in the basement and is ignited, an explosion and fire are likely. This is the greatest hazard. The broken sewer pipe and the water seepage can create health hazards and should be reported and repaired, but these corrections do not represent the same emergency

situations as the gas leak. An unlit basement is also a safety hazard, but is even less of an emergency.

8. **The correct answer is (B).** The most urgent hazard is that caused by the sparking wire. A quick call to the police department will get the area sealed off and a repair crew to attend to the wire. The health department could be notified of rodents in the building, but pest infestation is a chronic problem rather than an emergency. The parking enforcement agent can ticket the illegally parked car. The two men sharing one joint pose no immediate danger.

STRATEGIES FOR ANSWERING COMMUNICATION SKILL QUESTIONS

No one works entirely alone. Every person must at times communicate information to someone else. The communication may be in the form of written e-mails, memos, or reports, or it may be oral. No matter what form the communication takes, it must be clear and readily understood. It must convey all necessary information in a usable form.

Most city civil service exams include some measure of a candidate's ability to organize and communicate information. Where the communication is likely to be oral, such as a telephone call to a central post, communication questions offer a set of facts and ask how you would best organize those facts into a clear and accurate report. The following practice questions will help you answer this type of question, which measures your oral communication skills. The correct answers and explanations follow the exercise.

EXERCISE: COMMUNICATION SKILL

1. Police Officer Franks arrives at the scene of a two-family frame house in Brooklyn and observes flames leaping from the door onto the porch. A woman on the sidewalk gives him a description of a man she saw running from the house just before she noticed the fire. The information is:

   - Place of Occurrence: 1520 Clarendon Road, Brooklyn
   - Time of Occurrence: 6:32 a.m.
   - Type of Building: two-family frame dwelling
   - Event: fire, suspected arson
   - Suspect: male, white, approx. 6 ft., wearing blue jeans
   - Witness: Mary Smith of 1523 Clarendon Road, Brooklyn

   Officer Franks is about to radio an alert for the suspect. Which of the following expresses the information *most clearly and accurately?*

   (A) At 6:32 a.m., Mary Smith of 1523 Clarendon Road, Brooklyn, saw a white male wearing approximately 6-ft. blue jeans running from the building across the street.

   (B) A white male wearing blue jeans ran from the house at 1520 Clarendon Road at 6:32 a.m. Mary Smith saw him.

   (C) At 6:32 a.m., a 6-ft. white male wearing blue jeans ran from a burning two-family frame structure at 1520 Clarendon Road, Brooklyn. He was observed by a neighbor, Mary Smith.

   (D) A two-family frame house is on fire at 1520 Clarendon Road in Brooklyn. A white male in blue jeans probably did it. Mary Smith saw him run.

2. A woman runs to the token clerk at the platform of the subway station to report that her purse was just snatched. She gives the following information to the token clerk:

   - Time of Occurrence: 1:22 a.m.
   - Place of Occurrence: uptown-bound platform, 59th Street Station, 7th Avenue line
   - Victim: Juana Martinez
   - Crime: purse-snatching
   - Description of Suspect: unknown, fled down steps to lower platform

   The token clerk is about to call for assistance from the transit police. Which of the following expresses the information *most clearly and accurately?*

   (A) Juana Martinez had her purse snatched on the subway platform at 59th Street Station. She did not see him.

   (B) A purse was just snatched by a man who ran down the steps. This is the 7th Avenue token booth at 59th Street Station. Her name is Juana Martinez.

   (C) It is 1:22 a.m. The person who snatched Juana Martinez's purse is downstairs at 59th Street Station.

   (D) This is the 59th Street Station, uptown-bound 7th Avenue token booth. A Juana Martinez reports that her purse was just snatched by a person who fled down the steps to a lower platform.

ANSWER KEY AND EXPLANATIONS

| 1. C | 2. D |

1. **The correct answer is (C).** This statement tells what happened, where, and when. It gives a brief description of the suspect and identifies the witness. Choices (A) and (B) neglect to mention the fire; choice (D) omits the height of the suspect, which is an important fact, and does not identify the relationship of the witness for later questioning if necessary.

2. **The correct answer is (D).** This statement gives the precise location, the event, and a direction in which the suspect might be traced. Since the statement says that the event just occurred, the time is irrelevant. The recipient of the message knows to move quickly. Choice (A) does not give enough details to be of use. Choice (B) makes a disjointed statement. Choice (C) makes a flat statement that is not necessarily true; the purse-snatcher may have exited by another route.

STRATEGIES FOR ANSWERING OBSERVATION AND MEMORY QUESTIONS

Some government positions, such as firefighter, police officer, and corrections officer, require good observation and memory skills. Civil service exams for these and related positions may include questions that measure these skills. Typically, you are presented with a picture and are allowed to study it for a short period of time. Then, the picture is covered, and you must answer questions based on what you remember of the details that you observed in the picture.

The following exercise will help you practice for this type of question. You will need a timer so that you can correctly time the amount of time allowed for studying the picture.

EXERCISE: OBSERVATION AND MEMORY

Directions: You will have three minutes to study the following picture, to note details about people, time and place, and activities. Then you will have to answer five questions about the picture without looking back at the picture.

Directions: Answer questions 1 to 5 on the basis of the picture. Do not look at the picture again.

1. The teller is
   (A) wearing a striped tie.
   (B) wearing glasses.
   (C) making change.
   (D) left-handed.

2. The man wearing a hat is also
   (A) handing money to the teller.
   (B) wearing a bow tie.
   (C) talking to another man in the line.
   (D) smoking a pipe.

3. The teller's name is
   (A) R. Smith.
   (B) T. Jones.
   (C) T. Smith.
   (D) R. Jones.

4. The woman in the dark dress is
   (A) carrying a handbag.
   (B) wearing gloves.
   (C) holding a hat.
   (D) third in line.

5. The time of day is
   (A) early morning.
   (B) around noon.
   (C) mid-afternoon.
   (D) late afternoon.

ANSWER KEY

1. B   2. D   3. D   4. B   5. B

SUMMING IT UP

- Good judgment is a required skill for most federal, state, and local civil service positions. Almost all multiple-choice civil service exams include questions designed to directly or indirectly assess judgment skills.

- Judgment questions may resemble reading comprehension questions, but they differ in that you must choose the best answer based on your own knowledge and common sense, not on the meaning of the passage. The answer to a judgment question does not necessarily appear in the passage.

- To recognize and understand judgment questions when they appear on your exam, review the exercises in this chapter and review the answer explanations at the end.

- Like good judgment, communication skills are essential to doing your job effectively in the civil service. No matter what form it takes, all of your communication must be clear and easily understood, and it must convey the necessary information.

- Most civil service exams include assessments of your ability to organize and communicate effectively. Review the exercises in this chapter and review the answer explanations at the end to practice answering these types of questions.

- Good observation and memory skills are especially important for certain civil service positions, such as firefighter, police officer, and corrections officer. Civil service exams for these types of positions usually include questions designed to measure these skills. Typically, you're presented with a picture and asked to study it for a short time. Then, without looking at the picture again, you must answer questions based on what you remember of the details you observed.

Mechanical Aptitude

OVERVIEW

- What are mechanical aptitude questions?
- Summing it up

WHAT ARE MECHANICAL APTITUDE QUESTIONS?

Mechanical aptitude questions are useful in predicting success in jobs that require the ability to operate, service, or maintain machinery. Frequently, these questions draw upon your acquired knowledge through education, prior work experience, and what you have learned on your own.

Depending on the position that you are applying for, mechanical aptitude questions may test any or all of the following skills and aptitudes:

- Knowledge of tools and their uses
- Knowledge of shop practices
- Knowledge of electronics information
- Knowledge of automotive information
- Knowledge of maintenance work
- Your inherent feeling for machinery
- Your mechanical experience

Civil service exams that have a mechanical aptitude portion often include arithmetic questions that test your ability to solve reasoning problems and perform basic computations in typical shop situations. Turn to Part V of this book to learn how to answer arithmetic ability questions.

chapter 12

EXERCISE

Directions: Read each question carefully. Select the best answer from the choices given.

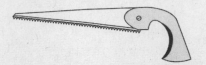

1. The saw shown above is used mainly to cut
   (A) plywood.
   (B) odd-shaped holes in wood.
   (C) along the grain of the wood.
   (D) across the grain of the wood.

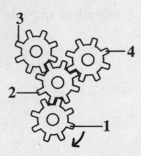

2. Four gears are shown in the figure above. If Gear 1 turns as shown, then which of the following gears are turning in the same direction?
   (A) 2 and 3
   (B) 2 and 4
   (C) 3 and 4
   (D) 2, 3, and 4

3. After brakes have been severely overheated, what should be checked?
   (A) Water condensation in brake fluid.
   (B) Glazed brake shoes
   (C) Wheels out of alignment
   (D) Crystallized wheel bearings

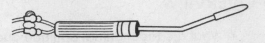

4. The tool shown above is used for
   (A) pressure lubricating.
   (B) welding a steel plate.
   (C) drilling small holes in tight places.
   (D) holding small parts for heat treating.

5. When working on live 600-volt equipment where rubber gloves might be damaged, an electrician should
   (A) work without gloves.
   (B) carry a spare pair of rubber gloves.
   (C) reinforce the fingers of the rubber gloves with rubber tape.
   (D) wear leather gloves over the rubber gloves.

6. Concrete is usually made by mixing
   (A) only sand and water.
   (B) only cement and water.
   (C) lye, cement, and water.
   (D) rock, sand, cement, and water.

7. The tool used to locate a point directly below a ceiling hook is a
   (A) plumb bob.
   (B) line level.
   (C) transit.
   (D) drop gauge.

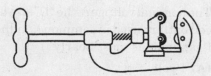

8. The tool above is a
   (A) marking gauge.
   (B) knurling tool.
   (C) thread cutter.
   (D) pipe cutter.

9. A "pinch bar" is used for
   (A) joining.
   (B) leveling.
   (C) prying.
   (D) tightening.

10. When marking wood, an allowance of $\frac{1}{16}''$ to $\frac{1}{8}''$ should be made to allow for
    (A) drying of the wood.
    (B) absorption of water by the wood.
    (C) the width of the saw.
    (D) knots in the wood.

11. The primary function of a power-driven saber saw is to
    (A) cut angles.
    (B) saw heavy wood stock.
    (C) cut curves in flat wood.
    (D) make perfectly straight cuts.

12. The best electrical connection between two wires is obtained when
    (A) the insulations are melted together.
    (B) all insulation is removed and the wires are bound together with friction tape.
    (C) both are wound on a common binding post.
    (D) they are soldered together.

13. If every time a washing machine is started the circuit breaker must be reset, the best solution would be to
    (A) oil the motor in the washer.
    (B) replace the circuit breaker.
    (C) tape the breaker switch closed.
    (D) repair the timing mechanism.

14. One use of a coaxial cable is to
    (A) ground a signal.
    (B) pass a signal from the set to the antenna of a mobile unit.
    (C) carry the signal from a ballast tube.
    (D) carry grid signals in high-altitude areas.

15. A black gummy deposit in the end of the tailpipe of an automobile indicates that
    (A) the automobile "burns" oil.
    (B) there is probably a leak in the exhaust manifold.
    (C) the timing is late.
    (D) there are leaks in the exhaust valves.

16. Of the following, the most important reason for not letting oily rags accumulate in an open storage bin is that they
    (A) may start a fire by spontaneous combustion.
    (B) will drip oil onto other items in the bin.
    (C) may cause a foul odor.
    (D) will make the area messy.

17. The best tool to use to make a hole in a concrete floor for a machine hold-down bolt is a
    (A) counterboring tool.
    (B) cold chisel.
    (C) drift punch.
    (D) star drill.

18. The best reason for overhauling a machine on a regular basis is
    (A) that overhauling is easier to do when done often.
    (B) to minimize breakdowns of the machine.
    (C) to make sure that the machine is properly lubricated.
    (D) to make sure that employees are familiar with the machine.

19. The best method to employ in putting out a gasoline fire is to
    (A) use a bucket of water.
    (B) smother it with rags.
    (C) use a carbon dioxide extinguisher.
    (D) use a carbon tetrachloride extinguisher.

20. What would be the most probable cause if an automobile has a weak spark at the plugs, "turns over" very slowly, and has dim headlights?
    (A) Weak battery
    (B) Faulty condenser
    (C) Faulty ignition cable
    (D) Worn contact breaker points

21. A miter box is used
    (A) for locating dowel holes in two pieces of wood to be joined together.
    (B) to hold a saw at a fixed angle while sawing.
    (C) to hold a saw while sharpening its teeth.
    (D) to clamp two pieces of wood together at 90 degrees.

22. The nominal voltage of the "D" size dry-cell battery used in common handheld flashlights is most nearly
    (A) 1 volt.
    (B) 1.5 volts.
    (C) 2.0 volts.
    (D) 2.5 volts.

23. The purpose of a water trap in a plumbing drainage system is to
    (A) prevent the leakage of water.
    (B) prevent freezing of the pipes.
    (C) block off sewer gases.
    (D) reduce the water pressure in the system.

24. Gaskets are commonly used between the flanges of large pipe joints to
    (A) make a leakproof connection.
    (B) provide for expansion.
    (C) provide space for assembly.
    (D) adjust for poor alignment.

25. To prevent damage to an air compressor, the air coming into the compressor is usually
    (A) cooled.
    (B) heated.
    (C) expanded.
    (D) filtered.

ANSWER KEY AND EXPLANATIONS

1. B	6. D	11. C	16. A	21. B
2. C	7. A	12. D	17. D	22. B
3. B	8. D	13. B	18. B	23. C
4. B	9. C	14. B	19. C	24. A
5. D	10. C	15. A	20. A	25. D

1. **The correct answer is (B).** The compass saw is used to cut odd-shaped holes in wood.

2. **The correct answer is (C).** Gear 1 turns clockwise; Gear 2 turns counterclockwise; Gears 3 and 4 turn clockwise.

3. **The correct answer is (B).** Overheating the brake shoe will cause the brake material to glaze and become slippery. Slippery brakes are dangerous because they take longer to stop a car.

4. **The correct answer is (B).** The tool is a welding torch used in making a metal joint. Welding is generally done with material made of steel.

5. **The correct answer is (D).** Leather gloves offer the best protection over the rubber gloves. The leather can withstand severe conditions before it will tear. The rubber acts as insulation.

6. **The correct answer is (D).** Rock, sand, cement, and water are used to make concrete.

7. **The correct answer is (A).** A plumb bob is used in this situation.

8. **The correct answer is (D).** The tool is a pipe cutter.

9. **The correct answer is (C).** The "pinch bar" is used for prying.

10. **The correct answer is (C).** You must make an allowance for the width of the saw.

11. **The correct answer is (C).** The saber saw is used to cut curves in flat wood.

12. **The correct answer is (D).** Soldering obtains the best electrical connection.

13. **The correct answer is (B).** In this situation, you should replace the circuit breaker.

14. **The correct answer is (B).** A coaxial cable can be used to pass a signal from the set to the antenna of a mobile unit.

15. **The correct answer is (A).** This situation indicates that the automobile is "burning" oil.

16. **The correct answer is (A).** The most important reason not to let the oily rags accumulate in the bin is to prevent a fire.

17. **The correct answer is (D).** The best tool to use is a star drill.

18. **The correct answer is (B).** The best reason to regularly overhaul a machine is to prevent breakdowns.

19. **The correct answer is (C).** Using a carbon dioxide extinguisher is the best way to put out a gasoline fire.

20. **The correct answer is (A).** This situation indicates a weak battery in the automobile.

21. **The correct answer is (B).** Use a miter box to hold a saw at a fixed angle while sawing.

22. **The correct answer is (B).** "D" size dry-cell batteries are most nearly 1.5 volts.

23. **The correct answer is (C).** The water trap blocks off sewer gases.

24. **The correct answer is (A).** Gaskets are used to make a leakproof connection.

25. **The correct answer is (D).** The air is usually filtered.

SUMMING IT UP

- Mechanical aptitude questions test specific abilities to operate, service, or maintain machinery. These questions assess your acquired knowledge through education, work experience, and self-learning.

- Depending on what position you're applying for, the exam may include questions on any or all of these skills and aptitudes: your mechanical experience, your "feel" for machinery, and your knowledge of tools and their uses, of shop practices, of electronics, of automotive information, and of maintenance work.

- Civil service exams with a mechanical aptitude portion usually involve arithmetic questions that test your ability to solve reasoning problems and perform basic computations.

PART IV
CLERICAL ABILITY

Alphabetizing and Filing

OVERVIEW

- **Rules of alphabetic filing**
- **Strategies for answering alphabetizing and filing questions**
- **Summing it up**

RULES OF ALPHABETIC FILING

The most important rule for putting names in alphabetical order is to consider each letter in the complete name in strict alphabetical order, exactly as it appears, starting with the last name for individuals. However, there are some specific rules that you should understand, and these can differ for names of people and names of organizations. The following sections outline all the rules that you should know to score well on this portion of the clerical ability exam.

Names of Individuals

The following rules apply to the alphabetizing of people's names:

- The names of individuals are filed in strict alphabetical order, first according to last name, then according to first name or initial, and finally according to middle name or initial. For example, *George Allen* comes before *Edward Bell*, and *Leonard P. Reston* comes before *Lucille B. Reston*.

- When last names and first initials are the same, the one with the initial comes before the one with the name written out. For example, *A. Green* comes before *Agnes Green*.

- When first and last names are the same, the name without a middle initial comes before the one with a middle name or initial. For example, *John Doe* comes before both *John A. Doe* and *John Alan Doe*.

- When first and last names are the same, the name with a middle initial comes before the one with a middle name beginning with the same initial. For example, *Jack R. Hertz* comes before *Jack Richard Hertz*.

- Prefixes like *De*, *O'*, *Mac*, *Mc*, and *Van* are filed exactly as written and treated as part of the names they come before. Ignore apostrophes for purposes of filing. For example, *Robert O'Dea* comes before *David Olsen*, and *Gladys McTeague* comes before *Frances Meadows*.

chapter 13

- Foreign names are filed as spelled. Prefixes are not considered separately. Likewise, foreign language articles (such as *Le*, *La*, *Les*, and *El*), whether they begin with a lowercase or capital letter, are considered part of the name with which they appear. For example, *Carl Da Costa* is filed before *Ugo D'Agnota*.

- Hyphenated surnames are indexed as though the hyphen joins the two parts, making one. Thus, *Amadeus Lyttonet* is filed before *John Lytton-Strachey*.

- Abbreviated names are treated as if they are spelled out. For example, *Chas.* is filed as *Charles*, and *Thos.* is filed as *Thomas*.

- Titles and designations, such as *Dr.*, *Mr.*, *Prof.*, *Jr.*, or *II*, are given last consideration in filing.

Names of Businesses

The following rules apply to the alphabetizing of business names:

- The names of organizations, institutions, and buildings are filed according to the order in which each word in the name appears, *except* where these names include the full names of individuals.

- When business names include the full names of individuals, the business names are filed using the rules for filing individual names. For example, *Edward Rice and Sons, Ltd.* is filed as *Rice, Edward, and Sons Ltd.*

- When *the*, *of*, *and*, or an apostrophe are parts of a business name, they are disregarded for purposes of filing.

- Names that include numerals should be filed as if the numerals were spelled out. Thus, *10th Street Bootery* is filed as *Tenth Street Bootery*.

- When the same names appear with different addresses, arrange them alphabetically according to town or city, considering state only when town or city names are duplicated. Example: *American Tobacco Co., Norfolk, VA; American Tobacco Co., Quincey, IL; American Tobacco Co., Quincey, MA.*

- Abbreviations are alphabetized as though the words were spelled out. Thus, *Indus. Bros. of America* is filed as *Industrial Brothers of America*.

- Hyphenated firm names are treated as separate words. For example, *Oil-O-Match Heating Co.* is filed before *Oilimatic Heating Co.*

- Compound geographic names written as separate words are always treated as separate words. For example, *West Chester* comes before *Westchester*.

- Bureaus, boards, offices, and government departments are filed under the names of the chief governing body. For example, *Bureau of the Budget* would be filed as if written *Budget, Bureau of the*.

STRATEGIES FOR ANSWERING ALPHABETIZING AND FILING QUESTIONS

There are four different kinds of alphabetizing and filing questions, and any of these may appear on your civil service exam. Therefore, you should read the directions closely and make certain that you mark your answers exactly as specified. Let's take a look at an example of each kind of question.

One type is a simple alphabetizing question. All you have to do is insert the given word into its correct alphabetical position in the list of words and choose the letter of the word it precedes. Try an example:

1. BIOGRAPHY
   (A) bible
   (B) bibliography
   (C) bilge
   (D) biology

The correct answer is (D). Biography should be filed *before* biology.

Another kind of alphabetizing question tests your knowledge of the rules for filing names of individuals. You are given a name, followed by four names in proper alphabetic order. The spaces between the names are lettered. You must mark the space where the given name should be filed. Try an example:

2. Kessler, Neilson
   (A) –
     Kessel, Carl
   (B) –
     Kessinger, D. J.
   (C) –
     Kessler, Karl
   (D) –
     Kessner, Lewis
   (E) –

The correct answer is (D). According to the rules for alphabetizing names of individuals, when the last names are the same, you should alphabetize by the first name. Thus, *Neilson* falls after *Karl*.

A third type of question tests your ability to alphabetize both individual and business names. One name in a group of names is bold. You must determine where this name should be filed in the entire group: mark (A) if it should be first, mark (B) if it should be second, mark (C) if it should be third, and mark (D) if it should be fourth. Try a question of this type:

3. Albert Brown
   James Borenstein
   Frieda Albrecht
   Samuel Brown

The correct answer is (D). The correctly alphabetized group would look like this: Albrecht, Frieda; Borenstein, James; Brown, Albert; **Brown, Samuel**. Because the bold name is fourth in the group, choice (D) is the correct answer.

The final kind of alphabetizing question also tests your ability to file individual and business names. You are given a group of four names, and you must select the name that would be *third* if the group were correctly alphabetized. Here's an example:

4. **(A)** Herbert Restman
   (B) H. Restman
   (C) Harry Restmore
   (D) H. Restmore

The correct answer is (D). The correctly alphabetized group would look like this: Restman, H.; Restman, Herbert; Restmore, H.; Restmore, Harry. Choice (D), *H. Restmore*, falls third in this group.

TIP

When answering the third and fourth types of alphabetizing questions, it's helpful to write out the group of names in alphabetical order in your test booklet or on your scratch paper.

EXERCISE 1

Directions: Each question consists of a CAPITALIZED word that is to be filed correctly among the alphabetized words listed. Choose the word that should come after the given word.

1. CATHOLIC
   - **(A)** catacombs
   - **(B)** catalogs
   - **(C)** catechisms
   - **(D)** cattle

2. DRAMA
   - **(A)** drawing
   - **(B)** Drayton
   - **(C)** Dreyfus
   - **(D)** drugs

3. INQUISITION
   - **(A)** industry
   - **(B)** insurance
   - **(C)** international
   - **(D)** intern

4. LUGUBRIOUS
   - **(A)** Lucretius
   - **(B)** lumber
   - **(C)** Luther
   - **(D)** Lutheran

5. OCEANIC
   - **(A)** occult
   - **(B)** Ohio
   - **(C)** Oklahoma
   - **(D)** optics

6. ENGLAND
   - **(A)** engineering
   - **(B)** English
   - **(C)** engraving
   - **(D)** entomology

7. IRRIGATION
   - **(A)** Ireland
   - **(B)** Irish
   - **(C)** iron
   - **(D)** Irving

8. MARINE
   - **(A)** Margolin
   - **(B)** marketing
   - **(C)** Mary
   - **(D)** Maryland

9. PALEONTOLOGY
   - **(A)** Pacific
   - **(B)** painting
   - **(C)** Palestine
   - **(D)** paltry

10. ASIATIC
    - **(A)** ascetic
    - **(B)** assyriology
    - **(C)** astronomy
    - **(D)** astrophysics

EXERCISE 2

Directions: In each of the following questions, you are given a name, followed by four names in proper alphabetic order. The spaces between the names are lettered. Decide where the given name belongs in the alphabetic series, and mark the letter of the space.

1. Eatley, Mary

(A) –

Eagin, John

(B) –

Eagley, Robert

(C) –

Ebert, Jack

(D) –

Eckert, Wallace

(E) –

2. Pinch, Nathaniel

(A) –

Payne, Briscoe

(B) –

Pearlman, Abe

(C) –

Pincus, Harry

(D) –

Pollaci, Angelina

(E) –

3. Raphan, Max

(A) –

Rankin, H.

(B) –

Rappan, Sol

(C) –

Rascoll, Jon

(D) –

Rich, Harold

(E) –

4. Schwartz, H.

(A) –

Scavone, John

(B) –

Schwartz, Harry

(C) –

Seiden, Burt

(D) –

Shields, Vera

(E) –

5. Hakim, Wm.

(A) –

Hakiel, R.

(B) –

Hakim, Louis

(C) –

Hakim, M.

(D) –

Halabi, Joe

(E) –

6. Horn, Sol

(A) –

Hormel, Max

(B) –

Horn, Harold

(C) –

Horn, Irving

(D) –

Hornbeck, J. W.

(E) –

7. Krommes, Selma

(A) –

Kromolitz, J.

(B) –

Kromowitz, L.

(C) –

Kromwitz, Abe

(D) –

Kron, Harold

(E) –

8. Melzer, Max

(A) –

Meltz, Lena

(B) –

Meltzer, Abe

(C) –

Meltzer, Alex

(D) –

Melzner, L.

(E) –

9. Nesbitt, Carl

(A) –

Nesbiet, Jerry

(B) –

Nesbitt, Al

(C) –

Nesbitt, Gloria

(D) –

Nesci, Jas.

(E) –

10. Perron, Homer

(A) –

Perrin, Larry

(B) –

Perron, Lewis

(C) –

Perrone, James

(D) –

Perrotta, Chas.

(E) –

exercises

EXERCISE 3

Directions: Consider each group of names as a unit. Determine where the name printed in boldface would be if the names in the group were correctly alphabetized. If the name in boldface is first, mark (A); if second, mark (B); if third, mark (C); and if fourth, mark (D).

1. Hugh F. Martenson
   A. S. Martinson
   Albert Martinsen
   Albert S. Martinson

2. Arthur Roberts
   James Robin
   J. B. Robin
   Arnold Robinson

3. **Eugene Thompkins**
   Alice Thompson
   Arnold G. Thomas
   B. Thomas

4. Albert Green
   Wm. Greenfield
   A. B. Green
   Frank E. Green

5. Dr. Francis Karell
   John Joseph Karelsen Jr.
   John J. Karelson Sr.
   Mrs. Jeanette Kelly

6. Norman Fitzgibbons
   Charles F. Franklin
   Jas. Fitzgerald
   Andrew Fitzsimmons

7. **Chas. R. Connolly**
   Frank Conlon
   Charles S. Connolly
   Abraham Cohen

8. **The 5th Ave. Bus Co.**
   The Baltimore and Ohio Railroad
   3rd Ave. Elevated Co.
   Pennsylvania Railroad

9. The Jane Miller Shop
   Joseph Millard Corp.
   John Muller & Co.
   Jean Mullins, Inc.

10. **Anthony Delaney**
    A. De Landri
    A. M. D'Elia
    Alfred De Monte

EXERCISE 4

Directions: Each question consists of four names. For each question, select the one of the four names that should be third if the four names were arranged in alphabetical order in accordance with the rules for alphabetical filing.

1. **(A)** Elm Trading Co.
   (B) El Dorado Trucking Corp.
   (C) James Eldred Jewelry Store
   (D) Eldridge Printing, Inc.

2. **(A)** Fifth Avenue Book Shop
   (B) Mr. Wm. A. Fifner
   (C) 52nd Street Association
   (D) Robert B. Fiffner

3. **(A)** Timothy Macalan
   (B) Fred McAlden
   (C) Tomas MacAllister
   (D) Mrs. Frank McAllen

4. **(A)** Peter La Vance
   (B) George Van Meer
   (C) Wallace De Vance
   (D) Leonard Vance

5. **(A)** 71st Street Theater
   (B) The Seven Seas Corp.
   (C) 7th Ave. Service Co.
   (D) Walter R. Sevan and Co.

6. **(A)** Dr. Chas. D. Peterson
   (B) Miss Irene F. Petersen
   (C) Lawrence E. Peterson
   (D) Prof. N. A. Petersen

7. **(A)** Edward La Gabriel
   (B) Marie Doris Gabriel
   (C) Marjorie N. Gabriel
   (D) Mrs. Marian Gabriel

8. **(A)** Adam Dunn
   (B) E. Dunn
   (C) A. Duncan
   (D) Edward Robert Dunn

9. **(A)** Paul Moore
   (B) William Moore
   (C) Paul A. Moore
   (D) William Allen Moore

10. **(A)** George Peters
    (B) Eric Petersen
    (C) G. Peters
    (D) E. Petersen

ANSWER KEY AND EXPLANATIONS

Exercise 1

1. D	3. B	5. B	7. D	9. C
2. A	4. B	6. B	8. B	10. B

Exercise 2

1. C	3. B	5. D	7. A	9. C
2. C	4. B	6. D	8. D	10. B

Exercise 3

1. D	3. C	5. B	7. C	9. A
2. C	4. A	6. A	8. B	10. B

1. **The correct answer is (D).** Martenson, Hugh F.; Martinsen, Albert; Martinson, A. S.; **Martinson, Albert S.**

2. **The correct answer is (C).** Roberts, Arthur; Robin, J. B.; **Robin, James**; Robinson, Arnold

3. **The correct answer is (C).** Thomas, Arnold G.; Thomas, B.; **Thompkins, Eugene**; Thompson, Alice

4. **The correct answer is (A). Green, A. B.**; Green, Albert; Green, Frank E.; Greenfield, Wm.

5. **The correct answer is (B).** Karell, Francis, Dr.; **Karelsen, John Joseph, Jr.**; Karelson, John J., Sr.; Kelly, Jeanette, Mrs.

6. **The correct answer is (A). Fitzgerald, Jas.**; Fitzgibbons, Norman; Fitzsimmons, Andrew; Franklin, Charles F.

7. **The correct answer is (C).** Cohen, Abraham; Conlon, Frank; **Connolly, Chas. R.**; Connolly, Charles S.

8. **The correct answer is (B).** Baltimore and Ohio Railroad, The; **5th (Fifth) Ave. Bus Co., The**; Pennsylvania Railroad; 3rd (Third) Ave. Elevated Co.

9. **The correct answer is (A). Millard, Joseph, Corp.**; Miller, Jane Shop, The; Muller, John & Co.; Mullins, Jean, Inc.

10. **The correct answer is (B).** De Landri, A.; **Delaney, Anthony**; D'Elia, A. M.; De Monte, Alfred

Exercise 4

1. D	3. B	5. C	7. C	9. B
2. A	4. D	6. A	8. B	10. D

1. **The correct answer is (D).** El Dorado Trucking Corp.; Eldred, James Jewelry Store; Eldridge Printing, Inc.; Elm Trading Co.

2. **The correct answer is (A).** Fiffner, Robert B.; Fifner, Wm. A., Mr.; Fifth Avenue Book Shop; 52nd (Fifty-second) Street Association

3. **The correct answer is (B).** Macalan, Timothy; MacAllister, Thomas; McAlden, Fred; McAllen, Frank, Mrs.

4. **The correct answer is (D).** De Vance, Wallace; La Vance, Peter; Vance, Leonard; Van Meer, George

5. **The correct answer is (C).** Sevan, Walter R. and Co.; Seven Seas Corp., The; 7th (Seventh) Ave. Service Co.; 71st (Seventy-first) Street Theater

6. **The correct answer is (A).** Petersen, Irene F., Miss; Petersen, N. A., Prof.; Peterson, Chas. D., Dr.; Peterson, Lawrence E.

7. **The correct answer is (C).** Gabriel, Marian, Mrs.; Gabriel, Marie Doris; Gabriel, Marjorie N.; La Gabriel, Edward

8. **The correct answer is (B).** Duncan, A.; Dunn, Adam; Dunn, E.; Dunn, Edward Robert

9. **The correct answer is (B).** Moore, Paul; Moore, Paul A.; Moore, William; Moore, William Allen

10. **The correct answer is (D).** Peters, G.; Peters, George; Petersen, E.; Petersen, Eric

SUMMING IT UP

- The most important rule of alphabetical filing is to consider each letter in the complete name or phrase in strict alphabetical order, exactly as it appears. Review this chapter for more specific rules on alphabetizing names of individuals and names of businesses.

- Civil service exams present four different types of questions about alphabetizing and filing. One type requires simple alphabetizing. Another type tests your knowledge of alphabetizing rules. A third type requires you to alphabetize both individual and business names, and a fourth tests your ability to correctly file individual and business names. Read all directions carefully and make sure you know what the question is asking you to do.

Clerical Speed and Accuracy

chapter 14

OVERVIEW

- Answering timed questions
- Strategies for answering comparison questions
- Coding questions
- Summing it up

ANSWERING TIMED QUESTIONS

Generally, time is a crucial factor in comparison questions. You'll probably find that there are more questions than you can answer in the time allowed. Since accuracy is of prime importance, you should follow these rules:

- Work steadily until time is called.
- Don't rush beyond your ability to focus on words and numbers.
- Don't guess.
- Don't randomly answer the remaining questions when time is called.

Tests of clerical speed and accuracy put such a premium on accuracy that the scoring formula is sometimes "score equals the correct answers minus the wrong answers." Don't allow the fear of making errors to slow you down so that you plod along and answer very few questions; speed is also important. However, you must work steadily until time is called and then stop promptly.

STRATEGIES FOR ANSWERING COMPARISON QUESTIONS

In comparison questions, you are given several sets of names or numbers. You must quickly compare them to find which is different or inaccurate. Lots of practice with various forms of comparison questions should improve your skills in this area.

In answering comparison questions, look for differences in one area at a time. If you narrow your focus to compare only short numbers, abbreviations, or just the words, you're more likely to notice differences and less apt to see what you expect to see rather than what is actually printed on the page.

Start with length of line, number of digits, middle initials, or small words. Once you spot *any difference* at all, you know that the two items being compared are different. If, while concentrating on one area, you happen to catch a difference in another area, consider the items to be different and go on to the next comparison. A system may be useful, but don't stick to it slavishly.

The best way to read names, numbers, and addresses being compared is to read exactly what you see and to sound out words by syllables. For example:

- If you see *St*, read "es-tee" not "street."
- If you see *NH*, read "en-aitch" not "New Hampshire."
- If you see *1035*, read "one-zero-three-five" not "one thousand thirty-five."
- Read *sassafras* as "sas-sa-fras."

Psychologists have discovered that the human mind always tries to complete a figure. If you read "Pky" as "Parkway," you'll probably read "Pkwy" as "Parkway" and never notice the difference between the two. Your mind will complete the word without allowing you to focus on the letters. If, however, you read the abbreviation as an abbreviation, you'll notice that the two are different.

Remember that although one type of question asks you to identify the difference between the given word or string of numbers and the answer choices, another type asks you to identify the answer that is the same as the given words or set of numbers. Directions for the third type of question ask you to identify mistakes; this is the same as finding the differences. You have to read the directions carefully.

Finally, trust yourself. Once you've decided that an answer is the same or there is no mistake, don't second guess yourself.

EXERCISE 1

Directions: Each question lists four names or numbers. The names or numbers may or may not be exactly the same. Compare the four names or numbers in each question, and choose your answer as follows:

Choose (A) if all four names or numbers are DIFFERENT.
Choose (B) if TWO of the names or numbers are exactly the same.
Choose (C) if THREE of the names or numbers are exactly the same.
Choose (D) if all FOUR names or numbers are exactly the same.

1. W.E. Johnston
   W.E. Johnson
   W.E. Johnson
   W.B. Johnson

2. Vergil L. Muller
   Vergil L. Muller
   Vergil L. Muller
   Vergil L. Muller

3. 5261383
   5263183
   5263183
   5623183

4. Atherton R. Warde
   Ashcton R. Warde
   Atherton P. Warde
   Athertin P. Warde

5. 8125690
   8126690
   8125609
   8125609

6. E. Owens McVey
   E. Owen McVey
   E. Owen McVay
   E. Owen McVey

7. Emily Neal Rouse
   Emily Neal Rowse
   Emily Neal Roose
   Emily Neal Rowse

8. Francis Ramsdell
   Francis Ransdell
   Francis Ramsdell
   Francis Ramsdell

9. 2395890
   2395890
   2395890
   2395890

10. 1926341
    1962341
    1963241
    1926341

EXERCISE 2

Directions: Each question gives the name and identification number of an employee. You are to choose the one answer that has exactly the same identification number and name as those given in the question.

1. 176823   Katherine Blau
   - **(A)** 176823   Catherine Blau
   - **(B)** 176283   Katherine Blau
   - **(C)** 176823   Katherine Blau
   - **(D)** 176823   Katherine Blaw

2. 673403   Boris T. Frame
   - **(A)** 673403   Boris P. Frame
   - **(B)** 673403   Boris T. Frame
   - **(C)** 673403   Boris T. Fraim
   - **(D)** 673430   Boris T. Frame

3. 498832   Hyman Ziebart
   - **(A)** 498832   Hyman Zeibart
   - **(B)** 498832   Hiram Ziebart
   - **(C)** 498832   Hyman Ziebardt
   - **(D)** 498832   Hyman Ziebart

4. 506745   Barbara O'Dey
   - **(A)** 507645   Barbara O'Day
   - **(B)** 506745   Barbara O'Day
   - **(C)** 506475   Barbara O'Day
   - **(D)** 506745   Barbara O'Dey

5. 344223   Morton Sklar
   - **(A)** 344223   Morton Sklar
   - **(B)** 344332   Norton Sklar
   - **(C)** 344332   Morton Sklaar
   - **(D)** 343322   Morton Sklar

6. 816040   Betsy B. Voight
   - **(A)** 816404   Betsy B. Voight
   - **(B)** 814060   Betsy B. Voight
   - **(C)** 816040   Betsy B. Voight
   - **(D)** 816040   Betsey B. Voight

7. 913576   Harold Howritz
   - **(A)** 913576   Harold Horwitz
   - **(B)** 913576   Harold Howritz
   - **(C)** 913756   Harold Horwitz
   - **(D)** 913576   Harald Howritz

8. 621190   Jayne T. Downs
   - **(A)** 621990   Janie T. Downs
   - **(B)** 621190   Janie T. Downs
   - **(C)** 622190   Janie T. Downs
   - **(D)** 621190   Jayne T. Downs

9. 004620   George McBoyd
   - **(A)** 006420   George McBoyd
   - **(B)** 006420   George MacBoyd
   - **(C)** 006420   George McBoid
   - **(D)** 004620   George McBoyd

10. 723495   Alice Appleton
    - **(A)** 723495   Alice Appleton
    - **(B)** 723594   Alica Appleton
    - **(C)** 723459   Alice Appleton
    - **(D)** 732495   Alice Appleton

EXERCISE 3

Directions: Each of the following questions consists of three sets of names and name codes. In each question, the two names and name codes on the same line are supposed to be exactly the same. Look carefully at each set of names and codes, and choose your answer as follows:

Choose (A) if there are mistakes in all THREE sets.
Choose (B) if there are mistakes in TWO of the sets.
Choose (C) if there are mistakes in only ONE set.
Choose (D) if there are NO MISTAKES in any of the sets.

1. Macabe, John N.   V 53162   Macade, John N.   V 53162
   Howard, Joan S.   J 24791   Howard, Joan S.   J 24791
   Ware, Susan B.   A 45068   Ware, Susan B.   A 45968

2. Powell, Michael C.   78537 F   Powell, Michael C.   78537 F
   Martinez, Pablo J.   24435 P   Martinez, Pablo J.   24435 P
   MacBane, Eliot M.   98674 E   MacBane, Eliot M.   98674 E

3. Fitz-Kramer Machines Inc. 259090   Fitz-Kramer Machines Inc. 259090
   Marvel Cleaning Service   482657   Marvel Cleaning Service   482657
   Donato, Carl G.   637418   Danato, Carl G.   687418

4. M. Davison Trading Corp.   43108 T   M. Davidson Trading Corp.   43108 T
   Cotwald Lighting Fixtures   76065 L   Cotwald Lighting Fixtures   70056 L
   R. Crawford Plumbers   23157 C   R. Crawford Plumbers   23157 G

5. Fraiman Engineering Corp.   M4773   Friaman Engineering Corp.   M4773
   Neuman, Walter B.   N7745   Neumen, Walter B.   N7745
   Pierce, Eric M.   W6304   Pierce, Eric M.   W6304

6. Constable, Eugene   B 64837   Comstable, Eugene   B 64837
   Derrick, Paul   H 27119   Derrik, Paul   H 27119
   Scalsi Office Furniture   R 36742   Scalsi Office Furniture   R 36742

7. H. Delivery Service Co.   D 7456   H. Delivery Service Co.   D 7456
   Barettz Electrical Supplies N 5392   Barettz Electrical Supplies N 5392
   Tanner, Abraham   M 4798   Tanner, Abraham   M 4798

8. Kalin Associates   R 38641   Kaline Associates   R 38641
   Sealey, Robert E.   P 63533   Sealey, Robert E.   P 63553
   Scalsi Office Furniture   R 36742   Scalsi Office Furniture   R 36742

9. Janowsky, Philip M.   742213   Janowsky, Philip M.   742213
   Hansen, Thomas H.   934816   Hanson, Thomas H.   934816
   L. Lester and Son Inc.   294568   L. Lester and Son Inc.   294568

10. Majthenyi, Alexander   P 4802   Majthenyi, Alexander   B 4802
Prisco Pools, Inc.   W 3641   Frisco Pools, Inc.   W 3641
DePaso, Nancy G.   X 4464   DePaso, Nancy G.   X 4464

ANSWER KEY AND EXPLANATIONS

Exercise 1

1. B	3. B	5. B	7. B	9. D
2. D	4. A	6. B	8. C	10. B

1. **The correct answer is (B).** The second and third names are the same.

2. **The correct answer is (D).** All four names are the same.

3. **The correct answer is (B).** The second and third numbers are the same.

4. **The correct answer is (A).** All the names are different.

5. **The correct answer is (B).** The third and fourth numbers are the same.

6. **The correct answer is (B).** The second and fourth names are the same.

7. **The correct answer is (B).** The second and fourth names are the same.

8. **The correct answer is (C).** The first, third, and fourth names are the same.

9. **The correct answer is (D).** All four numbers are the same.

10. **The correct answer is (B).** The first and fourth numbers are the same.

Exercise 2

1. C	3. D	5. A	7. B	9. D
2. B	4. D	6. C	8. D	10. A

Exercise 3

1. B	3. C	5. B	7. D	9. C
2. D	4. A	6. B	8. B	10. B

1. **The correct answer is (B).** There are mistakes in the first and third sets.

2. **The correct answer is (D).** There are no mistakes.

3. **The correct answer is (C).** There are mistakes in the third set.

4. **The correct answer is (A).** There are mistakes in all three sets.

5. **The correct answer is (B).** There are mistakes in the first and second sets.

6. **The correct answer is (B).** There are mistakes in the first and second sets.

7. **The correct answer is (D).** There are no mistakes.

8. **The correct answer is (B).** There are mistakes in the first and second sets.

9. **The correct answer is (C).** There is a mistake in the second set.

10. **The correct answer is (B).** There are mistakes in the first and second sets.

CODING QUESTIONS

The most common variety of coding questions found on civil service exams consists of a coding table (which need not be memorized) and a series of questions that requires you to demonstrate your understanding of the use of the code and your ability to follow directions in answering the questions. From one exam to another, the chief variations in coding questions tend to be in the number of digits and letters in each question line and in the directions. The best way to learn how to answer coding questions is to practice with some examples.

EXERCISE 1

Directions: Each letter should be matched with its number in accordance with the following table:

Letter	P	S	B	O	Q	K	A	M	E	Y
Number	0	1	2	3	4	5	6	7	8	9

For each question, compare each line of letters and numbers carefully to see if each letter is matched correctly to its corresponding number. Choose your answer according to the number of lines in which all the letters and numbers are matched correctly:

Choose (A) if NONE of the lines are matched correctly.
Choose (B) if only ONE of the lines is matched correctly.
Choose (C) if TWO of the lines are matched correctly.
Choose (D) if all THREE lines are matched correctly.

1. SEOB   1732
   YMQA   9756
   BEPM   2806

2. AOSY   6319
   EKQM   8547
   YBOP   9230

3. QABS   3621
   PKEO   0583
   SEYO   1983

4. AQOB   6432
   YSAP   9061
   BAKM   2657

5. SBOK   1234
   YEAQ   9854
   MPES   7081

EXERCISE 2

Directions: Each question contains three lines of letters and numbers. The numbers in each line should correspond with the code letters in this table:

Code Letter	M	Q	O	H	B	C	I	N	Y	V
Number	0	1	2	3	4	5	6	7	8	9

In some of the lines below, an error exists in the coding. Compare the numbers and letters in each question very carefully. Choose your answers according to the number of lines in which you find an error as follows:

Choose (A) if only ONE line contains an error.
Choose (B) if TWO lines contain errors.
Choose (C) if all THREE lines contain errors.
Choose (D) if NONE of the lines contains an error.

1. BCMHIOB   4503624
   VYBQNCO   8941752
   MHBCNIV   0345869

2. HYVNOQM   3987210
   NCOMHYQ   7520481
   QBCHIYN   1463687

3. MHBNYQO   0347812
   CONBMYH   5274083
   QBHNOMV   1430279

exercises

ANSWER KEY AND EXPLANATIONS

Exercise 1

| 1. A | 2. D | 3. B | 4. C | 5. B |

1. **The correct answer is (A).** None of the lines is matched correctly. In the first set, E is incorrectly matched with 7. In the second set, Q is incorrectly matched with 5. In the third set, M is incorrectly matched with 6.

2. **The correct answer is (D).** All three lines are matched correctly.

3. **The correct answer is (B).** Only the second set is matched correctly. In the first set, Q is incorrectly matched with 3. In the third set, E is incorrectly matched with 9, and Y is incorrectly matched with 8.

4. **The correct answer is (C).** The first and third sets are matched correctly. In the second set, S is incorrectly matched with 0, and P is incorrectly matched with 1.

5. **The correct answer is (B).** Only the last set is matched correctly. In the first set, K is incorrectly matched with 4. In the second set, A is incorrectly matched with 5.

Exercise 2

| 1. B | 2. C | 3. A |

1. **The correct answer is (B).** The first line contains no errors. On the second line, V is incorrectly coded as 8, and Y is incorrectly coded as 9. On the third line, N is incorrectly coded as 8.

2. **The correct answer is (C).** All three lines contain errors. In the first line, Y is incorrectly coded as 9, and V is incorrectly coded as 8. In the second line, H is incorrectly coded as 4. In the third line, C is incorrectly coded as 6.

3. **The correct answer is (A).** The first and second lines contain no errors. In the third line, N is incorrectly coded as 0, and M is incorrectly coded as 7.

SUMMING IT UP

- Time is crucial in answering comparison questions. To be sure you're as accurate as possible, follow these rules: Work steadily until time is called, don't rush beyond your ability to focus on words and numbers, don't guess at answers, and don't randomly answer remaining questions when time is called.

- Comparison questions measure speed and accuracy by presenting several sets of names or numbers and asking you to quickly compare them to learn which one is the same, or which has mistake(s). Be sure to practice with various forms of this question type to improve your ability to work quickly and accurately.

- A good strategy for answering comparison questions is to look for differences in one area at a time, so you're more likely to notice differences or errors. Once you spot any difference at all, you know that the two items being compared are different.

- An essential tip for reading names, numbers, and addresses being compared is to read them phonetically, syllable by syllable. If you see "St," don't read it as "street" but as "ess tee." You're more likely to notice differences this way.

- The directions for coding questions include a coding table that shows letters paired with numbers. You don't have to memorize the table; it will be available for you to refer to as you answer questions. The questions require that you identify any errors in the matching of the letters and numbers.

Typing and Stenography

OVERVIEW

- The typing test
- The stenography test
- Summing it up

THE TYPING TEST

For jobs in which typing is a very important skill, the typing test may be competitively scored. In those cases, the score on the typing test is part of the overall civil service exam score and affects hiring decisions. If typing is a requirement of the job, the job announcement will tell you the minimum number of words per minute an applicant must be able to input.

In the typing test, you're faced with a single task: copying material exactly as it is presented. You must demonstrate how rapidly you can do so and with what degree of accuracy.

What to Expect on the Typing Test

The typing test consists of a passage that you must copy exactly as it is presented to you. You'll have a specified length of time in which to type, and your score will be based upon the number of words per minute that you type within that time and upon the number of errors that you make.

You'll also be given a practice exercise before the test itself. The practice exercise, usually about ten lines in length, enables you to warm up. It is not scored.

How the Typing Test Is Scored

The length of the typing test varies from one governmental jurisdiction to another. Most typing tests last five minutes. The minimum performance standards also vary. For some positions, a minimum speed of 30 words per minute (wpm) is adequate; for others 35 wpm, 40 wpm, or even greater speeds are required. Likewise, the number of errors permitted varies according to department and the position for which you're applying.

The basic principles in charging typing errors are as follows:

- WORD or PUNCTUATION MARK incorrectly typed. (An error in spacing that follows an incorrect word or punctuation mark is not further charged.)
- SERIES of consecutive words omitted, repeated, inserted, or transposed, or erased. (A charge is made for errors within such series, but the total charge cannot exceed the number of words.)
- LINE or part of a line typed in all capitals, or apparently typed with the fingers on the wrong keys.
- CHANGE from the MARGIN where most lines are begun by the candidate or from the PARAGRAPH INDENTION most frequently used by the candidate.

Strategies for Taking the Typing Test

Assuming that you already know how to type, the best preparation for any typing test is typing. Choose any material at all and practice copying it line for line, exactly as you see it. As on the actual typing test, spell, capitalize, punctuate, and begin and end lines exactly as they appear on the page that you're copying. Try to balance yourself to meet speed requirements while maintaining a very high level of accuracy.

EXERCISE

Directions: Type the copy exactly as it is given below. Spell, space, begin and end each line, paragraph, punctuate, and capitalize precisely as shown. Make no insertions or other corrections in the copy. Keep on typing even though you detect an error in your copy. If you finish typing the passage before the time limit is up, simply double space once and continue typing from the beginning of the passage.

TIME: 5 minutes

Line Count

(1)   Under President Bill Clinton, the federal government un-
      derwent its own process of rationalization and consolidation.
(3) President Clinton appointed Vice President Al Gore to trim
      the federal government through a program known as "The
(5) National Performance Review." Known as reinventing govern-
      ment, the program undertook a broad review of departments,
(7) agencies, and personnel. The goal was to cut inefficient, un-
      necessary, and redundant programs, thereby saving the federal
(9) government and taxpayers millions of dollars. The reinvention
      of government was also intended to restore people's faith in
(11) government by providing improving service to people.
       President George W. Bush consolidated a number of pro-
(13) grams and agencies related to the nation's defense under a new
      Department of Homeland Security. This department, which
(15) includes the Federal Emergency Management Agency, is also
      responsible for preparedness, response, and recovery to natural
(17) disasters.

EACH TIME YOU REACH THIS POINT, DOUBLE SPACE ONCE AND BEGIN AGAIN.

TYPING SPEED ATTAINED: _____ words per minute

NUMBER OF ERRORS: _____

THE STENOGRAPHY TEST

Only stenographer competitors take a stenography test. You will be expected to take dictation at the rate of 80 words per minute. You must then consult your notes to fill in the missing words of a transcript from an alphabetic word list. The sample stenography test given in this section shows the length of the dictated material and will help you prepare if your exam includes a stenography test.

To take the practice stenography test, sit down with your pencil and notebook, and hand this book to a friend or family member. Have that person dictate the passage to you. Each pair of lines is dictated in 10 seconds. Your friend should dictate periods, but not commas, and should read the exercise with the expression that the punctuation indicates. Have your friend use a watch with a second hand to read the sentences at the proper speed.

EXERCISE 1

Directions: Exactly on a minute start dictating. Finish reading each line at the number of seconds indicated below.

I realize that this practice dictation	
is not a part of the examination	10 sec.
proper and is not to be scored. (Period)	
When making a study of the defined	20 sec.
contribution plan and its influence,	
the most striking feature of it is its	30 sec.
youth. (Period) As has been shown, the time	
of greatest growth began just a few years	40 sec.
ago. (Period) The influence that this	
growth has had on the labor market and	50 sec.
worker attitudes is hard to assess,	
partly because the effects have not yet fully	1 min.
evolved and many are still in the	
growing stage. (Period) Even so, most pension	10 sec.
plans continue to be defined benefit plans,	
which pay a specified amount of money regularly	20 sec.
to retirees. (Period). But the newer defined	
contribution plans, specify only the amount	30 sec.
contributed by the employee and usually by the	
employer. (Period). Employees whose	40 sec.
plans have been changed from a defined	
benefit to a defined contribution plan	50 sec.
find that they do not have the guaranteed	
retirement payments that they thought they	2 min.
would. (Period) This has angered many	
employees and raised concerns among workers'	10 sec.
advocates. (Period) As informal and formal	
information on these pension plans spread,	20 sec.
workers will become more aware of the plans	
and their provisions. (Period) Their impact	30 sec.
on employee attitudes will no doubt become	
stronger. (Period) Each year, more and more workers	40 sec.
will be retiring and as they do, those with defined	
contribution plans will be sounding the alarm for	50 sec.
younger workers. (Period) So, active workers may	
begin to pay more attention to their pensions. (Period)	3 min.

EXERCISE 2

Directions: The following transcript and word list is taken from the previous dictation. Many words have been omitted from the transcript. Compare your notes with it. When you come to a blank space in the transcript, decide what word (or words) belongs there. Look for the missing word in the word list. Notice which letter (A, B, C, or D) is printed beside the word. Write that letter in the blank. (B) is written in blank 1 to show how you are to record your choice. Write (E) if the exact answer is not in the word list. You may also write the word (or words) or the shorthand for it, if you wish. The same choice may belong in more than one blank.

Alphabetic Word List

Write (E) if the answer is not listed.

a — (D)	influence — (A)
attitudes — (C)	labor — (C)
be — (B)	main — (B)
been — (C)	make — (A)
began — (D)	making — (B)
being — (A)	market — (B)
completely — (A)	markets — (D)
contribution — (C)	marking — (D)
defined — (D)	never — (B)
examination — (A)	not — (D)
examine — (B)	over — (C)
examining — (D)	part — (C)
feat — (A)	partly — (D)
feature — (C)	plan — (D)
full — (B)	practical — (C)
fully — (D)	practice — (B)
greater — (D)	proper — (C)
grow — (B)	section — (D)
growing — (C)	so — (B)
had — (D)	still — (A)
has — (C)	striking — (B)
has been — (B)	to — (D)
has had — (A)	to be — (C)
has made — (A)	trial — (A)
in — (C)	turn — (D)
in part — (B)	values — (A)
	yet — (C)

I realize that this <u>B</u> dictation is __ a __ of the __ __ and is __ __
            1   2   3   4 5   6 7

scored. When __ a __ of the __ __ __ and its __, the most
           8   9   10 11 12   13

__ __ is its youth. As __ shown, the time of __ growth began just a few
14 15   16   17

years ago. The __ that this growth __ on the labor __ and worker __ is hard
          18   19   20   21

to assess, __ because the effects have not yet __ evolved and many are __ in the
     22   23   24

__ stage.
25

ANSWER KEY

Exercise 2

1. B	6. D	11. C	16. B	21. C
2. D	7. C	12. D	17. E	22. D
3. C	8. B	13. A	18. A	23. D
4. A	9. E	14. B	19. A	24. A
5. C	10. D	15. C	20. B	25. C

1. **The correct answer is (B),** practice (filled in for you).

2. **The correct answer is (D),** not.

3. **The correct answer is (C),** part.

4. **The correct answer is (A),** examination.

5. **The correct answer is (C),** proper.

6. **The correct answer is (D),** not.

7. **The correct answer is (C),** to be.

8. **The correct answer is (B),** making.

9. **The correct answer is (E),** study (not given).

10. **The correct answer is (D),** defined.

11. **The correct answer is (C),** contribution.

12. **The correct answer is (D),** plan.

13. **The correct answer is (A),** influence.

14. **The correct answer is (B),** striking.

15. **The correct answer is (C),** feature.

16. **The correct answer is (B),** has been.

17. **The correct answer is (E),** greatest (not given).

18. **The correct answer is (A),** influence.

19. **The correct answer is (A),** has had.

20. **The correct answer is (B),** market.

21. **The correct answer is (C),** attitudes.

22. **The correct answer is (D),** partly.

23. **The correct answer is (D),** fully.

24. **The correct answer is (A),** still.

25. **The correct answer is (C),** growing.

SUMMING IT UP

- The typing test consists of one task: Copying material exactly as it is presented within a specified period of time. Your score is based on the number of words per minute that you type minus the number of errors you make. Before the actual timed test, you'll be given an unscored practice test that allows you to warm up.

- The best preparation for any typing test is simply to practice typing. Choose any material and practice copying it exactly as it's presented, with the same punctuation, line breaks, capitalization, and spelling. Try timing yourself and aim for speed balanced with accuracy.

- Stenography tests are given only to those who are seeking a position as stenographer. You are expected to take dictation at 80 words per minute or better. You must then consult your notes and fill in the missing words of a transcript from an alphabetic word list.

PART V
ARITHMETIC ABILITY

Fractions and Decimals

OVERVIEW

- Fractions and mixed numbers
- Decimals
- Summing it up

FRACTIONS AND MIXED NUMBERS

Before going over the rules for solving arithmetic problems involving fractions and mixed numbers, let's review what fractions and mixed numbers are:

- A **fraction** is part of a unit. The two parts of the fraction are the numerator and the denominator. In the fraction $\frac{3}{4}$, 3 is the numerator and 4 is the denominator. In any fraction, the numerator is being divided by the denominator. So in the previous example, 3 is being divided by 4.

- A **mixed number** is an integer together with a fraction, such as $2\frac{3}{5}$. The integer is the integral part, and the fraction is the fractional part.

- An **improper fraction** is one in which the numerator is equal to or greater than the denominator, such as $\frac{19}{6}$, $\frac{25}{4}$, or $\frac{10}{10}$.

In a fraction problem, the whole quantity is 1, which can be expressed by a fraction in which the numerator and denominator are the same number. For example, if a problem involves $\frac{1}{8}$ of a quantity, the whole quantity is $\frac{8}{8}$, or 1.

Rules to Know

If you understand the rules outlined in this section, you'll be able to solve any arithmetic problem that involves fractions and mixed numbers. Study the rules and example problems, and be sure that you understand each rule before moving on to the practice exercises.

chapter 16

Converting Mixed Numbers and Improper Fractions

It's often helpful to convert mixed numbers to improper fractions to solve fraction problems. Follow these three steps:

❶ Multiply the denominator of the fraction by the integer.

❷ Add the numerator to this product.

❸ Place this sum over the denominator.

To change $3\frac{4}{7}$ to an improper fraction, for example, follow these steps:

- 7 (denominator) × 3 (integer) = 21
- 21 (product) + 4 (numerator) = 25
- The answer is $\frac{25}{7}$.

To convert an improper fraction to a mixed number, reverse the process and follow these two steps:

❶ Divide the numerator by the denominator. The quotient, disregarding the remainder, is the integral part of the mixed number.

❷ Place the remainder, if any, over the denominator. This is the fractional part of the mixed number.

Change $\frac{36}{13}$ to a mixed number using these steps:

- 36 (numerator) ÷ 13 (denominator) = 2 with a remainder of 10
- The answer is $2\frac{10}{13}$.

Reducing Fractions

The numerator and denominator of a fraction can be changed by dividing both by the same number, without affecting the value of the fraction. This process is called reducing the fraction. A fraction that has been reduced as much as possible is said to be in lowest terms.

For example, the value of the fraction $\frac{3}{12}$ is not altered if both the numerator and denominator are divided by 3, resulting in $\frac{1}{4}$. Likewise, if $\frac{6}{30}$ is reduced to lowest terms (by dividing both numerator and denominator by 6), the result is $\frac{1}{5}$.

Adding Fractions

Fractions can't be added unless the denominators are all the same. To convert all fractions to the same denominator, you must first find the least common denominator.

The least common denominator (LCD) is the lowest number that can be divided evenly by all the given denominators. If no two of the given denominators can be divided by the same number, the LCD is the product of all the denominators.

To find the LCD when two or more of the given denominators can be divided by the same number, follow these five steps:

1 Write down all the denominators.

2 Select the smallest number (other than 1) by which two or more of the denominators can be divided evenly.

3 Divide the denominators by this number, copying down those that cannot be divided evenly. Write this number to one side.

4 Repeat this process, writing each divisor to one side until there are no longer any denominators that can be divided evenly by the same number.

5 Multiply all the divisors to find the LCD.

To find the LCD of $\frac{1}{5}$, $\frac{1}{7}$, $\frac{1}{10}$, and $\frac{3}{14}$, follow these steps:

- Write down the denominators: 5, 7, 10, 14

- 10 and 14 can be divided by 2: 5, 7, 5, 7

- 5 and 5 can be divided by 5: 1, 7, 1, 7

- 7 and 7 can be divided by 7: 1, 1, 1, 1

- None of the remainders can be divided any further. Multiply the divisors: $2 \times 5 \times 7 = 70$.

70 is the least common denominator.

If two fractions have the same denominator, the one with the larger numerator is the greater fraction. If two fractions have the same numerator, the one with the larger denominator is the smaller fraction. To compare fractions with different numerators and denominators, change them to equivalent fractions by finding the LCD.

Now that you know how to find the LCD, you can add any fractions by following these four steps:

1 Find the LCD of the denominators.

2 Convert each fraction to an equivalent fraction with the LCD as its denominator.

3 Add all the numerators and place this sum over the common denominator.

4 Reduce the answer as far as possible. Change improper fractions to mixed numbers.

Add $\frac{1}{4}$, $\frac{3}{10}$, and $\frac{2}{5}$ using these steps:

- Find the LCD; your answer should be 20.

- Convert each fraction to one having a denominator of 20: $\frac{1}{4} \times \frac{5}{5} = \frac{5}{20}$; $\frac{3}{10} \times \frac{2}{2} = \frac{6}{20}$; $\frac{2}{5} \times \frac{4}{4} = \frac{8}{20}$.

- Add all the numerators: $5 + 6 + 8 = 19$.

- Place the sum over the common denominator: $\frac{19}{20}$. This is not an improper fraction and it cannot be reduced, so it is the final answer.
- If the problem contains any mixed numbers, add the fractions first, and then add the integers. You don't need to convert the mixed numbers to improper fractions.

Subtracting Fractions

In subtraction, as in addition, the denominators must be the same. Follow these steps to subtract fractions:

1 Find the LCD of the two fractions.

2 Convert both fractions to equivalent fractions with the LCD as the denominator.

3 Subtract the numerator of the second fraction from the numerator of the first, and place this difference over the LCD.

4 Reduce the fraction, if possible, and convert improper fractions to mixed numbers.

5 When subtracting mixed numbers, it may be necessary to "borrow," so that the fractional part of the first term is larger than the fractional part of the second term. Otherwise, subtract the fractions and integers separately.

Subtract $16\frac{4}{5}$ from $29\frac{1}{3}$ using these steps:

- Find the LCD: $5 \times 3 = 15$.
- Convert both fractions to ones with the LCD: $29\frac{5}{15} - 16\frac{12}{15}$.
- Note that $\frac{5}{15}$ is less than $\frac{12}{15}$. Borrow 1 from 29, which is equivalent to $\frac{15}{15}$, and add this to the fraction: $28\frac{20}{15} - 16\frac{12}{15}$.
- Subtract the numerators and the integers. The answer is $12\frac{8}{15}$.

Multiplying Fractions

Fractions don't need to have the same denominators to be multiplied. Follow these five steps to multiply fractions:

1 Change the mixed numbers, if any, to improper fractions.

2 Multiply all the numerators.

3 Multiply all the denominators.

4 Place the product of the numerators over the product of the denominators.

5 Reduce, if possible, and convert improper fractions to mixed numbers.

Multiply $\frac{2}{3} \times 2\frac{4}{7} \times \frac{5}{9}$ using these steps:

- Convert $2\frac{4}{7}$ to an improper fraction: $\frac{18}{7}$.

- Multiply the numerators and denominators, and put the products on top of each other: $\frac{2}{3} \times \frac{18}{7} \times \frac{5}{9} = \frac{180}{189}$.

- Reduce as much as possible: $\frac{180}{189} \div \frac{9}{9} = \frac{20}{21}$.

A whole number has an understood denominator of 1. To multiply a whole number by a mixed number, first multiply the fractional part of the mixed number by the whole number, and then the integral part of the mixed number; then add both products. For example, to multiply $23\frac{3}{4}$ by 95, first multiply $\frac{3}{4}$ by $\frac{95}{1}$, then multiply 23 by 95, and then add the results of each. You should get $2{,}256\frac{1}{4}$.

Dividing Fractions

To divide two fractions, multiply one fraction by the other's reciprocal. The reciprocal of a fraction is its invert; for example, the reciprocal of $\frac{3}{8}$ is $\frac{8}{3}$. Since every whole number has an understood denominator of 1, the reciprocal of a whole number has 1 as the numerator and the whole number as the denominator; for example, the reciprocal of 5 is $\frac{1}{5}$.

Follow these three steps to divide two fractions:

1 Convert all mixed numbers, if any, to improper fractions.

2 Invert the second fraction and multiply the two.

3 Reduce the answer, if possible. Convert improper fractions to mixed numbers.

Divide $\frac{2}{3}$ by $2\frac{1}{4}$ using these steps:

- Convert $2\frac{1}{4}$ to an improper fraction: $\frac{9}{4}$.

- Invert the second fraction and multiply the two: $\frac{2}{3} \div \frac{9}{4} = \frac{2}{3} \times \frac{4}{9}$.

- The answer is $\frac{8}{27}$.

A complex fraction has a fraction as the numerator and/or the denominator,

such as $\dfrac{\frac{2}{3}}{\frac{5}{14}}$.

To clear (or simplify) a complex fraction, divide the numerator by the denominator

and reduce.

TIP

Dividing a numerator and a denominator by the same number in a multiplication problem, or canceling, can facilitate multiplication. In the problem $\frac{4}{7} \times \frac{5}{6}$, the numerator 4 and the denominator 6 can both be divided by 2: $\frac{2}{7} \times \frac{5}{3} = \frac{10}{21}$.

Tackling Fraction Problems

Most fraction problems can be arranged in the form, "What fraction of a number is another number?" This form contains three important parts: the fractional part; the number following "of"; and the number following "is." Follow these three rules to find the answer:

1 If the fraction and the "of" number are given, multiply them to find the "is" number. For example, if asked, "What is $\frac{3}{4}$ of 20?" rewrite the question as "$\frac{3}{4}$ of 20 is what number?" Then multiply $\frac{3}{4}$ (the fraction) by 20 (the "of" number) to get $\frac{60}{4}$, which can be reduced to 15.

2 If the fraction and the "is" number are given, divide the "is" number by the fraction to find the "of" number. For example, if asked, "$\frac{4}{5}$ of what number is 40?" divide 40 (the "is" number) by $\frac{4}{5}$ (the fraction) to get $\frac{200}{4}$, which can be reduced to 50.

3 To find the fraction when the other two numbers are known, divide the "is" number by the "of" number. For example, if asked, "What part of 12 is 9?" divide 9 (the "is" number) by 12 (the "of" number). The answer is $\frac{9}{12}$, which can be reduced to $\frac{3}{4}$.

EXERCISE 1

Directions: Each question has four suggested answers. Select the correct one.

1. Reduce to lowest terms: $\frac{60}{108}$.

   (A) $\frac{1}{48}$

   (B) $\frac{1}{3}$

   (C) $\frac{5}{9}$

   (D) $\frac{10}{18}$

2. Change $\frac{27}{7}$ to a mixed number.

   (A) $2\frac{1}{7}$

   (B) $3\frac{6}{7}$

   (C) $6\frac{1}{3}$

   (D) $7\frac{1}{2}$

3. Find the LCD of $\frac{1}{6}$, $\frac{1}{10}$, $\frac{1}{18}$, and $\frac{1}{21}$.
   (A) 160
   (B) 330
   (C) 630
   (D) 1,260

4. Add $16\frac{3}{8}$, $4\frac{4}{5}$, $12\frac{3}{4}$, and $23\frac{5}{6}$.

   (A) $57\frac{91}{120}$

   (B) $57\frac{1}{4}$

   (C) 58

   (D) 59

5. Subtract $27\frac{5}{14}$ from $43\frac{1}{6}$.
   (A) 15
   (B) 16

   (C) $15\frac{8}{21}$

   (D) $15\frac{17}{21}$

6. Multiply $17\frac{5}{8}$ by 128.
   (A) 2,200
   (B) 2,305
   (C) 2,356
   (D) 2,256

7. Divide $1\frac{2}{3}$ by $1\frac{1}{9}$.

   (A) $\frac{2}{3}$

   (B) $1\frac{1}{2}$

   (C) $1\frac{23}{27}$

   (D) 6

EXERCISE 2

Directions: Each question has four suggested answers. Select the correct one.

1. The number of half-pound packages of tea that can be weighed out of a box that holds $10\frac{1}{2}$ pounds of tea is
   - **(A)** 5
   - **(B)** $10\frac{1}{2}$
   - **(C)** $20\frac{1}{2}$
   - **(D)** 21

2. If each bag of tokens weighs $5\frac{3}{4}$ pounds, how many pounds do three bags weigh?
   - **(A)** $7\frac{1}{4}$
   - **(B)** $15\frac{3}{4}$
   - **(C)** $16\frac{1}{2}$
   - **(D)** $17\frac{1}{4}$

3. During one week, a man traveled $3\frac{1}{2}, 1\frac{1}{4}, 1\frac{1}{16}$, and $2\frac{3}{8}$ miles. The next week he traveled $\frac{1}{4}, \frac{3}{8}, \frac{9}{16}, 3\frac{1}{16}, 2\frac{5}{8}$, and $3\frac{3}{16}$ miles. How many more miles did he travel the second week than the first week?
   - **(A)** $1\frac{7}{8}$
   - **(B)** $1\frac{1}{2}$
   - **(C)** $1\frac{3}{4}$
   - **(D)** 1

4. A certain type of board is sold only in lengths of multiples of 2 feet. The shortest board sold is 6 feet and the longest is 24 feet. A builder needs a large quantity of this type of board in $5\frac{1}{2}$-foot lengths. For minimum waste, the lengths to be ordered should be
   - **(A)** 6 feet
   - **(B)** 12 feet
   - **(C)** 22 feet
   - **(D)** 24 feet

5. A man spent $\frac{15}{16}$ of his assets in buying a car for $7,500. How much money did the man originally have?
   - **(A)** $6,000
   - **(B)** $6,500
   - **(C)** $7,000
   - **(D)** $8,000

6. The population of a town was 54,000 in the last census. It has increased $\frac{2}{3}$ since then. Its present population is
   - **(A)** 18,000
   - **(B)** 36,000
   - **(C)** 72,000
   - **(D)** 90,000

7. If one third of the liquid contents of a can evaporates on the first day, and three fourths of the remainder evaporates on the second day, the part of the original contents remaining at the close of the second day is
   - **(A)** $\frac{5}{12}$
   - **(B)** $\frac{7}{12}$
   - **(C)** $\frac{1}{6}$
   - **(D)** $\frac{1}{2}$

8. A car is run until the gas tank is $\frac{1}{8}$ full. The tank is then filled to capacity by putting in 14 gallons. The capacity of the gas tank of the car is
   - **(A)** 14 gal.
   - **(B)** 15 gal.
   - **(C)** 16 gal.
   - **(D)** 17 gal.

ANSWER KEY AND EXPLANATIONS

Exercise 1

1. C	3. C	5. D	7. B
2. B	4. A	6. D	

1. **The correct answer is (C).** Divide the numerator and denominator by 12 to get $\frac{5}{9}$.

2. **The correct answer is (B).** Divide the numerator (27) by the denominator (7) to get 3 with a remainder of 6; the answer is $3\frac{6}{7}$.

3. **The correct answer is (C).** You can divide the denominators by 2, 3, 3, 5, and 7. Multiply these divisors to find 630.

4. **The correct answer is (A).** The LCD is 120, so the mixed numbers convert to $16\frac{45}{120} + 4\frac{96}{120} + 12\frac{90}{120} + 23\frac{100}{120}$. Add the numerators and the integers: $55\frac{331}{120}$. Change the improper fraction to a mixed number: $57\frac{91}{120}$.

5. **The correct answer is (D).** The LCD is 42, so the mixed numbers convert to $43\frac{7}{42} - 27\frac{15}{42}$. "Borrow" to make the first numerator greater than the second: $42\frac{49}{42} - 27\frac{15}{42}$. Subtract the integers and numerators: $15\frac{34}{42}$. Reduce: $15\frac{17}{21}$.

6. **The correct answer is (D).** Convert $17\frac{5}{8}$ to an improper fraction: $\frac{141}{8}$. Multiply the numerators and denominators: $\frac{141}{8} \times \frac{128}{1} = \frac{18,048}{8}$. Reduce: 2,256.

7. **The correct answer is (B).** Convert the mixed numbers to improper fractions: $\frac{5}{3} \div \frac{10}{9}$. Invert the second fraction and multiply: $\frac{5}{3} \times \frac{9}{10} = \frac{45}{30}$. Reduce: $\frac{3}{2}$. Convert to a mixed number: $1\frac{1}{2}$.

Exercise 2

1. D	3. A	5. D	7. C
2. D	4. C	6. D	8. C

1. **The correct answer is (D).** Divide $10\frac{1}{2}$ pounds by $\frac{1}{2}$ pound: $\frac{21}{2} \div \frac{1}{2} = \frac{21}{2} \times \frac{2}{1} = \frac{42}{2} = 21$.

2. **The correct answer is (D).** Multiply $5\frac{3}{4}$ pounds by 3: $\frac{23}{4} \times \frac{3}{1} = \frac{69}{4} = 17\frac{1}{4}$.

3. **The correct answer is (A).** For the first week, the LCD is 16; add all the fractions to get $8\frac{3}{16}$ miles. For the second week, the LCD is 16; add all the fractions to get $10\frac{1}{16}$ miles. Subtract $8\frac{3}{16}$ from $10\frac{1}{16}$. "Borrow" to make the first numerator greater than the second: $9\frac{17}{16} - 8\frac{3}{16} = 1\frac{14}{16}$. Reduce to $1\frac{7}{8}$.

4. **The correct answer is (C).** Consider each choice. Each 6-foot board yields one $5\frac{1}{2}$-foot board with $\frac{1}{2}$ foot waste. Each 12-foot board yields two $5\frac{1}{2}$-foot boards with 1 foot waste ($2 \times 5 = 11$; $12 - 11 = 1$). Each 24-foot board yields four $5\frac{1}{2}$-foot boards with 2 feet waste ($4 \times 5\frac{1}{2} = 22$; $24 - 22 = 2$). Each 22-foot board yields four $5\frac{1}{2}$-foot boards with no waste ($4 \times 5\frac{1}{2} = 22$ exactly). So 22 feet is the best choice.

5. **The correct answer is (D).** $\frac{15}{16}$ of the assets is $7,500. Therefore, the fortune is $7,500 \div \frac{15}{16}$, or $8,000.

6. **The correct answer is (D).** The increase equals $\frac{2}{3}$ of 54,000. Therefore, the increase is $\frac{2}{3} \times \frac{54,000}{1}$, or 36,000. The present population is 54,000 + 36,000, or 90,000.

7. **The correct answer is (C).** On the first day, $\frac{1}{3}$ evaporates and $\frac{2}{3}$ remains. On the second day, $\frac{3}{4}$ of $\frac{2}{3}$ evaporates, and $\frac{1}{4}$ of $\frac{2}{3}$ remains. The amount remaining is $\frac{1}{4} \times \frac{2}{3}$, or $\frac{1}{6}$ of the original contents.

8. **The correct answer is (C).** $\frac{7}{8}$ of capacity equals 14 gal. Therefore, the capacity is $14 \div \frac{7}{8}$, or 16 gal.

DECIMALS

A decimal is actually a fraction, the denominator of which is understood to be a power of 10. The number of digits, or places, after a decimal point determines which power of 10 the denominator is. If there is one digit, the denominator is 10; if there are two digits, the denominator is 100, and so on. For example, $0.3 = \frac{3}{10}$, $0.57 = \frac{57}{100}$, and $0.643 = \frac{643}{1,000}$.

Convert a mixed number containing a decimal to a fraction by dividing the mixed number by the power of 10 indicated by its number of decimal places. The fraction doesn't count as a decimal place. To convert $0.25\frac{1}{3}$ to a fraction, for example, divide $25\frac{1}{3}$ by 100.

Rules to Know

Study the rules outlined in this section to learn how to solve any arithmetic problem that involves decimals. Be sure that you understand the rules before moving on to the practice problems.

Adding and Subtracting Decimals

Decimals are added and subtracted in the same way as whole numbers. However, decimal points must be kept in a vertical line to determine the place of the decimal point in the answer:

$$
\begin{array}{r}
2.3100 \\
0.0370 \\
4.0000 \\
+\ 5.0017 \\
\hline
11.3487
\end{array}
\qquad
\begin{array}{r}
15.3000 \\
-\ 4.0037 \\
\hline
11.2963
\end{array}
$$

Multiplying Decimals

Decimals are multiplied the same way as whole numbers. The number of decimal places in the product equals the sum of the decimal places in the multiplicand and the multiplier. If there are fewer places in the product than this sum, then a sufficient number of zeros must be added in front of the product to equal the number of places required, and the decimal point is placed in front of the zeros. For example, 2.372 (three decimal places) × 0.012 (three decimal places) = 0.028464 (six decimal places).

NOTE

Adding zeros after a decimal point doesn't change the value of the decimal: 0.7 = 0.70 = 0.700.

TIP

A decimal can be multiplied by a power of 10 by moving the decimal point to the right as many places as indicated by the power:

0.235 × 10 = 2.35
0.235 × 100 = 23.50

TIP

A decimal can be divided by a power of 10 by moving the decimal to the left as many places as indicated by the power. If there aren't enough places, add zeros in front of the number to make up the difference: $0.4 \div 10 = 0.04$.

Dividing Decimals

There are four types of division involving decimals:

❶ When the dividend only is a decimal, the division is the same as that of whole numbers; the number of decimal places in the answer must equal that in the dividend: $12.864 \div 32 = 0.402$.

❷ When the divisor only is a decimal, the decimal point in the divisor is omitted and as many zeros are placed to the right of the dividend as there are decimal points in the divisor: $211{,}327 \div 6.817 = 211{,}327{,}000 \div 6{,}817 = 31{,}000$.

❸ When both divisor and divided are decimals, the decimal point in the divisor is omitted, and the decimal point in the dividend is moved to the right as many decimal places as there are in the divisor. If there aren't enough places in the dividend, zeros must be added to make up the difference: $2.62 \div 0.131 = 2{,}620 \div 131 = 20$.

❹ When neither the divisor nor the dividend is a decimal, the problem may still involve decimals. This occurs when the dividend is a smaller number than the divisor, and when you must work out a division to a certain number of decimal places. In either case, write in a decimal point after the dividend, add as many zeros as necessary, and then divide: $7 \div 50 = 7.00 \div 50 = 0.14$.

Converting Fractions to Decimals

A fraction can be changed to a decimal by dividing the numerator by the denominator and working out the division to as many decimal points as required. For example, to change $\frac{5}{11}$ to a decimal of two places, divide 5.00 by 11, which equals $0.45\frac{5}{11}$.

Because decimal equivalents of fractions are often used, it's helpful to be familiar with the most common conversions (the decimal values have been rounded to the nearest ten-thousandth):

$\frac{1}{2} = 0.5$

$\frac{1}{3} = 0.3333$

$\frac{2}{3} = 0.6667$

$\frac{1}{4} = 0.25$

$\frac{3}{4} = 0.75$

$\frac{1}{5} = 0.2$

$\frac{1}{8} = 0.125$

EXERCISE 1

Directions: Each question has four suggested answers. Select the correct one.

1. Add 37.03; 11.5627; 3.4005; 3,423; and 1.141.
   - **(A)** 3,476.1342
   - **(B)** 3,500
   - **(C)** 3,524.4322
   - **(D)** 3,424.1342

2. Subtract 4.64324 from 7.
   - **(A)** 3.35676
   - **(B)** 2.35676
   - **(C)** 2.45676
   - **(D)** 2.36676

3. Multiply 27.34 by 16.943.
   - **(A)** 463.22162
   - **(B)** 453.52162
   - **(C)** 462.52162
   - **(D)** 462.53162

4. How much is 19.6 divided by 3.2 carried out to three decimal places?
   - **(A)** 6.125
   - **(B)** 6.124
   - **(C)** 6.123
   - **(D)** 5.123

5. What is $\frac{5}{11}$ in decimal form (to the nearest hundredth)?
   - **(A)** 0.44
   - **(B)** 0.55
   - **(C)** 0.40
   - **(D)** 0.45

6. What is $0.64\frac{2}{3}$ in fraction form?
   - **(A)** $\frac{97}{120}$
   - **(B)** $\frac{97}{150}$
   - **(C)** $\frac{97}{130}$
   - **(D)** $\frac{98}{130}$

7. What is the difference between $\frac{9}{8}$ and $\frac{3}{5}$ expressed decimally?
   - **(A)** 0.525
   - **(B)** 0.425
   - **(C)** 0.520
   - **(D)** 0.500

exercises

EXERCISE 2

Directions: Each question has four suggested answers. Select the correct one.

1. A boy saved up $4.56 the first month, $3.82 the second month, and $5.06 the third month. How much did he save in total?

   (A) $12.56
   (B) $13.28
   (C) $13.44
   (D) $14.02

2. The diameter of a certain rod is required to be 1.51 ± 0.015 inches. The rod would NOT be acceptable if the diameter measured

   (A) 1.490 inches
   (B) 1.500 inches
   (C) 1.510 inches
   (D) 1.525 inches

3. After an employer figures out an employee's salary of $190.57, he deducts $3.05 for Social Security and $5.68 for pension. What is the amount of the check after these deductions?

   (A) $181.84
   (B) $181.92
   (C) $181.93
   (D) $181.99

4. If the outer diameter of a metal pipe is 2.84 inches and the inner diameter is 1.94 inches, the thickness of the metal is

   (A) 0.45 inch
   (B) 0.90 inch
   (C) 1.94 inches
   (D) 2.39 inches

5. A boy earns $20.56 on Monday, $32.90 on Tuesday, and $20.78 on Wednesday. He spends half of all that he earned during the three days. How much has he left?

   (A) $29.19
   (B) $31.23
   (C) $34.27
   (D) $37.12

6. To the nearest cent, the total cost of $3\frac{1}{2}$ pounds of meat at $1.69 a pound and 20 lemons at $0.60 a dozen will be

   (A) $6.00
   (B) $6.40
   (C) $6.52
   (D) $6.92

7. A reel of cable weighs 1,279 pounds. If the empty reel weighs 285 pounds and the cable weighs 7.1 pounds per foot, the number of feet of cable on the reel is

   (A) 220
   (B) 180
   (C) 140
   (D) 100

8. To the nearest cent, 345 fasteners at $4.15 per hundred will cost

   (A) $0.14
   (B) $1.43
   (C) $14.32
   (D) $143.20

ANSWER KEY AND EXPLANATIONS

Exercise 1

1. A	3. A	5. D	7. A
2. B	4. A	6. B	

1. **The correct answer is (A).** Line up the decimal points one under the other before adding.

2. **The correct answer is (B).** Add a decimal point and five zeros to the 7 before subtracting.

3. **The correct answer is (A).** Because two decimal places are in the multiplicand and three decimal places are in the multiplier, there should be five decimal places in the product.

4. **The correct answer is (A).** Omit the decimal point in the divisor by moving it one place to the right. Move the decimal point in the dividend one place to the right and add three zeros in order to carry your answer out to three decimal places: $196.000 \div 32 = 6.125$.

5. **The correct answer is (D).** Divide the numerator by the denominator: $5.000 \div 11 = 0.45$ to the nearest hundredth.

6. **The correct answer is (B).** Divide by the power of 10 indicated by the number of decimal places. (The fraction doesn't count as a decimal place.) $64\frac{2}{3} \div 100 = \frac{97}{150}$.

7. **The correct answer is (A).** Convert each fraction to a decimal and subtract to find the difference: $\frac{9}{8} = 1.125$; $\frac{3}{5} = 0.60$; $1.125 - 0.60 = 0.525$.

Exercise 2

1. C	3. A	5. D	7. C
2. A	4. A	6. D	8. C

1. **The correct answer is (C).** Add the savings for each month: $13.44.

2. **The correct answer is (A).** The rod may have a diameter of 1.495 inches to 1.525 inches: 1.51 + 0.015 = 1.525; 1.510 − 0.015 = 1.495. Therefore, 1.490 inches is not acceptable.

3. **The correct answer is (A).** Add to find the total deductions: $3.05 + $5.68 = $8.73. Subtract total deductions from salary to find the amount of the check: $190.57 − $8.73 = $181.84.

4. **The correct answer is (A).** The difference of the two diameters equals the total thickness of the metal. Find the difference of the two diameters, and then divide by 2: 2.84 − 1.94 = 0.90; 0.90 ÷ 2 = 0.45 in. (the thickness of the metal).

5. **The correct answer is (D).** Add the daily earnings to find the total earnings: $20.56 + $32.90 + $20.78 = $74.24. Divide the total earnings by 2 (the inverse of ½) to find what he has left: $74.24 ÷ 2 = $37.12.

6. **The correct answer is (D).** Find the cost of $3\frac{1}{2}$ pounds of meat: $1.69 × 3.5 = $5.92 (to the nearest cent). Find the cost of 20 lemons: 0.60 ÷ 12 = $0.05 (for one lemon); $0.05 × 20 = $1.00 (for 20 lemons). Add the cost of the meat and the cost of the lemons: $5.92 + $1.00 = $6.92.

7. **The correct answer is (C).** Subtract the weight of the empty reel from the total weight to find the weight of the cable: 1,279 pounds − 285 pounds = 994 pounds. Each foot of cable weighs 7.1 pounds; therefore, to find the number of feet of cable on the reel, divide 994 by 7.1 = 140.

8. **The correct answer is (C).** Each fastener costs $4.15 ÷ 100 = $0.0415. 345 fasteners cost 345 × 0.0415 = $14.32 (rounded to the nearest cent).

SUMMING IT UP

- Be sure you know what fractions and mixed numbers are so that you'll do well on arithmetic problems on your civil service exam. Study the ways to convert mixed numbers and improper fractions; reduce fractions; and add, subtract, multiply, and divide fractions.

- Most fraction questions on the civil service exam ask you what fraction of a number another number is. This question type contains three important parts: the fractional part, the number following "of," and the number following "is." Any one of these three parts may be missing and what you need to find. Follow the rules outlined in this chapter and take the practice exercises to successfully and correctly answer this type of question on your exam.

- You can consider decimal questions as a type of fraction question. The denominator is understood to be a power of 10. The number of digits after the decimal point determines the power of the 10 of the denominator. To convert a mixed number containing a decimal to a fraction, divide the mixed number by the power of 10, which is indicated by the number of decimal points in the number. Follow the rules outlined in this chapter for adding, subtracting, multiplying, and dividing decimals and for converting fractions to decimals and vice versa.

Percents, Ratio, and Proportion

OVERVIEW

- **Percents**
- **Ratio and proportion**
- **Summing it up**

PERCENTS

The percent symbol (%) means "parts of a hundred." Some problems require you to express a fraction, mixed number, or a decimal as a percent. In other problems, you must convert a percent to a fraction, mixed number, or a decimal to perform the calculations.

Rules to Know

In order to answer percent problems, it's important to understand the following rules for making these conversions.

Converting Decimals to Percents

Follow these two steps to change a whole number or decimal to a percent:

1 Multiply the number by 100.

2 Affix a % sign to the product.

To change 3 to a percent, for example, multiply 3 by 100 and affix a percent sign: 300%. To change 0.67 to a percent, multiply 0.67 by 100 and affix a percent sign: 67%. To convert a percent to a decimal or whole number, divide the percent by 100. For example, 0.5% equals 0.005. You can then convert the resulting decimal to a fraction, if necessary: $\frac{1}{200}$

Converting Fractions to Percents

Follow these three steps to change a fraction or mixed number to a percent:

1 Multiply the fraction or mixed number by 100.

2 Reduce, if possible, and convert improper fractions to mixed numbers.

3 Affix a % sign to the result.

chapter 17

Change $4\frac{2}{3}$ to a percent using these steps:

- Multiply $4=\frac{2}{3}$ by 100: $\frac{14}{3} \times 100 = \frac{1,400}{3}$.

- Convert the improper fraction to a mixed number: $466\frac{2}{3}$.

- Affix a percent sign: $466\frac{2}{3}\%$.

Some fraction–percent equivalents are used so frequently that it's helpful to be familiar with them:

$$\frac{1}{25} = 4\%$$

$$\frac{1}{20} = 5\%$$

$$\frac{1}{10} = 10\%$$

$$\frac{1}{5} = 20\%$$

$$\frac{1}{4} = 25\%$$

$$\frac{1}{2} = 50\%$$

$$\frac{3}{4} = 75\%$$

To convert a fractional percent to a fraction, divide the fractional percent by 100 and reduce, if possible. For example, $\frac{3}{4}\% \div 100 = \frac{3}{400}$. You can then convert the resulting fraction to a decimal, if necessary: 0.075.

Tackling Percent Problems

Most percent problems involve three quantities:

- The rate (R), which is followed by a percent sign
- The base (B), which follows the word "of"
- The amount of percentage (P), which usually follows the word "is"

Depending on which two quantities you know, you can easily find the third quantity by following a formula:

- If the rate and the base are known, then $P = R \times B$.

- If the rate and the percentage are known, then $B = \frac{P}{R}$.

- If the percentage and the base are known, then $R = \frac{P}{B}$.

Try an example of each kind of problem:

- Find 15% of 50.

  In this problem, you know the rate (15%) and the base (50). To find the percentage, multiply 15% by 50: $0.15 \times 50 = 7.5$.

- 7% of what number is 35?

  In this problem, you know the rate (7%) and the percentage (35). To find the base, divide 35 by 7%: $35 \div 0.07 = 500$.

- There are 96 men in a group of 150 people. What percent of the group are men?

  Here you know the base (150) and the amount, or percentage, (96). To find the rate, divide 96 by 150: $96 \div 150 = 0.64$, or 64%.

In all percent problems, the whole is always 100%. Knowing this, you can often deduce a solution to a problem. If a problem involves 10% of a quantity, the rest of the quantity is 90%; if a quantity has been decreased by 15%, the new amount is 85% of the original quantity; or if a quantity has been increased by 5%, the new amount is 105% of the original quantity.

EXERCISE 1

Directions: Each question has four suggested answers. Select the correct one.

1. 10% written as a decimal is
   - **(A)** 1.0
   - **(B)** 0.01
   - **(C)** 0.001
   - **(D)** 0.1

2. What is 5.37% in fraction form?
   - **(A)** $\frac{537}{10,000}$
   - **(B)** $5\frac{37}{10,000}$
   - **(C)** $\frac{537}{1,000}$
   - **(D)** $5\frac{37}{100}$

3. What percent of $\frac{5}{6}$ is $\frac{3}{4}$?
   - **(A)** 75%
   - **(B)** 60%
   - **(C)** 80%
   - **(D)** 90%

4. What percent is 14 of 24?
   - **(A)** $62\frac{1}{4}\%$
   - **(B)** $58\frac{1}{3}\%$
   - **(C)** $41\frac{2}{3}\%$
   - **(D)** $33\frac{3}{5}\%$

5. 200% of 800 equals
   - **(A)** 2,500
   - **(B)** 16
   - **(C)** 1,600
   - **(D)** 4

EXERCISE 2

Directions: Each question has four suggested answers. Select the correct one.

1. If John must have a mark of 80% to pass a test of 35 items, the number of items he may miss and still pass the test is

   (A) 7

   (B) 8

   (C) 11

   (D) 28

2. The regular price of a TV set that sold for $118.80 at a 20% reduction sale is

   (A) $148.50

   (B) $142.60

   (C) $138.84

   (D) $95.04

3. A circle graph of a budget shows the expenditure of 26.2% for housing, 28.4% for food, 12% for clothing, 12.7% for taxes, and the balance for miscellaneous items. The percent for miscellaneous items is

   (A) 31.5

   (B) 79.3

   (C) 20.7

   (D) 68.5

4. Two dozen shuttlecocks and four badminton rackets are to be purchased for a playground. The shuttlecocks are priced at $0.35 each and the rackets at $2.75 each. The playground receives a discount of 30% from these prices. The total cost of this equipment is

   (A) $7.29

   (B) $11.43

   (C) $13.58

   (D) $18.60

5. A piece of wood weighing 10 ounces is found to have a weight of 8 ounces after drying. The moisture content was

   (A) 25%

   (B) $33\frac{1}{3}$%

   (C) 20%

   (D) 40%

6. A bag contains 800 coins. Of these, 10 percent are dimes, 30 percent are nickels, and the rest are quarters. The amount of money in the bag is

   (A) less than $150

   (B) between $150 and $300

   (C) between $301 and $450

   (D) more than $450

7. Six quarts of a 20% solution of alcohol in water are mixed with four quarts of a 60% solution of alcohol in water. The alcoholic strength of the mixture is

   (A) 80%

   (B) 40%

   (C) 36%

   (D) 72%

8. A man insures 80% of his property and pays a $2\frac{1}{2}$% premium amounting to $348. What is the total value of his property?

   (A) $17,000

   (B) $18,000

   (C) $18,400

   (D) $17,400

9. A clerk divided his 35-hour workweek as follows: $\frac{1}{5}$ of his time was spent in sorting mail; $\frac{1}{2}$ of his time in filing letters; and $\frac{1}{7}$ of his time in reception work. The rest of his time was devoted to messenger work. The percent of time spent on messenger work by the clerk during the week was most nearly

(A) 6%

(B) 10%

(C) 14%

(D) 16%

10. In a school in which 40% of the enrolled students are boys, 80% of the boys are present on a certain day. If 1,152 boys are present, what is the total school enrollment?

(A) 1,440

(B) 2,880

(C) 3,600

(D) 5,400

ANSWER KEY AND EXPLANATIONS

Exercise 1

| 1. D | 2. A | 3. D | 4. B | 5. C |

1. **The correct answer is (D).** $10\% \div 100 = 0.1$

2. **The correct answer is (A).** $5.37\% \div 100 = 0.0537 = \frac{537}{10,000}$

3. **The correct answer is (D).** Base (number following "of") = $\frac{5}{6}$; percentage (number following "is") = $\frac{3}{4}$; rate = percentage ÷ base = $\frac{3}{4} \div \frac{5}{6} = \frac{9}{10} = 0.9 = 90\%$

4. **The correct answer is (B).** Base (number following "of") = 24; percentage (number following "is") = 14; rate = percentage ÷ base = $14 \div 24 = 0.58\frac{1}{3} = 58\frac{1}{3}\%$

5. **The correct answer is (C).** Percentage = 200; base = 800; rate = percentage × base = $2.00 \times 800 = 1,600$

answers

Exercise 2

1. A	3. C	5. C	7. C	9. D
2. A	4. C	6. A	8. D	10. C

1. **The correct answer is (A).** He must answer 80% of 35 correctly. Therefore, he can miss 20% of 35. 20% of 35 (percentage) = 0.20 (rate) × 35 (base) = 7.

2. **The correct answer is (A).** Since $118.80 represents a 20% reduction, $118.80 equals 80% of the regular price. The regular price (base) = $118.80 (percentage) ÷ 80% (rate) = 118.80 ÷ 0.80 = $148.50.

3. **The correct answer is (C).** All the items in a circle graph total 100%. Add the figures given for housing, food, clothing, and taxes: 26.2 + 28.4 + 12 + 12.7 = 79.3%. Subtract this total from 100% to find the percent for miscellaneous items: 100 − 79.3 = 20.7%.

4. **The correct answer is (C).** The price of the shuttlecocks: 24 × $.35 = $8.40. The price of the rackets: 4 × $2.75 = $11.00. The total price: $8.40 + $11.00 = $19.40. The discount is 30%, and 100% minus 30% equals 70%. So the actual cost is 70% of $19.40: 0.70 (rate) × 19.40 (base) = $13.58 (percentage).

5. **The correct answer is (C).** Subtract the weight of the wood after drying from the original weight of the wood to find the amount of moisture in the wood: 10 − 8 = 2 ounces of moisture in the wood. The moisture content (rate) equals 2 ounces (percentage) divided by 10 ounces (base): 2 ÷ 10 = 0.2 = 20%.

6. **The correct answer is (A).** Find the number of each kind of coin: 10% of 800 = 0.10 × 800 = 80 dimes; 30% of 800 = 0.30 × 800 = 240 nickels; 60% of 800 = 0.60 × 800 = 480 quarters. Find the value of the coins: 80 dimes = 80 × 0.10 = $8.00; 240 nickels = 240 × 0.05 = $12.00; 480 quarters = 480 × 0.25 = $120.00; $8.00 + $12.00 + $120.00 = $140.00. So, there is less than $150 in the bag.

7. **The correct answer is (C).** The first solution contains 20% of 6 quarts of alcohol; the alcohol content is 0.20 × 6 = 1.2 quarts. The second solution contains 60% of 4 quarts of alcohol; the alcohol content is 0.60 × 4 = 2.4 quarts. The mixture contains 1.2 + 2.4 = 3.6 quarts alcohol, and 6 + 4 = 10 quarts liquid. So the alcoholic strength of the mixture (rate) = 3.6 (percentage) ÷ 10 (base) = 36%.

8. **The correct answer is (D).** $2\frac{1}{2}\%$, or 2.5%, of the insured value = $348; the insured value (base) = 348 (percentage) ÷ 2.5% (rate): 348 ÷ 0.025 = $13,920. The insured value ($13,920) is 80% of the total value; the total value (base) = $13,920 (percentage) ÷ 80% (rate): 13,290 ÷ 0.80 = $17,400.

9. **The correct answer is (D).** The workweek is 35 hours long. $\frac{1}{5} \times 35 = 7$ hours sorting mail; $\frac{1}{2} \times 35 = 17\frac{1}{2}$ hours filing; $\frac{1}{7} \times 35 = 5$ hours reception. $7 + 17\frac{1}{2} + 5 = 29\frac{1}{2}$ hours accounted

for. $35 - 29\frac{1}{2} = 5\frac{1}{2}$ hours left for messenger work. The percentage time spent on messenger work (rate) = 5 $\frac{1}{2}$ (percentage) ÷ 35 (base) = $\frac{11}{70}$ = $15\frac{5}{7}$ = most nearly 16%.

10. **The correct answer is (C).** 80% of the boys equals 1,152; the total number of boys (base) = 1,152 (percentage) ÷ 80% (rate) = 1,152 ÷ 0.80 = 1,440 boys. 40% of the students = 1,440, so the total number of students (base) = 1,440 (percentage) ÷ 40% (rate) = 1,440 ÷ 0.40 = 3,600 students.

answers

RATIO AND PROPORTION

Ratio and proportion questions have long been a popular type of arithmetic problem given on civil service exams. This section will help you understand the rules governing ratio and proportion problems.

Solving Ratio Problems

A ratio expresses the relationship between two (or more) quantities in terms of numbers. The mark used to indicate ratio is the colon (:) and is read "to." For example, the ratio 2:3 is read "2 to 3."

A ratio also represents division. Therefore, any ratio of two terms can be written as a fraction, and any fraction can be written as a ratio. For example, $3:4 = \frac{3}{4}$.

Follow these three steps to solve problems in which the ratio is given:

1 Add the terms in the ratio.

2 Divide the total amount that is to be put into a ratio by this sum.

3 Multiply each term in the ratio by this quotient.

For example, the sum of $360 is to be divided among three people according to the ratio 3:4:5. How much does each one receive? Follow these steps:

- Add the terms in the ratio: $3 + 4 + 5 = 12$.
- Divide the total amount to be put into the ratio by this sum: $360 ÷ 12 = 30.
- Multiply each term in the ratio by this quotient: $30 \times 3 = 90; $30 \times 4 = 120; $30 \times 5 = 150.

The money is divided thus: $90, $120, and $150.

To simplify any complicated ratio of two terms containing fractions, decimals, or percents, you only need to divide the first term by the second. Reduce the answer to its lowest terms, and write the fraction as a ratio. For example, simplify the ratio $\frac{5}{6}:\frac{7}{8} \rightarrow \frac{5}{6} \div \frac{7}{8} = \frac{20}{21} = 20:21$.

Solving Proportion Problems

A proportion indicates the equality of two ratios. For example, 2:4 = 5:10 is a proportion. This is read, "2 is to 4 as 5 is to 10." The two outside terms (2 and 10) are the extremes, and the two inside terms (4 and 5) are the means. Proportions are often written in fractional form. For example, the proportion 2:4 = 5:10 can be written as $\frac{2}{4} = \frac{5}{10}$.

In any proportion, the product of the means equals the product of the extremes. If the proportion is in fractional form, the products can be found by cross-multiplication. For example, in the proportion $\frac{2}{4} = \frac{5}{10}$, $4 \times 5 = 2 \times 10$.

Many problems in which three terms are given and one term is unknown can be solved using proportions. To solve such problems, follow these three steps:

1 Formulate the proportion very carefully according to the facts given. (If any term is misplaced, the solution will be incorrect.) Any symbol can be written in place of the missing term.

2 Determine by inspection whether the means or the extremes are known. Multiply the pair that has both terms given.

3 Divide this product by the third term given to find the unknown term.

Try this example problem:

1. The scale on a map shows that 2 centimeters represent 30 miles of actual length. What is the actual length of a road that is represented by 7 centimeters on the map?

In this problem, the map lengths and the actual lengths are in proportion; that is, they have equal ratios. If m stands for the unknown length, the proportion is $\frac{2}{7} = \frac{30}{m}$. As the proportion is written, m is an extreme and is equal to the product of the means, divided by the other extreme: $m = 7 \times 30 \div 2 = 210 \div 2 = 105$. Therefore, 7 cm on the map represent 105 miles.

EXERCISE 1

Directions: Each question has four suggested answers. Select the correct one.

1. The ratio of 24 to 64 is
   - **(A)** 8:3
   - **(B)** 24:100
   - **(C)** 3:8
   - **(D)** 64:100

2. The Baltimore Ravens won 8 games and lost 3. The ratio of games won to games played is
   - **(A)** 8:11
   - **(B)** 3:11
   - **(C)** 8:3
   - **(D)** 3:8

3. The ratio of $\frac{1}{4}$ to $\frac{3}{5}$ is
   - **(A)** 1 to 3
   - **(B)** 3 to 20
   - **(C)** 5 to 12
   - **(D)** 3 to 4

4. If there are 16 boys and 12 girls in a class, the ratio of the number of girls to the number of children in the class is
   - **(A)** 3 to 4
   - **(B)** 3 to 7
   - **(C)** 4 to 7
   - **(D)** 4 to 3

5. 259 is to 37 as
   - **(A)** 5 is to 1
   - **(B)** 63 is to 441
   - **(C)** 84 is to 12
   - **(D)** 130 is to 19

EXERCISE 2

Directions: Each question has four suggested answers. Select the correct one.

1. Two dozen cans of dog food at the rate of three cans for $1.45 would cost
   (A) $10.05
   (B) $11.20
   (C) $11.60
   (D) $11.75

2. A snapshot measures $2\frac{1}{2}$ inches by $1\frac{7}{8}$ inches. It is to be enlarged so that the longer dimension will be 4 inches. The length of the enlarged shorter dimension will be
   (A) $2\frac{1}{2}$ inches
   (B) 3 inches
   (C) $3\frac{3}{8}$ inches
   (D) None of these

3. Packs of tissues cost $2.29 for three. The cost per a dozen packs is
   (A) $27.48
   (B) $13.74
   (C) $9.16
   (D) $6.87

4. A certain pole casts a shadow 24 feet long. Another pole 3 feet high casts a shadow 4 feet long. How high is the first pole, given that the heights and shadows are in proportion?
   (A) 18 feet
   (B) 19 feet
   (C) 20 feet
   (D) 21 feet

5. The actual length represented by $3\frac{1}{2}$ inches on a drawing having a scale of $\frac{1}{8}$ inch to the foot is
   (A) 3.75 ft.
   (B) 28 ft.
   (C) 360 ft.
   (D) 120 ft.

6. Aluminum bronze consists of copper and aluminum, usually in the ratio of 10:1 by weight. If an object made of this alloy weighs 77 pounds, how many pounds of aluminum does it contain?
   (A) 7.7
   (B) 7.0
   (C) 70.0
   (D) 62.3

7. It costs 31 cents a square foot to lay vinyl flooring. To lay 180 square feet of flooring, it will cost
   (A) $16.20
   (B) $18.60
   (C) $55.80
   (D) $62.00

8. If a temp worker earns $352 in 16 days, the amount that he will earn in 117 days is most nearly
   (A) $3,050
   (B) $2,575
   (C) $2,285
   (D) $2,080

9. Assuming that on a blueprint $\frac{1}{8}$ inch equals 12 inches of actual length, the actual length in inches of a steel bar represented on the blueprint by a line $3\frac{3}{4}$ inches long is

(A) 3

(B) 30

(C) 450

(D) 360

10. Alan, Bonnie, and Chris invested $9,000, $7,000, and $6,000, respectively. Their profits were to be divided according to the ratio of their investments. If Bonnie uses her share of the firm's profit of $825 to pay a personal debt of $230, how much will she have left?

(A) $30.50

(B) $32.50

(C) $34.50

(D) $36.50

ANSWER KEY AND EXPLANATIONS

Exercise 1

1. C	2. A	3. C	4. B	5. C

1. **The correct answer is (C).** The ratio 24 to 64 can be written 24:64, or $\frac{24}{64}$. In fraction form, the ratio can be reduced to $\frac{3}{8}$, or 3:8.

2. **The correct answer is (A).** The number of games played was 3 + 8 = 11. The ratio of games won to games played is 8:11.

3. **The correct answer is (C).** $\frac{1}{4} : \frac{3}{5}$
   $= \frac{1}{4} \div \frac{3}{5} = \frac{5}{12} = 5:12$

4. **The correct answer is (B).** There are 16 + 12 = 28 children in the class. The ratio of number of girls to number of children is 12:28, which can be reduced to 3:7.

5. **The correct answer is (C).** The ratio $\frac{259}{37}$ reduces by 37 to $\frac{7}{1}$. The ratio $\frac{84}{12}$ also reduces to $\frac{7}{1}$. Therefore, $\frac{259}{37} = \frac{84}{12}$ is a proportion.

Exercise 2

1. C	3. C	5. B	7. C	9. D
2. B	4. A	6. B	8. B	10. B

1. **The correct answer is (C).** The number of cans is proportional to the price. Let p represent the unknown price: $\frac{3}{24} = \frac{1.45}{p}$. $p = 1.45 \times 24 \div 3 = 34.80 \div 3 = \$11.60$.

2. **The correct answer is (B).** Let s represent the unknown shorter dimension: $\frac{2\frac{1}{2}}{4} = \frac{1\frac{7}{8}}{s}$. $s = 4 \times 1\frac{7}{8} \div 2\frac{1}{2} = \frac{15}{2} \div 2\frac{1}{2} = 3$ inches.

3. **The correct answer is (C).** If p is the cost per dozen (12), the proportion is: $\frac{3}{12} = \frac{2.29}{p}$. $p = 12 \times 2.29 \div 3 = \$9.16$.

4. **The correct answer is (A).** If f is the height of the first pole, the proportion is: $\frac{f}{24} = \frac{3}{4}$. $f = 24 \times 3 \div 4 = 18$ ft.

5. **The correct answer is (B).** If y is the unknown length, the proportion is: $\frac{3\frac{1}{2}}{\frac{1}{8}} = \frac{y}{1}$. $y = 3\frac{1}{2} \times 1 \div \frac{1}{8} = 28$ ft.

6. **The correct answer is (B).** Because only two parts of a proportion are known (77 is the total weight), the problem must be solved by the ratio method. The ratio of 10:1 means that if the alloy were separated into equal parts, 10 of those parts would be copper and 1 would be aluminum, for a total of 11 parts. $77 \div 11 = 7$ pounds per part. The alloy has 1 part aluminum: $7 \times 1 = 7$ pounds aluminum.

7. **The correct answer is (C).** The cost (c) is proportional to the number of square feet: $\frac{0.31}{c} = \frac{1}{180}$. $c = 0.31 \times 180 \div 1 = \$55.80$.

8. **The correct answer is (B).** The amount earned is proportional to the number of days worked. If a is the unknown amount, the proportion is: $\frac{\$352}{a} = \frac{16}{117}$. $a = 352 \times 117 \div 16 = \$2,575$.

9. **The correct answer is (D).** If n is the unknown length, the proportion is: $\frac{\frac{1}{8}}{3\frac{3}{4}} = \frac{12}{n}$. $n = 12 \times 3\frac{3}{4} \div \frac{1}{8} = 360$.

10. **The correct answer is (B).** The ratio of investment is: 9000:7000:6000, or 9:7:6. $9 + 7 + 6 = 22$. Each share of the profit is $\$825 \div 22 = \$37.50$. Bonnie's share of the profit is $7 \times 37.50 = \$262.50$. The amount Bonnie has left is $\$262.50 - \$230.00 = \$32.50$.

SUMMING IT UP

- Percent questions often require you to change a fraction, mixed number, or decimal to a percent, or vice versa, so be sure you understand the rules for making these conversions. Follow the steps and exercises in this chapter to practice.

- Remember that in all percent problems, the whole is always 100%. Keeping this in mind may help you figure out the answer to a question. For example, if a problem involves 40% of a quantity, you know for certain that the rest of the quantity must be 60%.

- A ratio expresses the relationship between two or more quantities in terms of numbers. A ratio also represents division. Follow the steps and exercises in this chapter to practice.

- A proportion indicates the equality of two ratios. Remember that the product of the means (inner numbers) equals the products of the extremes (outer numbers) in a proportion. Follow the steps and exercises in this chapter to practice.

Graphs and Tables

OVERVIEW

- **Graphs**
- **Tabular completions**
- **Summing it up**

GRAPHS

A graph is a picture that illustrates comparisons and trends in statistical information. This section will prepare you to see the "complete picture" in a graph and supply the correct answers based on the data. The following are the most commonly used graphs:

- Bar graphs
- Line graphs
- Circle graphs
- Pictographs

Understanding Bar Graphs

Bar graphs compare various quantities using either horizontal or vertical bars. Each bar may represent a single quantity or may be divided to represent several quantities.

See Figure 18.1 for an example of a bar graph. The questions following the graph are typical of the kinds of questions found on the civil service exam.

chapter 18

FIGURE 18.1

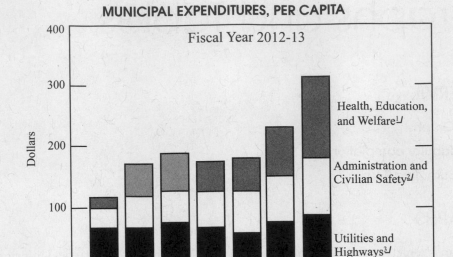

MUNICIPAL EXPENDITURES, PER CAPITA

Fiscal Year 2012-13

Health, Education, and Welfare[1]

Administration and Civilian Safety[2]

Utilities and Highways[3]

City population (Thousands)

1. Public welfare, education, hospitals, health, libraries, and housing and urban renewal.
2. Police and fire protection, file administration, general control, general public buildings, interest on general debt, and other.
3. Highway, sewage, sanitation, parks and recreation, and utilities.
   Source: Department of Commerce

1. What was the approximate municipal expenditure per capita in cities having populations of 200,000 to 299,000?

   The middle bar represents cities having populations from 200,000 to 299,000. This bar reaches about halfway between 100 and 200. Therefore, the per capita expenditure is approximately $150.

2. Which cities spent the most per capita on health, education, and welfare?

   The bar for cities having populations of 1 million and over has a larger gray section than the other bars. Therefore, those cities spent the most.

3. Of the three categories of expenditures, which was least dependent on city size?

   The expenditures for utilities and highways, the darkest part of each bar, varied least as city size increased.

Understanding Line Graphs

Line graphs illustrate trends, often over a period of time. A line graph may include more than one line, with each line representing a different item. Study the line graph in Figure 18.2 and answer the questions following the graph.

FIGURE 18.2

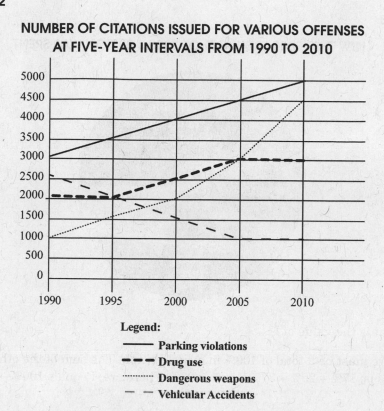

NUMBER OF CITATIONS ISSUED FOR VARIOUS OFFENSES AT FIVE-YEAR INTERVALS FROM 1990 TO 2010

Legend:
——— Parking violations
– – – Drug use
·········· Dangerous weapons
— — Vehicular Accidents

1. Over the 20-year period, which offense shows an average rate of increase of more than 150 citations per year?

   Dangerous weapons citations increased from 1,000 in 1990 to 4,500 in 2010. The average increase over the 20-year period is $\frac{3,500}{20} = 175$.

2. Over the 20-year period, which offense shows a constant rate of increase or decrease?

   A straight line indicates a constant rate of increase or decrease. Of the four lines, the one representing parking violations is the only straight one.

3. Which offense shows a total increase or decrease of 50% for the full 20-year period?

   Drug use citations increased from 2,000 in 1990 to 3,000 in 2010, an increase of 50%.

Understanding Circle Graphs

Circle graphs show the relationship of various parts of a quantity to each other and to the whole quantity. Each part of a circle graph is called a sector.

Study the circle graph in Figure 18.3 and answer the questions following the graph.

FIGURE 18.3

HOW THE FEDERAL BUDGET OF $300.4 BILLION WAS SPENT

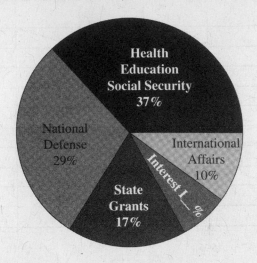

1. What is the value of I?

   There must be a total of 100% in a circle graph. The sum of the other sections is: 17% + 29% + 37% + 10% = 93%. Therefore, I equals 100% – 93% = 7%.

2. How much money was actually spent on national defense?

   29% × $300.4 billion = $87.116 billion, or $87,116,000,000.

3. How much more money was spent on state grants than on interest?

   17% – 7% = 10%; 10% × $300.4 billion = $30.04 billion, or $30,040,000,000.

Understanding Pictographs

Pictographs compare quantities using symbols. Each symbol represents a given number of a particular item. Take a look at the pictograph in Figure 18.4 and answer the questions following the graph.

FIGURE 18.4

THE NUMBER OF NEW HOUSES BUILT IN XYZ TOWN, 1995–2010

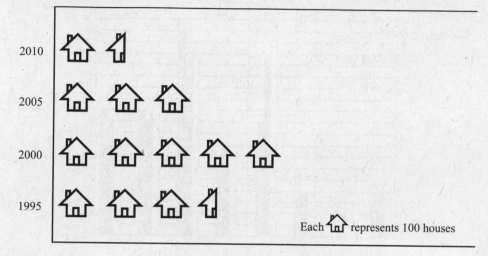

Each 🏠 represents 100 houses

1. How many more new houses were built in 2000 than in 2005?

   There are two more symbols for 2000 than for 2005. Each symbol represents 100 houses. Therefore, 200 more houses were built in 2000.

2. How many new houses were built in 1995?

   There are $3\frac{1}{2}$ symbols shown for 1995: $3\frac{1}{2} \times 100 = 350$ houses.

3. In which year were half as many houses built as in 2005?

   In 2005, $3 \times 100 = 300$ houses were built. Half of 300, or 150 houses, were built in 2010.

EXERCISE

Directions: Each question has four suggested answers. Select the correct one.

QUESTIONS 1–4 REFER TO THE FOLLOWING GRAPH:

Yearly Incidence of Major Crimes for Community Z 2010-12

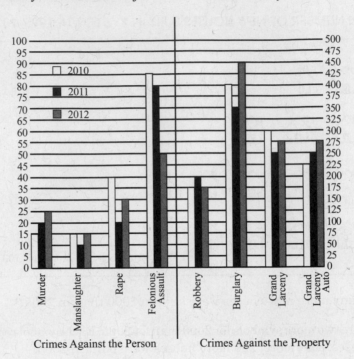

Crimes Against the Person　　　Crimes Against the Property

1. In 2012, the incidence of which of the following crimes was greater than in the previous two years?

(A) Grand larceny

(B) Murder

(C) Rape

(D) Robbery

2. If the incidence of burglary in 2013 had increased over 2012 by the same number as it had increased in 2012 over 2011, then the average for this crime for the period from 2010 to 2013 would be most nearly

(A) 100

(B) 400

(C) 425

(D) 440

3. The graph indicates that the percentage increase in grand larceny auto from 2011 to 2012 was

   (A) 5%

   (B) 10%

   (C) 15%

   (D) 20%

4. Which of the following cannot be determined because there is NOT enough information in the graph to do so?

   (A) For the three-year period, what percentage of all "Crimes Against the Person" involved murders committed in 2011?

   (B) For the three-year period, what percentage of all major crimes was committed in the first six months of 2011?

   (C) Which major crimes followed a pattern of continuing yearly increases for the three-year period?

   (D) For 2012, what was the ratio of robbery, burglary, and grand larceny crimes?

exercises

QUESTIONS 5–7 REFER TO THE FOLLOWING GRAPH:

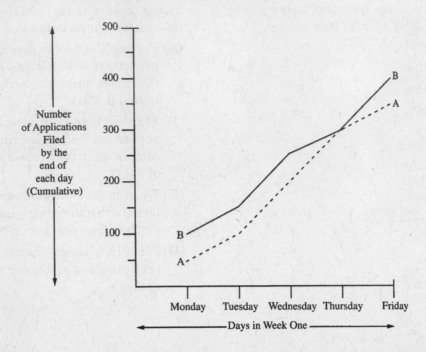

Directions: In the graph above, the lines labeled "A" and "B" represent the cumulative progress in the work of two file clerks, each of whom was given 500 consecutively numbered applications to file in the proper cabinets over a five-day workweek.

5. The day during which the largest number of applications was filed by both clerks was

(A) Monday.

(B) Tuesday.

(C) Wednesday.

(D) Friday.

6. At the end of the second day, the percentage of applications still to be filed was

(A) 25%

(B) 50%

(C) 66%

(D) 75%

7. Assuming that the production pattern continues during the following week as though there had been no days off, the day on which Clerk B will finish this assignment will be

(A) Monday.

(B) Tuesday.

(C) Wednesday.

(D) Friday.

QUESTIONS 8–11 REFER TO THE FOLLOWING GRAPHS:

**Characteristics of
U.S. Travelers Abroad...**
Based on Passports Issued
and Renewed in 2012

▲Occupation
1.2 Million = 100%

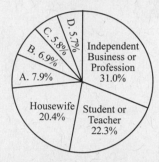

A. Skilled, Clerical, Technical
   or Sales Workers
B. Others
C. Retired
D. Civilian, Government and Military

▲ Based on nine months only

Note: Due to rounding, figures may not add up to 100%

Age
1.3 Million = 100%

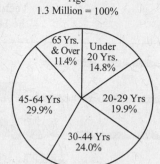

Residence
1.3 Million = 100%

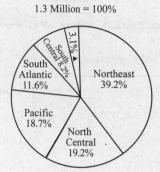

▲ Mountain

8. Approximately how many persons aged 29 or younger traveled abroad in 2012?

(A) 175,000

(B) 245,000

(C) 385,000

(D) 450,000

9. Of the people who did NOT live in the Northeast, what percent came from the North Central states?

(A) 19.2%

(B) 19.9%

(C) 26.5%

(D) 31.6%

10. The fraction of travelers from the four smallest occupation groups is most nearly equal to the fraction of travelers

(A) under age 20, and 65 and over, combined.

(B) from the North Central and Mountain states.

(C) between 45 and 64 years of age.

(D) from the Housewife and Other categories.

11. If the South Central, Mountain, and Pacific sections were considered as a single classification, how many degrees would its sector include?

(A) 30°

(B) 67°

(C) 108°

(D) 120°

QUESTIONS 12–15 REFER TO THE FOLLOWING GRAPH:

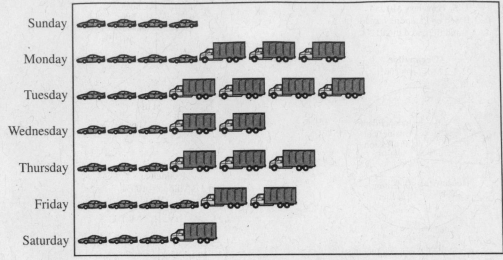

Vechicles Crossing the Hudson Bridge

Each symbol represents 500 vehicles

Passenger car

Truck

12. What percent of the total number of vehicles on Wednesday were cars?

(A) 30%

(B) 60%

(C) 20%

(D) 50%

13. What was the total number of vehicles crossing the bridge on Tuesday?

(A) 7

(B) 700

(C) 1,100

(D) 3,500

14. How many more trucks crossed on Monday than on Saturday?

(A) 200

(B) 1,000

(C) 1,500

(D) 2,000

15. If trucks paid a toll of $1.00 and cars paid a toll of $0.50, how much money was collected in tolls on Friday?

(A) $400

(B) $600

(C) $2,000

(D) $2,500

ANSWER KEY AND EXPLANATIONS

1. B	4. B	7. B	10. A	13. D
2. D	5. C	8. D	11. C	14. B
3. B	6. D	9. D	12. B	15. C

1. **The correct answer is (B).** The incidence of murder increased from 15 in 2010 to 20 in 2011 to 25 in 2012.

2. **The correct answer is (D).** The incidence of burglary in 2010 was 400; in 2011, it was 350; and in 2012, it was 450. The increase from 2011 to 2012 was 100. If there is the same increase of 100 from 2012 to 2013, the incidence of burglary would be 550 in 2013. The average of 400, 350, 450, and 550 is: 400 + 350 + 450 + 550 = 1,750 ÷ 4 = 437.5, which rounds up to 440.

3. **The correct answer is (B).** The incidence of grand larceny auto went from 250 in 2011 to 275 in 2012, an increase of 25. The percent increase is 25 ÷ 250 = 0.10 = 10%.

4. **The correct answer is (B).** This graph gives information by year, not month. It's impossible to determine from the graph the percentage of crimes committed during the first six months of any year.

5. **The correct answer is (C).** For Clerks A and B, the greatest increase in the cumulative totals occurred from the end of Tuesday until the end of Wednesday. Therefore, the largest number of applications was filed on Wednesday.

6. **The correct answer is (D).** By the end of Tuesday, Clerk A had filed 100 applications and Clerk B had filed 150, for a total of 250. This left 750 of the original 1,000 applications: 750 ÷ 1000 = 0.75 = 75%.

7. **The correct answer is (B).** During Week One, Clerk B filed 100 applications on Monday, 50 on Tuesday, 100 on Wednesday, 50 on Thursday, and 100 on Friday. If he follows this pattern, he will file 50 on the Monday of Week Two, for a total of 450, and the remaining 50 during Tuesday.

8. **The correct answer is (D).** 20 – 29 yrs. = 19.9%; under 20 yrs. = 14.8%; 19.9% + 14.8% = 34.7%; 34.7% × 1.3 million = 0.4511 million = 451,100, which rounds down to 450,000.

9. **The correct answer is (D).** 100% – 39.2% = 60.8% did not live in the Northeast. 19.2% lived in the North Central states. 19.2 ÷ 60.8 = approximately 0.316, or 31.6%.

10. **The correct answer is (A).** The four smallest groups of occupation: 7.9 + 6.9 + 5.8 + 5.7 = 26.3. Age groups under 20 and over 65: 14.8 + 11.4 = 26.2. Therefore, these two groups are most nearly equal.

11. **The correct answer is (C).** South Central: 8.2%; Mountain: 3.1%; Pacific: 18.7%; 8.2 + 3.1 + 18.7 = 30.0%; 30% × 360° = 108°.

12. **The correct answer is (B).** There are five vehicle symbols, of which three are cars: 3 ÷ 5 = 60%.

13. **The correct answer is (D).** On Tuesday, there were 3 × 500 = 1,500 cars and 4 × 500 = 2,000 trucks. The total number of vehicles was 3,500.

14. **The correct answer is (B).** The graph shows two more truck symbols on Monday than on Saturday. Each symbol represents 500 trucks, so there were 2 × 500 = 1,000 more trucks on Monday.

15. **The correct answer is (C).** On Friday there were 4 × 500 = 2,000 cars and 2 × 500 = 1,000 trucks; car tolls: 2,000 × $0.50 = $1,000; truck tolls: 1,000 × $1.00 = $1,000; total tolls: $1,000 + $1,000 = $2,000.

TABULAR COMPLETIONS

Numerically, tabular completion questions are among the easiest questions. The arithmetic involved is limited to addition and subtraction. The numbers may be large, but the process itself is simple.

Answering Tabular Completion Questions

The difficulty of answering tabular completion questions lies in choosing which numbers to add or subtract. The tables demand careful reading. You need to be careful as you read the tables. For example, if a question calls for you to add the entry for "Utilities" and the entry for "Transportation," don't make the mistake of adding (or subtracting) the major category "Utilities" and its subcategories. The subcategories are already included in the major category. For example:

Utilities	4,665,170
Gas-powered	1,065,080
Coal-powered	3,600,090

The category "Utilities" is the sum of its two subcategories.

In answering these questions, you must first determine which entries combine to create each total and subtotal. If you're unclear as to how a number is arrived at, you may have to look at a completed column to determine how certain figures were arrived at. Then move over into the column with the unknown that you're seeking, and calculate it by combining the appropriate entries.

Note that the directions for tabular completion questions give you five options. The final answer choice always is "(E) None of the above." The directions state that the exact answer may not always be among the answer choices. In that case, you should choose "(E) None of the above."

EXERCISE

Directions: These questions are based on information presented in tables. You must calculate the unknown values by using the known values given in the table. In some questions, the exact answer will not be given as one of the response choices. In such cases, you should select choice (E), "None of the above."

QUESTIONS 1–5 REFER TO THE FOLLOWING TABLE:

LOCAL GOVERNMENT EXPENDITURES OF FINANCES: 2009 TO 2012 (IN MILLIONS OF DOLLARS)

Item	2009	2010	2011	2012	Total Percent*
Expenditures	I	432,328	485,174	520,966	100.0
Direct General Expenditures	326,024	367,340	405,576	IV	83.2
Utility and Liquor Stores	30,846	II	43,016	47,970	9.2
Water and electric	20,734	24,244	28,453	31,499	6.0
Transit and others	10,112	11,947	14,563	16,471	3.2
Insurance Trust Expenditures	23,504	28,797	36,582	39,466	V
Employee retirement	12,273	14,008	III	17,835	3.4
Unemployment compensation	11,231	14,789	20,887	21,631	4.2

Rounded to one decimal place

1. What is the value of I in millions of dollars?

   (A) 380,374

   (B) 377,604

   (C) 356,870

   (D) 349,528

   (E) None of the above

2. What is the value of II in millions of dollars?

   (A) 338,543

   (B) 64,988

   (C) 53,041

   (D) 40,744

   (E) None of the above

3. What is the value of III in millions of dollars?

   (A) 57,469

   (B) 52,277

   (C) 20,887

   (D) 15,695

   (E) None of the above

4. What is the value of IV in millions of dollars?

   (A) 472,996

   (B) 433,530

   (C) 425,026

   (D) 134,807

   (E) None of the above

5. What is the percent value of V?

   (A) 7.6

   (B) 7.4

   (C) 6.7

   (D) 3.3

   (E) None of the above

QUESTIONS 6–10 REFER TO THE FOLLOWING TABLE:

REVENUE OF ALL GOVERNMENTS BY SOURCE AND LEVEL OF GOVERNMENT FISCAL YEAR 2012 (IN MILLIONS OF DOLLARS)*

Source	Total	Federal	State	Local
Total Revenue	1,259,421	660,759	310.828	V
Intergovernmental	184,033	1,804	70,786	111,443
From Federal Government	90,295	—	III	22,427
From state or local government	93,738	1,804	2,918	89,016
Revenue from Own Sources	1,075,388	II	240,042	176,391
General	820,814	487,706	187,373	145,735
Taxes	I	405,714	149,738	94,776
Property	74,969	—	2,949	72,020
Individual and corporate income	407,257	346,688	55,039	5,530
Sales and gross receipts	134,532	48,561	72,751	13,220
Other	33,470	10,465	18,999	4,006
Charges and miscellaneous	170,586	81,992	37,635	50,959
Utility and liquor stores	29,896	—	4,628	25,268
Insurance trust	224,678	171,249	48,041	5,388
Employee and railroad retirement	36,962	6,580	IV	5,260
Unemployment compensation	18,733	162	18,443	128
Old age, disability, and health insurance	168,983	164,507	4,476	—

* *Hypothetical data.*

6. What is the value of I in millions of dollars?

(A) 695,097

(B) 616,758

(C) 555,452

(D) 254,574

(E) None of the above

7. What is the value of II in millions of dollars?

(A) 835,346

(B) 662,563

(C) 658,955

(D) 417,433

(E) None of the above

8. What is the value of III in millions of dollars?

(A) 73,704

(B) 68,868

(C) 67,868

(D) 67,978

(E) None of the above

9. What is the value of IV in millions of dollars?

(A) 43,565

(B) 29,598

(C) 25,122

(D) 22,919

(E) None of the above

10. What is the value of V in millions of dollars?

(A) 821,567

(B) 464,175

(C) 318,490

(D) 287,834

(E) None of the above

QUESTIONS 11–15 REFER TO THE FOLLOWING TABLE:

FINANCE COMPANIES—ASSETS AND LIABILITIES: 2002 TO 2012 (IN MILLIONS OF DOLLARS)*

Item	2002	2007	2012
Total Receivables	I	85,994	183,341
Consumer Receivables	31,773	40,814	77,460
Retail passenger car paper and others	11,577	13,399	31,950
Retail consumer goods and loans	20,196	27,415	IV
Business Receivables	22,999	39,286	86,067
Wholesale paper and others	14,084	22,012	48,059
Lease paper and others	8,915	17,274	38,008
Other Receivables	2,341	5,894	19,814
Total Liabilities	60,577	III	175,025
Loans and Notes Payable to Banks	7,551	8,617	15,458
Short-term	II	7,900	7,885
Long-term	969	717	7,573
Commercial Paper	22,073	25,905	52,328
Other Debt	30,953	54,194	V

Hypothetical data.

11. What is the value of I in millions of dollars?

  (A) 54,772

  (B) 57,113

  (C) 63,546

  (D) 68,856

  (E) None of the above

12. What is the value of II in millions of dollars?

  (A) 6,582

  (B) 14,522

  (C) 53,026

  (D) 58,236

  (E) None of the above

13. What is the value of III in millions of dollars?

  (A) 62,811

  (B) 88,716

  (C) 94,610

  (D) 97,333

  (E) None of the above

14. What is the value of IV in millions of dollars?

  (A) 45,610

  (B) 47,610

  (C) 47,611

  (D) 54,117

  (E) None of the above

15. What is the value of V in millions of dollars?

  (A) 67,786

  (B) 85,147

  (C) 107,239

  (D) 107,259

  (E) None of the above

ANSWER KEY AND EXPLANATIONS

1. A	4. B	7. C	10. D	13. B
2. E	5. A	8. C	11. B	14. E
3. D	6. E	9. C	12. A	15. C

1. **The correct answer is (A).** To calculate the total 2009 *Expenditures,* add the 2009 values for *Direct General Expenditures, Utility and Liquor Stores,* and *Insurance Trust Expenditure:* 326,024 + 30,846 + 23,504 = 380,374. Did you remember to add the subcategories?

2. **The correct answer is (E).** The correct value (not given as an answer) is calculated by adding the value for *Water and electric* and the value for *Transit and others:* 24,244 + 11,947 = 36,191.

3. **The correct answer is (D).** To calculate the 2011 *Employee retirement costs,* subtract the 2011 value of *Unemployment compensation* from the total *Insurance Trust Expenditure:* 36,582 − 20,887 = 15,695.

4. **The correct answer is (B).** To calculate the value of 2012 *Direct General Expenditures,* add the 2012 values of *Utility and Liquor Stores* and *Insurance Trust Expenditure,* and subtract that sum from the total of 2012 *Expenditures:* 520,966 − (47,970 + 39,466) = 433,530.

5. **The correct answer is (A).** To calculate the percent of total 2012 *Expenditures* represented by *Insurance Trust Expenditures,* add the percents represented by *Direct General Expenditures* and *Utility and Liquor Stores,* and subtract from 100%: 100% − (83.2% + 9.2%) = 7.6%. Alternatively, add the two components of *Insurance Trust Expenditure (Employee retirement*

and *Unemployment compensation):* 3.4% + 4.2% = 7.6%.

6. **The correct answer is (E).** The correct value (not given as an answer) is calculated by subtracting the value for *Charges and miscellaneous* in the Total column from the value for *General* under *Revenue from Own Sources:* 820,814 − 170,586 = 650,228.

7. **The correct answer is (C).** Federal *Revenue from Own Sources* can be calculated by subtracting the value for *Intergovernmental* in the Federal column from the value for *Total Revenue* in the Federal column: 660,759 − 1,804 = 658,955.

8. **The correct answer is (C).** Calculate the value of state revenues *From Federal Government* by subtracting the value of revenues *From state or local government* in the State column from the value of *Intergovernmental* revenues in the State column: 70,786 − 2,918 = 67,868.

9. **The correct answer is (C).** Calculate the value of state revenues from *Employee and railroad retirement* by subtracting the combined values of *Unemployment compensation* and *Old age, disability, and health insurance* in the State column from the value of *Insurance trust:* 48,041 − (18,443 + 4,476) = 25,122.

10. **The correct answer is (D).** To calculate total local revenue, add together Local *Intergovernmental* revenue and *Revenue from Own Sources* in the Local column: 111,443 + 176,391 = 287,834.

11. **The correct answer is (B).** *Total 2002 Receivables* can be calculated by adding the values for 2002 *Consumer Receivables, Business Receivables,* and *Other Receivables:* 31,773 + 22,999 + 2,341 = 57,113.

12. **The correct answer is (A).** The value of 2002 *Short-term* can be calculated by subtracting the value for *Long-term* from the value for *Loans and Notes Payable to Banks:* 7,551 – 969 = 6,582.

13. **The correct answer is (B).** Calculate total 2007 liabilities by adding the value of 2007 *Loans and Notes Payable to Banks, Commercial Paper,* and *Other Debt:* 8,617 + 25,905 + 54,194 = 88,716.

14. **The correct answer is (E).** The correct answer (45,510) was not among the choices provided. To calculate the value of the 2012 *Retail consumer goods and loans,* subtract the 2012 *Retail passenger car paper and others* value from the 2012 *Consumer Receivables* value: 77,460 – 31,950 = 45,510.

15. **The correct answer is (C).** Calculate the value of 2012 *Other Debt* by subtracting the sum of the values of *Loans and Notes Payable to Banks* and *Commercial Paper* from 2012 *Total Liabilities:* 175,025 – (15,458 + 52,328) = 107,239.

answers

SUMMING IT UP

- Graphs are pictures that illustrate comparisons and trends in statistical information. On your civil service exam, you're likely to encounter the most commonly used types of graphs: bar graphs, line graphs, circle graphs (pie charts), and pictographs.

- A bar graph compares various quantities using either horizontal or vertical bars, each of which represents a single quantity (or is divided to represent several linked quantities).

- Line graphs illustrate trends over periods of time. Such a graph may include more than one line, each representing a different item.

- Circle graphs, sometimes called pie charts, show the relationship of various related parts to each other and to a whole. Each part of a circle graph is called a sector.

- Pictographs, as the name implies, compare quantities using pictures or symbols, each of which represents a given number of a particular item of data.

Reasoning

OVERVIEW

- Work problems
- Arithmetic reasoning problems
- Summing it up

WORK PROBLEMS

In work problems, three factors are involved: the number of people working; the time to complete the job, expressed in minutes, hours, or days; and the amount of work done. Work problems follow these rules:

- The number of people working is directly proportional to the amount of work done. The more people on the job, the more work will be done, and vice versa.

- The number of people working is inversely proportional to the time. The more people on the job, the less time it will take to finish it, and vice versa.

- The time expended on a job is directly proportional to the amount of work done. The more time expended on a job, the more work that is done, and vice versa.

Tackling Work Problems

In work problems, you are asked to find a rate, time, or number of workers. Depending on what information you have, you can solve the problem using various formulas, as outlined in this section.

Solving Problems Using Equal Rates

The rate at which a person works is the amount of work he or she can do in a unit of time. If all the workers work at equal rates to complete a job, you can easily find how long it will take any number of workers to finish the job. Follow these two steps:

1. Multiply the number of people by the time to find the amount of time required by one person to complete the job.

2. Divide this time by the number of people required to complete the job to find how long it will take them to finish it.

chapter 19

If four workers each working at the same rate can do a job in 48 days, how long will it take to finish the same job if only three of these workers are able to work on the job?

- Multiply the number of people by the time: $48 \times 4 = 192$ days. So one worker can do the job in 192 days.

- Divide this amount by three, the number of workers able to work: $192 \div 3 = 64$. So three workers can finish the job in 64 days.

In some work problems, the rates, though unequal, can be equalized by comparison. Follow these three steps to solve such problems:

1 Determine from the facts how many equal rates there are.

2 Multiply the number of equal rates by the time given.

3 Divide this time by the number of equal rates.

Three workers can do a job in 12 days. Two of the workers work twice as fast as the third. How long would it take one of the faster workers to do the job himself? Follow the steps:

- There are two fast workers and one slow worker, so there are actually five slow workers working at equal rates.

- One slow worker will take 12 days × 5 slow workers = 60 days to complete the job.

- One fast worker equals two slow workers; therefore, he will take $60 \div 2 = 30$ days to complete the job.

Solving Problems Using Time

If you're given the various times at which each person in a group can complete a job, you can find the time it will take to do the job if all work together by following these three steps:

1 Invert the time of each person to find how much work each person can do in one unit of time.

2 Add these reciprocals to find which part of the job all the workers working together can complete in one unit of time.

3 Invert this sum to find the time it will take all the workers to finish the entire job.

If it takes A three days to dig a ditch, whereas B can dig it in six days and C in twelve, how long would it take all three to do the job? Follow the steps:

- A can complete the job in three days; therefore, he can finish $\frac{1}{3}$ of the job in one day. B can complete the job in six days; therefore, he can finish $\frac{1}{6}$ of the job in one day. C can complete the job in 12 days; therefore, he can finish $\frac{1}{12}$ of the job in one day.

- $\frac{1}{3} + \frac{1}{6} + \frac{1}{12} = \frac{7}{12}$.

- A, B, and C can finish $\frac{7}{12}$ of the work in one day; therefore, it will take them $\frac{12}{7}$, or $1\frac{5}{7}$, days to complete the job working together.

When given the time it will take one person to finish a job, the reciprocal of that time is how much of the job can be completed in one particular unit of time. For example, if a worker can finish a job in six days, then she can finish $\frac{1}{6}$ of the job in one day. Conversely, the reciprocal of the work done in one unit of time is the time it will take to finish the entire job. For example, if a worker can complete $\frac{3}{7}$ of the work in one day, then he can finish the whole job in $\frac{7}{3}$, or $2\frac{1}{3}$, days.

If you're given the total time it requires a number of people working together to complete a job, and the times of all but one are known, follow these four steps to find the missing time:

❶ Invert the given times to find how much of the job each worker can complete in one unit of time.

❷ Add these reciprocals to find how much of the job can be completed in one unit of time by those workers whose rates are known.

❸ Subtract this sum from the reciprocal of the total time to complete the job to find the missing rate.

❹ Invert this rate to find the unknown time.

A, B, and C can finish a job in two days. B can finish it in five days, and C can finish it in four days. How long would it take A to finish the job by himself? Follow the steps:

- B can finish the job in five days; therefore, he can complete $\frac{1}{5}$ of the job in one day.

  C can finish the job in four days; therefore, he can complete $\frac{1}{4}$ of the job in one day.

- The part of the job that can be completed by B and C together in one day is: $\frac{1}{5} + \frac{1}{4} = \frac{9}{20}$.

- The total time to complete the job is two days; therefore, all the workers can complete $\frac{1}{2}$ the job in 1 day: $\frac{1}{2} - \frac{9}{20} = \frac{1}{20}$.

- A can complete $\frac{1}{20}$ of the job in one day; therefore, he can finish the whole job in 20 days.

Solving Problems Using All Factors

In some work problems, certain values are given for the three factors: the number of workers, the amount of work done, and the time. Usually you must find the changes that occur when one or two of the factors are given different values.

The best way to solve such problems is to directly make the necessary cancellations, divisions, and multiplications. Try this problem:

> If 60 workers can build four houses in twelve months, how many workers, working at the same rate, would be required to build six houses in four months?

In this problem, you can easily see that more workers would be required because more houses must be built in a shorter time:

- To build six houses instead of four in the same amount of time requires $\frac{6}{4}$ of the number of workers: $\frac{6}{4} \times 60 = 90$.
- Because you have four months to complete the job where previously twelve were required, you must triple $(12 \div 4 = 3)$ the number of workers: $90 \times 3 = 270$.

Therefore, 270 workers are needed to build six houses in four months.

EXERCISE

Directions: Each question has four suggested answers. Select the correct one.

1. If 314 clerks filed 6,594 papers in 10 minutes, what is the number filed per minute by the average clerk?

   (A) 2
   (B) 2.4
   (C) 2.1
   (D) 2.5

2. Four men working together can dig a ditch in 42 days. They begin, but one man works only half-days. How long will it take to complete the job?

   (A) 48 days
   (B) 45 days
   (C) 43 days
   (D) 44 days

3. A clerk is requested to file 800 cards. If he can file cards at the rate of 80 cards an hour, the number of cards remaining to be filed after seven hours of work is

   (A) 140
   (B) 240
   (C) 260
   (D) 560

4. If it takes four days for three machines to do a certain job, it will take two machines

   (A) 6 days
   (B) $5\frac{1}{2}$ days
   (C) 5 days
   (D) $4\frac{1}{2}$ days

5. A stenographer has been assigned to place entries on 500 forms. She places entries on 25 forms by the end of half an hour when she is joined by another stenographer. The second stenographer places entries at the rate of 45 an hour. Assuming that both stenographers continue to work at their respective rates of speed, the total number of hours required to carry out the entire assignment is

   (A) 5
   (B) $5\frac{1}{2}$
   (C) $6\frac{1}{2}$
   (D) 7

6. If in five days a clerk can copy 125 pages, 36 lines each, 11 words to the line, how many pages of 30 lines each and 12 words to the line can he copy in six days?

   (A) 145
   (B) 155
   (C) 160
   (D) 165

7. A and B do a job together in 2 hours. Working alone, A does the job in 5 hours. How long will it take B to do the job alone?

   (A) $3\frac{1}{3}$ hr.
   (B) $2\frac{1}{4}$ hr.
   (C) 3 hr.
   (D) 2 hr.

8. A stenographer transcribes her notes at the rate of one line typed in 10 seconds. At this rate, how long (in minutes and seconds) will it take her to transcribe notes that require seven pages of typing, 25 lines to the page?

(A) 29 min. and 10 sec.

(B) 17 min. and 50 sec.

(C) 40 min. and 10 sec.

(D) 20 min. and 30 sec.

9. A group of five clerks has been assigned to insert 24,000 letters into envelopes. The clerks perform this work at the following rates of speed: Clerk A, 1,100 letters an hour; Clerk B, 1,450 letters an hour; Clerk C, 1,200 letters an hour; Clerk D, 1,300 letters an hour; Clerk E, 1,250 letters an hour. At the end of two hours of work, Clerks C and D are assigned to another task. From the time that Clerks C and D were taken off the assignment, the number of hours required for the remaining clerks to complete this assignment is

(A) less than 3 hours.

(B) 3 hours.

(C) between 3 and 4 hours.

(D) more than 4 hours.

10. If a certain job can be performed by 18 workers in 26 days, the number of workers needed to perform the job in 12 days is

(A) 24

(B) 30

(C) 39

(D) 52

ANSWER KEY AND EXPLANATIONS

1. C	3. B	5. B	7. A	9. B
2. A	4. A	6. D	8. A	10. C

1. **The correct answer is (C).** 6,594 papers ÷ 314 clerks = 21 papers filed by each clerk in 10 minutes; 21 papers ÷ 10 minutes = 2.1 papers per minute filed by the average clerk.

2. **The correct answer is (A).** It takes one man $42 \times 4 = 168$ days to complete the job, working alone. If $3\frac{1}{2}$ men are working (one man works half-days, the other three work full days), the job takes $168 \div 3\frac{1}{2} = 48$ days.

3. **The correct answer is (B).** In seven hours, the clerk files $7 \times 80 = 560$ cards. Because 800 cards must be filed, there are $800 - 560 = 240$ remaining.

4. **The correct answer is (A).** It takes one machine $3 \times 4 = 12$ days to complete the job. Two machines can do the job in $12 \div 2 = 6$ days.

5. **The correct answer is (B).** At the end of the first half-hour, there are $500 - 25 = 475$ forms remaining. If the first stenographer completed 25 forms in half an hour, her rate is $25 \times 2 = 50$ forms per hour. The combined rate of the two stenographers is $50 + 45 = 95$ forms per hour. The remaining forms can be completed in $475 \div 95 = 5$ hours. Adding the first half-hour, the entire job requires $5\frac{1}{2}$ hours.

6. **The correct answer is (D).** 36 lines $\times 11$ words = 396 words on each page; 125 pages $\times 396$ words = 49,500 words copied in five days; $49,500 \div 5 = 9,900$ words copied in one day. 12 words $\times 30$ lines = 360 words on each page; $9,900 \div 360 = 27\frac{1}{2}$ pages copied in one day; $27\frac{1}{2} \times 6 = 165$ pages copied in six days.

7. **The correct answer is (A).** If A can finish the job alone in 5 hours, A can do $\frac{1}{5}$ of the job in one hour. Working together, A and B can complete the job in 2 hours; therefore, in one hour, they finish half the job. In one hour, B alone completes $\frac{1}{2} - \frac{1}{5} = \frac{3}{10}$ of the job. It would take B $\frac{10}{3}$ hours, or $3\frac{1}{3}$ hours, to finish the whole job alone.

8. **The correct answer is (A).** She must type $7 \times 25 = 175$ lines. At the rate of one line per 10 seconds, the job takes $175 \times 10 = 1,750$ seconds. 1,750 seconds $\div 60 = 29\frac{1}{6}$ minutes, or 29 minutes and 10 seconds.

9. **The correct answer is (B).** All five clerks working together process a total of $1,100 + 1,450 + 1,200 + 1,300 + 1,250 = 6,300$ letters per hour. After two hours, they process $6,300 \times 2 = 12,600$ letters. Of the original 24,000 letters, there are $24,000 - 12,600 = 11,400$ letters remaining. Clerks A, B, and E working together process a total of $1,100 + 1,450 + 1,250 = 3,800$ letters per hour. It takes them $11,400 \div 3,800 = 3$ hours to process the remaining letters.

10. **The correct answer is (C).** The job could be completed by one worker in $18 \times 26 = 468$ days. Completing the job in 12 days requires $468 \div 12 = 39$ workers.

ARITHMETIC REASONING PROBLEMS

Arithmetic reasoning problems are word problems that require you to reason out the answer based on the information given. No set formulas must be followed, other than the ones that you've already learned, so the best way to prepare is to practice with several different kinds of reasoning problems.

Arithmetic reasoning problems often require you to solve problems involving fractions, decimals, percents, ratios, and proportions. Turn back to Chapters 15, "Fractions and Decimals," and 16, "Percents, Ratio, and Proportion," to review the rules governing these problems.

Note that the five answer choices for this type of problem include "(E) None of the above." The directions state that the exact answer may not be given as one of the choices, so don't be surprised if, after you do your calculations, you don't see the answer you got. In that case, choose (E).

EXERCISE

Directions: These questions require you to solve problems formulated in both verbal and numeric form. You will have to analyze a paragraph in order to set up the problem and then solve it. If the exact answer is not given as one of the response choices, you should select choice (E), "None of the above."

1. An investigator rented a car for four days and was charged $200. The car rental company charged $10 per day plus $0.20 per mile driven. How many miles did the investigator drive the car?

   (A) 800

   (B) 950

   (C) 1,000

   (D) 1,200

   (E) None of the above

2. In one federal office, $\frac{1}{6}$ of the employees favored abandoning a flexible work schedule system. In a second office that had the same number of employees, $\frac{1}{4}$ of the workers favored abandoning it. What is the average of the fractions of the workers in the two offices who favored abandoning the system?

   (A) $\frac{1}{10}$

   (B) $\frac{1}{5}$

   (C) $\frac{5}{24}$

   (D) $\frac{5}{12}$

   (E) None of the above

3. A federal agency had a personal computer repaired at a cost of $49.20. This amount included a charge of $22 per hour for labor and a charge for a new switch that cost $18 before a 10% government discount was applied. How long did the repair job take?

   (A) 1 hr. and 6 min.

   (B) 1 hr. and 11 min.

   (C) 1 hr. and 22 min.

   (D) 1 hr. and 30 min.

   (E) None of the above

4. In a large agency where mail is delivered in motorized carts, two tires were replaced on a cart at a cost of $34 per tire. If the agency had expected to pay $80 for a pair of tires, what percent of its expected cost did it save?

   (A) 7.5%

   (B) 17.6%

   (C) 57.5%

   (D) 75.0%

   (E) None of the above

5. An interagency task force has representatives from three different agencies. Half of the task force members represent Agency A, one third represent Agency B, and three represent Agency C. How many people are on the task force?

   (A) 12

   (B) 15

   (C) 18

   (D) 24

   (E) None of the above

6. It has been established in recent productivity studies that, on the average, it takes a filing clerk 2 hours and 12 minutes to fill four drawers of a filing cabinet. At this rate, how long would it take two clerks to fill 16 drawers?

(A) 4 hr.

(B) 4 hr. and 20 min.

(C) 8 hr.

(D) 8 hr. and 40 min.

(E) None of the above

7. It costs $60,000 per month to maintain a small medical facility. The basic charge per person for treatment is $40, but 50% of those seeking treatment require laboratory work at an additional average charge of $20 per person. How many patients per month would the facility have to serve in order to cover its costs?

(A) 1,000

(B) 1,200

(C) 1,500

(D) 2,000

(E) None of the above

8. An experimental anti-pollution vehicle powered by electricity traveled 33 kilometers (km) at a constant speed of 110 kilometers per hour (km/h). How many minutes did it take this vehicle to complete its experimental run?

(A) 3

(B) 10

(C) 18

(D) 20

(E) None of the above

9. It takes 2 typists three 8-hour work days to type a report on a word processor. How many typists would be needed to type two reports of the same length in one 8-hour work day?

(A) 4

(B) 6

(C) 8

(D) 12

(E) None of the above

10. A clerk is able to process 40 unemployment compensation claims in one hour. After deductions of 18% for benefits and taxes, the clerk's net pay is $6.97 per hour. If the clerk processed 1,200 claims, how much would the government have to pay for the work, based on the clerk's hourly wage before deductions?

(A) $278.80

(B) $255.00

(C) $246.74

(D) $209.10

(E) None of the above

ANSWER KEY AND EXPLANATIONS

1. A	3. D	5. C	7. B	9. D
2. C	4. E	6. E	8. C	10. B

1. **The correct answer is (A).** The investigator rented the car for four days at $10 per day, which is $40; the portion of the total charge expended for miles driven is $200 − $40 = $160. The number of miles driven by the investigator is $160 ÷ $0.20 = 800.

2. **The correct answer is (C).** The average of the two fractions is ($\frac{1}{6}$ + $\frac{1}{4}$) ÷ 2 = $\frac{5}{24}$.

3. **The correct answer is (D).** The government discount is $18 × 10% = $1.80. The cost of the switch is $18.00 − $1.80 = $16.20. The charge for labor is $49.20 − $16.20 = $33.00. The number of hours worked is $33 ÷ $22 = 1.5 hours, or 1 hour and 30 minutes.

4. **The correct answer is (E).** The correct answer is not given. The difference between the actual cost of $34 per tire and the expected cost of $40 per tire ($80 ÷ 2) is $6: $6 ÷ $40 = 0.15, or 15% of the expected cost.

5. **The correct answer is (C).** Obtain the correct answer by computing $\frac{1}{2}x$ + $\frac{1}{3}x$ + 3 = x, where x is the total number of task force members; $\frac{1}{2}x$ is the number from Agency A; $\frac{1}{3}x$ is the number from Agency B; and 3 is the number from Agency C. Add the two fractions: $\frac{1}{2}x$ + $\frac{1}{3}x$ = $\frac{5}{6}x$. x (or $\frac{6}{6}x$) − $\frac{5}{6}x$ = $\frac{1}{6}x$ = 3. $\frac{1}{6}$ × 18 = 3, so the number of people on the task force is 18.

6. **The correct answer is (E).** The correct answer is not given. First, convert two hours and 12 minutes to 2.2 hours, and then set up a simple proportion: $\frac{2.2}{4}$ = $\frac{x}{16}$. The number of hours it takes one filing clerk to do the job is 2.2 × 16 ÷ 4 = 8.8 hours. If two clerks are filling 16 drawers, the job would be completed in half that time: 4.4 hours, or 4 hours, 24 minutes.

7. **The correct answer is (B).** The basic charge of $40 applies to all patients (x); the additional average charge of $20 applies to only 50% (or $\frac{1}{2}$) of them (0.5x). The combined charges—$40 times the total number of patients (40x) plus $20 times the total number of patients (20 × 0.5x, or 10x)—must equal $60,000, the cost of maintaining the medical facility: 40x + 10x = 60,000. Solve for x: 60,000 ÷ 50 = 1,200, the number of patients who must be served per month.

8. **The correct answer is (C).** Obtain the correct answer by setting up a simple proportion: $\frac{110 \text{ km}}{60 \text{ min}}$ = $\frac{33 \text{ km}}{x \text{ min}}$ min. 33 × 60 ÷ 110 = 18 min.

9. **The correct answer is (D).** The total number of 8-hour work days of typing required for the two reports is 3 days × 2 typists × 2 reports = 12 eight-hour work days of typing. If all of this had to be accomplished in one 8-hour work day, 12 typists would be needed to do the job.

10. **The correct answer is (B).** The clerk's net pay of $6.97 per hour represents 82% of his gross pay (100% − 18% = 82%). The clerk's hourly salary before deductions is $6.97 ÷ 82% = $8.50. The total number of hours of work involved is 1,200 forms ÷ 40 forms per hour = 30 hours. The amount the government would have to pay for the work is 30 hours × $8.50 = $255.00.

SUMMING IT UP

- Three factors are involved in work problems: the number of people working, the time required to complete a job, and the amount of work completed.

- In work problem questions, you're asked to find a rate, time, or number of workers. Depending on the information you're presented with, you must solve the problem using one or more of several formulas. Follow the tips in this chapter to solve using equal rates, time, or all three factors.

- Arithmetic reasoning problems require you to reason out an answer based on the information presented in the question. The formulas that you've already reviewed in Chapters 16, 17, and the first part of this chapter are all you'll need to know to understand and solve the problems on the test.

- The best way to prepare for this section of your exam is to practice answering a variety of arithmetic reasoning questions. Because they often involve calculating fractions, decimals, percents, ratios, and proportions, you may wish to review Chapters 15 and 16 for the rules on these types of calculations.

PART VI

FOUR PRACTICE TESTS

ANSWER SHEET PRACTICE TEST 2

Verbal Ability

1. Ⓐ Ⓑ Ⓒ Ⓓ Ⓔ
2. Ⓐ Ⓑ Ⓒ Ⓓ Ⓔ
3. Ⓐ Ⓑ Ⓒ Ⓓ Ⓔ
4. Ⓐ Ⓑ Ⓒ Ⓓ Ⓔ
5. Ⓐ Ⓑ Ⓒ Ⓓ Ⓔ
6. Ⓐ Ⓑ Ⓒ Ⓓ Ⓔ
7. Ⓐ Ⓑ Ⓒ Ⓓ Ⓔ
8. Ⓐ Ⓑ Ⓒ Ⓓ Ⓔ
9. Ⓐ Ⓑ Ⓒ Ⓓ Ⓔ
10. Ⓐ Ⓑ Ⓒ Ⓓ Ⓔ
11. Ⓐ Ⓑ Ⓒ Ⓓ Ⓔ
12. Ⓐ Ⓑ Ⓒ Ⓓ Ⓔ
13. Ⓐ Ⓑ Ⓒ Ⓓ Ⓔ
14. Ⓐ Ⓑ Ⓒ Ⓓ Ⓔ
15. Ⓐ Ⓑ Ⓒ Ⓓ Ⓔ
16. Ⓐ Ⓑ Ⓒ Ⓓ Ⓔ
17. Ⓐ Ⓑ Ⓒ Ⓓ Ⓔ
18. Ⓐ Ⓑ Ⓒ Ⓓ Ⓔ
19. Ⓐ Ⓑ Ⓒ Ⓓ Ⓔ
20. Ⓐ Ⓑ Ⓒ Ⓓ Ⓔ
21. Ⓐ Ⓑ Ⓒ Ⓓ Ⓔ
22. Ⓐ Ⓑ Ⓒ Ⓓ Ⓔ

23. Ⓐ Ⓑ Ⓒ Ⓓ Ⓔ
24. Ⓐ Ⓑ Ⓒ Ⓓ Ⓔ
25. Ⓐ Ⓑ Ⓒ Ⓓ Ⓔ
26. Ⓐ Ⓑ Ⓒ Ⓓ Ⓔ
27. Ⓐ Ⓑ Ⓒ Ⓓ Ⓔ
28. Ⓐ Ⓑ Ⓒ Ⓓ Ⓔ
29. Ⓐ Ⓑ Ⓒ Ⓓ Ⓔ
30. Ⓐ Ⓑ Ⓒ Ⓓ Ⓔ
31. Ⓐ Ⓑ Ⓒ Ⓓ Ⓔ
32. Ⓐ Ⓑ Ⓒ Ⓓ Ⓔ
33. Ⓐ Ⓑ Ⓒ Ⓓ Ⓔ
34. Ⓐ Ⓑ Ⓒ Ⓓ Ⓔ
35. Ⓐ Ⓑ Ⓒ Ⓓ Ⓔ
36. Ⓐ Ⓑ Ⓒ Ⓓ Ⓔ
37. Ⓐ Ⓑ Ⓒ Ⓓ Ⓔ
38. Ⓐ Ⓑ Ⓒ Ⓓ Ⓔ
39. Ⓐ Ⓑ Ⓒ Ⓓ Ⓔ
40. Ⓐ Ⓑ Ⓒ Ⓓ Ⓔ
41. Ⓐ Ⓑ Ⓒ Ⓓ Ⓔ
42. Ⓐ Ⓑ Ⓒ Ⓓ Ⓔ
43. Ⓐ Ⓑ Ⓒ Ⓓ Ⓔ

44. Ⓐ Ⓑ Ⓒ Ⓓ Ⓔ
45. Ⓐ Ⓑ Ⓒ Ⓓ Ⓔ
46. Ⓐ Ⓑ Ⓒ Ⓓ Ⓔ
47. Ⓐ Ⓑ Ⓒ Ⓓ Ⓔ
48. Ⓐ Ⓑ Ⓒ Ⓓ Ⓔ
49. Ⓐ Ⓑ Ⓒ Ⓓ Ⓔ
50. Ⓐ Ⓑ Ⓒ Ⓓ Ⓔ
51. Ⓐ Ⓑ Ⓒ Ⓓ Ⓔ
52. Ⓐ Ⓑ Ⓒ Ⓓ Ⓔ
53. Ⓐ Ⓑ Ⓒ Ⓓ Ⓔ
54. Ⓐ Ⓑ Ⓒ Ⓓ Ⓔ
55. Ⓐ Ⓑ Ⓒ Ⓓ Ⓔ
56. Ⓐ Ⓑ Ⓒ Ⓓ Ⓔ
57. Ⓐ Ⓑ Ⓒ Ⓓ Ⓔ
58. Ⓐ Ⓑ Ⓒ Ⓓ Ⓔ
59. Ⓐ Ⓑ Ⓒ Ⓓ Ⓔ
60. Ⓐ Ⓑ Ⓒ Ⓓ Ⓔ
61. Ⓐ Ⓑ Ⓒ Ⓓ Ⓔ
62. Ⓐ Ⓑ Ⓒ Ⓓ Ⓔ
63. Ⓐ Ⓑ Ⓒ Ⓓ Ⓔ
64. Ⓐ Ⓑ Ⓒ Ⓓ Ⓔ

65. Ⓐ Ⓑ Ⓒ Ⓓ Ⓔ
66. Ⓐ Ⓑ Ⓒ Ⓓ Ⓔ
67. Ⓐ Ⓑ Ⓒ Ⓓ Ⓔ
68. Ⓐ Ⓑ Ⓒ Ⓓ Ⓔ
69. Ⓐ Ⓑ Ⓒ Ⓓ Ⓔ
70. Ⓐ Ⓑ Ⓒ Ⓓ Ⓔ
71. Ⓐ Ⓑ Ⓒ Ⓓ Ⓔ
72. Ⓐ Ⓑ Ⓒ Ⓓ Ⓔ
73. Ⓐ Ⓑ Ⓒ Ⓓ Ⓔ
74. Ⓐ Ⓑ Ⓒ Ⓓ Ⓔ
75. Ⓐ Ⓑ Ⓒ Ⓓ Ⓔ
76. Ⓐ Ⓑ Ⓒ Ⓓ Ⓔ
77. Ⓐ Ⓑ Ⓒ Ⓓ Ⓔ
78. Ⓐ Ⓑ Ⓒ Ⓓ Ⓔ
79. Ⓐ Ⓑ Ⓒ Ⓓ Ⓔ
80. Ⓐ Ⓑ Ⓒ Ⓓ Ⓔ
81. Ⓐ Ⓑ Ⓒ Ⓓ Ⓔ
82. Ⓐ Ⓑ Ⓒ Ⓓ Ⓔ
83. Ⓐ Ⓑ Ⓒ Ⓓ Ⓔ
84. Ⓐ Ⓑ Ⓒ Ⓓ Ⓔ
85. Ⓐ Ⓑ Ⓒ Ⓓ Ⓔ

answer sheet

Clerical Ability

1. Ⓐ Ⓑ Ⓒ Ⓓ Ⓔ	31. Ⓐ Ⓑ Ⓒ Ⓓ Ⓔ	61. Ⓐ Ⓑ Ⓒ Ⓓ Ⓔ	91. Ⓐ Ⓑ Ⓒ Ⓓ Ⓔ
2. Ⓐ Ⓑ Ⓒ Ⓓ Ⓔ	32. Ⓐ Ⓑ Ⓒ Ⓓ Ⓔ	62. Ⓐ Ⓑ Ⓒ Ⓓ Ⓔ	92. Ⓐ Ⓑ Ⓒ Ⓓ Ⓔ
3. Ⓐ Ⓑ Ⓒ Ⓓ Ⓔ	33. Ⓐ Ⓑ Ⓒ Ⓓ Ⓔ	63. Ⓐ Ⓑ Ⓒ Ⓓ Ⓔ	93. Ⓐ Ⓑ Ⓒ Ⓓ Ⓔ
4. Ⓐ Ⓑ Ⓒ Ⓓ Ⓔ	34. Ⓐ Ⓑ Ⓒ Ⓓ Ⓔ	64. Ⓐ Ⓑ Ⓒ Ⓓ Ⓔ	94. Ⓐ Ⓑ Ⓒ Ⓓ Ⓔ
5. Ⓐ Ⓑ Ⓒ Ⓓ Ⓔ	35. Ⓐ Ⓑ Ⓒ Ⓓ Ⓔ	65. Ⓐ Ⓑ Ⓒ Ⓓ Ⓔ	95. Ⓐ Ⓑ Ⓒ Ⓓ Ⓔ
6. Ⓐ Ⓑ Ⓒ Ⓓ Ⓔ	36. Ⓐ Ⓑ Ⓒ Ⓓ Ⓔ	66. Ⓐ Ⓑ Ⓒ Ⓓ Ⓔ	96. Ⓐ Ⓑ Ⓒ Ⓓ Ⓔ
7. Ⓐ Ⓑ Ⓒ Ⓓ Ⓔ	37. Ⓐ Ⓑ Ⓒ Ⓓ Ⓔ	67. Ⓐ Ⓑ Ⓒ Ⓓ Ⓔ	97. Ⓐ Ⓑ Ⓒ Ⓓ Ⓔ
8. Ⓐ Ⓑ Ⓒ Ⓓ Ⓔ	38. Ⓐ Ⓑ Ⓒ Ⓓ Ⓔ	68. Ⓐ Ⓑ Ⓒ Ⓓ Ⓔ	98. Ⓐ Ⓑ Ⓒ Ⓓ Ⓔ
9. Ⓐ Ⓑ Ⓒ Ⓓ Ⓔ	39. Ⓐ Ⓑ Ⓒ Ⓓ Ⓔ	69. Ⓐ Ⓑ Ⓒ Ⓓ Ⓔ	99. Ⓐ Ⓑ Ⓒ Ⓓ Ⓔ
10. Ⓐ Ⓑ Ⓒ Ⓓ Ⓔ	40. Ⓐ Ⓑ Ⓒ Ⓓ Ⓔ	70. Ⓐ Ⓑ Ⓒ Ⓓ Ⓔ	100. Ⓐ Ⓑ Ⓒ Ⓓ Ⓔ
11. Ⓐ Ⓑ Ⓒ Ⓓ Ⓔ	41. Ⓐ Ⓑ Ⓒ Ⓓ Ⓔ	71. Ⓐ Ⓑ Ⓒ Ⓓ Ⓔ	101. Ⓐ Ⓑ Ⓒ Ⓓ Ⓔ
12. Ⓐ Ⓑ Ⓒ Ⓓ Ⓔ	42. Ⓐ Ⓑ Ⓒ Ⓓ Ⓔ	72. Ⓐ Ⓑ Ⓒ Ⓓ Ⓔ	102. Ⓐ Ⓑ Ⓒ Ⓓ Ⓔ
13. Ⓐ Ⓑ Ⓒ Ⓓ Ⓔ	43. Ⓐ Ⓑ Ⓒ Ⓓ Ⓔ	73. Ⓐ Ⓑ Ⓒ Ⓓ Ⓔ	103. Ⓐ Ⓑ Ⓒ Ⓓ Ⓔ
14. Ⓐ Ⓑ Ⓒ Ⓓ Ⓔ	44. Ⓐ Ⓑ Ⓒ Ⓓ Ⓔ	74. Ⓐ Ⓑ Ⓒ Ⓓ Ⓔ	104. Ⓐ Ⓑ Ⓒ Ⓓ Ⓔ
15. Ⓐ Ⓑ Ⓒ Ⓓ Ⓔ	45. Ⓐ Ⓑ Ⓒ Ⓓ Ⓔ	75. Ⓐ Ⓑ Ⓒ Ⓓ Ⓔ	105. Ⓐ Ⓑ Ⓒ Ⓓ Ⓔ
16. Ⓐ Ⓑ Ⓒ Ⓓ Ⓔ	46. Ⓐ Ⓑ Ⓒ Ⓓ Ⓔ	76. Ⓐ Ⓑ Ⓒ Ⓓ Ⓔ	106. Ⓐ Ⓑ Ⓒ Ⓓ Ⓔ
17. Ⓐ Ⓑ Ⓒ Ⓓ Ⓔ	47. Ⓐ Ⓑ Ⓒ Ⓓ Ⓔ	77. Ⓐ Ⓑ Ⓒ Ⓓ Ⓔ	107. Ⓐ Ⓑ Ⓒ Ⓓ Ⓔ
18. Ⓐ Ⓑ Ⓒ Ⓓ Ⓔ	48. Ⓐ Ⓑ Ⓒ Ⓓ Ⓔ	78. Ⓐ Ⓑ Ⓒ Ⓓ Ⓔ	108. Ⓐ Ⓑ Ⓒ Ⓓ Ⓔ
19. Ⓐ Ⓑ Ⓒ Ⓓ Ⓔ	49. Ⓐ Ⓑ Ⓒ Ⓓ Ⓔ	79. Ⓐ Ⓑ Ⓒ Ⓓ Ⓔ	109. Ⓐ Ⓑ Ⓒ Ⓓ Ⓔ
20. Ⓐ Ⓑ Ⓒ Ⓓ Ⓔ	50. Ⓐ Ⓑ Ⓒ Ⓓ Ⓔ	80. Ⓐ Ⓑ Ⓒ Ⓓ Ⓔ	110. Ⓐ Ⓑ Ⓒ Ⓓ Ⓔ
21. Ⓐ Ⓑ Ⓒ Ⓓ Ⓔ	51. Ⓐ Ⓑ Ⓒ Ⓓ Ⓔ	81. Ⓐ Ⓑ Ⓒ Ⓓ Ⓔ	111. Ⓐ Ⓑ Ⓒ Ⓓ Ⓔ
22. Ⓐ Ⓑ Ⓒ Ⓓ Ⓔ	52. Ⓐ Ⓑ Ⓒ Ⓓ Ⓔ	82. Ⓐ Ⓑ Ⓒ Ⓓ Ⓔ	112. Ⓐ Ⓑ Ⓒ Ⓓ Ⓔ
23. Ⓐ Ⓑ Ⓒ Ⓓ Ⓔ	53. Ⓐ Ⓑ Ⓒ Ⓓ Ⓔ	83. Ⓐ Ⓑ Ⓒ Ⓓ Ⓔ	113. Ⓐ Ⓑ Ⓒ Ⓓ Ⓔ
24. Ⓐ Ⓑ Ⓒ Ⓓ Ⓔ	54. Ⓐ Ⓑ Ⓒ Ⓓ Ⓔ	84. Ⓐ Ⓑ Ⓒ Ⓓ Ⓔ	114. Ⓐ Ⓑ Ⓒ Ⓓ Ⓔ
25. Ⓐ Ⓑ Ⓒ Ⓓ Ⓔ	55. Ⓐ Ⓑ Ⓒ Ⓓ Ⓔ	85. Ⓐ Ⓑ Ⓒ Ⓓ Ⓔ	115. Ⓐ Ⓑ Ⓒ Ⓓ Ⓔ
26. Ⓐ Ⓑ Ⓒ Ⓓ Ⓔ	56. Ⓐ Ⓑ Ⓒ Ⓓ Ⓔ	86. Ⓐ Ⓑ Ⓒ Ⓓ Ⓔ	116. Ⓐ Ⓑ Ⓒ Ⓓ Ⓔ
27. Ⓐ Ⓑ Ⓒ Ⓓ Ⓔ	57. Ⓐ Ⓑ Ⓒ Ⓓ Ⓔ	87. Ⓐ Ⓑ Ⓒ Ⓓ Ⓔ	117. Ⓐ Ⓑ Ⓒ Ⓓ Ⓔ
28. Ⓐ Ⓑ Ⓒ Ⓓ Ⓔ	58. Ⓐ Ⓑ Ⓒ Ⓓ Ⓔ	88. Ⓐ Ⓑ Ⓒ Ⓓ Ⓔ	118. Ⓐ Ⓑ Ⓒ Ⓓ Ⓔ
29. Ⓐ Ⓑ Ⓒ Ⓓ Ⓔ	59. Ⓐ Ⓑ Ⓒ Ⓓ Ⓔ	89. Ⓐ Ⓑ Ⓒ Ⓓ Ⓔ	119. Ⓐ Ⓑ Ⓒ Ⓓ Ⓔ
30. Ⓐ Ⓑ Ⓒ Ⓓ Ⓔ	60. Ⓐ Ⓑ Ⓒ Ⓓ Ⓔ	90. Ⓐ Ⓑ Ⓒ Ⓓ Ⓔ	120. Ⓐ Ⓑ Ⓒ Ⓓ Ⓔ

Practice Test 2

VERBAL ABILITY

85 Questions • 35 Minutes

Directions: Read each question carefully and select the best answer.

1. *Flexible* means most nearly
   - (A) breakable
   - (B) flammable
   - (C) pliable
   - (D) weak

2. *Option* means most nearly
   - (A) use
   - (B) choice
   - (C) value
   - (D) blame

3. To *verify* means most nearly to
   - (A) examine
   - (B) explain
   - (C) confirm
   - (D) guarantee

4. *Indolent* means most nearly
   - (A) moderate
   - (B) hopeless
   - (C) selfish
   - (D) lazy

5. *Respiration* means most nearly
   - (A) recovery
   - (B) breathing
   - (C) pulsation
   - (D) sweating

6. PLUMBER is related to WRENCH as PAINTER is related to
   - (A) brush
   - (B) pipe
   - (C) shop
   - (D) hammer

7. LETTER is related to MESSAGE as PACKAGE is related to
   - (A) sender
   - (B) merchandise
   - (C) insurance
   - (D) business

8. FOOD is related to HUNGER as SLEEP is related to
   - (A) night
   - (B) dream
   - (C) weariness
   - (D) rest

9. ATONEMENT is related to SIN as REPARATION is related to
   - (A) clemency
   - (B) peace
   - (C) virtue
   - (D) war

NOTE

The directions stated here pertain to taking the exam in a paper-and-pencil format. If you will be taking the exam on a computer, each section will have directions specific to how to answer questions on computer.

Directions: In questions 10 and 11 and all similar questions, decide which sentence is best with respect to grammar and usage suitable for a formal letter or report.

10. **(A)** I think that they will promote whoever has the best record.
    (B) The firm would have liked to have promoted all employees with good records.
    (C) Such of them that have the best records have excellent prospects of promotion.
    (D) I feel sure they will give the promotion to whomever has the best record.

11. **(A)** The receptionist must answer courteously the questions of all them callers.
    (B) The receptionist must answer courteously the questions what are asked by the callers.
    (C) There would have been no trouble if the receptionist had have always answered courteously.
    (D) The receptionist should answer courteously the questions of all callers.

Directions: In questions 12–15 and all similar questions, find the correct spelling of the word. If no suggested spelling is correct, choose choice (D).

12. **(A)** collapsible
    (B) collapseable
    (C) collapseble
    (D) None of the above

13. **(A)** ambigeuous
    (B) ambigeous
    (C) ambiguous
    (D) None of the above

14. **(A)** predesessor
    (B) predecesar
    (C) predecesser
    (D) None of the above

15. **(A)** sanctioned
    (B) sancktioned
    (C) sanctionned
    (D) None of the above

16. "Some fire-resistant buildings, although wholly constructed of materials that will not burn, may be completely gutted by the spread of fire through their contents by way of hallways and other openings. They may even suffer serious structural damage by the collapse of metal beams and columns."

The quotation best supports the statement that some fire-resistant buildings

(A) can be damaged seriously by fire.

(B) have specially constructed halls and doors.

(C) afford less protection to their contents than would ordinary buildings.

(D) will burn readily.

17. Civilization started to move ahead more rapidly when people freed themselves of the shackles that restricted their search for the truth.

The paragraph best supports the statement that the progress of civilization

(A) came as a result of people's dislike for obstacles.

(B) did not begin until restrictions on learning were removed.

(C) has been aided by people's efforts to find the truth.

(D) is based on continually increasing efforts.

18. *Vigilant* means most nearly

(A) sensible

(B) watchful

(C) suspicious

(D) restless

19. *Incidental* means most nearly

(A) independent

(B) needless

(C) infrequent

(D) accompanying

20. *Conciliatory* means most nearly

(A) pacific

(B) contentious

(C) obligatory

(D) offensive

21. *Altercation* means most nearly

(A) defeat

(B) concurrence

(C) controversy

(D) vexation

22. *Irresolute* means most nearly

(A) wavering

(B) insubordinate

(C) impudent

(D) unobservant

23. DARKNESS is related to SUNLIGHT as STILLNESS is related to

(A) quiet

(B) moonlight

(C) sound

(D) dark

24. DESIGNED is related to INTENTION as ACCIDENTAL is related to

(A) purpose

(B) caution

(C) damage

(D) chance

25. ERROR is related to PRACTICE as SOUND is related to

(A) deafness

(B) noise

(C) muffler

(D) horn

26. RESEARCH is related to FINDINGS as TRAINING is related to

(A) skill

(B) tests

(C) supervision

(D) teaching

27. **(A)** If properly addressed, the letter will reach my mother and I.

(B) The letter had been addressed to myself and my mother.

(C) I believe the letter was addressed to either my mother or I.

(D) My mother's name, as well as mine, was on the letter.

28. **(A)** The supervisors reprimanded the typists, whom she believed had made careless errors.

(B) The typists would have corrected the errors had they of known that the supervisor would see the report.

(C) The errors in the typed reports were so numerous that they could hardly be overlooked.

(D) Many errors were found in the reports which they typed and could not disregard them.

29. **(A)** minieture

(B) minneature

(C) mineature

(D) None of the above

30. **(A)** extemporaneous

(B) extempuraneus

(C) extemperaneous

(D) None of the above

31. **(A)** problemmatical

(B) problematical

(C) problematicle

(D) None of the above

32. **(A)** descendant

(B) decendant

(C) desendant

(D) None of the above

33. The likelihood of America's exhausting its natural resources seems to be growing less. All kinds of waste are being reworked and new uses are constantly being found for almost everything. We are getting more use out of our goods and are making many new byproducts out of what was formerly thrown away.

The paragraph best supports the statement that we seem to be in less danger of exhausting our resources because

(A) economy is found to lie in the use of substitutes.

(B) more service is obtained from a given amount of material.

(C) we are allowing time for nature to restore them.

(D) supply and demand are better controlled.

34. The key to making a good presentation is simple. First, tell your audience what you're going to tell them. Second, tell them. Third, tell them what you just told them. This may seem silly, but think about how you were taught to write essays. Begin with an introduction that lays the groundwork for your essay. Expand on the introduction by adding facts, details, and possibly your own observations. For the conclusion, summarize what you just wrote.

The paragraph best supports the statement that in developing a presentation

(A) one should think he/she is writing an essay.

(B) one should always include a summary statement.

(C) the comparison to writing an essay is easy to see.

(D) one should use a three-part format.

35. To *counteract* means most nearly to

(A) undermine

(B) censure

(C) preserve

(D) neutralize

36. *Deferred* means most nearly
    (A) reversed
    (B) delayed
    (C) considered
    (D) forbidden

37. *Feasible* means most nearly
    (A) capable
    (B) justifiable
    (C) practicable
    (D) beneficial

38. To *encounter* means most nearly to
    (A) meet
    (B) recall
    (C) overcome
    (D) retreat

39. *Innate* means most nearly
    (A) eternal
    (B) well-developed
    (C) native
    (D) prospective

40. STUDENT is related to TEACHER as DISCIPLE is related to
    (A) follower
    (B) master
    (C) principal
    (D) pupil

41. LECTURE is related to AUDITORIUM as EXPERIMENT is related to
    (A) scientist
    (B) chemistry
    (C) laboratory
    (D) discovery

42. BODY is related to FOOD as ENGINE is related to
    (A) wheels
    (B) fuel
    (C) motion
    (D) smoke

43. SCHOOL is related to EDUCATION as THEATER is related to
    (A) management
    (B) stage
    (C) recreation
    (D) preparation

44. (A) Most all these statements have been supported by persons who are reliable and can be depended upon.
    (B) The persons which have guaranteed these statements are reliable.
    (C) Reliable persons guarantee the facts with regards to the truth of these statements.
    (D) These statements can be depended on, for their truth has been guaranteed by reliable persons.

45. (A) The success of the book pleased both the publishers and the authors.
    (B) Both the publisher and they was pleased with the success of the book.
    (C) Neither they or their publisher was disappointed with their success of the book.
    (D) Their publisher was as pleased as them with the success of the book.

46. (A) extercate
    (B) extracate
    (C) extricate
    (D) None of the above

47. (A) hereditory
    (B) hereditary
    (C) hereditairy
    (D) None of the above

48. (A) auspiceous
    (B) auspiseous
    (C) auspicious
    (D) None of the above

49. (A) sequance
   (B) sequence
   (C) sequense
   (D) None of the above

50. In order to prevent accidents, safety devices must be used to guard exposed machinery. In addition, mechanics must be instructed in safety rules that they must follow for their own protection. Finally, the lighting in the plant must be adequate.

The paragraph best supports the statement that industrial accidents

   (A) may be due to lack of knowledge.
   (B) are always avoidable.
   (C) usually result from inadequate machinery.
   (D) cannot be entirely overcome.

51. The English language is peculiarly rich in synonyms, and there is scarcely a language spoken that has not some representative in English speech. The spirit of the Anglo-Saxon has subjugated these various elements to one idiom, making not a patchwork, but a composite language.

The paragraph best supports the statement that the English language

   (A) has few idiomatic expressions.
   (B) is difficult to translate.
   (C) is used universally.
   (D) has absorbed words from other languages.

52. To *acquiesce* means most nearly to
   (A) assent
   (B) acquire
   (C) complete
   (D) participate

53. *Unanimity* means most nearly
   (A) emphasis
   (B) namelessness
   (C) harmony
   (D) impartiality

54. *Precedent* means most nearly
   (A) example
   (B) theory
   (C) law
   (D) conformity

55. *Versatile* means most nearly
   (A) broad-minded
   (B) well-known
   (C) up-to-date
   (D) many-sided

56. *Authentic* means most nearly
   (A) detailed
   (B) reliable
   (C) valuable
   (D) practical

57. BIOGRAPHY is related to FACT as NOVEL is related to
   (A) fiction
   (B) literature
   (C) narration
   (D) book

58. HD is related to TELEVISION as 3D is related to
   (A) cable
   (B) movies
   (C) digital
   (D) cameras

59. EFFICIENCY is related to REWARD as CARELESSNESS is related to
   (A) improvement
   (B) disobedience
   (C) reprimand
   (D) repetition

60. ABUNDANT is related to CHEAP as SCARCE is related to
    (A) ample
    (B) costly
    (C) inexpensive
    (D) unobtainable

61. (A) Brown's & Company employees have recently received increases in salary.
    (B) Brown & Company recently increased the salaries of all its employees.
    (C) Recently Brown & Company has increased their employees' salaries.
    (D) Brown & Company have recently increased the salaries of all its employees.

62. (A) In reviewing the typists' work reports, the job analyst found records of unusual typing speeds.
    (B) It says in the job analyst's report that some employees type with great speed.
    (C) The job analyst found that, in reviewing the typists' work reports, that some unusual typing speeds had been made.
    (D) In the reports of typists' speeds, the job analyst found some records that are kind of unusual.

63. (A) oblitorate
    (B) oblitterat
    (C) obbliterate
    (D) None of the above

64. (A) diagnoesis
    (B) diagnossis
    (C) diagnosis
    (D) None of the above

65. (A) contenance
    (B) countenance
    (C) countinance
    (D) None of the above

66. (A) conceivably
    (B) concieveably
    (C) conceiveably
    (D) None of the above

67. Through advertising, manufacturers exercise a high degree of control over consumers' desires. However, the manufacturer assumes enormous risks in attempting to predict what consumers will want and thereby producing goods in quantity and distributing them before consumers have bought a single item of that product.

    The paragraph best supports the statement that manufacturers

    (A) can eliminate the risk of overproduction by advertising.
    (B) distribute goods directly to the consumers.
    (C) must depend upon the final consumers for the success of their undertakings.
    (D) can predict with great accuracy the success of any product they put on the market.

68. In the relations of humans to nature, the procuring of food and shelter is fundamental. With the migration of humans to various climates, ever new adjustments to the food supply and to the climate became necessary.

    The paragraph best supports the statement that the means by which the humans have, over time, supplied their material needs are

    (A) accidental.
    (B) varied.
    (C) limited.
    (D) inadequate.

69. *Strident* means most nearly

   (A) swaggering

   (B) domineering

   (C) angry

   (D) harsh

70. To *confine* means most nearly to

   (A) hide

   (B) restrict

   (C) eliminate

   (D) punish

71. To *accentuate* means most nearly to

   (A) modify

   (B) hasten

   (C) sustain

   (D) intensify

72. *Banal* means most nearly

   (A) commonplace

   (B) forceful

   (C) tranquil

   (D) indifferent

73. *Incorrigible* means most nearly

   (A) intolerable

   (B) undeveloped

   (C) irreformable

   (D) brazen

74. POLICE OFFICER is related to OR-DER as DOCTOR is related to

   (A) physician

   (B) hospital

   (C) sickness

   (D) health

75. ARTIST is related to PAINTS as SCULPTOR is related to

   (A) stone

   (B) art

   (C) statues

   (D) pottery

76. CROWD is related to PERSONS as FLEET is related to

   (A) expedition

   (B) officers

   (C) navy

   (D) ships

77. CALENDAR is related to DATE as MAP is related to

   (A) drive

   (B) trip

   (C) location

   (D) vacation

78. (A) Since the report lacked the needed information, it was of no use to them.

   (B) This report was useless to them because there were no needed information in it.

   (C) Since the report did not contain the needed information, it was not real useful to them.

   (D) Being that the report lacked the needed information, they could not use it.

79. (A) The company had hardly declared the dividend till the notices were prepared for mailing.

   (B) They had no sooner declared the dividend when they sent the notices to the stockholders.

   (C) No sooner had the dividend been declared than the notices were prepared for mailing.

   (D) Scarcely had the dividend been declared than the notices were sent out.

80. (A) compitition
(B) competition
(C) competetion
(D) None of the above

81. (A) occassion
(B) occasion
(C) ocassion
(D) None of the above

82. (A) knowlege
(B) knolledge
(C) knowledge
(D) None of the above

83. (A) deliborate
(B) deliberate
(C) delibrate
(D) None of the above

84. What constitutes skill in any line of work is not always easy to determine. Economy of time must be carefully distinguished from economy of energy, as the quickest method may require the greatest expenditure of muscular effort and may not be essential or at all desirable.

The paragraph best supports the statement that

(A) the most efficiently executed task is not always the one done in the shortest time.

(B) energy and time cannot both be conserved in performing a single task.

(C) a task is well done when it is performed in the shortest time.

(D) skill in performing a task should not be acquired at the expense of time.

85. It is difficult to distinguish between bookkeeping and accounting. In attempts to do so, bookkeeping is called the art, and accounting the science, of recording business transactions. Bookkeeping gives the history of the business in a systematic matter; and accounting classifies, analyzes, and interprets the facts thus recorded.

The paragraph best supports the statement that

(A) accounting is less systematic than bookkeeping.

(B) accounting and bookkeeping are closely related.

(C) bookkeeping and accounting cannot be distinguished from one another.

(D) bookkeeping has been superseded by accounting.

STOP

END OF SECTION. IF YOU HAVE ANY TIME LEFT, GO OVER YOUR WORK IN THIS SECTION ONLY. DO NOT WORK IN ANY OTHER SECTION OF THE TEST.

practice test

CLERICAL ABILITY

120 Questions • 15 Minutes

Directions: Read each question carefully and select the best answer.

In questions 1–5, compare the three names or numbers, and choose the answer:

(A) if ALL THREE names or numbers are exactly ALIKE.
(B) if only the FIRST and SECOND names or numbers are exactly ALIKE.
(C) if only the FIRST and THIRD names or numbers are exactly ALIKE.
(D) if only the SECOND and THIRD names or numbers are exactly ALIKE.
(E) if ALL THREE names or numbers are DIFFERENT.

1. 5261383   5261383   5261338

2. 8125690   8126690   8125609

3. W. E. Johnston   W. E. Johnson   W. E. Johnson

4. Vergil L. Muller   Vergil L. Muller   Vergil L. Muller

5. Atherton R. Warde   Asheton R. Warde   Atherton P. Warde

Directions: In questions 6–10 and all similar questions, find the correct place for the given name.

6. Hackett, Gerald
   (A) –
       Habert, James
   (B) –
       Hachett, J. J.
   (C) –
       Hachetts, K. Larson
   (D) –
       Hachettson, Leroy
   (E) –

7. Margenroth, Alvin
   (A) –
       Margeroth, Albert
   (B) –
       Margestein, Dan
   (C) –
       Margestein, David
   (D) –
       Margue, Edgar
   (E) –

8. Bobbitt, Olivier E.

   (A) –

   Bobbitt, D. Olivier

   (B) –

   Bobbitt, Olive B.

   (C) –

   Bobbitt, Olivia H.

   (D) –

   Bobbitt, R. Olivia

   (E) –

9. Mosely, Werner

   (A) –

   Mosely, Albert J.

   (B) –

   Mosley, Alvin

   (C) –

   Mosley, S. M.

   (D) –

   Mosley, Vinson N.

   (E) –

10. Youmuns, Frank L.

   (A) –

   Youmons, Frank G.

   (B) –

   Youmons, Frank H.

   (C) –

   Youmons, Frank K.

   (D) –

   Youmons, Frank M.

   (E) –

11. $\begin{array}{r} 43 \\ +\ 32 \\ \hline \end{array}$

   (A) 55

   (B) 65

   (C) 66

   (D) 75

   (E) None of the above

12. $\begin{array}{r} 83 \\ -\ 4 \\ \hline \end{array}$

   (A) 73

   (B) 79

   (C) 80

   (D) 90

   (E) None of the above

13. $\begin{array}{r} 41 \\ \times\ 7 \\ \hline \end{array}$

   (A) 281

   (B) 287

   (C) 291

   (D) 297

   (E) None of the above

14. $\begin{array}{r} 306 \\ \div\ 6 \\ \hline \end{array}$

   (A) 44

   (B) 51

   (C) 52

   (D) 60

   (E) None of the above

15. $\begin{array}{r} 37 \\ +\ 15 \\ \hline \end{array}$

   (A) 42

   (B) 52

   (C) 53

   (D) 62

   (E) None of the above

Directions: In questions 16–20 and all similar questions, find which one of the suggested answers appears in that question.

								Suggested Answers
16. 6	2	5	K	4	P	T	G	**A** = 4, 5, K, T
17. L	4	7	2	T	6	V	K	**B** = 4, 7, G, K
18. 3	5	4	L	9	V	T	G	**C** = 2, 5, G, L
19. G	4	K	7	L	3	5	Z	**D** = 2, 7, L, T
20. 4	K	2	9	N	5	T	G	**E** = None of the above

Directions: In questions 21–25, compare the three names or numbers, and choose the answer:

    (A) if ALL THREE names or numbers are exactly ALIKE.
    (B) if only the FIRST and SECOND names or numbers are exactly ALIKE.
    (C) if only the FIRST and THIRD names or numbers are exactly ALIKE.
    (D) if only the SECOND and THIRD names or numbers are exactly ALIKE.
    (E) if ALL THREE names or numbers are DIFFERENT.

21.   2395890   2395890   2395890

22.   1926341   1926347   1926314

23. E. Owens McVey   E. Owen McVey   E. Owen McVay

24. Emily Neal Rouse   Emily Neal Rowse   Emily Neal Rowse

25. H. Merritt Audubon   H. Merriott Audubon   H. Merritt Audubon

26. Watters, N. O.

    (A) –

        Waters, Charles L.

    (B) –

        Waterson, Nina P.

    (C) –

        Watson, Nora J.

    (D) –

        Wattwood, Paul A.

    (E) –

27. Johnston, Edward

    (A) –

        Johnston, Edgar R.

    (B) –

        Johnston, Edmond

    (C) –

        Johnston, Edmund

    (D) –

        Johnstone, Edmund A.

    (E) –

28. Rensch, Adeline

    (A) –

        Ramsay, Amos

    (B) –

        Remschel, Augusta

    (C) –

        Renshaw, Austin

    (D) –

        Rentzel, Becky

    (E) –

29. Schnyder, Maurice

    (A) –

        Schneider, Martin

    (B) –

        Schneider, Mertens

    (C) –

        Schnyder, Newman

    (D) –

        Schreibner, Norman

    (E) –

30. Freedenburg, C. Erma

  (A) –

    Freedenberg, Emerson

  (B) –

    Freedenberg, Erma

  (C) –

    Freedenberg, Erma E.

  (D) –

    Freedinberg, Erma F.

  (E) –

31. Subtract: 68 – 47

  (A) 10

  (B) 11

  (C) 20

  (D) 22

  (E) None of the above

32. Multiply: 50 • 8

  (A) 400

  (B) 408

  (C) 450

  (D) 458

  (E) None of the above

33. Divide: 180 ÷ 9

  (A) 20

  (B) 29

  (C) 30

  (D) 39

  (E) None of the above

34. Add: 78 + 63

  (A) 131

  (B) 140

  (C) 141

  (D) 151

  (E) None of the above

35. Subtract: 89 – 70

  (A) 9

  (B) 18

  (C) 19

  (D) 29

  (E) None of the above

#								Suggested Answers
36. 9	G	Z	3	L	4	6	N	**A** = 4, 9, L, V
37. L	5	N	K	4	3	9	V	**B** = 4, 5, N, Z
38. 8	2	V	P	9	L	Z	5	**C** = 5, 8, L, Z
39. V	P	9	Z	5	L	8	7	**D** = 8, 9, N, V
40. 5	T	8	N	2	9	V	L	**E** = None of the above

Directions: In questions 41–45, compare the three names or numbers, and choose the answer:

(A) if ALL THREE names or numbers are exactly ALIKE.
(B) if only the FIRST and SECOND names or numbers are exactly ALIKE.
(C) if only the FIRST and THIRD names or numbers are exactly ALIKE.
(D) if only the SECOND and THIRD names or numbers are exactly ALIKE.
(E) if ALL THREE names or numbers are DIFFERENT.

41. 6219354   6219354   6219354

42. 2311.2793   2312793   2312793

43. 1065407   1065407   1065047

44. Francis Ransdell   Frances Ramsdell   Francis Ramsdell

45. Cornelius Detwiler Cornelius Detwiler Cornelius Detwiler

46. DeMattia, Jessica
   (A) –
       DeLong, Jesse
   (B) –
       DeMatteo, Jessie
   (C) –
       Derby, Jessie S.
   (D) –
       DeShazo, L. M.
   (E) –

47. Theriault, Louis
   (A) –
       Therien, Annette
   (B) –
       Therien, Elaine
   (C) –
       Thibeault, Gerald
   (D) –
       Thiebeault, Pierre
   (E) –

48. Gaston, M. Hubert
   (A) –
       Gaston, Dorothy M.
   (B) –
       Gaston, Henry N.
   (C) –
       Gaston, Isabel
   (D) –
       Gaston, M. Melvin
   (E) –

49. SanMiguel, Carlos
   (A) –
       SanLuis, Juana
   (B) –
       Santilli, Laura
   (C) –
       Stinnett, Nellie
   (D) –
       Stoddard, Victor
   (E) –

50. DeLaTour, Hall F.

(A) –

Delargy, Harold

(B) –

DeLathouder, Hilda

(C) –

Lathrop, Hillary

(D) –

LaTour, Hulbert E.

(E) –

51. Multiply: 62 • 5

(A) 300

(B) 310

(C) 315

(D) 360

(E) None of the above

52. Divide: 153 ÷ 3

(A) 41

(B) 43

(C) 51

(D) 53

(E) None of the above

53. Add: 47 + 21

(A) 58

(B) 59

(C) 67

(D) 68

(E) None of the above

54. Subtract: 87 – 42

(A) 34

(B) 35

(C) 44

(D) 45

(E) None of the above

55. Multiply: 37 • 3

(A) 91

(B) 101

(C) 104

(D) 114

(E) None of the above

									Suggested Answers
56. N	5	4	7	T	K	3	Z		**A** = 3, 8, K, N
57. 8	5	3	V	L	2	Z	N		**B** = 5, 8, N, V
58. 7	2	5	N	9	K	L	V		**C** = 3, 9, V, Z
59. 9	8	L	2	5	Z	K	V		**D** = 5, 9, K, Z
60. Z	6	5	V	9	3	P	N		**E** = None of the above

Directions: In questions 61–65, compare the three names or numbers, and choose the answer:

(A) if ALL THREE names or numbers are exactly ALIKE.
(B) if only the FIRST and SECOND names or numbers are exactly ALIKE.
(C) if only the FIRST and THIRD names or numbers are exactly ALIKE.
(D) if only the SECOND and THIRD names or numbers are exactly ALIKE.
(E) if ALL THREE names or numbers are DIFFERENT.

61.	6452054	6452654	6452054
62.	8501268	8501268	8501286
63.	Ella Burk Newham	Ella Burk Newnham	Elena Burk Newnham
64.	Jno. K. Ravencroft	Jno. H. Ravencroft	Jno. H. Ravencroft
65.	Martin Wills Pullen	Martin Wills Pulen	Martin Wills Pullen

66. O'Bannon, M. J.

(A) –

O'Beirne, B. B.

(B) –

Oberlin, E. L.

(C) –

Oberneir, L. P.

(D) –

O'Brian, S. F.

(E) –

67. Entsminger, Jacob

(A) –

Ensminger, J.

(B) –

Entsminger, J. A.

(C) –

Entsminger, Jack

(D) –

Entsminger, James

(E) –

68. Iacone, Pete R.

(A) –

Iacone, Pedro

(B) –

Iacone, Pedro M.

(C) –

Iacone, Peter F.

(D) –

Iascone, Peter W.

(E) –

69. Sheppard, Gladys

(A) –

Shepard, Dwight

(B) –

Shepard, F. H.

(C) –

Shephard, Louise

(D) –

Shepperd, Stella

(E) –

70. Thackton, Melvin T.

   (A) –

      Thackston, Milton G.

   (B) –

      Thackston, Milton W.

   (C) –

      Thackston, Theodore

   (D) –

      Thackston, Thomas G.

   (E) –

71. Divide: 357 ÷ 7

   (A) 51

   (B) 52

   (C) 53

   (D) 54

   (E) None of the above

72. Add: 58 + 27

   (A) 75

   (B) 84

   (C) 85

   (D) 95

   (E) None of the above

73. Subtract: 86 – 57

   (A) 18

   (B) 29

   (C) 38

   (D) 39

   (E) None of the above

74. Multiply: 68 • 4

   (A) 242

   (B) 264

   (C) 272

   (D) 274

   (E) None of the above

75. Divide: 639 ÷ 9

   (A) 71

   (B) 73

   (C) 81

   (D) 83

   (E) None of the above

Suggested Answers

76. 6	Z	T	N	8	7	4	V	**A** = 2, 7, L, N
77. V	7	8	6	N	5	P	L	**B** = 2, 8, T, V
78. N	7	P	V	8	4	2	L	**C** = 6, 8, L, T
79. 7	8	G	4	3	V	L	T	**D** = 6, 7, N, V
80. 4	8	G	2	T	N	6	L	**E** = None of the above

Directions: In questions 81–85, compare the three names or numbers, and choose the answer:

(A) if ALL THREE names or numbers are exactly ALIKE.
(B) if only the FIRST and SECOND names or numbers are exactly ALIKE.
(C) if only the FIRST and THIRD names or numbers are exactly ALIKE.
(D) if only the SECOND and THIRD names or numbers are exactly ALIKE.
(E) if ALL THREE names or numbers are DIFFERENT.

81. 3457988	3457986	3457986
82. 4695682	4695862	4695682
83. Sticklund Kanedy	Stricklund Kanedy	Stricklund Kanedy
84. Joy Harlor Witner	Joy Harloe Witner	Joy Harloe Witner
85. R. M. O. Uberroth	R. M. O. Uberroth	R. N. O. Uberroth

86. Dunlavey, M. Hilary
   (A) –
   Dunleavy, Hilary G.
   (B) –
   Dunleavy, Hilary K.
   (C) –
   Dunleavy, Hilary S.
   (D) –
   Dunleavy, Hilery W.
   (E) –

87. Yarbrough, Maria
   (A) –
   Yabroudy, Margy
   (B) –
   Yarboro, Marie
   (C) –
   Yarborough, Marina
   (D) –
   Yarborough, Mary
   (E) –

88. Prouty, Martha
   (A) –
   Proutey, Margaret
   (B) –
   Proutey, Maude
   (C) –
   Prouty, Myra
   (D) –
   Prouty, Naomi
   (E) –

89. Pawlowicz, Ruth M.
   (A) –
   Pawalek, Edward
   (B) –
   Pawelek, Flora G.
   (C) –
   Pawlowski, Joan M.
   (D) –
   Pawtowski, Wanda
   (E) –

90. Vanstory, George

 (A) –

 Vanover, Eva

 (B) –

 VanSwinderen, Floyd

 (C) –

 VanSyckle, Harry

 (D) –

 Vanture, Laurence

 (E) –

91. Add: 28 + 35

 (A) 53

 (B) 62

 (C) 64

 (D) 73

 (E) None of the above

92. Subtract: 78 – 69

 (A) 7

 (B) 8

 (C) 18

 (D) 19

 (E) None of the above

93. Multiply: 86 • 6

 (A) 492

 (B) 506

 (C) 516

 (D) 526

 (E) None of the above

94. Divide: 648 ÷ 8

 (A) 71

 (B) 76

 (C) 81

 (D) 89

 (E) None of the above

95. Add: 97 + 34

 (A) 131

 (B) 132

 (C) 140

 (D) 141

 (E) None of the above

								Suggested Answers
96. V	5	7	Z	N	9	4	T	**A** = 2, 5, N, Z
97. 4	6	P	T	2	N	K	9	**B** = 4, 5, N, P
98. 6	4	N	2	P	8	Z	K	**C** = 2, 9, P, T
99. 7	P	5	2	4	N	K	T	**D** = 4, 9, T, Z
100. K	T	8	5	4	N	2	P	**E** = None of the above

Directions: In questions 101–105, compare the three names or numbers, and choose the answer:

(A) if ALL THREE names or numbers are exactly ALIKE.
(B) if only the FIRST and SECOND names or numbers are exactly ALIKE.
(C) if only the FIRST and THIRD names or numbers are exactly ALIKE.
(D) if only the SECOND and THIRD names or numbers are exactly ALIKE.
(E) if ALL THREE names or numbers are DIFFERENT.

101.	1592514	1592574	1592574
102.	2010202	2010202	2010220
103.	6177396	6177936	6177396

104. Drusilla S. Ridgeley   Drusilla S. Ridgeley   Drusilla S. Ridgeley

105. Andrei I. Toumantzev   Andrei I. Tourmantzev   Andrei I. Toumantzov

106. Fitzsimmons, Hugh

(A) –

Fitts, Harold

(B) –

Fitzgerald, June

(C) –

FitzGibbon, Junius

(D) –

FitzSimons, Martin

(E) –

107. D'Amato, Vincent

(A) –

Daly, Steven

(B) –

D'Amboise, S. Vincent

(C) –

Daniel, Vail

(D) –

DeAlba, Valentina

(E) –

108. Schaeffer, Roger D.

(A) –

Schaffert, Evelyn M.

(B) –

Schaffner, Margaret M.

(C) –

Schafhirt, Milton G.

(D) –

Shafer, Richard E.

(E) –

109. White-Lewis, Cecil

(A) –

Whitelaw, Cordelia

(B) –

White-Leigh, Nancy

(C) –

Whitely, Rodney

(D) –

Whitlock, Warren

(E) –

110. VanDerHeggen, Don

    (A) –

        VanDemark, Doris

    (B) –

        Vandenberg, H. E.

    (C) –

        VanDercook, Marie

    (D) –

        vanderLinden, Robert

    (E) –

111. Add: 75 + 49

    (A) 124

    (B) 125

    (C) 134

    (D) 225

    (E) None of the above

112. Subtract: 69 – 45

    (A) 14

    (B) 23

    (C) 24

    (D) 26

    (E) None of the above

113. Multiply: 36 • 8

    (A) 246

    (B) 262

    (C) 288

    (D) 368

    (E) None of the above

114. Divide: 328 ÷ 8

    (A) 31

    (B) 41

    (C) 42

    (D) 48

    (E) None of the above

115. Multiply: 58 • 9

    (A) 472

    (B) 513

    (C) 521

    (D) 522

    (E) None of the above

Suggested Answers

116. Z	3	N	P	G	5	4	2	**A** = 2, 3, G, N
117. 6	N	2	8	G	4	P	T	**B** = 2, 6, N, T
118. 6	N	4	T	V	G	8	2	**C** = 3, 4, G, K
119. T	3	P	4	N	8	G	2	**D** = 4, 6, K, T
120. 6	7	K	G	N	2	L	5	**E** = None of the above

STOP

END OF SECTION. IF YOU HAVE ANY TIME LEFT, GO
OVER YOUR WORK IN THIS SECTION ONLY. DO NOT
WORK IN ANY OTHER SECTION OF THE TEST.

ANSWER KEY AND EXPLANATIONS

Verbal Ability

1. C	18. B	35. D	52. A	69. D
2. B	19. D	36. B	53. C	70. B
3. C	20. A	37. C	54. A	71. D
4. D	21. C	38. A	55. D	72. A
5. B	22. A	39. C	56. B	73. C
6. A	23. C	40. B	57. A	74. D
7. B	24. D	41. C	58. B	75. A
8. C	25. D	42. B	59. C	76. D
9. D	26. A	43. C	60. B	77. C
10. A	27. D	44. D	61. B	78. A
11. D	28. C	45. A	62. A	79. C
12. A	29. D	46. C	63. D	80. B
13. C	30. A	47. B	64. C	81. B
14. D	31. B	48. C	65. B	82. C
15. A	32. A	49. B	66. A	83. B
16. A	33. B	50. A	67. C	84. A
17. C	34. D	51. D	68. B	85. B

1. **The correct answer is (C).** *Flexible* means "adjustable" or "pliable."

2. **The correct answer is (B).** An *option* is a choice.

3. **The correct answer is (C).** To *verify* is to check the accuracy of or to confirm.

4. **The correct answer is (D).** *Indolent* means "idle" or "lazy."

5. **The correct answer is (B).** *Respiration* is breathing.

6. **The correct answer is (A).** A *brush* is a tool of the *painter's* trade, as a *wrench* is a tool of the *plumber's* trade.

7. **The correct answer is (B).** A *package* transports *merchandise* just as a *letter* transmits a *message*.

8. **The correct answer is (C).** *Sleep* alleviates *weariness* just as *food* alleviates *hunger*.

9. **The correct answer is (D).** *Reparation* is a compensation for *war*, just as *atonement* is a compensation for *sin*.

10. **The correct answer is (A).** *Whoever* is the subject of the phrase "whoever has the best record" and is used incorrectly in choice (D). Choices (B) and (C) are wordy and awkward.

11. **The correct answer is (D).** All the other choices contain obvious errors.

12. **The correct answer is (A).** The correct spelling is *collapsible*.

13. **The correct answer is (C).** The correct spelling is *ambiguous*.

14. **The correct answer is (D).** The correct spelling is *predecessor*.

15. **The correct answer is (A).** The correct spelling is *sanctioned*.

16. **The correct answer is (A).** The paragraph presents the problems of

fire in fire-resistant buildings. It suggests that the contents of the buildings may burn even though the structural materials themselves do not, and the ensuing fire may even cause the collapse of the buildings. The paragraph does not compare the problem of fire in fire-resistant buildings with that of fire in ordinary buildings, as stated in choice (C).

17. **The correct answer is (C).** The search for truth has speeded the progress of civilization. Choice (B) is incorrect in its statement that "civilization did not begin until . . ."; rather, civilization moved ahead slowly even before restrictions on learning were removed.

18. **The correct answer is (B).** *Vigilant* means "alert" or "watchful."

19. **The correct answer is (D).** *Incidental* means "likely to ensue as a chance or minor consequence" or "accompanying."

20. **The correct answer is (A).** *Conciliatory* means "tending to reconcile" or "to make peace."

21. **The correct answer is (C).** An *altercation* is a quarrel or a controversy.

22. **The correct answer is (A).** *Irresolute* means "indecisive" or "wavering."

23. **The correct answer is (C).** *Stillness* and *sound* are opposites, as are *darkness* and *sunlight*.

24. **The correct answer is (D).** That which is *accidental* happens by *chance* as that which is *designed* happens by *intention*.

25. **The correct answer is (C).** A *muffler* reduces *sound* as *practice* reduces *errors*.

26. **The correct answer is (A).** The desired result of *training* is the development of *skill* as the desired result of *research* is scientific *findings*.

27. **The correct answer is (D).** Choices (A) and (C) are incorrect in use of the subject form "I" instead of the object of the preposition "me." Choice (B) incorrectly uses the reflexive "myself." Only I can address a letter to myself.

28. **The correct answer is (C).** Choice (B) can't be right because the subject of the dependent clause is "she," but its antecedent is "supervisors." Choice (B) uses the incorrect construction "of known"; all you need is "known." Who is "they" in choice (D)? The pronoun has nothing to refer back to.

29. **The correct answer is (D).** The correct spelling is *miniature*.

30. **The correct answer is (A).** The correct spelling is *extemporaneous*.

31. **The correct answer is (B).** The correct spelling is *problematical*.

32. **The correct answer is (A).** The correct spelling of first choice is *descendant*. An alternate spelling, which is also correct, is *descendent*. A correct spelling is offered among the choices, so choice (A) is the best answer.

33. **The correct answer is (B).** In a word, we are preserving our natural resources through recycling.

34. **The correct answer is (D).** The main idea of the paragraph is that a three-part format is the most useful for developing a presentation. The other answers relate a specific idea in the paragraph, not the general idea.

35. **The correct answer is (D).** To *counteract* is to act directly against or to neutralize.

36. **The correct answer is (B).** *Deferred* means "postponed" or "delayed."

37. **The correct answer is (C).** *Feasible* means "possible" or "practicable."

38. **The correct answer is (A).** To *encounter* is to come upon or to meet.

39. **The correct answer is (C).** *Innate* means "existing naturally" or "native."

40. **The correct answer is (B).** The *disciple* learns from a *master* as a *student* learns from a *teacher*.

41. **The correct answer is (C).** In this analogy of place, an *experiment* occurs in a *laboratory* as a *lecture* occurs in an *auditorium*.

42. **The correct answer is (B).** *Fuel* powers the *engine* as *food* powers the *body*.

43. **The correct answer is (C).** *Recreation* occurs in the *theater* as *education* occurs in a *school*.

44. **The correct answer is (D).** Choice (A) might state either "most" or "all" but not both; choice (B) should read "persons who"; choice (C) should read "with regard to . . ."

45. **The correct answer is (A).** Choice (B) is incorrect because it requires the plural verb "were"; choice (C) requires the correlative construction "neither . . . nor"; choice (D) requires the subjective "they."

46. **The correct answer is (C).** The correct spelling is *extricate*.

47. **The correct answer is (B).** The correct spelling is *hereditary*.

48. **The correct answer is (C).** The correct spelling is *auspicious*.

49. **The correct answer is (B).** The correct spelling is *sequence*.

50. **The correct answer is (A).** If instruction in safety rules will help to prevent accidents, some accidents must occur because of lack of knowledge.

51. **The correct answer is (D).** Words from other languages have been absorbed into English.

52. **The correct answer is (A).** To *acquiesce* is to give in or to assent.

53. **The correct answer is (C).** *Unanimity* is complete agreement or harmony.

54. **The correct answer is (A).** A *precedent* is an example that sets a standard.

55. **The correct answer is (D).** *Versatile* means "adaptable" or "many-sided."

56. **The correct answer is (B).** *Authentic* means "genuine" or "reliable."

57. **The correct answer is (A).** The information and substance of a *novel* is *fiction*, while the information and substance of *biography* is *fact*.

58. **The correct answer is (B).** *HD* is a format for *television* as *3D* is a format for *movies*.

59. **The correct answer is (C).** *Carelessness* earns a *reprimand* as *efficiency* merits a *reward*.

60. **The correct answer is (B).** This analogy refers to the marketplace and the law of supply and demand. That which is *scarce* is likely to be *costly*, while that which is *abundant* will be *cheap*.

61. **The correct answer is (B).** In choice (A), the placement of the apostrophe is inappropriate; choices (C) and (D) use the plural, but there is only one company.

62. **The correct answer is (A).** Choice (C) is incorrect because it has *that* twice to introduce the same clause, and the clause is awkwardly stated. Choice (D) is incorrect because "kind of" is considered an error in Standard English. Choice (B) is wordy but not incorrect. A better version is "The job analyst's report notes that some employees type with great speed." Choice (A) is the best choice.

63. **The correct answer is (D).** The correct spelling is *obliterate*.

64. **The correct answer is (C).** The correct spelling is *diagnosis*.

65. The correct answer is (B). The correct spelling is *countenance*.

66. The correct answer is (A). The correct spelling is *conceivably*.

67. The correct answer is (C). Since manufacturers are assuming risks in attempting to predict what consumers will want, their success depends on the ultimate purchases made by the consumers.

68. The correct answer is (B). Humans migrate to various climates and adjust the food supply in each climate. The means by which they supply their needs are varied.

69. The correct answer is (D). *Strident* means "grating" or "harsh-sounding."

70. The correct answer is (B). To *confine* is to limit or to restrict.

71. The correct answer is (D). To *accentuate* is to stress, emphasize, or intensify.

72. The correct answer is (A). *Banal* means "insipid" or "commonplace."

73. The correct answer is (C). One who is *incorrigible* cannot be changed or corrected; the person is irreformable.

74. The correct answer is (D). A *doctor* promotes *health* as a *police officer* promotes *order*.

75. The correct answer is (A). An *artist* creates with *paints* as a *sculptor* creates with *stone*.

76. The correct answer is (D). Many *ships* make up the *fleet* as many *persons* make up a *crowd*.

77. The correct answer is (C). A *calendar* visually represents *dates* as a *map* visually represents *locations*.

78. The correct answer is (A). *Information* is a singular noun so its verb must be singular *(was)*, making choice (B) incorrect. Choice (C) is incorrect because *useful* is an adverb, and any word modifying an adverb must be an adverb itself. *Real* is an adjective form; the adverb form is *really*, so this answer can't be correct. The clause *Being that the report lacked the needed information* has no place in the sentence. It doesn't modify *they*, the subject of the sentence. It's just dangling at the beginning of the sentence, so choice (D) is incorrect.

79. The correct answer is (C). Choices (A) and (B) use adverbs incorrectly; choice (D) is awkward and not part of everyday speech.

80. The correct answer is (B). The correct spelling is *competition*.

81. The correct answer is (B). The correct spelling is *occasion*.

82. The correct answer is (C). The correct spelling is *knowledge*.

83. The correct answer is (B). The correct spelling is *deliberate*.

84. The correct answer is (A). Time and effort cannot be equated. Efficiency must be measured in terms of results.

85. The correct answer is (B). The first sentence of the paragraph makes this statement.

Clerical Ability

1. B	25. C	49. B	73. B	97. C
2. E	26. D	50. C	74. C	98. E
3. D	27. D	51. B	75. A	99. B
4. A	28. C	52. C	76. D	100. B
5. E	29. C	53. D	77. D	101. D
6. E	30. D	54. D	78. A	102. B
7. A	31. E	55. E	79. E	103. C
8. D	32. A	56. E	80. C	104. A
9. B	33. A	57. B	81. D	105. E
10. E	34. C	58. E	82. C	106. D
11. D	35. C	59. D	83. D	107. B
12. B	36. E	60. C	84. D	108. A
13. B	37. A	61. C	85. B	109. C
14. B	38. C	62. B	86. A	110. D
15. B	39. C	63. E	87. E	111. A
16. A	40. D	64. D	88. C	112. C
17. D	41. A	65. C	89. C	113. C
18. E	42. D	66. A	90. B	114. B
19. B	43. B	67. D	91. E	115. D
20. A	44. E	68. C	92. E	116. A
21. A	45. A	69. D	93. C	117. B
22. E	46. C	70. E	94. C	118. B
23. E	47. A	71. A	95. A	119. A
24. D	48. D	72. C	96. D	120. E

1. **The correct answer is (B).** The third number is different.

2. **The correct answer is (E).** All three numbers are different.

3. **The correct answer is (D).** The first name is different.

4. **The correct answer is (A).** All three names are exactly alike.

5. **The correct answer is (E).** All three names are different.

6. **The correct answer is (E).** Hachettson; Hackett

7. **The correct answer is (A).** Margenroth; Margeroth

8. **The correct answer is (D).** Bobbitt, Olivia H.; Bobbitt, Olivier E.; Bobbitt, R. Olivia

9. **The correct answer is (B).** Mosely, Albert J.; Mosely, Werner; Mosley, Alvin.

10. **The correct answer is (E).** Youmons; Youmuns

11. **The correct answer is (D).** 75

12. **The correct answer is (B).** 79

13. **The correct answer is (B).** 287

14. **The correct answer is (B).** 51

15. **The correct answer is (B).** 52

16. **The correct answer is (A).** 6 2 5 K 4 P T G

17. **The correct answer is (D).** L 4 7 2 T 6 V K

18. **The correct answer is (E).** The answer cannot be (A) or (B) because there is no **K;** it cannot be (C) or (D) because there is no **2.**

19. **The correct answer is (B).** G 4 K 7 L 3 5 Z

20. **The correct answer is (A).** 4 K 2 9 N 5 T G

21. **The correct answer is (A).** All three numbers are exactly alike.

22. **The correct answer is (E).** All three numbers are different.

23. **The correct answer is (E).** All three names are different.

24. **The correct answer is (D).** The first name is different.

25. **The correct answer is (C).** The second name is different.

26. **The correct answer is (D).** Watson; Watters; Wattwood

27. **The correct answer is (D).** Johnston, Edmund; Johnston, Edward; Johnstone, Edmund A.

28. **The correct answer is (C).** Remschel; Rensch; Renshaw

29. **The correct answer is (C).** Schneider, Mertens; Schnyder, Maurice; Schnyder, Newman

30. **The correct answer is (D).** Freedenberg; Freedenburg; Freedinberg

31. **The correct answer is (E).** 21

32. **The correct answer is (A).** 400

33. **The correct answer is (A).** 20

34. **The correct answer is (C).** 141

35. **The correct answer is (C).** 19

36. **The correct answer is (E).** The answer cannot be (A) because there is no **V;** it cannot be (B) or (C) because

there is no **5;** it cannot be (D) because there is no **8** or **V.**

37. **The correct answer is (A).** L 5 N K 4 3 9 V

38. **The correct answer is (C).** 8 2 V P 9 L Z 5

39. **The correct answer is (C).** V P 9 Z 5 L 8 7

40. **The correct answer is (D).** 5 T 8 N 2 9 V L

41. **The correct answer is (A).** All three numbers are exactly alike.

42. **The correct answer is (D).** The first number is different.

43. **The correct answer is (B).** The third number is different.

44. **The correct answer is (E).** All three names are different.

45. **The correct answer is (A).** All three names are exactly alike.

46. **The correct answer is (C).** DeMatteo; DeMattia; Derby

47. **The correct answer is (A).** Theriault; Therien

48. **The correct answer is (D).** Gaston, Isabel; Gaston, M. Hubert; Gaston, M. Melvin

49. **The correct answer is (B).** SanLuis; SanMiguel; Santilli

50. **The correct answer is (C).** DeLathouder; DeLaTour; Lathrop

51. **The correct answer is (B).** 310

52. **The correct answer is (C).** 51

53. **The correct answer is (D).** 68

54. **The correct answer is (D).** 45

55. **The correct answer is (E).** 111

56. **The correct answer is (E).** The answer cannot be (A) or (B) because there is no **8;** it cannot be (C) or (D) because there is no **9.**

57. **The correct answer is (B).** 8 5 3 V L 2 Z N

58. **The correct answer is (E).** The answer cannot be (A) or (B) because there is no **8**; it cannot be (C) or (D) because there is no **Z**.

59. **The correct answer is (D).** 9 8 L 2 5 **Z K** V

60. **The correct answer is (C).** **Z** 6 5 V 9 3 **P N**

61. **The correct answer is (C).** The second number is different.

62. **The correct answer is (B).** The third number is different.

63. **The correct answer is (E).** All three names are different.

64. **The correct answer is (D).** The first name is different.

65. **The correct answer is (C).** The second name is different.

66. **The correct answer is (A).** O'Bannon; O'Beirne

67. **The correct answer is (D).** Entsminger, Jack; Entsminger, Jacob; Entsminger, James

68. **The correct answer is (C).** Iacone, Pedro M.; Iacone, Pete R.; Iacone, Peter F.

69. **The correct answer is (D).** Shephard; Sheppard; Shepperd

70. **The correct answer is (E).** Thackston; Thackton

71. **The correct answer is (A).** 51

72. **The correct answer is (C).** 85

73. **The correct answer is (B).** 29

74. **The correct answer is (C).** 272

75. **The correct answer is (A).** 71

76. **The correct answer is (D).** 6 **Z** T **N** 8 7 4 V

77. **The correct answer is (D).** V 7 8 6 **N** 5 **P L**

78. **The correct answer is (A).** **N** 7 P V 8 4 2 **L**

79. **The correct answer is (E).** The answer cannot be choice (A) or (B) because there is no **2**; it cannot be choice (C) or (D) because there is no **6**.

80. **The correct answer is (C).** 4 8 G 2 **T N** 6 **L**

81. **The correct answer is (D).** The first number is different.

82. **The correct answer is (C).** The second number is different.

83. **The correct answer is (D).** All three names are exactly alike.

84. **The correct answer is (D).** The first name is different.

85. **The correct answer is (B).** The third name is different.

86. **The correct answer is (A).** Dunlavey; Dunleavy

87. **The correct answer is (E).** Yarborough; Yarbrough

88. **The correct answer is (C).** Proutey, Maude; Prouty, Martha; Prouty, Myra

89. **The correct answer is (C).** Pawalek; Pawlowicz; Pawlowski

90. **The correct answer is (B).** Vanover; Vanstory; VanSwinderen

91. **The correct answer is (E).** 63

92. **The correct answer is (E).** 9

93. **The correct answer is (C).** 516

94. **The correct answer is (C).** 81

95. **The correct answer is (A).** 131

96. **The correct answer is (D).** V 5 7 **Z** **N** 9 4 **T**

97. **The correct answer is (C).** 4 6 **P T** 2 **N K** 9

98. **The correct answer is (E).** The answer cannot be choice (A) or (B) because there is no **5**; it cannot be choice (C) or (D) because there is no **9**.

99. **The correct answer is (B).** 7 **P** 5 2 4 **N K T**

100. The correct answer is (B). K T 8 5 4 N 2 P

101. The correct answer is (D). The first number is different.

102. The correct answer is (B). The third number is different.

103. The correct answer is (C). The second number is different.

104. The correct answer is (A). All three names are exactly alike.

105. The correct answer is (E). All three names are different.

106. The correct answer is (D). FitzGibbon; Fitzsimmons; FitzSimons

107. The correct answer is (B). Daly; D'Amato; D'Amboise

108. The correct answer is (A). Schaeffer; Schaffert

109. The correct answer is (C). White-Leigh; White-Lewis; Whitely

110. The correct answer is (D). VanDercook; VanDerHeggen; VanderLinden

111. The correct answer is (A). 124

112. The correct answer is (C). 24

113. The correct answer is (C). 288

114. The correct answer is (B). 41

115. The correct answer is (D). 522

116. The correct answer is (A). Z 3 N P G 5 4 2

117. The correct answer is (B). 6 N 2 8 G 4 P T

118. The correct answer is (B). 6 N 4 T V G 8 2

119. The correct answer is (A). T 3 P 4 N 8 G 2

120. The correct answer is (E). The answer cannot be choice (A) or (C) because there is no **3**; it cannot be choice (B) or (D) because there is no **T**.

SELF-EVALUATION

On your answer sheet, mark the numbers of the questions that you answered incorrectly and check them against the following charts. If you missed several of any question type, you need more practice with that kind of question. Return to the appropriate chapter and review the rules and practice exercises before moving on to the next sample exam.

SELF-EVALUATION CHART: VERBAL ABILITY TEST

Question Type	Question Numbers	Chapter to Review
Grammar and Usage	10–11; 27–28; 44–45; 61–62; 78–79	4
Spelling	12–15; 29–32; 46–49; 63–66; 80–83	5
Synonyms	1–5; 18–22; 35–39; 52–56; 69–73	6
Verbal Analogies	6–9; 23–26; 40–43; 57–60; 74–77	8
Reading Comprehension	16–17; 33–34; 50–51; 67–68; 84–85	10

SELF-EVALUATION CHART: CLERICAL ABILITY TEST

Question Type	Question Numbers	Chapter to Review
Alphabetizing and Filing	6–10; 26–30; 46–50; 66–70; 86–90; 106–110	13
Speed and Accuracy	1–5; 16–25; 36–45; 56–65; 76–85; 96–105; 116–120	14
Simple Arithmetic	11–15; 31–35; 51–55; 71–75; 91–95; 111–115	(Be careful of careless mistakes.)

ANSWER SHEET PRACTICE TEST 3

Clerical Ability

1. Ⓐ Ⓑ Ⓒ Ⓓ Ⓔ   23. Ⓐ Ⓑ Ⓒ Ⓓ Ⓔ   44. Ⓐ Ⓑ Ⓒ Ⓓ Ⓔ   65. Ⓐ Ⓑ Ⓒ Ⓓ Ⓔ

2. Ⓐ Ⓑ Ⓒ Ⓓ Ⓔ   24. Ⓐ Ⓑ Ⓒ Ⓓ Ⓔ   45. Ⓐ Ⓑ Ⓒ Ⓓ Ⓔ   66. Ⓐ Ⓑ Ⓒ Ⓓ Ⓔ

3. Ⓐ Ⓑ Ⓒ Ⓓ Ⓔ   25. Ⓐ Ⓑ Ⓒ Ⓓ Ⓔ   46. Ⓐ Ⓑ Ⓒ Ⓓ Ⓔ   67. Ⓐ Ⓑ Ⓒ Ⓓ Ⓔ

4. Ⓐ Ⓑ Ⓒ Ⓓ Ⓔ   26. Ⓐ Ⓑ Ⓒ Ⓓ Ⓔ   47. Ⓐ Ⓑ Ⓒ Ⓓ Ⓔ   68. Ⓐ Ⓑ Ⓒ Ⓓ Ⓔ

5. Ⓐ Ⓑ Ⓒ Ⓓ Ⓔ   27. Ⓐ Ⓑ Ⓒ Ⓓ Ⓔ   48. Ⓐ Ⓑ Ⓒ Ⓓ Ⓔ   69. Ⓐ Ⓑ Ⓒ Ⓓ Ⓔ

6. Ⓐ Ⓑ Ⓒ Ⓓ Ⓔ   28. Ⓐ Ⓑ Ⓒ Ⓓ Ⓔ   49. Ⓐ Ⓑ Ⓒ Ⓓ Ⓔ   70. Ⓐ Ⓑ Ⓒ Ⓓ Ⓔ

7. Ⓐ Ⓑ Ⓒ Ⓓ Ⓔ   29. Ⓐ Ⓑ Ⓒ Ⓓ Ⓔ   50. Ⓐ Ⓑ Ⓒ Ⓓ Ⓔ   71. Ⓐ Ⓑ Ⓒ Ⓓ Ⓔ

8. Ⓐ Ⓑ Ⓒ Ⓓ Ⓔ   30. Ⓐ Ⓑ Ⓒ Ⓓ Ⓔ   51. Ⓐ Ⓑ Ⓒ Ⓓ Ⓔ   72. Ⓐ Ⓑ Ⓒ Ⓓ Ⓔ

9. Ⓐ Ⓑ Ⓒ Ⓓ Ⓔ   31. Ⓐ Ⓑ Ⓒ Ⓓ Ⓔ   52. Ⓐ Ⓑ Ⓒ Ⓓ Ⓔ   73. Ⓐ Ⓑ Ⓒ Ⓓ Ⓔ

10. Ⓐ Ⓑ Ⓒ Ⓓ Ⓔ   32. Ⓐ Ⓑ Ⓒ Ⓓ Ⓔ   53. Ⓐ Ⓑ Ⓒ Ⓓ Ⓔ   74. Ⓐ Ⓑ Ⓒ Ⓓ Ⓔ

11. Ⓐ Ⓑ Ⓒ Ⓓ Ⓔ   33. Ⓐ Ⓑ Ⓒ Ⓓ Ⓔ   54. Ⓐ Ⓑ Ⓒ Ⓓ Ⓔ   75. Ⓐ Ⓑ Ⓒ Ⓓ Ⓔ

12. Ⓐ Ⓑ Ⓒ Ⓓ Ⓔ   34. Ⓐ Ⓑ Ⓒ Ⓓ Ⓔ   55. Ⓐ Ⓑ Ⓒ Ⓓ Ⓔ   76. Ⓐ Ⓑ Ⓒ Ⓓ Ⓔ

13. Ⓐ Ⓑ Ⓒ Ⓓ Ⓔ   35. Ⓐ Ⓑ Ⓒ Ⓓ Ⓔ   56. Ⓐ Ⓑ Ⓒ Ⓓ Ⓔ   77. Ⓐ Ⓑ Ⓒ Ⓓ Ⓔ

14. Ⓐ Ⓑ Ⓒ Ⓓ Ⓔ   36. Ⓐ Ⓑ Ⓒ Ⓓ Ⓔ   57. Ⓐ Ⓑ Ⓒ Ⓓ Ⓔ   78. Ⓐ Ⓑ Ⓒ Ⓓ Ⓔ

15. Ⓐ Ⓑ Ⓒ Ⓓ Ⓔ   37. Ⓐ Ⓑ Ⓒ Ⓓ Ⓔ   58. Ⓐ Ⓑ Ⓒ Ⓓ Ⓔ   79. Ⓐ Ⓑ Ⓒ Ⓓ Ⓔ

16. Ⓐ Ⓑ Ⓒ Ⓓ Ⓔ   38. Ⓐ Ⓑ Ⓒ Ⓓ Ⓔ   59. Ⓐ Ⓑ Ⓒ Ⓓ Ⓔ   80. Ⓐ Ⓑ Ⓒ Ⓓ Ⓔ

17. Ⓐ Ⓑ Ⓒ Ⓓ Ⓔ   39. Ⓐ Ⓑ Ⓒ Ⓓ Ⓔ   60. Ⓐ Ⓑ Ⓒ Ⓓ Ⓔ   81. Ⓐ Ⓑ Ⓒ Ⓓ Ⓔ

18. Ⓐ Ⓑ Ⓒ Ⓓ Ⓔ   40. Ⓐ Ⓑ Ⓒ Ⓓ Ⓔ   61. Ⓐ Ⓑ Ⓒ Ⓓ Ⓕ   82. Ⓐ Ⓑ Ⓒ Ⓓ Ⓕ

19. Ⓐ Ⓑ Ⓒ Ⓓ Ⓔ   41. Ⓐ Ⓑ Ⓒ Ⓓ Ⓔ   62. Ⓐ Ⓑ Ⓒ Ⓓ Ⓔ   83. Ⓐ Ⓑ Ⓒ Ⓓ Ⓔ

20. Ⓐ Ⓑ Ⓒ Ⓓ Ⓔ   42. Ⓐ Ⓑ Ⓒ Ⓓ Ⓔ   63. Ⓐ Ⓑ Ⓒ Ⓓ Ⓔ   84. Ⓐ Ⓑ Ⓒ Ⓓ Ⓔ

21. Ⓐ Ⓑ Ⓒ Ⓓ Ⓔ   43. Ⓐ Ⓑ Ⓒ Ⓓ Ⓔ   64. Ⓐ Ⓑ Ⓒ Ⓓ Ⓔ   85. Ⓐ Ⓑ Ⓒ Ⓓ Ⓔ

22. Ⓐ Ⓑ Ⓒ Ⓓ Ⓔ

answer sheet

Verbal Ability

1. Ⓐ Ⓑ Ⓒ Ⓓ Ⓔ   15. Ⓐ Ⓑ Ⓒ Ⓓ Ⓔ   29. Ⓐ Ⓑ Ⓒ Ⓓ Ⓔ   43. Ⓐ Ⓑ Ⓒ Ⓓ Ⓔ

2. Ⓐ Ⓑ Ⓒ Ⓓ Ⓔ   16. Ⓐ Ⓑ Ⓒ Ⓓ Ⓔ   30. Ⓐ Ⓑ Ⓒ Ⓓ Ⓔ   44. Ⓐ Ⓑ Ⓒ Ⓓ Ⓔ

3. Ⓐ Ⓑ Ⓒ Ⓓ Ⓔ   17. Ⓐ Ⓑ Ⓒ Ⓓ Ⓔ   31. Ⓐ Ⓑ Ⓒ Ⓓ Ⓔ   45. Ⓐ Ⓑ Ⓒ Ⓓ Ⓔ

4. Ⓐ Ⓑ Ⓒ Ⓓ Ⓔ   18. Ⓐ Ⓑ Ⓒ Ⓓ Ⓔ   32. Ⓐ Ⓑ Ⓒ Ⓓ Ⓔ   46. Ⓐ Ⓑ Ⓒ Ⓓ Ⓔ

5. Ⓐ Ⓑ Ⓒ Ⓓ Ⓔ   19. Ⓐ Ⓑ Ⓒ Ⓓ Ⓔ   33. Ⓐ Ⓑ Ⓒ Ⓓ Ⓔ   47. Ⓐ Ⓑ Ⓒ Ⓓ Ⓔ

6. Ⓐ Ⓑ Ⓒ Ⓓ Ⓔ   20. Ⓐ Ⓑ Ⓒ Ⓓ Ⓔ   34. Ⓐ Ⓑ Ⓒ Ⓓ Ⓔ   48. Ⓐ Ⓑ Ⓒ Ⓓ Ⓔ

7. Ⓐ Ⓑ Ⓒ Ⓓ Ⓔ   21. Ⓐ Ⓑ Ⓒ Ⓓ Ⓔ   35. Ⓐ Ⓑ Ⓒ Ⓓ Ⓔ   49. Ⓐ Ⓑ Ⓒ Ⓓ Ⓔ

8. Ⓐ Ⓑ Ⓒ Ⓓ Ⓔ   22. Ⓐ Ⓑ Ⓒ Ⓓ Ⓔ   36. Ⓐ Ⓑ Ⓒ Ⓓ Ⓔ   50. Ⓐ Ⓑ Ⓒ Ⓓ Ⓔ

9. Ⓐ Ⓑ Ⓒ Ⓓ Ⓔ   23. Ⓐ Ⓑ Ⓒ Ⓓ Ⓔ   37. Ⓐ Ⓑ Ⓒ Ⓓ Ⓔ   51. Ⓐ Ⓑ Ⓒ Ⓓ Ⓔ

10. Ⓐ Ⓑ Ⓒ Ⓓ Ⓔ   24. Ⓐ Ⓑ Ⓒ Ⓓ Ⓔ   38. Ⓐ Ⓑ Ⓒ Ⓓ Ⓔ   52. Ⓐ Ⓑ Ⓒ Ⓓ Ⓔ

11. Ⓐ Ⓑ Ⓒ Ⓓ Ⓔ   25. Ⓐ Ⓑ Ⓒ Ⓓ Ⓔ   39. Ⓐ Ⓑ Ⓒ Ⓓ Ⓔ   53. Ⓐ Ⓑ Ⓒ Ⓓ Ⓔ

12. Ⓐ Ⓑ Ⓒ Ⓓ Ⓔ   26. Ⓐ Ⓑ Ⓒ Ⓓ Ⓔ   40. Ⓐ Ⓑ Ⓒ Ⓓ Ⓔ   54. Ⓐ Ⓑ Ⓒ Ⓓ Ⓔ

13. Ⓐ Ⓑ Ⓒ Ⓓ Ⓔ   27. Ⓐ Ⓑ Ⓒ Ⓓ Ⓔ   41. Ⓐ Ⓑ Ⓒ Ⓓ Ⓔ   55. Ⓐ Ⓑ Ⓒ Ⓓ Ⓔ

14. Ⓐ Ⓑ Ⓒ Ⓓ Ⓔ   28. Ⓐ Ⓑ Ⓒ Ⓓ Ⓔ   42. Ⓐ Ⓑ Ⓒ Ⓓ Ⓔ

Practice Test 3

CLERICAL ABILITY

85 Questions • 19 Minutes

There are four types of questions in this part of the exam. Each question type has its own set of directions, and each portion is timed separately.

Sequencing
20 Questions • 3 Minutes

Directions: For each question, you are given a name, number, or code, followed by four other names or codes in alphabetical or numerical order. Find the correct space for the given name or number so that it will be in alphabetical and/or numerical order with the others.

1. Mathison, J. John
   (A) –
      Mathers, Doris
   (B) –
      Matherson, Judy
   (C) –
      Mathews, J. R.
   (D) –
      Mathewson, Jerome
   (E) –

2. 59233362
   (A) –
      58146020
   (B) –
      59233162
   (C) –
      59233262
   (D) –
      5923662
   (E) –

3. MYP-6734
   (A) –
      NYP-6733
   (B) –
      NYS-7412
   (C) –
      NZT-4899
   (D) –
      PYZ-3636
   (E) –

4. Morin, Jose
   (A) –
      Morin, J. B.
   (B) –
      Morin, J. James
   (C) –
      Morin, James J.
   (D) –
      Morin, Joseph F.
   (E) –

NOTE

The directions are stated as if you are taking the exam in a paper-and-pencil format. If you will be taking the exam on computer, each section will have directions specific to how to answer questions on computer.

5. 00102032

(A) –
    00120312

(B) –
    00120323

(C) –
    00120324

(D) –
    00200303

(E) –

6. LPD-6100

(A) –
    LPD-5865

(B) –
    LPD-6001

(C) –
    LPD-6101

(D) –
    LPD-6106

(E) –

7. Vonbrunner, Carl

(A) –
    Von Alton, Karl

(B) –
    Vonderson, Michael

(C) –
    Von Lolhoffel, Darlene

(D) –
    Vonlolhoffel, M. E.

(E) –

8. Sanchez, R. R.

(A) –
    Sanchez, Alvira

(B) –
    Sanchez, Juanita

(C) –
    Sanchez, R. Juanita

(D) –
    Sanchez, S. Robert

(E) –

9. 01066010

(A) –
    01006040

(B) –
    01006051

(C) –
    01016053

(D) –
    01016060

(E) –

10. AAZ-2687

(A) –
    AAA-2132

(B) –
    AAS-4623

(C) –
    ASA-3216

(D) –
    ASZ-5490

(E) –

11. Kowalski, Raymond M.
    (A) –
    Kawalski, Raymond M.
    (B) –
    Kawalski, Robert
    (C) –
    Kowalsky, Robert S.
    (D) –
    Kowolsky, S.T., Jr.
    (E) –

12. NCD-7834
    (A) –
    NBJ-4682
    (B) –
    NBT-5066
    (C) –
    NCD-7710
    (D) –
    NCD-7868
    (E) –

13. 36270013
    (A) –
    36260006
    (B) –
    36270000
    (C) –
    36270030
    (D) –
    36670012
    (E) –

14. Ketchener, Glen
    (A) –
    Ketchner, Alan
    (B) –
    Ketchum, George
    (C) –
    Kichner, A. George
    (D) –
    Kitchiner, Samuel
    (E) –

15. Figuaro, Estevanico
    (A) –
    Figaro, Fernando
    (B) –
    Figaro, Francis
    (C) –
    Figuaro, Francisco
    (D) –
    Figurao, Geraldo
    (E) –

16. 58006021
    (A) –
    58006130
    (B) –
    58097222
    (C) –
    59000599
    (D) –
    59909000
    (E) –

17. EKK-1443

(A) –

EGK-1164

(B) –

EKG-1329

(C) –

EKK-1331

(D) –

EKK-1403

(E) –

18. D'Arcy, Fabrice

(A) –

D'Arcy, F.W.

(B) –

Darren, Jordan

(C) –

Defoe, Christopher

(D) –

Defoe, Wallace

(E) –

19. Schuster, Robert

(A) –

Shugusta, H. Thomas

(B) –

Shugusta, Ilsa

(C) –

Shuster, Alma

(D) –

Shuster, P. A.

(E) –

20. SPP-4856

(A) –

PPS-4838

(B) –

PSP-4921

(C) –

SPS-4906

(D) –

SSP-4911

(E) –

Comparisons

30 Questions • 5 Minutes

Directions: In each line across the page are three names, addresses, or codes that are very much alike. Compare the three and choose the answer:

(A) if ALL THREE names, addresses, or codes are exactly ALIKE.
(B) if only the FIRST and SECOND names, addresses, or codes are exactly ALIKE.
(C) if only the FIRST and THIRD names, addresses, or codes are exactly ALIKE.
(D) if only the SECOND and THIRD names, addresses, or codes are exactly ALIKE.
(E) if ALL THREE names, addresses, or codes are DIFFERENT.

21.	Rickard E. VonHofstadter	Rickard E. VonHofstadter	Rickard E. VonHofstadter
22.	Sergei Kuznets	Serge Kusnetz	Sergei Kuznetts
23.	6-78912-e3e42	6-78912-3e3e42	6-78912-e3e42
24.	86529 Dunwoodie Drive	86529 Dunwoodie Drive	85629 Dunwoodie Drive
25.	9566110	9565101	9565101
26.	Becca Katherine Hines	Becca Catherine Hanes	Becca Catharine Hane
27.	5416R-1952TZ-op	5416R-1952TZ-op	5416R-1952TZ-op
28.	60646 West Touhy Ave.	60646 West Touhy Ave.	60646 West Touhey Ave.
29.	Mardikian & Moore, Inc.	Mardikian and Moore, Inc.	Mardikian & Moore, Inc.
30.	9670243	9670423	9670423
31.	Eduardo Ingles	Eduardo Inglese	Eduardo Inglese
32.	Roger T. DeAngelis	Roger T. D'Angelis	Roger T. DeAngelcs
33.	7692138	7692138	7692138
34.	2695 East 3435 South	2695 East 3435 South	2695 East 3435 South
35.	63qs5-95YT3-001	63qs5-95YT3-001	62qs5-95YT3-001
36.	2789350	2789350	2798350
37.	Helmut V. Lochner	Helmut V. Lockner	Helmut W. Lochner
38.	2454803	2548403	2454803
39.	Lemberger, WA 28094	Lemberger, VA 28094	Lemberger, VA 28094
40.	4168-GNP-78852	4168-GNP-78852	4168-GNP-78852

41. Yoshihito Saito	Yoshihito Saito	Yoshihito Saito
42. 5927681	5927861	5927681
43. O'Reilly Bay, LA 56212	O'Reillys Bay, LA 56212	O'Reilly Bay, LA 56212
44. Myra Simpson	Myra Sampson	Myra Simpson
45. 5634-OotV5a-16867	5634-Ootv5a-16867	5634-Ootv5a-16867
46. Dolores Mollicone	Dolores Mollicone	Doloras Mollicone
47. David C. Routzon	David E. Routzon	David C. Routzron
48. 8932 Shimabui Hwy.	8932 Shimabui Hwy.	8932 Shimabui Hwy.
49. 3479103	3497130	3479103
50. A8987-B73245	A8987-B73245	A8987-B73245

Spelling
20 Questions • 3 Minutes

Directions: Find the correct spelling of the word and darken the appropriate space on the answer sheet. If none of the spellings is correct, select choice (D).

51. **(A)** anticipate
    (B) antisipate
    (C) anticapate
    (D) None of the above

52. **(A)** similiar
    (B) simmilar
    (C) similar
    (D) None of the above

53. **(A)** sufficiantly
    (B) suficeintly
    (C) sufficiently
    (D) None of the above

54. **(A)** intelligence
    (B) inteligence
    (C) intellegence
    (D) None of the above

55. **(A)** referance
    (B) referrence
    (C) referense
    (D) None of the above

56. **(A)** conscious
    (B) consious
    (C) conscius
    (D) None of the above

57. **(A)** paralell
    (B) parellel
    (C) parellell
    (D) None of the above

58. **(A)** abundence
    (B) abundance
    (C) abundants
    (D) None of the above

59. **(A)** corregated
    (B) corrigated
    (C) corrugated
    (D) None of the above

60. **(A)** accumalation
    (B) accumulation
    (C) accumullation
    (D) None of the above

61. **(A)** resonance
    (B) resonence
    (C) resonnance
    (D) None of the above

62. **(A)** benaficial
    (B) benefitial
    (C) beneficial
    (D) None of the above

63. **(A)** spesifically
    (B) specificially
    (C) specifically
    (D) None of the above

64. **(A)** elemanate
    (B) elimenate
    (C) elliminate
    (D) None of the above

65. **(A)** collosal
    (B) colosal
    (C) collossal
    (D) None of the above

66. **(A)** auxillary
    (B) auxilliary
    (C) auxiliary
    (D) None of the above

67. **(A)** inimitable
    (B) inimitible
    (C) inimatable
    (D) None of the above

68. **(A)** disapearance
    (B) dissapearance
    (C) disappearence
    (D) None of the above

69. **(A)** coaltion
    (B) coalition
    (C) co-alition
    (D) None of the above

70. **(A)** esential
    (B) essential
    (C) essencial
    (D) None of the above

Computations
15 Questions • 8 Minutes

Directions: Perform the computation as indicated in the question, and find the answer among the list of alternative responses. If the correct answer is not given among the choices, choose choice (E).

71.   83
   − 56

(A) 23
(B) 29
(C) 33
(D) 37
(E) None of the above

72.   15
   + 17

(A) 22
(B) 32
(C) 39
(D) 42
(E) None of the above

73.   32
   × 7

(A) 224
(B) 234
(C) 324
(D) 334
(E) None of the above

74.   39
   × 2

(A) 77
(B) 78
(C) 79
(D) 81
(E) None of the above

75.   43
   − 15

(A) 23
(B) 32
(C) 33
(D) 35
(E) None of the above

76.   50
   + 49

(A) 89
(B) 90
(C) 99
(D) 109
(E) None of the above

77. 6)366

(A) 11
(B) 31
(C) 36
(D) 66
(E) None of the above

78.   38
   × 3

(A) 111
(B) 113
(C) 115
(D) 117
(E) None of the above

STOP

79.   19
     + 21

(A) 20
(B) 30
(C) 40
(D) 50
(E) None of the above

80.   13
     − 6

(A) 5
(B) 7
(C) 9
(D) 11
(E) None of the above

81. 6)180

(A) 29
(B) 31
(C) 33
(D) 39
(E) None of the above

82.   10
     × 1

(A) 0
(B) 1
(C) 10
(D) 100
(E) None of the above

83. 7)287

(A) 21
(B) 27
(C) 31
(D) 37
(E) None of the above

84.   12
     + 11

(A) 21
(B) 22
(C) 23
(D) 24
(E) None of the above

85.   85
     − 64

(A) 19
(B) 21
(C) 29
(D) 31
(E) None of the above

STOP

END OF SECTION. IF YOU HAVE ANY TIME LEFT, GO
OVER YOUR WORK IN THIS SECTION ONLY. DO NOT
WORK IN ANY OTHER SECTION OF THE TEST.

VERBAL ABILITY

55 Questions • 50 Minutes

There are four kinds of questions in this part of the exam. Each kind of question has its own set of directions, but the portions containing the different kinds of questions are not separately timed.

Directions: Questions 1–20 test your ability to follow instructions. Each question directs you to mark a specific number and letter combination on your answer sheet. The questions require your total concentration because the answers that you are instructed to mark are, for the most part, NOT in numerical sequence (i.e., you would not use Number 1 on your answer sheet to answer Question 1; Number 2 for Question 2; etc.). Instead, you must mark the number and space specifically designated in each test question.

1. Look at the letters below. Draw a circle around the letter that comes first in the alphabet. Now, on your answer sheet, find Number 12 and darken the space for the letter you just circled.

    E   G   D   Z   B   F

2. Draw a line under the odd number below that is more than 5 but less than 10. Find this number on your answer sheet and darken space (E).

    8   10   5   6   11   9

3. Divide the number 16 by 4 and write your answer on the line below. Now find this number on your answer sheet and darken space (A).

    _____

4. Write the letter C on the line next to the left-hand number below. Now, on your answer sheet, darken the space for the number–letter combination you see.

    5 _____   19 _____   7 _____

5. If in any week Wednesday comes before Tuesday, write the number 15 on the line below. If not, write the number 18. Now, on your answer sheet, darken the letter (A) for the number you just wrote.

    _____

6. Count the number of Bs in the line below and write that number at the end of the line. Now, on your answer sheet, darken the letter (D) for the number you wrote.

    A D A E B D C A _____

7. Write the letter B on the line with the highest number. Now, on your answer sheet, darken the number–letter combination that appears on that line.

    16 _____   9 _____   20 _____   11 _____

8. If the product of 6 • 4 is greater than the product of 8 • 3, write the letter E on the line below. If not, write the letter C. Now, on your answer sheet, find number 8 and darken the space for the letter you just wrote.

_____

9. Write the number 2 in the larger circle below. Now, on your answer sheet, darken the space for the number–letter combination in that circle.

10. Write the letter D on the line next to the number that is the sum of 7 + 4 + 4. Now, on your answer sheet, darken the space for that number–letter combination.

13 _____   14 _____   15 _____   16 _____   17 _____

11. If 5 • 5 equals 25, and 5 + 5 equals 10, write the number 17 on the line below. If not, write the number 10. Now, on your answer sheet, darken space (E) for the number you just wrote.

_____

12. Circle the second letter from the left below. On the line beside that letter, write the number that represents the number of days in a week. Now, on your answer sheet, darken the space for that number–letter combination.

_____ C   _____ D   _____ B   _____ E

13. If a triangle has more angles than a rectangle, write the number 13 in the circle below. If not, write the number 14 in the square. Now, on your answer sheet, darken the space for the number–letter combination in the figure that you just wrote in.

_A   _C   _E

14. Count the number of Bs below and write that number at the end of the line. Subtract 2 from that number. Now, on your answer sheet, darken space (E) for the number that represents 2 less than the number of Bs in the line.

B E A D E C C B B B A E B D _____

15. The numbers below represent morning pick-up times from neighborhood letter-boxes. Draw a line under the number that represents the latest pick-up time. Now, on your answer sheet, darken space (D) for the number that is the same as the "minutes" of the time that you underlined.

9:19   10:16   10:10

16. If a person who is 6 feet tall is taller than a person who is 5 feet tall and if a pillow is softer than a rock, darken space 11(A) on your answer sheet. If not, darken space 6(B).

17. Write the fourth letter of the alphabet on the line next to the third number from the left below. Now, on your answer sheet, darken that number–letter combination.

10 ＿＿＿ 19 ＿＿＿ 13 ＿＿＿ 4 ＿＿＿

18. Write the letter B in the box containing the next-to-smallest number. On your answer sheet, darken the space for that number–letter combination.

| 10 ＿＿ | 19 ＿＿ | 11 ＿＿ | 6 ＿＿ |

19. Directly below, you will see three boxes and three words. Write the third letter of the first word on the line in the second box. Now, on your answer sheet, darken the space for that number-letter combination.

| 6 ＿＿ | 19 ＿＿ | 12 ＿＿ | BAD DRAB ALE

20. Count the number of points on the figure below. If there are five or more points, darken the space for 6(E) on your answer sheet. If there are fewer than five points, darken 6(A).

Directions: Each question from 21–40 consists of a sentence written in four different ways. Choose the sentence that is most appropriate with respect to grammar, usage, and punctuation to be suitable for a business letter or report.

21. **(A)** Double parking is when you park your car alongside one that is already having been parked.

 (B) When one double parks, you park your car alongside one that is already parked.

 (C) Double parking is parking alongside a car already parked.

 (D) To double park is alongside a car already parked.

22. **(A)** This is entirely among you and he.

 (B) This is completely among him and you.

 (C) This is between you and him.

 (D) This is between he and you.

23. **(A)** As I said, "neither of them are guilty."

 (B) As I said, "neither of them are guilty".

 (C) As I said, "neither of them is guilty."

 (D) As I said, neither of them is guilty.

24. **(A)** A promotion means more responsibility and more money, but not everyone wants one.

 (B) A promotion means more responsibility and more money, not everyone wants one.

 (C) More responsibility comes with a promotion and more harder work.

 (D) Not every one wants be promoted even the more money that comes with it.

25. **(A)** The data-entry positions offers real good work experience and pay.

 (B) A candidate he'll get good experience with a data-entry job and pay.

 (C) There is good experience and pay associated with data-entry jobs.

 (D) The data-entry position offers a candidate work experience and good pay.

26. **(A)** Having been told that she had interviewed well, she left feeling confident.

 (B) Feeling confident, the interview went well.

 (C) She felt the interview went good and left confident.

 (D) She felt confident, and it went well.

27. **(A)** His document was misfiled so they were more difficult to find then hers.

 (B) Someone mis-filed his document, hers were filed okay.

 (C) His document was misfiled so it was more difficult to find than hers.

 (D) Because of filing his document in the wrong place, his file was misplaced.

28. **(A)** The final report was input in less than four hours by three typists and whom should be thanked for their hard work.

   (B) If the three typists had know they'd be working four hours to finish the report.

   (C) The three typists who input the final report in less than four hours should be thanked.

   (D) To who should the thanks be given for inputting the final report in less than four hours.

29. **(A)** "Are you absolutely certain, she asked, that you are right?"

   (B) "Are you absolutely certain," she asked, "that you are right?"

   (C) "Are you absolutely certain," she asked, "That you are right"?

   (D) "Are you absolutely certain", she asked, "That you are right?"

30. **(A)** In agreeing to a deadline, her and me negotiated an extra day just in case.

   (B) Our supervisor worked with her and I to set a realistic deadline.

   (C) No one asked she and I if we thought we could the work done in two days.

   (D) She and I negotiated an extra day for finishing the work in case there was a problem.

31. **(A)** Most all these statements have been supported by persons who are reliable and can be depended upon.

   (B) The persons which have guaranteed these statements are reliable.

   (C) Reliable persons guarantee the facts with regards to the truth of these statements.

   (D) These statements can be depended on, for their truth has been guaranteed by reliable persons.

32. **(A)** Neither the department head nor the agency head realized the problem was so severe.

   (B) Noone realized the severity of the problem.

   (C) Both the department head and they was unaware of the problems severity.

   (D) The department head was as unaware of the problem as them.

33. **(A)** The number of applications for that position has declined greatly over the last three years.

   (B) In the last three years the application's numbers have declined greatly.

   (C) The number of applications for that position have declined greatly over the last three years.

   (D) The applications for that particular position shows a trend downward.

34. **(A)** Every carrier should always have something to throw; not something to throw at the dog but something what will divert its attention.

   (B) Every carrier should have something to throw—not something to throw at the dog, but something to divert its attention.

   (C) Every carrier should always carry something to throw not something to throw at the dog but something that will divert it's attention.

   (D) Every carrier should always carry something to throw, not something to throw at the dog, but, something that will divert its' attention.

35. **(A)** O'Brien's and Associates are hiring five lawyers.

    (B) O'Brien and Associates is taking on several new cases and hiring more lawyers.

    (C) O'Brien and Associates must be doing good because they have hired five more lawyers.

    (D) O'Brien and Associates have hired five more lawyers in the recently month.

36. **(A)** He couldn't find his family in all the chaos of the storm around himself.

    (B) He never felt himself was in danger, it was his family he worried about.

    (C) Worrying about his family, his own self was not a concern.

    (D) He never felt himself in danger, but he couldn't find his family.

37. **(A)** One of us have to make the reply before tomorrow.

    (B) Making the reply before tomorrow will have to be done by one of us.

    (C) One of us has to reply before tomorrow.

    (D) Anyone has to reply before tomorrow.

38. **(A)** You have got to get rid of some of these people if you expect to have the quality of the work improve.

    (B) The quality of the work would improve if they would leave fewer people do it.

    (C) I believe it would be desirable to have fewer persons doing this work.

    (D) If you had planned on employing fewer people than this to do the work, this situation would not have arose.

39. **(A)** The paper we use for this purpose must be light, glossy, and stand hard usage as well.

    (B) Only a light and a glossy, but durable, paper must be used for this purpose.

    (C) For this purpose, we want a paper that is light, glossy, but that will stand hard wear.

    (D) For this purpose, paper that is light, glossy, and durable is essential.

40. **(A)** This letter, together with the reports, are to be sent to the postmaster.

    (B) The reports, together with this letter, is to be sent to the postmaster.

    (C) The reports and this letter is to be sent to the postmaster.

    (D) This letter, together with the reports, is to be sent to the postmaster.

Directions: Each question from 41–48 consists of a sentence containing a word in boldface type. Choose the best meaning for the word in boldface type.

41. Please consult your office **manual** to learn the proper operation of our copying machine.

    Manual means most nearly

    (A) labor
    (B) handbook
    (C) typewriter
    (D) handle

42. There is a specified punishment for each **infraction** of the rules.

    Infraction means most nearly

    (A) violation
    (B) use
    (C) interpretation
    (D) part

43. The order was **rescinded** within the week.

    Rescinded means most nearly

    (A) revised
    (B) canceled
    (C) misinterpreted
    (D) confirmed

44. If you have a question, please raise your hand to **summon** the test proctor.

    Summon means most nearly

    (A) ticket
    (B) fine
    (C) give
    (D) call

45. We dared not bring charges against our employer for fear of **reprisal**.

    Reprisal means most nearly

    (A) retaliation
    (B) advantage
    (C) warning
    (D) denial

46. The use of the personal computer by office managers has severely **reduced** the need for assistants.

    Reduced means most nearly

    (A) enlarged
    (B) cut out
    (C) lessened
    (D) expanded

47. Frequent use of marijuana may **impair** your judgment.

    Impair means most nearly

    (A) weaken
    (B) conceal
    (C) improve
    (D) expose

48. It is altogether **fitting** that the parent discipline the child.

    Fitting means most nearly

    (A) illegal
    (B) bad practice
    (C) appropriate
    (D) required

Directions: For questions 49–55, read each paragraph and answer the question that follows.

49. A survey to determine the subjects that have helped students most in their jobs shows that typing leads all other subjects in the business group. It also leads among the subjects college students consider most valuable and would take again if they were to return to high school.

The paragraph best supports the statement that

(A) the ability to type is an asset in business and in school.

(B) students who return to night school take typing.

(C) students with a knowledge of typing do superior work in college.

(D) success in business is assured those who can type.

50. The Supreme Court's power to invalidate legislation that violates the Constitution is a strong restriction on the powers of Congress. If an act of Congress is deemed unconstitutional by the Supreme Court, then the act is voided. Unlike a presidential veto, which can be overridden by a two-thirds vote of the House and the Senate, a constitutional ruling by the Supreme Court must be accepted by the Congress.

The paragraph best supports the statement that

(A) if an act of Congress is voided, then it has been deemed unconstitutional by the Supreme Court.

(B) if an act of Congress has not been voided, then it has not been deemed unconstitutional by the Supreme Court.

(C) if an act of Congress has not been deemed unconstitutional by the Supreme Court, then it is voided.

(D) if an act of Congress is deemed unconstitutional by the Supreme Court, then it is not voided.

51. Since the government can spend only what it obtains from the people, and this amount is ultimately limited by their capacity and willingness to pay taxes, it is very important that the people be given full information about the full work of the government.

The paragraph best supports the statement that

(A) governmental employees should be trained not only in their own work, but also in how to perform the duties of other employees in their agency.

(B) taxation by the government rests upon the consent of the people.

(C) the release of full information on the work of the government will increase the efficiency of governmental operations.

(D) the work of the government, in recent years, has been restricted because of reduced tax collection.

52. Both high schools and colleges should take responsibility for preparing students to get jobs. Since the ability to write a good application letter is one of the first steps toward this goal, every teacher should be willing to do what he or she can to help the student learn to write such letters.

The paragraph best supports the statement that

(A) inability to write a good letter often reduces one's job prospects.

(B) the major responsibility of the school is to obtain jobs for its students.

(C) success is largely a matter of the kind of work the student applies for first.

(D) every teacher should teach a course in the writing of application letters.

53. Direct lighting is the least satisfactory lighting arrangement. The desk or ceiling light with a reflector that diffuses all the rays downward is sure to cause a glare on the work surface.

The paragraph best supports the statement that direct lighting is least satisfactory as a method of lighting chiefly because

(A) the light is diffused, causing eyestrain.

(B) the shade on the individual desk lamp is not constructed along scientific lines.

(C) the working surface is usually obscured by the glare.

(D) direct lighting is injurious to the eyes.

54. *White collar* is a term used to describe one of the largest groups of workers in U.S. industry and trade. It distinguishes those who work in offices in professional, managerial, and administrative functions from those who depend for their living on their hands and large-scale machinery. The term suggests occupations in which physical exertion and handling of materials are not primary job features.

The paragraph best supports the statement that "white collar" workers are

(A) not so strong physically as those who work with their hands.

(B) those who supervise workers handling materials.

(C) all whose work is entirely indoors.

(D) not likely to use machines as much as are other groups of workers.

55. In large organizations, a standardized, simple, inexpensive method of giving employees information about company policies and rules, as well as specific instructions regarding their duties, is practically essential. This is the purpose of all office manuals of whatever type.

The paragraph best supports the statement that office manuals

(A) are all about the same.

(B) should be simple enough for the average employee to understand.

(C) are necessary to large organizations.

(D) act as constant reminders to the employee of his or her duties.

STOP

END OF SECTION. IF YOU HAVE ANY TIME LEFT, GO OVER YOUR WORK IN THIS SECTION ONLY. DO NOT WORK IN ANY OTHER SECTION OF THE TEST.

ANSWER KEY AND EXPLANATIONS

Clerical Ability

1. E		18. B		35. B		52. C		69. B
2. D		19. A		36. B		53. C		70. B
3. A		20. C		37. E		54. A		71. E
4. D		21. A		38. C		55. D		72. B
5. A		22. E		39. D		56. A		73. A
6. C		23. C		40. A		57. D		74. B
7. B		24. B		41. A		58. B		75. E
8. D		25. D		42. C		59. C		76. C
9. E		26. E		43. C		60. B		77. E
10. C		27. A		44. C		61. A		78. E
11. C		28. B		45. D		62. C		79. C
12. D		29. C		46. B		63. C		80. B
13. C		30. C		47. E		64. D		81. E
14. A		31. D		48. A		65. D		82. C
15. C		32. E		49. C		66. C		83. E
16. A		33. A		50. A		67. A		84. C
17. E		34. A		51. A		68. D		85. B

1. **The correct answer is (E).** Mattewson; Mathison

2. **The correct answer is (D).** 59233262; 59233362; 59233662

3. **The correct answer is (A).** MYP-6734; NYP-6733

4. **The correct answer is (D).** Morin, J.B.; Morin, J. James; Morin, James J.; Morin, Jose; Morin, Joseph F.

5. **The correct answer is (A).** 00102032; 00120312

6. **The correct answer is (C).** LPD-6001; LPD-6100; LPD-6101

7. **The correct answer is (B).** Von Alton; Vonbrunner; Vonderson

8. **The correct answer is (D).** Sanchez, R. Juanita; Sanchez, R.R.; Sanchez, S. Robert

9. **The correct answer is (E).** 01016060; 01066010

10. **The correct answer is (C).** AAS-4623; AAZ-2687; ASA-3216

11. **The correct answer is (C).** Kawalski, Robert; Kowalski, Raymond M.; Kowalsky, Robert S.

12. **The correct answer is (D).** NCD-7710; NCD-7834; NCD-7868

13. **The correct answer is (C).** 36270000; 36270013; 36270030

14. **The correct answer is (A).** Ketchener, Glen; Ketchner, Alan

15. **The correct answer is (C).** Figaro, Francis; Figuaro, Estevanico; Figuaro, Francisco

16. **The correct answer is (A).** 58006021; 58006130

17. **The correct answer is (E).** EKK-1403; EKK-1443

18. **The correct answer is (B).** D'Arcy, F.W.; D'Arcy, Fabrece; Darren, Jordan

19. **The correct answer is (A).** Schuster, Robert; Shugusta, H. Thomas.

20. **The correct answer is (C).** PSP-4921; SPP-4856; SPS-4906

21. **The correct answer is (A).** All three names are exactly alike.

22. **The correct answer is (E).** Sergei Kuznets, Serge Kusnetz, Sergei Kuznetts.

23. **The correct answer is (C).** The middle number is different: 6-78912-3e3e42.

24. **The correct answer is (B).** The last address is different: 85629 Dunwoodie Drive.

25. **The correct answer is (D).** The first number is different: 9566110.

26. **The correct answer is (E).** All three names are different: Becca Katherine Hines; Becca Catherine Hanes, Becca Catharine Hane.

27. **The correct answer is (A).** All three codes are exactly alike.

28. **The correct answer is (B).** The last address is different: 60646 West Touhey Avenue.

29. **The correct answer is (C).** The second name is different: Mardikian and Moore, Inc.

30. **The correct answer is (D).** The first number is different: 9670243.

31. **The correct answer is (D).** The first name is different: Ingles (missing the final "e").

32. **The correct answer is (E).** All three names are different: DeAngelis; D'Angelis; DeAngeles.

33. **The correct answer is (A).** All three numbers are exactly alike.

34. **The correct answer is (A).** All three addresses are exactly alike.

35. **The correct answer is (B).** The third number is different: 62qs5-95yT3-001.

36. **The correct answer is (B).** The last number is different: 2798350.

37. **The correct answer is (E).** All three names are different: Helmut V. Lochner; Helmut V. Lockner; Helmut W. Lochner.

38. **The correct answer is (C).** The second number is different: 2548403.

39. **The correct answer is (D).** The first address is different: Lemberger, WA 28094-9182.

40. **The correct answer is (A).** All three codes are exactly alike.

41. **The correct answer is (A).** All three names are exactly alike.

42. **The correct answer is (C).** The second number is different: 5927861.

43. **The correct answer is (C).** The second address is different: O'Reillys Bay, LA 56212.

44. **The correct answer is (C).** The second name is different: Myra Sampson.

45. **The correct answer is (D).** The first code is different: 5634-OotV5a-16867.

46. **The correct answer is (B).** The last name is different: Doloras.

47. **The correct answer is (E).** All three names are different: David C. Routzon; David E. Routzon; David C. Routzron.

48. **The correct answer is (A).** All three addresses are exactly alike.

49. **The correct answer is (C).** The second number is different: 3497130.

50. **The correct answer is (A).** All three codes are exactly alike.

51. **The correct answer is (A).** The correct spelling is *anticipate*.

52. **The correct answer is (C).** The correct spelling is *similar*.

53. **The correct answer is (C).** The correct spelling is *sufficiently*.

54. **The correct answer is (A).** The correct spelling is *intelligence*.

55. **The correct answer is (D).** The correct spelling is *reference*.

56. **The correct answer is (A).** The correct spelling is *conscious*.

57. **The correct answer is (D).** The correct spelling is *parallel*.

58. **The correct answer is (B).** The correct spelling is *abundance*.

59. **The correct answer is (C).** The correct spelling is *corrugated*.

60. **The correct answer is (B).** The correct spelling is *accumulation*.

61. **The correct answer is (A).** The correct spelling is *resonance*.

62. **The correct answer is (C).** The correct spelling is *beneficial*.

63. **The correct answer is (C).** The correct spelling is *specifically*.

64. **The correct answer is (D).** The correct spelling is *eliminate*.

65. **The correct answer is (D).** The correct spelling is *colossal*.

66. **The correct answer is (C).** The correct spelling is *auxiliary*.

67. **The correct answer is (A).** The correct spelling is *inimitable*.

68. **The correct answer is (D).** The correct spelling is *disappearance*.

69. **The correct answer is (B).** The correct spelling is *coalition*.

70. **The correct answer is (B).** The correct spelling is *essential*.

71. **The correct answer is (E).** 27

72. **The correct answer is (B).** 32

73. **The correct answer is (A).** 224

74. **The correct answer is (B).** 78

75. **The correct answer is (E).** 28

76. **The correct answer is (C).** 99

77. **The correct answer is (E).** 61

78. **The correct answer is (E).** 114

79. **The correct answer is (C).** 40

80. **The correct answer is (B).** 7

81. **The correct answer is (E).** 30

82. **The correct answer is (C).** 10

83. **The correct answer is (E).** 41

84. **The correct answer is (C).** 23

85. **The correct answer is (B).** 21

Verbal Ability

1. D	12. B	23. D	34. B	45. A
2. C	13. D	24. A	35. B	46. C
3. E	14. A	25. D	36. D	47. A
4. A	15. D	26. A	37. C	48. C
5. C	16. D	27. C	38. C	49. A
6. E	17. E	28. C	39. D	50. B
7. D	18. A	29. B	40. D	51. B
8. C	19. D	30. D	41. B	52. A
9. E	20. B	31. D	42. A	53. C
10. B	21. C	32. A	43. B	54. D
11. A	22. C	33. A	44. D	55. C

1. **The correct answer is (D).** This answer goes with question 6. There is one B on the line; choice (D) is correct.

2. **The correct answer is (C).** This answer goes with question 9. The larger circle is around the letter C, so choice (C) is correct.

3. **The correct answer is (E).** This answer goes with question 14. There are five Bs in the line, and 5 − 2 = 3.

4. **The correct answer is (A).** This answer goes with question 3. 16 ÷ 4 = 4.

5. **The correct answer is (C).** This answer goes with question 4. The left-hand number is 5.

6. **The correct answer is (E).** This answer goes with question 20. There are five points on a star, so choice (E) is correct.

7. **The correct answer is (D).** This answer goes with question 12. The second letter from the left is D, and the number of days in a week is seven, so choice (D) is correct.

8. **The correct answer is (C).** This answer goes with question 8. 6 • 4 = 24 and 8 • 3 = 24, so 6 • 4 is not greater than 8 • 3.

9. **The correct answer is (E).** This answer goes with question 2. 9 is the only odd number listed that is greater than 5 and less than 10, so choice (E) is correct.

10. **The correct answer is (B).** This answer goes with question 18. The next-to-smallest number listed is 10.

11. **The correct answer is (A).** This answer goes with question 16. It is true that a 6-foot-tall person is taller than a 5-foot-tall person and that a pillow is softer than a rock.

12. **The correct answer is (B).** This answer goes with question 1. Of the letters listed, the one that comes first in the alphabet is B.

13. **The correct answer is (D).** This answer goes with question 17. The fourth letter in the alphabet is D, and the third number listed is 13.

14. **The correct answer is (A).** This answer goes with question 13. It is not true that a triangle has more angles than a rectangle, so you should have written 14 beside letter A, which is enclosed by a square.

15. **The correct answer is (D).** This answer goes with question 10. 7 + 4 + 4 = 15, so choice (D) is correct.

16. **The correct answer is (D).** This answer goes with question 15. The latest time is 10:16.

17. **The correct answer is (E).** This answer goes with question 11. It is true that 5 • 5 = 25 and 5 + 5 = 10.

18. **The correct answer is (A).** This answer goes with question 5. Wednesday never comes before Tuesday, so you should have written down the number 18.

19. **The correct answer is (D).** This answer goes with question 19. The third letter in the first word is D, and the second box contains the number 19.

20. **The correct answer is (B).** This answer goes with question 7. The highest number listed is 20.

21. **The correct answer is (C).** Choice (A) has two grammatical errors: it uses when to introduce a definition and the unacceptable verb form *already having been parked*. Choice (B) incorrectly shifts subjects from *one* to *you*. Choice (D) does not make sense.

22. **The correct answer is (C).** Choices (A) and (B) are incorrect because only two persons are involved in the statement; *between* is used when there are only two, and *among* is reserved for three or more. Choices (A) and (D) use the pronoun *he*; the object of a preposition, in this case *between*, must be in the objective case, *him*.

23. **The correct answer is (D).** Punctuation aside, both choices (A) and (B) incorrectly place the verb in the plural, *are*; *neither* is a singular indefinite pronoun and requires a singular verb. The choice between choices (C) and (D) is more difficult, but this is a simple statement and not a direct quote.

24. **The correct answer is (A).** Choice (B) is a run-on sentence; it needs a period or a semicolon, or it needs a conjunction such as *but*. The correct way to form the comparative of a one-syllable adjective (or adverb) is to add *–er*; for words of more than one syllable, add the word *more*. You don't need both so choice (C) is incorrect. Choice (D) has two errors. *Every one* should be one word, and the second part of the sentence has a word or words missing so that it doesn't make sense.

25. **The correct answer is (D).** Subject and verbs must agree in number, so eliminate choice (A). Either *candidate* or *he* can be the subject, but not both without a conjunction to connect them in some way; this rules out choice (B). In Choice (C), which is trickier, the verb agrees with *experience and pay*; those are the subject of the predicate, not *there*.

26. **The correct answer is (A).** As written, choice (B) says that the interview felt confident and left. Choice (C) uses the adjective *good* when the word that is needed is the adverb *well*. With choice (D), there is no antecedent for *it* so you don't know what went well.

27. **The correct answer is (C).** There are two errors in choice (A). *Document* is singular so the pronoun referring to it should be *it*, not *they*. In addition, *then* should be *than*, which is used for comparisons. Choice (B) also has two errors. It's a run-on sentence, and *okay* is too informal for writing related to a work situation. Choice (D) has a misplaced location problem of its own. There is no antecedent for the phrase *Because of filing his document in the wrong place*. His file didn't misfile itself.

28. **The correct answer is (C).** The error in choice (A) is *whom*. The sentence requires the subject form *who*. Choice (D) has the opposite problem. The

correct form here should be *whom* because the relative pronoun is the object of the preposition *to*. Choice (B) is a dependent clause with no main sentence to attach itself to. In addition, the incorrect form of *to know* is used. The clause requires the past participle, *known*.

29. **The correct answer is (B).** Only the quoted material should be enclosed by quotation marks, so choice (A) is incorrect. Only the first word of a sentence should begin with a capital letter, so choices (C) and (D) are wrong. In addition, only the quoted material itself is a question; the entire sentence is a statement. Therefore, the question mark must be placed inside the quotes.

30. **The correct answer is (D).** The misuse of the personal pronouns is a common error in spoken and written English. Fix the rules in your mind now. *Her* and *me* are object pronouns; choice (A) requires the subject pronouns *she* and *I*. In choice (B), *her* is correct because it's the object of the preposition, and *I* is incorrect because the object form—*me*—is required. Choice (C) requires *her* and *me* as objects of the predicate *asked*.

31. **The correct answer is (D).** Choice (A) might state that *most or all* but not both. Choice (B) should read *persons who*. Choice (C) should read *with regard to. . .*

32. **The correct answer is (A).** *No one* is always two words, so eliminate choice (B). Choice (C) has multiple problems. If *they* is the correct pronoun, then *both* and *was* are incorrect. Also, if it's a single problem, then the word should be *problem's*; if there are several problems, then the word should be *problems'*. You need to finish choice (D) in order to see that *them* is incorrect: "as

unaware of the problem as they were," not "them were."

33. **The correct answer is (A).** Choice (B) says that there has been only one application, which makes no sense. Choice (C) is incorrect because *number* is a collective noun, and the context in which a collective noun is used indicates whether it should take a singular or plural verb. In this case, because *number* relates to a single type of thing, an application, it is considered singular and should take the singular form of the verb. This also explains why choice (A) is correct. Choice (D) puts a phrase between the subject and verb. The noun closest to the verb is plural, but the subject is singular so the verb should be *show*.

34. **The correct answer is (B).** Choice (A) incorrectly uses a semicolon to separate a complete clause from a sentence fragment; it also incorrectly uses *what* in place of *that*. Choice (C) is a run-on sentence that also misuses an apostrophe—*it's* is the contraction for *it is*, not the possessive of *it*. Choice (D) uses commas indiscriminately; it also misuses the apostrophe.

35. **The correct answer is (B).** In choice (A), the placement of the apostrophe is inappropriate. Choice (C) uses the adjective *good* when it should use the adverb *well*. It also uses the plural pronoun *they* when the pronoun should be *it* because the firm is considered a single thing. Choice (D) has the same error and also introduces the use of the adverb *recently* to modify a noun; adverbs modify verbs, adjectives, and other adverbs.

36. **The correct answer is (D).** There is no reason to use the reflexive pronoun *himself*; the pronoun *him* would have been sufficient in choice (A). Choice (B) has the same problem and is also a run-on sentence. Having one's self worrying doesn't make sense, so eliminate choice (C).

37. **The correct answer is (C).** Choice (A) incorrectly uses the plural verb form *have* with the singular subject *one*. Choice (B) is awkward and wordy. Choice (D) incorrectly changes the subject from *one of us* to *anyone*.

38. **The correct answer is (C).** Choice (A) is wordy. In choice (B), the correct verb should be *have* in place of *leave*. In choice (D), the word *arose* should be *arisen*.

39. **The correct answer is (D).** The first three sentences lack parallel construction. All of the words that modify *paper* must appear in the same form.

40. **The correct answer is (D).** The phrase *together with. . .* is extra information and not a part of the sentence; therefore, choices (A) and (B) contain errors of agreement. Choice (C) also presents subject-verb disagreement, but in this case, the compound subject, indicated by the conjunction *and*, requires a plural verb.

41. **The correct answer is (B).** Even if you do not recognize the root "manu" as meaning "hand" and relating directly to *handbook*, you should have no trouble getting this question right. If you substitute each of the choices in the sentence, you will see that only one makes sense.

42. **The correct answer is (A).** Within the context of the sentence, punishment for *use*, *interpretation*, or *part* of the rules does not make sense. Since it is reasonable to expect punishment for negative behavior with relation to the rules, *violation*, which is the meaning of infraction, is the proper answer.

43. **The correct answer is (B).** The prefix "re," meaning "back" or "again," should help narrow your choices to (A) or (B). To *rescind* is to take back or to *cancel*.

44. **The correct answer is (D).** First eliminate choice (C) since it does not make sense in the sentence. Your experience with the word *summons* may be with relation to tickets and fines, but tickets and fines have nothing to do with asking questions while taking a test. Even if you are unfamiliar with the word *summon*, you should be able to choose *call* as the best synonym in this context.

45. **The correct answer is (A).** *Reprisal* means "injury done for injury received," or *retaliation*.

46. **The correct answer is (C).** To *reduce* is to make smaller or *lessen*.

47. **The correct answer is (A).** To *impair* is to make worse, to injure, or to *weaken*.

48. **The correct answer is (C).** *Fitting* in this context means "suitable" or *appropriate*.

49. **The correct answer is (A).** The survey showed that of all subjects, typing helped most in business. It was also considered valuable by college students in their schoolwork.

50. **The correct answer is (B).** You can infer the answer from the information in the second sentence, which states that if an act of Congress has been deemed unconstitutional, then it is voided. In choice (B), we are told that an act of Congress is not voided; therefore, we can conclude that it has not been deemed unconstitutional by the Supreme Court.

51. **The correct answer is (B).** According to the paragraph, the government can spend only what it obtains from the people. The government obtains money from the people by taxation. If the people are unwilling to pay taxes, the government has no source of funds.

answers

52. The correct answer is (A). Step one in the job application process is often the application letter. If the letter is not effective, the applicant will not move on to the next step, and job prospects will be greatly lessened.

53. The correct answer is (C). The second sentence of the paragraph states that direct lighting causes glare on the working surface.

54. The correct answer is (D). While all of the answer choices are likely to be true, the answer suggested by the paragraph is that "white collar" workers work with their pencils and their minds, rather than with their hands and machines.

55. The correct answer is (C). All the paragraph says is that office manuals are a necessity in large organizations.

SELF-EVALUATION

Since there is only a single exam score, your performance on any single question type does not matter. In order to earn a high score, however, you must do well on all parts of the exam. Using the following self-evaluation charts, check how many of each question type you missed to gauge your performance on that question type. Then, concentrate your efforts toward improvement in the areas with which you had the most difficulty. It will be worth your while to return to the chapter indicated and review.

SELF-EVALUATION CHART: CLERICAL ABILITY TEST

Question Type	Question Numbers	Chapter to Review
Alphabetizing and Filing	1–20	13
Clerical Speed and Accuracy	21–50	14
Spelling	51–70	5
Computations	71–85	(Watch out for careless errors.)

SELF-EVALUATION CHART: VERBAL ABILITY TEST

Question Type	Question Numbers	Chapter to Review
Following Written Instructions	1–20	(Read and follow instructions carefully.)
English Grammar and Usage	21–40	4
Synonyms	41–48	6
Reading Comprehension	49–55	10

Use the following chart to find out where your total score falls on a scale from Poor to Excellent.

SCORE RATING CHART

	Excellent	Good	Average	Fair	Poor
Score	125–140	109–124	91–108	61–90	0–6

ANSWER SHEET PRACTICE TEST 4: MUNICIPAL OFFICE AIDE

1. Ⓐ Ⓑ Ⓒ Ⓓ Ⓔ   14. Ⓐ Ⓑ Ⓒ Ⓓ Ⓔ   27. Ⓐ Ⓑ Ⓒ Ⓓ Ⓔ   40. Ⓐ Ⓑ Ⓒ Ⓓ Ⓔ

2. Ⓐ Ⓑ Ⓒ Ⓓ Ⓔ   15. Ⓐ Ⓑ Ⓒ Ⓓ Ⓔ   28. Ⓐ Ⓑ Ⓒ Ⓓ Ⓔ   41. Ⓐ Ⓑ Ⓒ Ⓓ Ⓔ

3. Ⓐ Ⓑ Ⓒ Ⓓ Ⓔ   16. Ⓐ Ⓑ Ⓒ Ⓓ Ⓔ   29. Ⓐ Ⓑ Ⓒ Ⓓ Ⓔ   42. Ⓐ Ⓑ Ⓒ Ⓓ Ⓔ

4. Ⓐ Ⓑ Ⓒ Ⓓ Ⓔ   17. Ⓐ Ⓑ Ⓒ Ⓓ Ⓔ   30. Ⓐ Ⓑ Ⓒ Ⓓ Ⓔ   43. Ⓐ Ⓑ Ⓒ Ⓓ Ⓔ

5. Ⓐ Ⓑ Ⓒ Ⓓ Ⓔ   18. Ⓐ Ⓑ Ⓒ Ⓓ Ⓔ   31. Ⓐ Ⓑ Ⓒ Ⓓ Ⓔ   44. Ⓐ Ⓑ Ⓒ Ⓓ Ⓔ

6. Ⓐ Ⓑ Ⓒ Ⓓ Ⓔ   19. Ⓐ Ⓑ Ⓒ Ⓓ Ⓔ   32. Ⓐ Ⓑ Ⓒ Ⓓ Ⓔ   45. Ⓐ Ⓑ Ⓒ Ⓓ Ⓔ

7. Ⓐ Ⓑ Ⓒ Ⓓ Ⓔ   20. Ⓐ Ⓑ Ⓒ Ⓓ Ⓔ   33. Ⓐ Ⓑ Ⓒ Ⓓ Ⓔ   46. Ⓐ Ⓑ Ⓒ Ⓓ Ⓔ

8. Ⓐ Ⓑ Ⓒ Ⓓ Ⓔ   21. Ⓐ Ⓑ Ⓒ Ⓓ Ⓔ   34. Ⓐ Ⓑ Ⓒ Ⓓ Ⓔ   47. Ⓐ Ⓑ Ⓒ Ⓓ Ⓔ

9. Ⓐ Ⓑ Ⓒ Ⓓ Ⓔ   22. Ⓐ Ⓑ Ⓒ Ⓓ Ⓔ   35. Ⓐ Ⓑ Ⓒ Ⓓ Ⓔ   48. Ⓐ Ⓑ Ⓒ Ⓓ Ⓔ

10. Ⓐ Ⓑ Ⓒ Ⓓ Ⓔ   23. Ⓐ Ⓑ Ⓒ Ⓓ Ⓔ   36. Ⓐ Ⓑ Ⓒ Ⓓ Ⓔ   49. Ⓐ Ⓑ Ⓒ Ⓓ Ⓔ

11. Ⓐ Ⓑ Ⓒ Ⓓ Ⓔ   24. Ⓐ Ⓑ Ⓒ Ⓓ Ⓔ   37. Ⓐ Ⓑ Ⓒ Ⓓ Ⓔ   50. Ⓐ Ⓑ Ⓒ Ⓓ Ⓔ

12. Ⓐ Ⓑ Ⓒ Ⓓ Ⓔ   25. Ⓐ Ⓑ Ⓒ Ⓓ Ⓔ   38. Ⓐ Ⓑ Ⓒ Ⓓ Ⓔ

13. Ⓐ Ⓑ Ⓒ Ⓓ Ⓔ   26. Ⓐ Ⓑ Ⓒ Ⓓ Ⓔ   39. Ⓐ Ⓑ Ⓒ Ⓓ Ⓔ

answer sheet

Practice Test 4

MUNICIPAL OFFICE AIDE

50 Questions • 60 Minutes

Directions: Choose the best answer to each question and mark its letter on the answer sheet.

1. In order to maintain office coverage during working hours, your supervisor has scheduled your lunch hour from 1 p.m. to 2 p.m., and your coworker's lunch hour is from 12 p.m. to 1 p.m. Lately, your coworker has been returning late from lunch each day. As a result, you do not get a full hour, since you must return to the office by 2 p.m. Of the following, the best action for you to take first is to

   (A) explain to your coworker in a courteous manner that his or her lateness is interfering with your right to a full hour for lunch.

   (B) tell your coworker that his or her lateness must stop, or you will report him or her to your supervisor.

   (C) report your coworker's lateness to your supervisor.

   (D) leave at 1 p.m. for lunch, whether your coworker has returned or not.

2. Assume that, as an office worker, one of your jobs is to open mail sent to your unit, read the mail for content, and send the mail to the appropriate person for handling. You accidentally open and begin to read a letter marked "personal" addressed to a coworker. Of the following, the best action for you to take is

   (A) report to your supervisor that your coworker is receiving personal mail at the office.

   (B) destroy the letter so that your coworker doesn't know you saw it.

   (C) reseal the letter and place it on the coworker's desk without saying anything.

   (D) bring the letter to your coworker and explain that you opened it by accident.

3. Suppose that in evaluating your work, your supervisor gives you an overall good rating, but states that you sometimes turn in work with careless errors. The best action for you to take would be to

   (A) ask a coworker who is good at details to proofread your work.

   (B) take time to do a careful job, paying more attention to detail.

   (C) continue working as usual since occasional errors are to be expected.

   (D) ask your supervisor if he or she would mind correcting your errors.

351

NOTE

The directions are stated as if you are taking the exam in a paper-and-pencil format. If you will be taking the exam on computer, each section will have directions specific to how to answer questions on computer.

Directions: Questions 4–8 consist of a sentence that may or may not be an example of good English. The underlined parts of each sentence may be correct or incorrect. Examine each sentence, considering grammar, punctuation, spelling, and capitalization. If the English usage in the underlined parts of the sentence given is better than any of the changes in the underlined words suggested in choices (B), (C), or (D), choose (A). If the changes in the underlined words suggested in choices (B), (C), or (D) would make the sentence correct, choose the correct option. Do not choose an option that will change the meaning of the sentence.

4. This manual <u>discribes the duties performed</u> by an office aide.
   (A) Correct as is
   (B) describe the duties performed
   (C) discribe the duties performed
   (D) describes the duties performed

5. There <u>weren't no</u> paper in the supply closet.
   (A) Correct as is
   (B) weren't any
   (C) wasn't any
   (D) wasn't no

6. The new employees left <u>there</u> office to attend a meeting.
   (A) Correct as is
   (B) they're
   (C) their
   (D) thier

7. The office worker started working at <u>8;30 a.m.</u>
   (A) Correct as is
   (B) 8:30 a.m.
   (C) 8;30 A,M.
   (D) 8:30 AM.

8. The <u>alphabet, or A to Z sequence are</u> the basis of most filing systems.
   (A) Correct as is
   (B) alphabet, or A to Z sequence, is
   (C) alphabet, or A to Z, sequence are
   (D) alphabet, or A too Z sequence, is

Directions: Questions 9–13 have two lists of numbers. Each list contains three sets of numbers. Check each of the three sets in the list on the right to see if they are the same as the corresponding set in the list on the left. Choose your answers as follows:

(A) if NONE of the sets in the right list is the SAME as those in the left list.
(B) if ONLY ONE of the sets in the right list is the SAME as those in the left list.
(C) if ONLY TWO of the sets in the right list are the SAME as those in the left list.
(D) if ALL THREE sets in the right list are the SAME as those in the left list.

9. 7143592185   7143892185

   8344517699   8344518699

   9178531263   9178531263

10. 2572114731   257214731

   8806835476   8806835476

   8255831246   8255831246

11. 331476853821   331476858621

   6976658532996   6976655832996

   3766042113715   3766042113745

12. 8806663315   880663315

   74477138449   74477138449

   211756663666   211756663666

13. 990006966996   99000696996

   53022219743   53022219843

   4171171117717   4171171177717

Directions: Questions 14–16 have two lists of numbers. Each list contains three sets of numbers. Check each of the three sets in the list on the right to see if they are the same as the corresponding set in the list on the left. Choose your answers as follows:

(A) if NONE of the sets in the right list is the SAME as those in the left list.
(B) if ONLY ONE of the sets in the right list is the SAME as those in the left list.
(C) if ONLY TWO of the sets in the right list are the SAME as those in the left list.
(D) if ALL THREE sets in the right list are the SAME as those in the left list.

14. Mary T. Berlinger
2351 Hampton St.
Monsey, NY 20117

Eduardo Benes
473 Kingston Avenue
Central Islip, NY 11734

Alan Carrington Fuchs
17 Gnarled Hollow Road
Los Angeles, California 91635

Mary T. Berlinger
2351 Hampton St.
Monsey, NY 20117

Eduardo Benes
473 Kingston Avenue
Central Islip, NY 11734

Alan Carrington Fuchs
17 Gnarled Hollow Road
Los Angeles, California 91685

15. David John Jacobson
178 35 St. Apt. 4C
New York, NY 00927

Ann-Marie Calonella
7243 South Ridge Blvd.
Bakersfield, California 96714

Pauline M. Thompson
872 Linden Ave.
Houston, Texas 70321

David John Jacobson
178 53 St. Apt. 4C
New York, NY 00927

Ann-Marie Calonella
7243 South Ridge Blvd.
Bakersfield, California 96714

Pauline M. Thomson
872 Linden Ave.
Houston, Texas 70321

16. Chester LeRoy Masterton
152 Lacy Rd.
Kankakee, IL 54532

William Maloney
S. LaCrosse Pla.
Wausau, Wisconsin 52146

Cynthia V. Barnes
16 Pines Rd.
Greenpoint, Mississippi 20376

Chester LeRoy Masterson
152 Lacy Rd.
Kankakee, IL 54532

William Maloney
S. LaCross Pla.
Wausau, Wisconsin 52146

Cynthia V. Barnes
16 Pines Rd.
Greenpoint, Mississippi 20376

In a survey of U.S. businesses, the American Management Association and the ePolicy Institute found that 66 percent of companies monitored their employees' use of the Internet, and 65 percent blocked access to websites that the companies considered inappropriate. It's not only private business that limits use of the Internet by employees. Federal, state, and local governments also have Internet policies. The following is an excerpt from the Executive Branch of the Federal government's policy/guidance on "Limited Personal Use" of information technology:

GENERAL POLICY

Federal employees are permitted limited use of government office equipment for personal needs if the use does not interfere with official business. . . . This limited personal use of government office equipment should take place during the employee's non-work time. . . .

C. Inappropriate Personal Use

Any personal use that could cause congestion, delay, or disruption of service to any government system or equipment. For example, greeting cards, video, sound, or other large file attachments can degrade the performance of the entire network. . . .

1. The creation, copying, transmission, or retransmission of chain letters or other unauthorized mass mailings regardless of the subject matter.

2. Using government office equipment for activities that are illegal, inappropriate, or offensive to fellow employees or the public. Such activities include, but are not limited to: hate speech or material that ridicules others on the basis of race, creed, religion, color, sex, disability, national origin, or sexual orientation.

3. The creation, download, viewing, storage, copying, or transmission of sexually explicit or sexually oriented materials.

4. The creation, download, viewing, storage, copying, or transmission of materials related to illegal gambling, illegal weapons, terrorist activities, and any other illegal activities otherwise prohibited, etc.

5. Use for commercial purposes or in support of "for-profit" activities or in support of other outside employment or business activity (e.g., consulting for pay, sales or administration of business transactions, sale of goods or services).

6. Engaging in any outside fundraising activity, endorsing any product or service, participating in any lobbying activity, or engaging in any prohibited partisan political activity.

7. Use for posting agency information to external newsgroups, bulletin boards, or other public forums without authority.

17. Which point refers to terrorist activities?

(A) Statement 5

(B) Statement 7

(C) Statement 4

(D) Statement 2

18. The abbreviation *e.g.* (statement 5) means

(A) indeed

(B) for example

(C) that is

(D) the following

19. Which of the following is NOT mentioned as restricted?

(A) creating a chain letter

(B) checking personal e-mail

(C) signing an online petition in support of school reform

(D) retransmitting a cartoon that makes fun of a politician

20. Which of the following is not listed as covered under statement 2?

(A) race

(B) age

(C) disability

(D) religion

Directions: For questions 21–23, select the choice that is closest in meaning to the underlined word.

21. A central file eliminates the need to underline{retain} duplicate material.

The word *retain* means most nearly

(A) keep

(B) change

(C) locate

(D) process

22. Filing is a underline{routine} office task.

Routine means most nearly

(A) proper

(B) regular

(C) simple

(D) difficult

23. Sometimes a word, phrase, or sentence must be underline{deleted} to correct an error.

Deleted means most nearly

(A) removed

(B) added

(C) expanded

(D) improved

Directions: The code table below shows 10 letters with matching numbers. For questions 24–28, there are three sets of letters. Each set of letters is followed by a set of numbers that may or may not match their correct letters according to the code table. For each question, check all three sets of letters and numbers and choose your answer as follows:

(A) if NO PAIRS are CORRECTLY MATCHED.
(B) if only ONE PAIR is CORRECTLY MATCHED.
(C) if only TWO PAIRS are CORRECTLY MATCHED.
(D) if ALL THREE PAIRS are CORRECTLY MATCHED.

CODE TABLE

T	M	V	D	S	P	R	G	B	H
1	2	3	4	5	6	7	8	9	0

24. DSPRGM   456782
    MVDBHT   234902
    HPMDBT   062491

25. BVPTRD   936184
    GDPHMB   807029
    GMRHMV   827032

26. MGVRSH   283750
    TRDMBS   174295
    SPRMGV   567283

27. SGBSDM   489542
    MGHPTM   290612
    MPBMHT   269301

28. TDPBHM   146902
    VPBMRS   369275
    GDMBHM   842902

Directions: For questions 29–32, choose the name that should be filed first according to the usual system of alphabetical filing of names.

29. (A) Howard J. Black
    (B) Howard Black
    (C) J. Howard Black
    (D) John H. Black

30. (A) Theodora Garth Kingston
    (B) Theadore Barth Kingston
    (C) Thomas Kingston
    (D) Thomas T. Kingston

31. (A) Paulette Mary Huerta
    (B) Paul M. Huerta
    (C) Paulette L. Huerta
    (D) Peter A. Huerta

32. (A) Martha Hunt Morgan
    (B) Martin Hunt Morgan
    (C) Mary H. Morgan
    (D) Martine H. Morgan

33. Which one of the following statements about proper telephone usage is NOT always correct? When answering the telephone, you should

    (A) know who you are speaking to.
    (B) give the caller your undivided attention.
    (C) identify yourself to the caller.
    (D) obtain the information the caller wishes before you do your other work.

34. Assume that, as a member of a Worker's Safety Committee in your agency, you are responsible for encouraging other employees to follow correct safety practices. While you are working on your regular assignment, you observe an employee violating a safety rule. Of the following, the best action for you to take first is to

(A) speak to the employee about safety practices and order him or her to stop violating the safety rule.

(B) speak to the employee about safety practices and point out the safety rule he or she is violating.

(C) bring up the matter in the next committee meeting.

(D) report this violation of the safety rule to the employee's supervisor.

35. Assume that you have been temporarily assigned by your supervisor to do a job that you do not want to do. The best action for you to take is

(A) discuss the job with your supervisor, explaining why you do not want to do it.

(B) discuss the job with your supervisor and tell him or her that you will not do it.

(C) ask a coworker to take your place on this job.

(D) do some other job that you like; your supervisor may give the job you do not like to someone else.

NOTE

The directions are stated as if you are taking the exam in a paper-and-pencil format. If you will be taking the exam on computer, each section will have directions specific to how to answer questions on computer.

Directions: You are to answer questions 36–38 solely on the basis of the information contained in the following passage.

The city government is committed to providing a safe and healthy work environment for all city employees. An effective agency safety program reduces accidents by educating employees about the types of careless acts that can cause accidents. Even in an office, accidents can happen. If each employee is aware of possible safety hazards, the number of accidents on the job can be reduced.

Careless use of office equipment can cause accidents and injuries. For example, file cabinet drawers that are filled with papers can be so heavy that the entire cabinet could tip over from the weight of one open drawer.

The bottom drawers of desks and file cabinets should never be left open, since employees could easily trip over open drawers and injure themselves.

When reaching for objects on a high shelf, an employee should use a strong, sturdy object such as a stepstool to stand on. Makeshift platforms made out of books, papers, or boxes can easily collapse. Even chairs can slide out from underfoot, causing serious injury.

Even at an employee's desk, safety hazards can occur. The tangle of wires from phones, computers, surge protectors, and other electrical equipment pose a hazard if not tucked neatly at the rear of the desk and away from a woman's high heels, which could easily catch on them. Computer towers need to be out of the walkway so that people can't trip over them. Proper seat height in relation to computers is also important to reduce the number of absences due to back pain and wrist and arm stress.

36. The goal of an effective safety program is to

(A) reduce office accidents.

(B) stop employees from smoking on the job.

(C) encourage employees to continue their education.

(D) eliminate high shelves in offices.

37. Desks and file cabinets can become safety hazards when

(A) their drawers are left open.

(B) they are used as wastebaskets.

(C) they are makeshift.

(D) they are not anchored securely to the floor.

38. What could cause a female employee to trip?

(A) Her chair may be too low.

(B) The computer might fall if its too close to the edge of the desk.

(C) She could catch her heels on the wires under her desk.

(D) A filing cabinet might be too heavy and collapse.

39. Assume that you are assigned to work as a receptionist and your duties are to answer phones, greet visitors, and do other general office work. You are busy with a routine job when several visitors approach your desk. The best action to take is to

(A) ask the visitors to have a seat and assist them after your work is completed.

(B) tell the visitors that you are busy and they should return at a more convenient time.

(C) stop working long enough to assist the visitors.

(D) continue working and wait for the visitors to ask you for assistance.

40. Assume that your supervisor has chosen you to take a special course during working hours to learn a new payroll procedure. Although you know that you were chosen because of your good work record, a coworker who feels that he or she should have been chosen has been telling everyone in your unit that the choice was unfair. Of the following, the best way to handle this situation first is to

(A) suggest to the coworker that everything in life is unfair.

(B) contact your union representative in case your coworker presents a formal grievance.

(C) tell your supervisor about your coworker's complaints and let him or her handle the situation.

(D) tell the coworker that you were chosen because of your superior work record.

Directions: You are to answer questions 41–45 solely on the basis of the information contained in the following passage.

The purpose of performance management systems is to facilitate the creation and nurturing of a performance-based culture where the individual employee's performance is aligned with agency and administration objectives, and employees are rewarded for the results they achieve.

Performance management defines the relationship that should exist between state employees and their supervisors. It is an interactive process where upper management communicates the agency's strategic vision and objectives to every manager, supervisor, and employee who then develop program, division, and individual goals designed to achieve the agency's strategic objectives. The agency's strategic objectives should cascade down to the employees in such a way that there is a clear path that connects the individual goals to that agency plan. To be effective, employees must understand how their work contributes to the success of the organization.

Agency management must send a clear and unequivocal message to all employees that performance matters. Each employee at every level of the organization must be held accountable for their participation in this process. Management is also obligated to provide sufficient resources for the training and support of all supervisors and managers in the essential components of employee-level performance management. Successful implementation of performance management will enable agencies to create and sustain a performance-based, high-achieving culture.

Performance objectives must be specific, measurable, achievable, and timely and expressed as an outcome or result.

Key components include regular, ongoing coaching, feedback, and communication with employees. Feedback should not be limited to the annual written performance appraisal in which the employee's actual performance is assessed relative to the performance objectives. This annual review is the minimum. Timely, meaningful recognition and reward of the desired performance should be part of a performance management system. An annual performance-based increase in base salary tied to the performance rating on the appraisal is also an important aspect of the program.

41. What is management obligated to provide supervisors and managers?

(A) performance objectives

(B) annual performance appraisals

(C) resources for training and support

(D) feedback and results

42. What will be the result of the successful implementation of a performance management program?

(A) annual performance reviews

(B) achievable performance objectives

(C) a performance-based, high achieving culture

(D) effective feedback

43. *Unequivocal* most nearly means

(A) unchangeable

(B) unfeeling

(C) unmistakable

(D) indecisive

44. In addition to being specific and timely, performance objectives must be

(A) measurable and achievable

(B) desired and recognized

(C) communicated and annual

(D) expressed and effective

45. How often must performance appraisals be conducted?

(A) at least every 6 months

(B) at least once a year

(C) at regular intervals

(D) as needed based on performance

46. Assume that your unit ordered 14 staplers at a total cost of $30.20, and each stapler cost the same amount. The cost of one stapler was most nearly

(A) $1.02.

(B) $1.61.

(C) $2.16.

(D) $2.26.

47. Assume that you are responsible for counting and recording licensing fees collected by your department. On a particular day, your department collected in fees 40 checks in the amount of $6 each; 80 checks in the amount of $4 each; 45 $20 bills; 30 $10 bills; 42 $5 bills; and 186 $1 bills. The total amount in fees collected on that day was

(A) $1,406.

(B) $1,706.

(C) $2,156.

(D) $2,356.

48. Assume that you are responsible for your agency's petty cash fund. During the month of February, you pay out seven subway fares at $1.25 each and one taxi fare for $7.30. You pay out nothing else from the fund. At the end of February, you count the money left in the fund and find three $1 bills, four quarters, five dimes, and four nickels. The amount of money you had available in the petty cash fund at the beginning of February was

(A) $4.70.

(B) $11.35.

(C) $16.05.

(D) $20.75.

49. Assume that you are assigned to sell tickets at a city-owned ice skating rink. An adult ticket costs $3.75, and a children's ticket costs $2. At the end of the day, you find that you have sold 36 adult tickets and 80 children's tickets. The total amount of money you collected for that day was

(A) $285.50.

(B) $295.00.

(C) $298.75.

(D) $301.00.

50. If each office worker files 487 index cards in one hour, how many cards can 26 office workers file in one hour?

(A) 10,662

(B) 12,175

(C) 12,662

(D) 14,266

STOP

END OF TEST. IF YOU HAVE ANY TIME LEFT, GO OVER YOUR WORK IN THIS TEST ONLY.

ANSWER KEY AND EXPLANATIONS

1. A	11. A	21. A	31. B	41. C
2. D	12. C	22. B	32. A	42. C
3. B	13. A	23. A	33. D	43. C
4. D	14. C	24. C	34. B	44. A
5. C	15. B	25. A	35. A	45. B
6. C	16. B	26. D	36. A	46. C
7. B	17. C	27. A	37. A	47. C
8. B	18. B	28. D	38. C	48. D
9. B	19. B	29. B	39. C	49. B
10. C	20. B	30. B	40. C	50. C

1. **The correct answer is (A).** The first step is to discuss the problem with your coworker. Remember that calm, polite discussion is almost always the correct answer when given as a choice.

2. **The correct answer is (D).** Obviously, the best thing to do is to be honest with your coworker and to deliver the letter.

3. **The correct answer is (B).** The best solution is to work on the areas that your supervisor has told you need improvement so that you can do a better job. If you're committing many careless errors, you need to be more careful when doing your work.

4. **The correct answer is (D).** The subject of the sentence, the manual, is singular, so the verb must be singular as well. The correct spelling is *describes*.

5. **The correct answer is (C).** Paper is a singular noun taking the singular verb *wasn't*. The construction *weren't no* constitutes an unacceptable double negative.

6. **The correct answer is (C).** *Their* is the possessive. *They're* is the contraction for *they are*. *There* refers to a place. Choice (D) is a misspelling.

7. **The correct answer is (B).** The correct way to express time is 8:30 a.m. Alternatively, 8:30 A.M. is also correct, but it is not one of the choices.

8. **The correct answer is (B).** The alphabet—singular—*is*. The phrase *or A to Z sequence* is extra information about the alphabet, so it is enclosed by commas. *Too* means "also" or "excessive" and is the incorrect spelling of *to*.

9. **The correct answer is (B).** The numbers in the first and second sets are different: 7143592185 and 7143892185; 8344517699 and 8344518699.

10. **The correct answer is (C).** The numbers in the first set are different: 2572114731 and 257214731.

11. **The correct answer is (A).** None of the sets are alike: 331476853821 and 331476858621; 6976658532996 and 6976655832996; 3766042113715 and 3766042113745.

12. **The correct answer is (C).** The numbers in the first set are different: 8806663315 and 880663315.

13. **The correct answer is (A).** None of the sets are alike: 990006966996 and 99000696996; 53022219743 and

53022219843; 4171171117717 and 4171171177717.

14. **The correct answer is (C).** The ZIP Codes in the third set are different: Los Angeles, California 91635 and Los Angeles, California 91685.

15. **The correct answer is (B).** The first and third sets are different: 178 35 St. Apt. 4C and 178 53 St. Apt. 4C; Pauline M. Thompson and Pauline M. Thomson.

16. **The correct answer is (B).** The first and second sets are different: Chester LeRoy Masterton and Chester LeRoy Masterson; S. LaCrosse Pla. and S. LaCross Pla.

17. **The correct answer is (C).** See the first sentence of the fourth paragraph.

18. **The correct answer is (B).** See the second sentence of the third paragraph.

19. **The correct answer is (B).** In choices (C) and (D), the numbers are too high for the fluid process. Five copies would be most efficiently reproduced by the photocopy process without preparing a master.

20. **The correct answer is (B).** See the second sentence of the last paragraph.

21. **The correct answer is (A).** To retain is to hold or to keep.

22. **The correct answer is (B).** A routine is a course of action that is followed regularly.

23. **The correct answer is (A).** To delete is to strike out or to remove.

24. **The correct answer is (C).** The second set is incorrectly coded: MVDBHT–234902 (should be 1).

25. **The correct answer is (A).** No sets are correctly coded: BVPTRD–936184 (should be 7); GDPHMB–807029 (should be 46); GMRHMV–827032 (should be 23).

26. **The correct answer is (D).** All three sets are correctly coded.

27. **The correct answer is (A).** No sets are correctly coded: SGBSDM–489542 (should be 5); MGHPTM–290612 (should be 8); MPBMHT–269301 (should be 2).

28. **The correct answer is (D).** All three sets are correctly coded.

29. **The correct answer is (B).** The correct alphabetization is: Black, Howard; Black, Howard J.; Black, J. Howard; Black, John H.

30. **The correct answer is (B).** The correct alphabetization is: Kingston, Theadore Barth; Kingston, Theodora Garth; Kingston, Thomas; Kingston, Thomas T.

31. **The correct answer is (B).** The correct alphabetization is: Huerta, Paul M.; Huerta, Paulette L.; Huerta, Paulette Mary; Huerta, Peter A.

32. **The correct answer is (A).** The correct alphabetization is: Morgan, Martha Hunt; Morgan, Martin Hunt; Morgan, Martine H.; Morgan, Mary H.

33. **The correct answer is (D).** You must always identify yourself, find out to whom you are speaking, and be courteous to the caller, but sometimes a return call could give information at a later hour or date.

34. **The correct answer is (B).** The first thing to do is speak to the employee who may not even be aware of the rule.

35. **The correct answer is (A).** Be "up front" with your supervisor. Refusing to do a distasteful task or trying to hand it off to someone else is not proper business procedure.

36. **The correct answer is (A).** See the second sentence of the first paragraph.

37. **The correct answer is (A).** See the third paragraph.

38. **The correct answer is (C).** See the second sentence in the last paragraph.

39. **The correct answer is (C).** A receptionist receives visitors.

40. **The correct answer is (C).** No matter how you approach the co-worker, you are likely to create ill feeling. Let your supervisor handle this tricky office morale problem.

41. **The correct answer is (C).** See sentence 3 in paragraph 3.

42. **The correct answer is (C).** See the last sentence in paragraph 3.

43. **The correct answer is (C).** *Unequivocal* means "unmistakable."

44. **The correct answer is (A).** See paragraph 4.

45. **The correct answer is (B).** See the last paragraph, where it says that "Feedback should not be limited to the annual written performance appraisal . . . This annual review is the minimum."

46. **The correct answer is (C).** $30.20 ÷ 14 = $2.157; round up to $2.16.

47. **The correct answer is (C).** 40 checks • $6 = $240; 80 checks • $4 = $320; 45 bills • $20 = $900; 30 bills • $10 = $300; 42 bills • $5 = $210; 186 bills • $1 = $186; $240 + $320 + $900 + $300 + $210 + $186 = $2,156.

48. **The correct answer is (D).** 7 subway fares • $1.25 = $8.75; 1 taxi fare • $7.30 = $7.30; $8.75 + $7.30 = $16.05, the total amount spent during the month. 3 dollar bills = $3; 4 quarters = $1; 5 dimes = $0.50; 4 nickels = $0.20; $3 + $1 + $0.50 + $0.20 = $4.70, the total amount left at the end of the month. $16.05 + $4.70 = $20.75, the total amount at the beginning of the month.

49. **The correct answer is (B).** 36 adults • $3.75 = $135; 80 children • $2 = $160; $135 + $160 = $295.

50. **The correct answer is (C).** 487 cards • 26 workers = 12,662.

SELF-EVALUATION

Since there is only a single exam score, your performance on any single question type does not matter. In order to earn a high score, however, you must do well on all parts of the exam. Using the following self-evaluation chart, check how many of each question type you missed to gauge your performance on that question type. Then, concentrate your efforts toward improvement in the areas with which you had the most difficulty. It will be worth your while to return to the chapter indicated and review.

SELF-EVALUATION CHART

Question Type	Question Numbers	Chapter(s) to Review
Judgment	1–3, 33–35, 39–40	11
English Grammar and Usage; Spelling	4–8	4 and 5
Clerical Speed and Accuracy	9–16	13
Reading Comprehension	17–20, 36–38, 41–45	10
Synonyms	21–23	6
Coding	24–28	14
Alphabetizing and Filing	29–32	13
Decimals	46–49	16
Work Problems	50	19

ANSWER SHEET PRACTICE TEST 5: SENIOR OFFICE TYPIST

1. Ⓐ Ⓑ Ⓒ Ⓓ Ⓔ   26. Ⓐ Ⓑ Ⓒ Ⓓ Ⓔ   51. Ⓐ Ⓑ Ⓒ Ⓓ Ⓔ   76. Ⓐ Ⓑ Ⓒ Ⓓ Ⓔ
2. Ⓐ Ⓑ Ⓒ Ⓓ Ⓔ   27. Ⓐ Ⓑ Ⓒ Ⓓ Ⓔ   52. Ⓐ Ⓑ Ⓒ Ⓓ Ⓔ   77. Ⓐ Ⓑ Ⓒ Ⓓ Ⓔ
3. Ⓐ Ⓑ Ⓒ Ⓓ Ⓔ   28. Ⓐ Ⓑ Ⓒ Ⓓ Ⓔ   53. Ⓐ Ⓑ Ⓒ Ⓓ Ⓔ   78. Ⓐ Ⓑ Ⓒ Ⓓ Ⓔ
4. Ⓐ Ⓑ Ⓒ Ⓓ Ⓔ   29. Ⓐ Ⓑ Ⓒ Ⓓ Ⓔ   54. Ⓐ Ⓑ Ⓒ Ⓓ Ⓔ   79. Ⓐ Ⓑ Ⓒ Ⓓ Ⓔ
5. Ⓐ Ⓑ Ⓒ Ⓓ Ⓔ   30. Ⓐ Ⓑ Ⓒ Ⓓ Ⓔ   55. Ⓐ Ⓑ Ⓒ Ⓓ Ⓔ   80. Ⓐ Ⓑ Ⓒ Ⓓ Ⓔ
6. Ⓐ Ⓑ Ⓒ Ⓓ Ⓔ   31. Ⓐ Ⓑ Ⓒ Ⓓ Ⓔ   56. Ⓐ Ⓑ Ⓒ Ⓓ Ⓔ   81. Ⓐ Ⓑ Ⓒ Ⓓ Ⓔ
7. Ⓐ Ⓑ Ⓒ Ⓓ Ⓔ   32. Ⓐ Ⓑ Ⓒ Ⓓ Ⓔ   57. Ⓐ Ⓑ Ⓒ Ⓓ Ⓔ   82. Ⓐ Ⓑ Ⓒ Ⓓ Ⓔ
8. Ⓐ Ⓑ Ⓒ Ⓓ Ⓔ   33. Ⓐ Ⓑ Ⓒ Ⓓ Ⓔ   58. Ⓐ Ⓑ Ⓒ Ⓓ Ⓔ   83. Ⓐ Ⓑ Ⓒ Ⓓ Ⓔ
9. Ⓐ Ⓑ Ⓒ Ⓓ Ⓔ   34. Ⓐ Ⓑ Ⓒ Ⓓ Ⓔ   59. Ⓐ Ⓑ Ⓒ Ⓓ Ⓔ   84. Ⓐ Ⓑ Ⓒ Ⓓ Ⓔ
10. Ⓐ Ⓑ Ⓒ Ⓓ Ⓔ   35. Ⓐ Ⓑ Ⓒ Ⓓ Ⓔ   60. Ⓐ Ⓑ Ⓒ Ⓓ Ⓔ   85. Ⓐ Ⓑ Ⓒ Ⓓ Ⓔ
11. Ⓐ Ⓑ Ⓒ Ⓓ Ⓔ   36. Ⓐ Ⓑ Ⓒ Ⓓ Ⓔ   61. Ⓐ Ⓑ Ⓒ Ⓓ Ⓔ   86. Ⓐ Ⓑ Ⓒ Ⓓ Ⓔ
12. Ⓐ Ⓑ Ⓒ Ⓓ Ⓔ   37. Ⓐ Ⓑ Ⓒ Ⓓ Ⓔ   62. Ⓐ Ⓑ Ⓒ Ⓓ Ⓔ   87. Ⓐ Ⓑ Ⓒ Ⓓ Ⓔ
13. Ⓐ Ⓑ Ⓒ Ⓓ Ⓔ   38. Ⓐ Ⓑ Ⓒ Ⓓ Ⓔ   63. Ⓐ Ⓑ Ⓒ Ⓓ Ⓔ   88. Ⓐ Ⓑ Ⓒ Ⓓ Ⓔ
14. Ⓐ Ⓑ Ⓒ Ⓓ Ⓔ   39. Ⓐ Ⓑ Ⓒ Ⓓ Ⓔ   64. Ⓐ Ⓑ Ⓒ Ⓓ Ⓔ   89. Ⓐ Ⓑ Ⓒ Ⓓ Ⓔ
15. Ⓐ Ⓑ Ⓒ Ⓓ Ⓔ   40. Ⓐ Ⓑ Ⓒ Ⓓ Ⓔ   65. Ⓐ Ⓑ Ⓒ Ⓓ Ⓔ   90. Ⓐ Ⓑ Ⓒ Ⓓ Ⓔ
16. Ⓐ Ⓑ Ⓒ Ⓓ Ⓔ   41. Ⓐ Ⓑ Ⓒ Ⓓ Ⓔ   66. Ⓐ Ⓑ Ⓒ Ⓓ Ⓔ   91. Ⓐ Ⓑ Ⓒ Ⓓ Ⓔ
17. Ⓐ Ⓑ Ⓒ Ⓓ Ⓔ   42. Ⓐ Ⓑ Ⓒ Ⓓ Ⓔ   67. Ⓐ Ⓑ Ⓒ Ⓓ Ⓔ   92. Ⓐ Ⓑ Ⓒ Ⓓ Ⓔ
18. Ⓐ Ⓑ Ⓒ Ⓓ Ⓔ   43. Ⓐ Ⓑ Ⓒ Ⓓ Ⓔ   68. Ⓐ Ⓑ Ⓒ Ⓓ Ⓔ   93. Ⓐ Ⓑ Ⓒ Ⓓ Ⓔ
19. Ⓐ Ⓑ Ⓒ Ⓓ Ⓔ   44. Ⓐ Ⓑ Ⓒ Ⓓ Ⓔ   69. Ⓐ Ⓑ Ⓒ Ⓓ Ⓔ   94. Ⓐ Ⓑ Ⓒ Ⓓ Ⓔ
20. Ⓐ Ⓑ Ⓒ Ⓓ Ⓔ   45. Ⓐ Ⓑ Ⓒ Ⓓ Ⓔ   70. Ⓐ Ⓑ Ⓒ Ⓓ Ⓔ   95. Ⓐ Ⓑ Ⓒ Ⓓ Ⓔ
21. Ⓐ Ⓑ Ⓒ Ⓓ Ⓔ   46. Ⓐ Ⓑ Ⓒ Ⓓ Ⓔ   71. Ⓐ Ⓑ Ⓒ Ⓓ Ⓔ
22. Ⓐ Ⓑ Ⓒ Ⓓ Ⓔ   47. Ⓐ Ⓑ Ⓒ Ⓓ Ⓔ   72. Ⓐ Ⓑ Ⓒ Ⓓ Ⓔ
23. Ⓐ Ⓑ Ⓒ Ⓓ Ⓔ   48. Ⓐ Ⓑ Ⓒ Ⓓ Ⓔ   73. Ⓐ Ⓑ Ⓒ Ⓓ Ⓔ
24. Ⓐ Ⓑ Ⓒ Ⓓ Ⓔ   49. Ⓐ Ⓑ Ⓒ Ⓓ Ⓔ   74. Ⓐ Ⓑ Ⓒ Ⓓ Ⓔ
25. Ⓐ Ⓑ Ⓒ Ⓓ Ⓔ   50. Ⓐ Ⓑ Ⓒ Ⓓ Ⓔ   75. Ⓐ Ⓑ Ⓒ Ⓓ Ⓔ

answer sheet

Practice Test 5

SENIOR OFFICE TYPIST
95 Questions • 180 Minutes

Directions: Select the best answer from the choices given and mark its letter on your answer sheet. The exam is divided into several sections, but they are timed together.

Spelling

Directions: For questions 1–10, choose the word that is correctly spelled.

1. (A) apellate
   (B) appelate
   (C) appeallate
   (D) appellate

2. (A) presumption
   (B) presoumption
   (C) presumsion
   (D) presumptsion

3. (A) litigiant
   (B) litigent
   (C) litigant
   (D) litigint

4. (A) committment
   (B) commitment
   (C) comittment
   (D) comitment

5. (A) affidavid
   (B) afidavis
   (C) affidavit
   (D) afidavit

6. (A) arraign
   (B) arrain
   (C) arreign
   (D) areign

7. (A) cumalative
   (B) cummuletive
   (C) cummalative
   (D) cumulative

8. (A) sevarance
   (B) severance
   (C) severence
   (D) severants

9. (A) adjurnment
   (B) adjuornment
   (C) ajournment
   (D) adjournment

10. (A) comenced
    (B) commentced
    (C) commenced
    (D) commensced

NOTE

The directions are stated as if you are taking the exam in a paper-and-pencil format. If you will be taking the exam on computer, each section will have directions specific to how to answer questions on computer.

Directions: Each of questions 11–20 consists of three sentences with <u>one underlined word</u>. One of the underlined words might be spelled incorrectly. Mark the letter of the sentence that contains the incorrectly spelled word. If no sentence contains a misspelled word, choose choice (D).

11. **(A)** Punishment must be a planned part of a <u>comprehensive</u> program of treating delinquency.

    (B) It is easier to spot inexperienced check <u>forjers</u> than other criminals.

    (C) Even young vandals and <u>hooligans</u> can be reformed if given adequate attention.

    (D) No error.

12. **(A)** The court officer does not have the authority to make <u>exceptions</u>.

    (B) Usually the violations are the result of <u>illegal</u> and dangerous driving behavior.

    (C) The safety division is required to investigate if the <u>dispatcher</u> files a complaint.

    (D) No error.

13. **(A)** Violent video games may have a distinct <u>influence</u> on impressionable teens, especially males.

    (B) Some of the people behind bars are <u>innocent</u> people who have been put there by mistake.

    (C) Educational <u>achievment</u> is closely associated with delinquency.

    (D) No error.

14. **(A)** <u>Disciplinary</u> action is most effective when it is taken promptly.

    (B) Release on "personal <u>recognizance</u>" refers to release without bail.

    (C) Parole violators <u>forfeit</u> their freedom.

    (D) No error.

15. **(A)** Some responsibilities take <u>precedence</u> over preservation of evidence.

    (B) Objects should not be touched unless there is some <u>compelling</u> reason.

    (C) A juvenile, or youth, <u>detension</u> center houses youth awaiting court hearings or placement in long-term facilities.

    (D) No error.

16. **(A)** Evidence is <u>inmaterial</u> if it does not prove the truth of a fact at issue.

    (B) Without <u>qualms</u>, the offender will lie and manipulate others.

    (C) If spectators become disorderly, the court officer may threaten to <u>cite</u> them for contempt of court.

    (D) No error.

17. **(A)** Under certain conditions, circumstantial evidence may be <u>admissible</u>.

    (B) Just because evidence is circumstantial does not mean that it is <u>irrelevant</u>.

    (C) An <u>aggressive</u> offender may appear to be very hostile.

    (D) No error.

18. **(A)** A victim of <u>assault</u> may want to take revenge.

    (B) The result of the trial was put in doubt when the <u>prosecuter</u> produced a surprise witness.

    (C) The court officer must maintain order and <u>decorum</u> in the courtroom.

    (D) No error.

19. **(A)** A person whose accident record can be explained by a <u>correctable</u> physical defect cannot be called "accident prone."

(B) A <u>litigant</u> should not be permitted to invoke the aid of technical rules.

(C) Refusal to <u>waive</u> immunity automatically terminates employment.

(D) No error.

20. **(A)** Court employees may be fired for <u>malfeasance</u>.

(B) A common tactic used by defense lawyers is <u>embarrassment</u> of the witness.

(C) The criminal justice system may be called an "<u>adversary</u> system."

(D) No error.

NOTE

The directions are stated as if you are taking the exam in a paper-and-pencil format. If you will be taking the exam on computer, each section will have directions specific to how to answer questions on computer.

Grammar

Directions: For questions 21–27, choose the sentence that is grammatically incorrect.

21. **(A)** One of us had to reply before tomorrow.
    (B) All employees who had served from 40 to 51 years were retired.
    (C) The personnel office takes care of employment, dismissals, and etc.
    (D) We often come across people with whom we disagree.

22. **(A)** The jurors have been instructed to deliver a sealed verdict.
    (B) The court may direct the convict to be imprisoned in a county penitentiary instead of a state prison.
    (C) Conveying self-confidence is displaying assurance.
    (D) He devotes as much, if not more, time to his work than the rest of the employees.

23. **(A)** In comparison with that laptop, this one is more preferable.
    (B) The jurors may go to dinner only with the permission of the judge.
    (C) There was neither any intention to commit a crime nor any injury incurred.
    (D) It is the sociological view that all weight should be given to the history and development of the individual.

24. **(A)** The supervisor, not the employee, makes the suggestions for improvement.
    (B) Violations of traffic laws and illegal and dangerous driving behavior constitutes bad driving.
    (C) Cynics take the position that the criminal is rarely or never reformed.
    (D) The ultimate solution to the crime problem may be better schools and better job prospects.

25. **(A)** No crime can occur unless there is a written law forbidding the act or omission in question.
    (B) If one wants to prevent crime, we must deal with the possible criminals before they reach the prison.
    (C) One could reasonably say that the same type of correctional institution is not desirable for the custody of all prisoners.
    (D) When you have completed the report, you may give it to me or directly to the judge.

26. **(A)** The structure of an organization should be considered in determining the organization's goals.
    (B) Complaints are welcomed because they frequently bring into the open conditions and faults in service that should be corrected.
    (C) The defendant had a very unique alibi, so the judge dismissed the case.
    (D) Court officers must direct witnesses to seats when the latter present themselves in court to testify.

27. **(A)** The clerk promptly notified the judge of the fire for which he was highly praised.
    (B) There is justice among thieves; the three thieves divided the goods equally among themselves.
    (C) If he had been notified promptly, he might have been here on time.
    (D) Though doubt may exist about the mailability of some matter, the sender is fully liable for law violation if such matter should be non-mailable.

Directions: For questions 28–34, choose the sentence that is grammatically correct.

28. **(A)** In high-visibility crimes, it is apparent to all concerned that they are criminal acts at the time when they are committed.

   (B) Statistics tell us that more people are killed by guns than by any kind of weapon.

   (C) Reliable persons guarantee the facts with regards to the truth of these statements.

   (D) Messengers sort and carry mail, documents, or other materials between offices or buildings.

29. **(A)** She suspects that the service is so satisfactory as it should be.

   (B) The court officer goes to the exhibit table and discovered that Exhibit B is an entirely different document.

   (C) The jurors and alternates comprise a truly diverse group.

   (D) Our aim should be not merely to reform lawbreakers but striking at the roots of crime.

30. **(A)** Close examination of traffic accident statistics reveal that traffic accidents are frequently the result of violations of traffic laws.

   (B) If you had planned on employing fewer people than this to do the work, this situation would not have arose.

   (C) As far as good looks and polite manners are concerned, they are both alike.

   (D) If a murder has been committed with a bow and arrow, it is irrelevant to show that the defendant was well acquainted with firearms.

31. **(A)** An individual engages in criminal behavior if the number of criminal patterns that he or she has acquired exceeds the number of non-criminal patterns.

   (B) Every person must be informed of the reason for their arrest unless arrested in the actual commission of a crime.

   (C) The one of the following motorists to which it would be most desirable to issue a summons is the one which was late for an important business appointment.

   (D) The officer should glance around quickly but with care to determine whether his entering the area will damage any evidence.

32. **(A)** State troopers typically work on a rotating shift basis, must be available for duty 24 hours a day, they work on holidays in snow and rain.

   (B) If the budget allows, we are likely to reemploy anyone whose training fits them to do the work.

   (C) The investigative team went quietly about its work, sifting through the dirt and rubble looking for evidence.

   (D) Traffic control and enforcement are the mains concerns of state troopers and have limited general police authority.

33. **(A)** Due to the age of the defendant, the trial will be heard in Juvenile Court and the record will be sealed.

(B) Calculate the average amount stolen per incident by dividing the total value by the amount of offenses.

(C) The combination to the office safe is known only to the chief clerk and myself.

(D) Hearsay is evidence based on repeating the words told by another but is not based on personal observation or knowledge.

34. **(A)** A court officer needs specific qualifications that are different than those required of police officers.

(B) Understanding how one's own work contributes to the effort of the entire agency indicates an appreciation for the importance of that job.

(C) If only one guard was assigned to the jury room, the chances of wrong-doing would be heightened.

(D) One should not use an improved method for performing a task until you have obtained approval of the supervisor.

Clerical Checking

Directions: For questions 35–50, compare the name/address/number listings in all three columns. Then choose your answers as follows:

(A) if the listings in ALL THREE columns are exactly ALIKE.
(B) if only the listings in the FIRST and THIRD columns are exactly ALIKE.
(C) if only the listings in the FIRST and SECOND columns are exactly ALIKE.
(D) if the listings in ALL THREE columns are DIFFERENT.

35. John H. Smith
238 N. Monroe Street
Phila., PA 19147
176-54-326
5578-98765-33

John H. Smith
238 N. Monroe Street
Phila, PA 19147
176-54-326
5578-98765-33

John H. Smith
238 N. Monroe Street
Phila., PA 19147
176-54-326
5578-98765-33

36. Evan A. McKinley
2872 Broadway
East Amherst, NY 14051
212-883-5184
9803-115-6848

Evan A. McKinley
2872 Broadway
East Amherst, NY 14051
212-883-5184
9083-115-6848

Evan A. McKinley
2872 Broadway
East Amherst, NV 14051
212-883-5184
9803-115-6848

37. Luigi Antonio Cruz Jr.
2695 East 3435 South
Salt Lake City, UT 84109
801-485-1563, x.233
013-5589734-9

Luigi Antonio Cruz Jr.
2695 East 3435 South
Salt Lake City, UT 84109
801-485-1563, x.233
013-5589734-9

Luigi Antonio Cruz Jr.
2695 East 3435 South
Salt Lake City, UT 84109
801-485-1563, x.233
013-5589734-9

38. Educational Records Inst.
P.O. Box 44268a
Atlanta, Georgia 30337
18624-40-9128
63qs5-95YT3-001

Educational Records Inst.
P.O. Box 44268a
Atlanta, Georgia 30337
18624-40-9128
63qs5-95YT3-001

Educational Records Inst.
P.O. Box 44286a
Atlanta, Georgia 30337
18624-40-9128
63qs5-95YT3-001

39. Sr. Consultant, Labor Rel.
Benner Mgmt. Group
86408 W. 3rd Ave.
Trowbridge, MA 02178
617-980-1136

Sr. Consultant, Labor Rel.
Banner Mgmt. Group
86408 W. 3rd Ave.
Trowbridge, MA 02178
617-980-1136

Sr. Consultant, Labor Rel.
Benner Mgmt. Group
84608 W. 3rd Ave.
Trowbridge, MA 02178
617-980-1136

40. Marina Angelika Salvis
P.O.B. 11283 Gracie Sta.
Newtown, PA 18940-0998
215-382-0628
4168-GNP-78852

Marina Angelika Salvis
P.O.B. 11283 Gracie Sta.
Newtown, PA 18940-0998
215-382-0628
4168-GNP-78852

Marina Angelika Salvis
P.O.B. 11283 Gracie Sta.
Newtown, PA 18940-0998
215-382-0628
4168-GNP-78852

41. Durham Reichard III
8298 Antigua Terrace
Gaithersburg, MD 20879
301-176-9887-8
0-671-843576-X

Durham Reichard III
8298 Antigua Terrace
Gaithersburg, MD 20879
301-176-9887-8
0-671-843576-X

Durham Reichard III
8298 Antigua Terrace
Gaithersberg, MD 20879
301-176-9887-8
0-671-843576-X

42. L. Chamberlain Smythe
Mardikian & Moore, Inc.
Cor. Mott Street at Pell
San Francisco, CA
58312-398401-25

L. Chamberlain Smythe
Mardikian and Moore, Inc.
Cor. Mott Street at Pell
San Francisco, CA
58312-398401-25

L. Chamberlain Smythe
Markdikian & Moore, Inc.
Cor. Mott Street at Pell
San Francisco, CA
58312-398401-25

43. Ramona Fleischer-Chris
60646 West Touhy Avenue
Sebastopol, CA 95472
707-998-0104
0-06-408632-0

Ramona Fleisher-Chris
60646 West Touhy Avenue
Sebastopol, CA 95472
707-998-0104
0-06-408632-0

Ramona Fleischer-Chris
60646 West Touhey Avenue
Sepabstopol, CA 95472
707-998-0104
0-06-408632-0

44. George Sebastian Barnes
Noble/Encore/Dalton
43216 M Street, NE
Washington, DC 20036
202-222-1272

George Sebastian Barnes
Noble/Encore/Dalton
43216 M. Street, NE
Washington, DC 20036
202-222-1272

George Sebastian Barnes
Noble/Encore/Dalton
43216 M Street, NE
Washington, DC 20036
202-222-1272

45. Baldwin Algonquin III
2503 Bartholemew Way
Lemberger, VA 28094-9182
9-1-303-558-8536
683-64-0828

Baldwin Algonquin III
2503 Bartholemew Way
Lemberger, VA 28094-9182
9-1-303-558-8536
683-64-0828

Baldwin Algonquin III
2503 Bartholomew Way
Lemberger, VA 28094-9182
9-1-303-558-8536
683-64-0828

46. Huang Ho Cheung
612 Gallopade Gallery, E.
Seattle, WA 98101-2614
001-206-283-7722
5416R-1952TZ-op

Huang Ho Cheung
612 Gallopade Gallery, E.
Seattle, WA 98101-2614
001-206-283-7722
5416R-1952TZ-op

Huang Ho Cheung
612 Gallopade Gallery, E.
Seattle, WA 98101-2614
001-206-283-7722
5416R-1952TZ-op

47. Hilliard H. Hyacinth
86529 Dunwoodie Drive
Kanakao, HI 91132
808-880-8080
6-78912-e3e42

Hilliard H. Hyacinth
86529 Dunwoodie Drive
Kanakao, HI 91132
808-880-8080
6-78912-3e3e42

Hilliard H. Hyacinth
85629 Dunwoodie Drive
Kanakao, HI 91132
808-880-8080
6-78912-e3e42

48. Anoko Kawamoto
8932 Shimabui Hwy.
O'Reilly Bay, LA 56212
713-864-7253-4984
5634-Ootv5a-16867

Anoko Kawamoto
8932 Shimabui Hwy.
O'Reillys Bay, LA 56212
713-864-7253-4984
5634-Ootv5a-16867

Anoko Kawamoto
8932 Shimabui Hwy.
O'Reilly Bay, LA 56212
713-864-7253-4984
5634-Ootv5a-16867

49. Michael Chrzanowski
312 Colonia del Valle
4132 ES, Mexico DF
001-45-67265
A8987-B73245

Michael Chrzanowski
312 Colonia del Valle
4132 ES, Mexico DF
001-45-67265
A8987-B73245

Michael Chrzanowski
312 Colonia del Valle
4132 ES, Mexico D.F.
001-45-67265
A8987-B73245

50. Leonard Wilson-Wood
6892 Grand Boulevard, W.
St. Georges South, DE
302-333-4273
0-122365-3987

Leonard Wilson-Wood
6892 Grand Boulevard, W.
St. Goerges South, DE
302-333-4273
0-122365-3987

Leonard Wilson-Wood
6892 Grand Boulevard, W.
St. Georges South, DE
302-333-4273
0-122365-3987

Office Record Keeping

Directions: Study the information given in the tables and combine the information as indicated. Answer questions 51–65 in accordance with the information on the tables. You are NOT permitted to use a calculator to arrive at totals.

DAILY LOG OF CASES

Monday

Judge	Date Filed	Sum at Issue	Disposition	Award
Baron	6/5/11	$9,500	Adjourned	X
Lee	4/2/12	$20,000	Dismissed	X
Conlon	12/8/10	$12,000	Settled	X
Ramos	3/31/12	$5,500	Settled	X
Lee	10/8/11	$10,000	Dismissed	X
Jones	1/5/12	$14,000	Found for plaintiff	$15,000
Baron	5/1/13	$7,600	Adjourned	X

Tuesday

Judge	Date Filed	Sum at Issue	Disposition	Award
Ramos	2/2/12	$3,000	Found for plaintiff	$3,375
Amati	8/6/12	$8,000	Dismissed	X
Moro	4/8/11	$11,500	Found for plaintiff	$9,000
Jones	11/17/10	$12,000	Adjourned	X
Conlon	12/4/10	$4,500	Adjourned	X
Amati	6/12/11	$2,000	Settled	$15,000

Wednesday

Judge	Date Filed	Sum at Issue	Disposition	Award
Conlon	1/7/13	$10,000	Dismissed	X
Baron	5/3/12	$5,000	Adjourned	X
Ramos	6/22/11	$7,500	Found for plaintiff	$6,000
Moro	2/15/13	$22,000	Settled	X
Lee	9/7/12	$8,000	Settled	X
Conlon	11/30/10	$16,000	Found for plaintiff	$17,250
Amati	7/10/12	$10,000	Found for plaintiff	$10,850

Thursday

Judge	Date Filed	Sum at Issue	Disposition	Award
Jones	5/18/12	$7,500	Found for plaintiff	$6,000
Amati	3/6/12	$9,250	Settled	X
Conlon	3/31/12	$6,000	Adjourned	X
Moro	8/28/11	$12,000	Adjourned	X
Conlon	10/30/10	$4,600	Found for plaintiff	$5,000

Friday

Judge	Date Filed	Sum at Issue	Disposition	Award
Lee	4/12/12	$6,000	Adjourned	X
Baron	1/28/13	$9,500	Dismissed	X
Ramos	7/17/12	$28,000	Found for plaintiff	$20,000
Amati	12/2/11	$15,000	Settled	X
Lee	2/21/12	$8,000	Found for plaintiff	$8,625
Moro	5/10/11	$22,000	Settled	X
Baron	8/25/11	$11,000	Dismissed	X
Jones	11/4/10	$5,500	Settled	X

NOTE

The directions are stated as if you are taking the exam in a paper-and-pencil format. If you will be taking the exam on computer, each section will have directions specific to how to answer questions on computer.

DAILY BREAKDOWN OF CASES

	Mon.	Tue.	Wed.	Thurs.	Fri.	Total
Case Status						
Dismissed	2	1	1		2	6
Adjourned	2	2	1	2	1	8
Settled	2	1	2	1	3	9
Found for Plaintiff	1	2	3	2	2	10
Total Cases	7	6	7	5	8	33
Cases by Year Using Original Numbers						
2010	1	2	1	1	1	6
2011	2	2	1	1	3	9
2012	3	2	3	3	3	14
2013	1		2		1	4
Total Cases	7	6	7	5	8	33

SUMMARY OF CASES BY JUDGE/DISPOSITION

Judge	Dismissed	Adjourned	Settled	Found for Plaintiff	Total
Amati	1		3	1	5
Baron	2	3			5
Conlon	1	2	1	2	6
Jones		1	1	2	4
Lee	2	1	1	1	5
Moro		1	2	1	4
Ramos			1	3	4
Total	6	8	9	10	33

51. The judge scheduled to hear the greatest number of cases in this week was

(A) Amati.

(B) Lee.

(C) Conlon.

(D) Ramos.

52. The judge who determined no cash awards in this week was

(A) Moro.

(B) Jones.

(C) Baron.

(D) Lee.

53. How many judges were assigned to hear more than one case in one day?

(A) 1

(B) 2

(C) 3

(D) 4

54. In how many cases was the sum finally awarded lower than the sum at issue?

(A) 2

(B) 3

(C) 4

(D) 5

55. How many of the cases filed in 2010 were dismissed?

(A) 0

(B) 1

(C) 2

(D) 3

56. Of the cases adjourned, the greatest number were filed in

(A) 2010.

(B) 2011.

(C) 2012.

(D) 2013.

57. Which two judges were scheduled to sit on only three days?

(A) Jones and Baron

(B) Baron and Lee

(C) Lee and Moro

(D) Ramos and Jones

58. In which month were the greatest number of cases filed?

(A) February

(B) May

(C) August

(D) November

59. The total amount of money awarded on Wednesday was

(A) $33,500.

(B) $34,100.

(C) $35,300.

(D) $45,000.

60. The total amount of money awarded by Jones was

(A) $39,000.

(B) $21,500.

(C) $21,000.

(D) $17,500.

61. The amount at issue in the cases that were adjourned on Thursday was

(A) $12,100.

(B) $18,000.

(C) $21,350.

(D) $29,250.

62. When the amount of an award is greater than the sum at issue, the higher award represents an additional sum meant to cover plaintiff's costs in the suit. The total amount awarded this week to cover costs was

(A) $4,800.

(B) $9,000.

(C) $3,500.

(D) $17,500.

63. If all the plaintiffs who filed cases in 2003 were awarded exactly the sums for which they sued, they would have received a total of

(A) $41,500.

(B) $45,100.

(C) $48,600.

(D) $49,100.

64. The total amount awarded to plaintiffs who filed their cases in 2000 was

(A) $1,650.

(B) $20,600.

(C) $22,250.

(D) $22,650.

65. Comparing cases filed in 2001 with cases filed in 2002,

(A) Four more of the 2001 cases were settled than 2002 cases.

(B) Two fewer 2002 cases were settled than 2001 cases.

(C) An equal number of cases was settled from the two years.

(D) Three more of the 2001 cases were settled than 2002 cases.

NOTE

The directions are stated as if you are taking the exam in a paper-and-pencil format. If you will be taking the exam on computer, each section will have directions specific to how to answer questions on computer.

Reading, Understanding, and Interpreting Written Material

Directions: Questions 66–95 are based on the following passages. Each passage contains several numbered blanks. Read the passage once quickly to get the overall idea. Below each passage are listed sets of words numbered to match the blanks. Read the passage through a second time more slowly, and choose the word from each set that makes the most sense both in the sentence and in the total paragraph.

A large proportion of people __66__ bars are __67__ convicted criminals, __68__ people who have been arrested and are being __69__ until __70__ trials in __71__. Experts have often pointed out that this __72__ system does not operate fairly. For instance, a person who can afford to pay bail usually will not get locked up. The theory of the bail system is that the person will make sure to show up in court when he or she is supposed to; __73__, bail will be forfeited—the person will __74__ the __75__ that was put up. Sometimes a person __76__ can show that he or she is a stable __77__ with a job and a family will be released on "personal recognizance" (without bail). The result is that the well-to-do, the __78__, and family men can often __79__ the detention system. The people who do wind up in detention tend to __80__ the poor, the unemployed, the single, and the young.

66. **(A)** under
    (B) at
    (C) tending
    (D) behind

67. **(A)** always
    (B) not
    (C) hardened
    (D) very

68. **(A)** but
    (B) and
    (C) also
    (D) although

69. **(A)** hanged
    (B) freed
    (C) held
    (D) judged

70. **(A)** your
    (B) his
    (C) daily
    (D) their

71. **(A)** jail
    (B) court
    (C) fire
    (D) judgment

72. **(A)** school
    (B) court
    (C) detention
    (D) election

73. **(A)** otherwise
    (B) therefore
    (C) because
    (D) then

74. (A) save
    (B) spend
    (C) lose
    (D) count

75. (A) wall
    (B) money
    (C) front
    (D) pretense

76. (A) whom
    (B) which
    (C) what
    (D) who

77. (A) citizen
    (B) horse
    (C) cleaner
    (D) clown

78. (A) handsome
    (B) athletic
    (C) employed
    (D) alcoholic

79. (A) survive
    (B) avoid
    (C) provide
    (D) institute

80. (A) become
    (B) help
    (C) be
    (D) harm

___81___ acts are classified according to ___82___ standards. One is whether the ___83___ is major or minor. A major offense, such as murder, would be ___84___ a felony, ___85___ , a minor offense, such as reckless driving, would be considered a misdemeanor. ___86___ standard of classification is the specific kind of crime committed. Examples are burglary and robbery, which are ___87___ often used incorrectly by individuals who are ___88___ aware of the actual ___89___ as defined by law. A person who breaks ___90___ a building to commit a ___91___ or other major crime is ___92___ of burglary, while robbery is the felonious taking of an individual's ___93___ from his person or ___94___ his immediate ___95___ by the use of violence or threat.

81. (A) People's
    (B) Criminal
    (C) Felonious
    (D) Numerous

82. (A) decent
    (B) published
    (C) community
    (D) several

83. (A) crime
    (B) act
    (C) offender
    (D) standard

84. (A) labeled
    (B) convicted
    (C) executed
    (D) tried

NOTE

The directions are stated as if you are taking the exam in a paper-and-pencil format. If you will be taking the exam on computer, each section will have directions specific to how to answer questions on computer.

85. **(A)** moreover
    (B) because
    (C) whereas
    (D) hence

86. **(A)** Gold
    (B) Juried
    (C) Another
    (D) My

87. **(A)** crimes
    (B) terms
    (C) verdicts
    (D) sentences

88. **(A)** sometimes
    (B) very
    (C) not
    (D) angrily

89. **(A)** difference
    (B) definitions
    (C) crimes
    (D) victims

90. **(A)** down
    (B) into
    (C) apart
    (D) from

91. **(A)** felony
    (B) burglary
    (C) robbery
    (D) theft

92. **(A)** accused
    (B) convicted
    (C) freed
    (D) guilty

93. **(A)** life
    (B) liberty
    (C) property
    (D) weapon

94. **(A)** throughout
    (B) in
    (C) by
    (D) for

95. **(A)** lifetime
    (B) home
    (C) presence
    (D) concern

STOP

END OF TEST. IF YOU HAVE ANY TIME LEFT, GO OVER YOUR WORK IN THIS TEST ONLY.

ANSWER KEY AND EXPLANATIONS

1. D	20. D	39. D	58. B	77. A
2. A	21. C	40. A	59. B	78. C
3. C	22. D	41. C	60. C	79. B
4. B	23. A	42. D	61. B	80. C
5. C	24. B	43. D	62. D	81. B
6. A	25. B	44. B	63. D	82. D
7. D	26. C	45. C	64. C	83. A
8. B	27. A	46. A	65. C	84. A
9. D	28. D	47. D	66. D	85. C
10. C	29. C	48. B	67. B	86. C
11. B	30. D	49. C	68. A	87. B
12. D	31. A	50. B	69. C	88. C
13. C	32. C	51. C	70. D	89. A
14. D	33. A	52. C	71. B	90. B
15. C	34. B	53. D	72. C	91. D
16. A	35. B	54. C	73. A	92. D
17. D	36. D	55. A	74. C	93. C
18. B	37. A	56. C	75. B	94. B
19. D	38. C	57. B	76. D	95. C

1. **The correct answer is (D).** The correct spelling is *appellate*.

2. **The correct answer is (A).** The correct spelling is *presumption*.

3. **The correct answer is (C).** The correct spelling is *litigant*.

4. **The correct answer is (B).** The correct spelling is *commitment*.

5. **The correct answer is (C).** The correct spelling is *affidavit*.

6. **The correct answer is (A).** The correct spelling is *arraign*.

7. **The correct answer is (D).** The correct spelling is *cumulative*.

8. **The correct answer is (B).** The correct spelling is *severance*.

9. **The correct answer is (D).** The correct spelling is *adjournment*.

10. **The correct answer is (C).** The correct spelling is *commenced*.

11. **The correct answer is (B).** The correct spelling is *forgers*.

12. **The correct answer is (D).** None of the words are misspelled.

13. **The correct answer is (C).** The correct spelling is *achievement*.

14. **The correct answer is (D).** None of the words are misspelled.

15. **The correct answer is (C).** The correct spelling is *detention*.

16. **The correct answer is (A).** The correct spelling is *immaterial*.

17. **The correct answer is (D).** None of the words are misspelled.

18. **The correct answer is (B).** The correct spelling is *prosecutor*.

19. **The correct answer is (D).** None of the words are misspelled.

20. **The correct answer is (D).** None of the words are misspelled.

21. **The correct answer is (C).** There should be no *and* before the "etc." at the end of a series of words.

22. **The correct answer is (D).** This is an incomplete comparison. It should read, "He devotes as much as, if not more, time to his work than the rest of the employees."

23. **The correct answer is (A).** *More preferable* is a redundancy; *preferable* alone is quite adequate.

24. **The correct answer is (B).** The compound subject *violations . . .and. . . behavior* requires the plural form of the verb *constitute*.

25. **The correct answer is (B).** This sentence shifts point of view midstream. It could read either "If one wants to prevent crime, one must deal. . .," or, "If we want to prevent crime, we must deal. . ."

26. **The correct answer is (C).** *Unique* means that there is only one; therefore, the word can take no qualifier.

27. **The correct answer is (A).** This is an ambiguous statement. Was the judge praised for the fire? Was the clerk praised for the fire? It would be better to say "The clerk was highly praised for promptly notifying the judge of the fire."

28. **The correct answer is (D).** Sentence (A) reads as if all concerned are criminal acts. Since guns are a kind of weapon, sentence (B) would have to read ". . .than any other kind of weapon." In sentence (C), *regards* is the wrong word; the word required is *regard*.

29. **The correct answer is (C).** In sentence (A), the idiomatic form is *as satisfactory*. Sentence (B) confuses two verb tenses in the same sentence; it would be correct to say that the court officer *went. . .and discovered. . .* Sen-

tence (D) requires a parallel construction, either *reforming and striking* or *to reform and to strike*.

30. **The correct answer is (D).** In sentence (A), *examination*, being singular, requires the singular verb *reveals*. The correct form of sentence (B) is ". . .would not have arisen." As for sentence (C), the word *alike* obviously includes both, so the word *both* is redundant.

31. **The correct answer is (A).** In sentence (B), *Every person* is singular and therefore must be informed of the reason for his or her arrest. In sentence (C), a motorist is a person, not a thing, so use *to whom* and *who* rather than *to which* and *which*. Sentence (D) requires the parallelism of *quickly but carefully*.

32. **The correct answer is (C).** Sentence (A) has several problems. First, it's a run-on sentence. A punctuation mark or conjunction is required between "day" and "they." The sentence also reads as though the troopers work only on holidays if it snows or rains. The sentence would be clearer if it read: "They work on holidays and in bad weather." In sentence (B), *anyone* is singular, so the referent pronoun must also be singular, *him or her*. Sentence (D) has a problem with clarity. As written, it reads that traffic control and enforcement have limited general police authority.

33. **The correct answer is (A).** Sentence (D) is wordy and clearly wrong. In sentence (B), what is meant is the number of offenses. In sentence (C), we need a simple objective case pronoun: ". . .is known only to the chief clerk and me."

34. **The correct answer is (B).** In sentence (A), the correct idiomatic form is *different from*. Sentence (C) requires a subjunctive form because

the statement is contrary to fact: "If only one guard were. . ." Sentence (D) shifts point of view; for consistency, the pronoun throughout may be either *one* or *you*.

35. **The correct answer is (B).** There is a difference in the second column: Phila., PA 19147 and Phila, PA 19147

36. **The correct answer is (D).** All three columns are different: East Amherst, NY 14051 and East Amherst, NV 14051 (third column); 9803-115-6848 and 9083-115-6848 (second column)

37. **The correct answer is (A).** All three columns are alike.

38. **The correct answer is (C).** There is a difference in the third column: P.O. Box 44268a and P.O. Box 44286a

39. **The correct answer is (D).** All three columns are different: Benner Mgmt. Group and Banner Mgmt. Group (second column); 86408 W. 3rd Ave. and 84608 W. 3rd Ave. (third column)

40. **The correct answer is (A).** All three columns are alike.

41. **The correct answer is (C).** The third column is different: Gaithersburg, MD 20879 and Gaithersberg, MD 20879

42. **The correct answer is (D).** All three columns are different: Mardikian & Moore, Inc., Mardikian and Moore, Inc., and Markdikian & Moore, Inc.

43. **The correct answer is (D).** All three columns are different: Ramona Fleischer-Chris and Ramona Fleischer-Chris (second column); 60646 West Touhy Avenue and 60646 West Touhey Avenue (third column)

44. **The correct answer is (B).** The second column is different: 43216 M Street, NE and 43216 M. Street, NE

45. **The correct answer is (C).** The third column is different: 2503 Bartholemew Way and 2503 Bartholomew Way

46. **The correct answer is (A).** All three columns are alike.

47. **The correct answer is (D).** All three columns are different: 86529 Dunwoodie Drive and 85629 Dunwoodie Drive (third column); 6-78912-e3e42 and 6-78912-3e3e42 (second column)

48. **The correct answer is (B).** The second column is different: O'Reilly Bay, LA 56212 and O'Reillys Bay, LA 56212

49. **The correct answer is (C).** The third column is different: 4132 ES, Mexico DF and 4132 ES, Mexico D.F.

50. **The correct answer is (B).** The second column is different: St. Georges South, DE, and St. Goerges South, DE.

51. **The correct answer is (C).** Conlon was scheduled to hear 6 cases: 1 on Monday, 1 on Tuesday, 2 on Wednesday, and 2 on Thursday. Amati, Baron, and Lee were scheduled for 5 cases apiece. Jones, Moro, and Ramos were only scheduled for 4.

52. **The correct answer is (C).** Of the cases Baron was scheduled to hear, 3 were adjourned (2 on Monday and 1 on Wednesday) and 2 were dismissed (on Friday), so he didn't give any cash awards. Jones gave cash awards in 2 cases, and Moro and Lee gave cash awards in 1 case each.

53. **The correct answer is (D).** Lee and Baron were both scheduled for 2 trials on Monday and Friday, Amati was scheduled for 2 on Tuesday, and Conlon was scheduled for 2 on Wednesday and Thursday, for a total of 4 judges.

54. **The correct answer is (C).** On Tuesday, Moro awarded $9,000 in a suit for $11,500; on Wednesday, Ramos awarded $6,000 in a suit for $7,500; on Thursday, Jones awarded $6,000 in a suit for $7,500; and on Friday,

Ramos awarded $20,000 in a suit for $28,000, for a total of 4 cases.

55. **The correct answer is (A).** Of the 6 cases filed in 2010, 2 were settled (1 on Monday and 1 on Friday), 2 were adjourned (both on Tuesday), and 2 were adjudicated (1 on Wednesday and 1 on Thursday). None was dismissed.

56. **The correct answer is (C).** Three of the 2012 cases were adjourned: 1 on Wednesday, 1 on Thursday, and 1 on Friday. Only one 2013 case was adjourned, and 2 each of 2010 and 2011 cases were adjourned.

57. **The correct answer is (B).** Lee and Baron each sat on Monday, Wednesday, and Friday. Jones sat on Monday, Tuesday, Thursday, and Friday. Moro sat on Tuesday, Wednesday, Thursday, and Friday. Ramos sat on Monday, Tuesday, Wednesday, and Friday.

58. **The correct answer is (B).** Four cases were filed in May (see the tables for Monday, Wednesday, Thursday, and Friday). Three cases were filed in each of February, August, and November.

59. **The correct answer is (B).** $6,000 + $17,250 + $10,850 = $34,100

60. **The correct answer is (C).** $15,000 (on Monday) + $6,000 (on Thursday) = $21,000

61. **The correct answer is (B).** $6,000 (Conlon's first case) + $12,000 (Moro's case) = $18,000

62. **The correct answer is (D).** $15,000 – $14,000 = $1,000 (Jones on Monday); $3,375 – $3,000 = $375 (Ramos on Tuesday); $15,000 – $2,000 = $13,000 (Amati on Wednesday); $17,250 – $16,000 = $1,250 (Conlon on Wednesday); $10,850 – $10,000 = $850 (Amati on Wednesday); $5,000 – $4,600 = $400 (Conlon on Thursday); $8,625 – $8,000 = $625 (Lee on Friday); $1,000

+ $375 + $13,000 + $1,250 + $850 + $400 + $625 = $17,500

63. **The correct answer is (D).** $7,600 (filed on 5/1/13 and heard on Monday) + $10,000 (filed on 1/7/13 and heard on Wednesday) + $22,000 (filed on 2/15/13 and heard on Wednesday) + $9,500 (filed on 1/28/13 and heard on Friday) = $49,100

64. **The correct answer is (C).** On Wednesday, Conlon awarded $17,350 in a 11/30/10 case; on Thursday, Conlon awarded $5,000 in a 10/30/10 case; $17,350 + $5,000 = $22,250

65. **The correct answer is (C).** An equal number of cases was settled from the two years. Three 2011 cases were settled—one on Tuesday and two on Friday; three 2012 cases were settled—one on Monday, one on Wednesday, and one on Thursday.

66. **The correct answer is (D).** People are generally said to be behind bars.

67. **The correct answer is (B).** The second part of the sentence should lead you to choose the contrasting word *not*.

68. **The correct answer is (A).** Again, a contrasting word, *but*, fits best.

69. **The correct answer is (C).** The word that makes the most sense in the context of the sentence is *held*.

70. **The correct answer is (D).** Since *people* is plural, you must choose the plural possessive, *their*.

71. **The correct answer is (B).** Trials are generally held in court.

72. **The correct answer is (C).** The paragraph is discussing jailing of people awaiting trial, a form of detention.

73. **The correct answer is (A).** Reading the two parts of the sentence shows that you need a contrasting word, *otherwise*.

74. **The correct answer is (C).** To forfeit bail, as stated earlier in the sentence, means that you lose your money.

75. **The correct answer is (B).** Since bail is a set amount of cash, money is the best choice here.

76. **The correct answer is (D).** Since the pronoun refers to a person, you must choose *who*.

77. **The correct answer is (A).** The only choice that makes sense is *citizen*.

78. **The correct answer is (C).** As stated earlier ("a stable citizen with a job"), people who are employed can often avoid the detention system.

79. **The correct answer is (B).** Since these people are released on personal recognizance, they avoid the detention system.

80. **The correct answer is (C).** *Be* makes the most sense in the context of the sentence.

81. **The correct answer is (B).** A quick reading of the paragraph reveals that it is discussing criminal acts.

82. **The correct answer is (D).** Again, reading over the paragraph reveals that it is discussing more than one, or several, standards.

83. **The correct answer is (A).** Since the previous sentence was discussing criminal acts, *crime* is the best choice here.

84. **The correct answer is (A).** *Labeled* fits best in the context of the sentence.

85. **The correct answer is (C).** Major and minor offenses are being contrasted here, so choose the contrasting word, *whereas*.

86. **The correct answer is (C).** This sentence discusses a second standard, so the best choice is *Another*.

87. **The correct answer is (B).** This sentence is talking about definitions, so *terms* is the best choice.

88. **The correct answer is (C).** Since the terms are used incorrectly, the people who use them are not aware of their legal definitions.

89. **The correct answer is (A).** This sentence is clearly discussing the difference between the two terms.

90. **The correct answer is (B).** Typically, a person breaks into a building.

91. **The correct answer is (D).** Eliminate *felony* for one of the more specific terms. Since this part of the sentence is defining robbery, you can't reuse that term, and you already know that a burglary isn't the same thing as a robbery. Therefore, the best choice is *theft*.

92. **The correct answer is (D).** When a person commits the crime of burglary, he or she is *guilty* of burglary.

93. **The correct answer is (C).** Robbery generally means taking someone's property.

94. **The correct answer is (B).** *In* fits the context of the sentence best.

95. **The correct answer is (C).** You can eliminate *home*—you already know that that's a burglary. The only other choice that makes sense is *presence*.

SELF-EVALUATION

In order to earn a high score, you must do well on all parts of the exam. Using the following chart, check how many of each question type you missed to gauge your performance on that kind of question. Then, concentrate your efforts toward improvement in the areas with which you had the most difficulty; it will be worth your while to return to the indicated chapter and review.

SELF-EVALUATION CHART

Question Type	Question Numbers	Chapter to Review
Spelling	1–20	5
English Grammar and Usage	21–34	4
Clerical Speed and Accuracy	35–50	14
Tabular Completions	51–65	18
Effective Expression	66–95	9

PART VII

APPENDIXES

Occupations Available in the Federal Government

FROM USAJOBS® HELP

Occupations in the Federal Government are placed in one of two categories—either professional (general schedule) or trade, crafts, or labor (wage grade). The jobs are further categorized and defined by their series and/or grade. The following is a list of the occupational "families" and a description of what types of positions are included in each.

- **Professional**—Positions whose primary duty requires knowledge or experience of an administrative, clerical, scientific, artistic, or technical nature and is not related to trade, craft, or manual labor work.

- **Trade, Craft, or Labor**—Positions whose primary duty involves the performance of physical work and requires knowledge or experience of a trade, craft, or manual labor nature.

In terms of job availability, the three federal government departments projected to hire the most employees in the next years are the Departments of Homeland Security, Veterans Affairs, and Defense. Their needs cross a variety of occupations. For example, the Department of Defense not only enlists military personnel, but it also employs teachers for its Department of Defense schools overseas. Veterans Affairs' employees include doctors, nurses, pharmacists, and physical therapists as well as maintenance workers. The Department of Homeland Security also hires police officers, asylum officers, intelligence analysts, and human resources professionals. All three departments employ clerical staff.

PROFESSIONAL OCCUPATIONS

0000 – Miscellaneous Occupations
These positions include those whose duties are to administer, supervise, or perform work that cannot be included in other occupational groups either because the duties are unique or because they are complex and come in part under various groups.

0100 – Social Science, Psychology, and Welfare
This category includes those positions whose duties are to advise on, administer, supervise, or perform research or other professional and scientific work, subordinate technical work, or related clerical work in one or more of the social sciences; in psychology; in social work; in recreational activities; or in the administration of public welfare and insurance programs.

0200 – Human Resources Management

These positions include those whose duties are to advise on, administer, supervise, or perform work involved in the different phases of human resources management.

0300 – General Administrative, Clerical, and Office Services

This category includes those positions whose duties are to administer, supervise, or perform work involved in management analysis; stenography, typing, correspondence, and secretarial work; mail and file work; the operation of office equipment; the operation of communications equipment, use of codes and ciphers, and procurement of the most effective and efficient communications services; the operation of microform equipment, peripheral equipment, mail processing equipment, duplicating equipment, and copier/duplicating equipment; and other work of a general clerical and administrative nature.

0400 – Natural Resources Management and Biological Sciences

These positions include those whose duties are to advise on, administer, supervise, or perform research or other professional and scientific work or subordinate technical work in any of the fields of science concerned with living organisms, their distribution, characteristics, life processes, and adaptations and relations to the environment; the soil (its properties and distribution) and the living organisms growing in or on the soil; and the management, conservation, or utilization thereof for particular purposes or uses.

0500 – Accounting and Budget

This category includes those positions whose duties are to advise on, administer, supervise, or perform professional, technical, or related clerical work of an accounting, budget administration, related financial management, or similar nature.

0600 – Medical, Hospital, Dental, and Public Health

These positions include those whose duties are to advise on, administer, supervise, or perform research or other professional and scientific work, subordinate technical work, or related clerical work in the several branches of medicine, surgery, and dentistry or in related patient-care services such as dietetics, nursing, occupational therapy, physical therapy, pharmacy, and others.

0700 – Veterinary Medical Science

This category includes positions whose duties are to advise on, administer, manage, supervise, or perform professional or technical support work in the various branches of veterinary medical science.

0800 – Engineering and Architecture

These positions include those whose duties are to advise on, administer, supervise, or perform professional, scientific, or technical work concerned with engineering or architectural projects, facilities, structures, systems, processes, equipment, devices, material, or methods. Positions in this group require knowledge of the science or art, or both, by which materials, natural resources, and powers are made useful.

0900 – Legal and Kindred

This category includes positions whose duties are to advise on, administer, supervise, or perform work of a legal or similar nature. (See also 1200 below.)

1000 – Information and Arts

These positions include those that involve professional, artistic, technical, or clerical work in one of the following areas:

- the communication of information and ideas through verbal, visual, or pictorial means
- the collection, custody, presentation, display, and interpretation of art works, cultural objects, and other artifacts
- a branch of fine or applied arts such as industrial design, interior design, or musical composition

Positions in this group require writing, editing, and language ability; artistic skill and ability; knowledge of foreign languages; the ability to evaluate and interpret informational and cultural materials; or the practical application of technical or esthetic principles combined with manual skill and dexterity or related clerical skills.

1100 – Business and Industry

These positions include those whose duties are to advise on, administer, supervise, or perform work pertaining to and requiring a knowledge of business and trade practices, characteristics and use of equipment, products, or property, or industrial production methods and processes, including the conduct of investigations and studies; the collection, analysis, and dissemination of information; the establishment and maintenance of contacts with industry and commerce; the provision of advisory services; the examination and appraisement of merchandise or property; and the administration of regulatory provisions and controls.

1200 – Copyright, Patent, and Trademark

This category includes positions whose duties are to advise on, administer, supervise, or perform professional scientific, technical, and legal work involved in the cataloging and registration of copyrights, in the classification and issuance of patents, in the registration of trademarks, in the prosecution of applications for patents before the Patent Office, and in the giving of advice to Government officials on patent matters.

1300 – Physical Sciences

These positions include those whose duties are to advise on, administer, supervise, or perform research or other professional and scientific work, or subordinate technical work, in any of the fields of science concerned with matter, energy, physical space, time, nature of physical measurement, and fundamental structural particles; and the nature of the physical environment.

1400 – Library and Archives

These positions are for those whose duties are to advise on, administer, supervise, or perform professional and scientific work or subordinate technical work in the various phases of library and archival science.

1500 – Mathematical Sciences

This category includes positions whose duties are to advise on, administer, supervise, or perform research or other professional and scientific work or related clerical work in basic mathematical principles, methods, procedures, or relationships, including the development and application of mathematical methods for the investigation and solution of problems; the development and application of statistical theory in the selection, collection, classification, adjustment, analysis, and interpretation of data; the development and application of mathematical, statistical, and financial principles to programs or problems involving life and property risks; and any other professional and scientific or related clerical work requiring primarily and mainly the understanding and use of mathematical theories, methods, and operations.

1600 – Equipment, Facilities, and Services

These positions include those whose duties are to advise on, manage, or provide instructions and information concerning the operation, maintenance, and use of equipment, shops, buildings, laundries, printing plants, power plants, cemeteries, or other Government facilities, or other work involving services provided predominantly by persons in trades, crafts, or manual labor operations.

1700 – Education

This category includes positions whose duties are to involve administering, managing, supervising, performing, or supporting education or training work when the paramount requirement of the position is knowledge of, or skill in, education, training, or instruction processes.

1800 – Inspection, Investigation, Enforcement, and Compliance

These positions include those whose duties are to advise on, administer, supervise, or perform inspection, investigation, enforcement, or compliance work primarily concerned with alleged or suspected offenses against the laws of the United States, or such work primarily concerned with determining compliance with laws and regulations.

1900 – Quality Assurance, Inspection, and Grading

This category includes positions whose duties are to advise on, supervise, or perform administrative or technical work primarily concerned with the quality assurance or inspection of material, facilities, and processes; or with the grading of commodities under official standards.

2000 – Supply

The positions in this category involve work concerned with furnishing all types of supplies, equipment, material, property (except real estate), and certain services to components of the Federal Government, industrial, or other concerns under contract to the Government, or receiving supplies from the Federal Government. Included are positions concerned with one or more aspects of supply activities from initial planning, including requirements analysis and determination, through acquisition, cataloging, storage, distribution, and utilization to ultimate issue for consumption or disposal.

2100 – Transportation

This category includes positions whose duties are to advise on, administer, supervise, or perform clerical, administrative, or technical work involved in the provision of transportation service to the Government, the regulation of transportation utilities by the Government, or the management of Government-funded transportation programs, including transportation research and development projects.

2200 – Information Technology

The administrative positions in this category involve managing, supervising, leading, administering, developing, delivering, and supporting information technology (IT) systems and services. This series covers only those positions for which the principal requirement is knowledge of IT principles, concepts, and methods; e.g., data storage, software applications, networking. Information technology refers to systems and services used in the automated acquisition, storage, manipulation, management, movement, control, display, switching, interchange, transmission, assurance, or reception of information. Information technology includes computers, network components, peripheral equipment, software, firmware, services, and related resources.

TRADE, CRAFT, OR LABOR OCCUPATIONS

2500 – Wire Communications Equipment Installation and Maintenance

The occupations here are involved in the construction, installation, maintenance, repair, and testing of all types of wire communications systems and associated equipment that are predominantly electrical-mechanical.

2600 – Electronic Equipment Installation and Maintenance

These occupations involve the installation, repair, overhaul, fabrication, tuning, alignment, modification, calibration, and testing of electronic equipment and related devices such as radio, radar, loran, sonar, television, and other communications equipment; industrial controls; fire control, flight/landing control, bombing-navigation, and other integrated systems; and electronic computer systems and equipment.

2800 –   Electrical Installation and Maintenance

Occupations in this category are involved in the fabrication, installation, alteration, maintenance, repair, and testing of electrical systems, instruments, apparatus, and equipment.

3100 – Fabric and Leather Work

This category includes occupations that involve the fabrication, modification, and repair of clothing and equipment made of: (1) woven textile fabrics of animal, vegetable, or synthetic origin; (2) plastic film and filaments; (3) natural and simulated leather; (4) natural and synthetic fabrics; and (5) paper.

3300 – Instrument Work

These occupations involve fabricating, assembling, calibrating, testing, installing, repairing, modifying, and maintaining instruments and instrumentation systems for measuring, regulating, and computing physical quantities such as mass, moment, force, acceleration, displacement, stress, strain, vibration or oscillation frequency, phase and amplitude, linear or angular velocity, space-time position and attitude, pressure, temperature, density, viscosity, humidity, thermal or electrical conductivity, voltage, current, power, power factor, impedance, and radiation.

3400 – Machine Tool Work

Occupations in this category involve setting up and operating machine tools and using hand tools to make or repair (shape, fit, finish, assemble) metal parts, tools, gauges, models, patterns, mechanisms, and machines; and machining explosives and synthetic materials.

3500 – General Services and Support Work

These occupations are not specifically covered by another work family and require little or no specialized training or work experience. These occupations usually involve work such as moving and handling materials (e.g., loading, unloading, digging, hauling, hoisting, carrying, wrapping, mixing, pouring, spreading); washing and cleaning laboratory apparatus, cars, and trucks, etc; cleaning and maintaining living quarters, hospital rooms and wards, office buildings, grounds, and other areas; and doing other general maintenance work by hand or using common hand tools and power equipment. They may involve heavy or light physical work and various skill levels.

3600 – Structural and Finishing Work

Occupations in this category are not specifically covered by another work family and involve doing structural and finishing work in construction, maintenance, and repair of surfaces and structures (e.g., laying brick, block, and stone; setting tile; finishing cement and concrete; plastering; installing, maintaining, and repairing asphalt, tar, and gravel; roofing; insulating and glazing).

3700 – Metal Processing

These occupations involve processing or treating metals to alter their properties or produce desirable qualities such as hardness or workability, using processes such as welding, plating, melting, alloying, casting, annealing, heat treating, and refining.

3800 – Metal Work

The occupations in this category involves shaping and forming metal and making and repairing metal parts or equipment and includes such work as the fabrication and assembly of sheet metal parts and equipment; forging and press operations; structural iron working, boiler making, ship fitting, and other plate metal work; rolling, cutting, stamping, riveting, etc. It does not include machine tool work.

3900 – Motion Picture, Radio, Television, and Sound Equipment Operation

These occupations involve setting up, testing, operating, and making minor repairs to equipment such as microphones, sound and radio controls, sound recording equipment, lighting and sound effects devices, television cameras, magnetic video tape recorders, motion picture projectors, and broadcast transmitters used in the production of motion pictures and radio and television programs. It also includes occupations that involve related work such as operating public address system equipment.

4000 – Lens and Crystal Work

Occupations in this category involve making precision optical elements, crystal blanks or wafers, or other items of glass, crystalline substances, synthetics, polished metals, or similar materials, using such methods as cutting, etching, grinding, and polishing.

4100 – Painting and Paperhanging

The occupations listed here are those that involve hand or spray painting and decorating interiors and exteriors of buildings, structures, aircraft, vessels, mobile equipment, fixtures, furnishings, machinery, and other surfaces; finishing hardwoods, furniture, and cabinetry; painting signs; covering interiors of rooms with strips of wallpaper or fabric, and so on.

4200 – Plumbing and Pipefitting

Occupations in this category involve the installation, maintenance, and repair of water, air, steam, gas, sewer, and other pipelines and systems as well as related fixtures, apparatus, and accessories.

4300 – Pliable Materials Work

These occupations involve shaping, forming, and repairing items and parts from non-metallic moldable materials such as plastic, rubber, clay, wax, plaster, glass, sand, or other similar materials.

4400 – Printing Family

Occupations in this category involve letterpress (relief), offset-lithographic, gravure (intaglio), or screen printing. These occupations include layout, hand composition, photoengraving, plate making, printing, and finishing operations.

4600 – Wood Work

Occupations here are involved in the construction, alteration, repair, and maintenance of wooden buildings and other structures as well as the fabrication and repair of wood products such as furniture, foundry patterns, and form blocks, using power and hand tools.

4700 – General Maintenance and Operations Work

Occupations in this category consist of various combinations of work that are involved in constructing, maintaining, and repairing buildings, roads, grounds, and related facilities; manufacturing, modifying, and repairing items or apparatus made from a variety of materials or types of components; or repairing and operating equipment or utilities. These jobs require the application of a variety of trade practices associated with occupations in more than one job family (unless otherwise indicated) and the performance of the highest level of work in at least two of the trades involved.

4800 – General Equipment Maintenance

In this category, occupations involve the maintenance or repair of equipment, machines, or instruments that are not coded to other job families because the equipment is not characteristically related to one of the established subject matter areas, such as electronics, electrical, industrial, transportation, instruments, engines, aircraft, ordnance, and so on, or because the nature of the work calls for limited knowledge/skill in a variety of crafts or trades as they relate to the repair of such equipment, but not a predominate knowledge of any one trade or craft.

5000 – Plant and Animal Work

These occupations involve general or specialized farming operations; gardening, including the general care of grounds, roadways, nurseries, greenhouses, and so on; trimming and felling trees; and propagating, caring for, handling, and controlling animals and insects, including pest species.

5200 – Miscellaneous Occupations

Occupations in this category are not covered by the definition of any other job family or are of such a general or miscellaneous character as to preclude placing them within another job family.

5300 – Industrial Equipment Maintenance

These occupations involve the general maintenance, installation, and repair of portable and stationary industrial machinery, tools, and equipment such as sewing machines, machine tools, woodworking and metalworking machines, printing equipment, processing equipment, driving machinery, power generating equipment, air conditioning equipment, heating and boiler plant equipment, and other types of machines and equipment used in the production of goods and services.

5400 – Industrial Equipment Operation

The occupations in this category are involved in the operation of portable and stationary industrial equipment, tools, and machines to generate and distribute utilities such as electricity, steam, and gas for heat or power; treat and distribute water; collect, treat, and dispose of waste; open and close bridges, locks, and dams; lift and move workers, materials, and equipment; manufacture and process materials and products, and so on.

5700 – Transportation/Mobile Equipment Operation

These occupations involve the operation and operational maintenance of self-propelled transportation and other mobile equipment (except aircraft) used to move materials or passengers, including motor vehicles, engineering and construction equipment, tractors, and so on, some of which may be equipped with power takeoff and controls to operate special purpose equipment; ocean-going and inland waterway vessels, harbor craft, and floating plants; and trains, locomotives, and train cars.

5800 – Transportation/Mobile Equipment Maintenance

Occupations in this category involve repairing, adjusting, and maintaining self-propelled transportation and other mobile equipment (except aircraft), including any special purpose features with which they may be equipped.

6500 – Ammunition, Explosives, and Toxic Materials Work

The occupations in this category involve the manufacturing, assembling, disassembling, renovating, loading, deactivating, modifying, destroying, testing, handling, placing, and discharging of ammunition, propellants, chemicals and toxic materials, and other conventional and special munitions and explosives.

6600 – Armament Work

These occupations are involved in the installation, repair, rebuilding, adjustment, modification, and testing of small arms and artillery weapons and allied accessories. Artillery includes, but is not limited to, field artillery, antitank artillery, anti-aircraft weapons, aircraft and shipboard weapons, recoilless rifles, rocket launchers, mortars, cannons, and allied accessories. Small arms includes, but is not limited to, rifles, carbines, pistols, revolvers, helmets, body armor, shoulder-type rocket launchers, machine guns, and automatic rifles.

7000 – Packing and Processing

These occupations involve determining the measures required to protect items against damage during movement or storage; selecting proper method of packing, including type and size of container; cleaning, drying, and applying preservatives to materials, parts, or mechanical equipment; and packing equipment, parts, and materials.

7300 – Laundry, Dry Cleaning, and Pressing

Occupations in this category involve receiving, sorting, washing, drying, dry cleaning, dyeing, pressing, and preparing for delivery clothes, linens, and other articles requiring laundering, dry cleaning, or pressing.

7400 – Food Preparation and Serving

These occupations are involved in the preparation and serving of food.

7600 – Personal Services

In this category, the occupations are concerned with providing grooming, beauty, or other personal services to individuals, patrons, guests, passengers, entertainers, etc., or attending to their personal effects.

8200 – Fluid Systems Maintenance

Occupations in this category involve the repair, modification, assembly, and testing of fluid systems and fluid system components of aircraft, aircraft engines, missiles, and mobile and support equipment.

8600 – Engine Overhaul

These occupations are concerned primarily with the manufacture, repair, modification, and major overhaul of engines (except where covered by another group), including the disassembly, reassembly, and test phases of engine overhaul programs.

8800 – Aircraft Overhaul

In this category, the occupations are concerned primarily with the overhaul of aircraft, including the disassembly, reassembly, and test phases of aircraft overhaul programs.

9000 – Film Processing

These occupations involve processing film—for example, operating motion picture developers and printers; cleaning, repairing, matching, cutting, splicing, and assembling films; and mixing developing solutions. The work does not include processing work that requires specialized subject-matter knowledge or artistic ability.

*Source: http://help.usajobs.gov/index.php/What_occupations_are_available_in_the_federal_government

State and Municipal Government Jobs

The list below shows representative jobs in state and local government entities. The list is typical of all states and the largest municipalities. The number of jobs in a municipality depends on the size of the city, township, or village. The larger the governmental unit, the more jobs there are. At the local municipal level, the school district is often the largest employer.

The responsibilities of state and local governments are typically divided among a number of departments, agencies, offices, commissions, boards, and councils at the administrative and legislative levels. The titles depend on the state or locality. Jobs range from administrative assistants and clerks to lawyers and paralegals to facilities managers and food service workers. States and local governments also have judiciaries and employ lawyers, bailiffs and corrections officers, court reporters, and administrators. State and municipal office buildings and courthouses require maintenance personnel and security guards.

Some states also have strong county governmental structures. (In Louisiana, they are called parishes.) These may include county prosecutor/district attorney offices, county welfare departments, municipal water districts that connect several cities or townships, county public works departments that take care of county roads, and transportation districts that coordinate countywide networks of buses, subways, trolleys, and trains. All these services need to be staffed.

To find out about state or local government jobs in your area, go online to your state government website, and look for buttons related to employment, careers, or jobs. Some states list local government job postings as well as state openings. If you can't find local job announcements on the state site, check the website for the municipality you're interested in working for.

Not all jobs on the state and municipal levels require civil service exams. Some jobs are listed as non-civil service while others—such as administrative and clerical positions—may be either, depending on the department or agency the job is with.

ADMINISTRATIVE, ACCOUNTING, AND FISCAL CONTROL

Government officials need updated financial information to make decisions. Accountants and auditors prepare, analyze, and verify financial reports that inform those decisions. In addition, auditors, economists, and statisticians work for other areas of government that require their expertise. Lawyers also provide services to many departments within state and local governments as well as staff the Attorney General's office at the state level and the district attorney/prosecutor level at municipal and county levels.

appendix b

Accident record reviewer
Accountant
Actuary
Appeals examiner
Auditor/examiner
Audit account clerk
Budget analyst
Business analyst
Economist
Human resources assistant, supervisor
Insurance investigator
Legal assistant/paralegal
Life and health insurance policy examiner
Management analyst
Medical malpractice claims examiner, supervisor
Municipal court administrator
Pensions benefit specialist
Purchasing agent
Real estate appraiser, technician, specialist
Retirement administrator
Retirement benefits specialist, supervisor, technician
Staff attorney
Statistician
Unemployment compensation tax agent
Workers' compensation analyst

CLERICAL

Clerks perform a variety of administrative and clerical duties necessary to run state and local governments. Often, applicants must pass a written clerical and verbal abilities test.

Cashier
Clerk bookkeeper
Clerical and secretarial
Clerk transcriber
Clerk typist
Computer operator: keyboarding clerk, purchasing assistant, account clerk
Payroll clerk
Records specialist, supervisor
Secretarial supervisor
Stenographer
Stock clerk

EDUCATION

In addition to the traditional pre-kindergarten to 12th-grade educational systems, states and local municipalities offer other types of educational services. Correctional institutions on the state and county level may offer high school and vocational courses.

Adult basic and literacy education teacher
Adult basic education teacher
Alcohol education teacher
Business occupations teacher
Career and technical education teacher
Corrections activities specialist
Corrections education teacher
Corrections school principal
Curriculum specialist
Early childhood education teacher
Education administrator
Education aide
Education certification evaluator
Educational assessment specialist
Educator, K–12
Environmental education specialist
Food and nutrition services advisor
Guidance counselor
Nursing educator
Professional librarian
Special education teacher
Vocational teacher

ENGINEERING AND ENVIRONMENTAL CONTROL

Although many engineers work in design and development positions, others work in testing, production, operations, and maintenance.

Air monitoring equipment specialist
Air quality engineer and engineering specialist
Aquatic resources program specialist
Architect
Bridge and structural designer
Chemist
Civil engineer, manager: hydraulic, bridge, transportation
District utility manager
Drafter, drafter/designer
Ecological program specialist
Electrical engineer
Environmental engineer, interpretive technician
Environmental project construction inspector, supervisor

Environmental protection compliance specialist
Forester, program specialist, technician
Geologic scientist, specialist
Highway drafter, designer
Materials technicians
Mechanical engineer
Mineral resources program specialist
Mining engineer, specialist, permit and compliance specialist
Natural resources specialist
Nuclear safety specialist
Park manager, ranger
Plant pathologist
Radiation health physicist
Roadway programs specialist, manager, coordinator
Surveyor, technician
Traffic control specialist, technician
Transportation construction inspector, supervisor, manager
Wildlife biologist

INFORMATION TECHNOLOGY

A great variety of opportunities exist in the area of information technology. Jobs range from data-entry operators to computer specialists in applied programming. Much of the work involves database entry and management.

Applications developer and administrator
Data administrator
Data analyst
Database analyst and administrator
Information technology generalists and administrators
Information technology technicians
Computer service technician
Network specialists and administrators
Telecommunications specialists

LAW ENFORCEMENT, INVESTIGATION, AND SAFETY

The federal government has 65 federal agencies and 27 offices of inspector general that deal with law enforcement and investigation. There are more than 17,000 state and local law enforcement agencies divided among local police forces such as municipal, county, tribal, and regional forces; state police and highway patrol; special jurisdiction police such as housing authority police and school security; and deputy sheriffs who police local jails and serve court summonses and warrants. Other jobs in enforcement include corrections officers who oversee prisons.

Investigative positions include investigators who examine claims for benefits or compensation to ensure that they are valid and conform to regulations, gather evidence of fraud and other wrongdoing that is then used in legal actions, and discover violations of rules and regulations.

While villages and small towns and cities may rely heavily on volunteer firefighters, they may also have some full-time firefighters. Larger cities have paid fire companies. Some include EMTs. In addition to putting out fires, fire departments are responsible for fire prevention and education.

Agricultural commodity inspector
Agricultural products inspector, technician
Campus police officer
Capitol police officer
Case monitor, juvenile justice
Code enforcement officer
Commissioned boiler inspector, supervisor,
Community corrections center director
Corrections officer
Court clerk
Court liaison program specialist
Domestic animal health inspector
Driver license center manager, inspector
Emergency management watch officer, specialist
Forensic scientist
Institutional parole assistant
Institutional safety manager
Laboratory system quality specialist
Milk sanitarian
Mine electrical inspector
Mine inspector
Mine safety emergency response and training specialist
Mortuary inspector
Operations center monitor
Parole agent, supervisor, counselor
Plant industry field technician, inspector
Public utility enforcement officer
Railroad safety inspector
Regional traffic management center operator and supervisor
Regulatory enforcement inspector, supervisor
Securities investigator
Security officer
Seed analyst
Special investigator
Building inspector, supervisor, plans examiner
Elevator inspector, supervisor
Workers' compensation health and safety training specialist

MEDICAL AND HEALTH SERVICES

With the continuing growth of medical knowledge and the increasing demands of an aging population, state and local governments increasingly need physicians, medical researchers, nurses, physician's assistants, physical therapists, occupational therapists, and similar health-care workers.

Certified registered nurse practitioner
Clinic nurse
Clinical dietitian
Community health nurse
Dental hygienist, dentist
Disability physician specialist
Drug program specialist
Epidemiologist, epidemiology program specialist, research associate
Health facility quality examiner, supervisor
Health systems specialist
Laboratory technologists
Licensed occupational therapist, assistant
Licensed practical nurse
Medical assistance program technician
Medical facility and records examiner, supervisor
Medical records assistant, supervisor
Medical technologist
Nurse manager, nursing director
Nursing practice adviser
Nursing services consultant
Occupational therapist
Pharmacist, assistant
Physical therapist, registered assistant
Public health nutrition consultant, physician
Registered nurse
Registry technician, specialist
Speech, language, and hearing specialist
Veterinary laboratory diagnostician
Veterinary medical field officer

SOCIAL AND EMPLOYMENT SERVICES

People who work in the social welfare field are community troubleshooters. Through direct counseling, referral to other services, or policymaking and advocacy, they help individuals, families, and groups cope with their problems. Often, the problems are related to unemployment. State employment offices, known as American Job Centers, are a major source of help for the unemployed.

Aging care manager, case aide, program assessor
Childcare caseworker, supervisor

County care management manager, supervisor, caseworker, program specialist

Drug and alcohol case management specialist, prevention program specialist, program analyst, treatment specialist

Employment counselor

Meal transporter and van driver

Mental health/mental retardation staff specialist, county social work training specialist, community services area manager, unit manager

Senior Center manager, program specialists, aides

Social worker, supervisor, manager

Therapeutic activities aide

Unemployment claims examiner, supervisor, intake interviewer

Veterans' employment representative

Vocational rehabilitation counselor

Youth development counselor, aide, supervisor

TRADES AND MAINTENANCE

Increasingly, formal training acquired in high school, vocational or technical school, community college, or in the armed services is an asset for those entering the trades. Some trades also provide apprenticeship programs, but the number of apprentices accepted in any location is usually small. Many maintenance positions require no formal education, qualification, or experience. Some jobs, such as those that involve lifting heavy objects, may require a physical exam.

Automotive and diesel mechanic, supervisor, equipment foreman

Boiler plant operator

Building construction inspector

Carpenter

Construction inspector supervisor and manager

Corrections industry foreman and supervisor

Custodial supervisor and manager

Electrical construction inspector

Electrician

Food service personnel

Forest and park maintenance supervisor

Highway drilling operator

Housekeeper

Maintenance repairer, foreman, supervisor

Mason

Painter

Parks maintenance

Plasterer

Plumber

Semi-skilled laborer

Steamfitter

Wastewater treatment plant operator

Water treatment plant operator

Hiring Veterans

"Feds Hire Vets" (www.fedshirevets.gov) is the "single site for Federal employment information for Veterans, transitioning military service members, their families, and Federal hiring officials." Feds Hire Vets is the Office of Personnel Management's government-wide Veterans Employment website, a joint effort of the Departments of Defense, Labor, Veterans Affairs, Homeland Security, and other federal agencies. The website is part of the federal government's strategy for recruiting and employing veterans.

On November 9, 2009, President Barack Obama signed the act establishing the Veterans Employment Initiative, a plan for helping men and women who have served in the military find employment in the federal government. As the website says, the plan "underscores the importance of aligning the talents of these individuals with key positions so the Government is better positioned to meet mission objectives and citizens are better served."

On the Feds Hire Vets website, you can find a dashboard with buttons for job seekers and hiring officials; a directory of federal agencies with contact names, numbers, and e-mail addresses; and buttons for multimedia and success stories to provide an overview of how other veterans and their family members have gotten jobs in the federal government. There is also an "About Us" button that offers a list of FAQs about government policies for hiring veterans. In addition, the site offers lists of tips for job hunters and scheduled webinars on topics of interest to those wishing to work for the federal government.

Like other federal jobseekers, the primary tool for veterans looking for jobs is www.usajobs.gov, the employment site of the Office of Personnel Management. The site lists all the federal job openings available anywhere in the nation. The site offers tutorials, FAQs, and a "Resume Builder". You can set up an account, work on your resume and store it for later submission, and apply for jobs through usajobs.gov.

VETERANS PREFERENCE POINTS

Giving veterans preference in hiring has been a federal government policy since the Civil War. A law enacted in 1944 and amended several times since sets up a hiring preference system for disabled veterans and those who served on active duty during certain military actions or time periods. Members of all five branches of the armed forces are eligible: Army, Navy, Air Force, Marine Corps, and Coast Guard. The law entitles them "to preference over others in hiring from competitive lists of [those] eligible and also in retention during reductions in force." The law also applies to family members under certain circumstances. Not all jobs in the federal government are open to the use of preference points, but many are.

To be eligible for preference points, a veteran must have received an honorable or general discharge. Veterans with ranks at or above major and lieutenant commander are not eligible for preference points.

Candidates for jobs who are veterans may have five points added to their examination score or rating if they served:

- During a war.

- During the period April 28, 1952 through July 1, 1955.

- For more than 180 consecutive days, not counting training, any part of which occurred after January 31, 1955, and before October 15, 1976.

- During the Gulf War from August 2, 1990, through January 2, 1992.

- For more than 180 consecutive days, not including training, any part of which occurred during the period beginning September 11, 2001, and ending on the date prescribed by Presidential proclamation or by law as the last day of Operation Iraqi Freedom.

- In a campaign or expedition for which a campaign medal has been authorized.

In addition, any Armed Forces Expeditionary medal or campaign badge, including El Salvador, Lebanon, Grenada, Panama, Southwest Asia, Somali, and Haiti, qualifies for preference.

Veterans with service-connected disabilities have 10 preference points added to their examination score or rating if they have served at any time and have a

- compensable service-connected disability rating of between 10 percent and 30 percent or higher.

- current service-connected disability, or are receiving compensation, disability retirement benefits, or pension, or have received a Purple Heart.

In addition to veterans, family members may be eligible for preference points. Ten points are added to the passing examination score or rating of the following family members:

- Spouse of a disabled veteran who cannot work in his or her usual occupation because of a service-connected disability

- Widow or widower of a veteran who served honorably during a particular campaign, expedition, or time period or who died while on active duty

- Mother of a deceased veteran who served and died honorably during a particular campaign, expedition, or time period

- Mother of a disabled veteran who served honorably including training in the Reserves or National Guard and is permanently and totally disabled because of a service-connected injury or illness

For additional information on preference points, check the "Veterans" button on the OPM.gov main site and then click on "Veterans Services," which has links to a number of information sources including the Vet Guide.

STATE RECOGNITION OF VETERANS PREFERENCE POINTS

State governments also have programs providing preference points to veterans who have served in the armed forces honorably, whether sustaining a service-connected disability or not. The state programs generally follow the federal government's criteria and points system, but some states also grant preference points for service in their state's National Guard. Spouses, including partners in civil unions, may also be included in some state programs.

Hiring People with Disabilities

The federal government actively recruits and hires people with disabilities. President Barack Obama signed an Executive Order in 2010 directing the federal government to "become a model for the employment of individuals with disabilities." Under the Executive Order, departments and agencies are to increase their recruitment, hiring, and retention of people with disabilities. The goal is 100,000 new employees with disabilities by 2015. The reasons for these activities are twofold: it's the right thing to do, and it enlarges the candidate pool of highly qualified people.

There are two routes to employment for those with disabilities. One is noncompetitively through Schedule A Authority, and the other is through the traditional or competitive process.

To be eligible to be considered for employment under Schedule A, a person must have a severe physical disability, a psychiatric disability, or an intellectual disability. To prove eligibility, a candidate must be qualified for the job, that is, have the competencies and relevant experience; show proof of disability, which is a Schedule A letter of disability; and possibly (but not necessarily) provide a certification of job readiness, meaning that he or she is able to perform the duties of the job under consideration.

A doctor, licensed medical professional, or licensed vocational rehabilitation specialist may write the letter documenting a candidate's disability. The hiring agency will also accept a letter from any federal, state, or local agency that issues or provides disability benefits. Some agencies may accept the certification of job readiness as part of the proof of disability letter or they may require a separate letter. You may find that an agency will accept your resume as enough proof of your ability to perform the duties of the job you're interested in.

The Office of Personnel Management (OPM) is very clear that being eligible for a Schedule A appointment does not guarantee a person a job, but it does help in the hiring process. Once hired, a person who received a Schedule A appointment undergoes a probationary period, which may last up to two years. The amount of time depends on the job. While on probation, the employee is expected to perform the job at the same level of competency as other employees.

The U.S. Equal Employment Opportunity Commission's initiative to tackle the declining number of employees with targeted disabilities in the federal workforce is known as LEAD (Leadership for the Employment of Americans with Disabilities). On the LEAD website, www.eeoc.gov/eeoc/initiatives/lead/index.cfm, you can download a PDF or HTML copy of *The ABCs of Schedule A,* which is a handy reference guide for applying for federal jobs under Schedule A.

GETTING HELP IN THE FEDERAL HIRING PROCESS

One of the first things that the OPM website advises potential candidates to do is to contact their Selective Placement Program Coordinator (SSPC) for help and advice. To aid potential candidates in finding jobs, most federal agencies have established the position of Selective Placement Program Coordinator (SPPC). SPCCs help agencies recruit, hire, and accommodate people with disabilities and assist potential candidates to navigate the hiring process.

Each agency with SPPCs maintains regional field offices with coordinators who are there to assist hiring managers and candidates. Selective Placement Program Coordinators can help individuals learn about job opportunities and the types of jobs that become available in their agencies. SSPCs can also advise on reasonable accommodations for jobs. Among their duties for hiring managers, SPPCs identify the essential duties of a job and any physical barriers to successful employment of a person with a disability for that job. They suggest possible modifications to the physical environment and reasonable accommodations.

On the SPPC website, http://apps.opm.gov/sppc_directory/, you can find a directory of regional field offices with the names and contact information of the local coordinators. You can search by state to find all SSPCs in the state or by department if you are interested in a job in a particular department such as Agriculture or Homeland Security. Many agencies also have a Disability Program Manager.

Veterans with service-connected disabilities are eligible for special consideration in the hiring process. They may have 10 preference points added to their passing exam score or rating. Families members of veterans with service-connected disabilities may also under certain circumstances receive 10 preference points toward their passing exam score or rating. For more information, check out www.fedshirevets.gov.

PROVIDING ACCOMMODATIONS

Federal agencies are required under the Rehabilitation Act of 1973 to provide reasonable adjustments to the work environment for employees and candidates for jobs who have disabilities. A reasonable accommodation as defined by the OPM is "any change in the work environment or the way things are usually done that enables an individual with a disability to enjoy Equal Employment Opportunity." A reasonable accommodation would be a sign language interpreter or a workstation that is accessible for an employee in a wheelchair.

The Americans with Disabilities Act of 1990 (ADA), as amended, extended reasonable accommodations to all Americans in work situations, among other rights. State and local governments also cannot discriminate in hiring practices against those with disabilities and must provide reasonable accommodations as defined by law.

The Law

The ADA extends to applicants and employees of most private employers, state and local governments, educational institutions, employment agencies, and labor organizations. Titles I and V of the ADA protect qualified individuals with disabilities from discrimination in hiring, promotion, termination, pay, fringe benefits, job training, classification, referral, and other aspects of employment.

Disability discrimination includes refraining from making reasonable accommodation to the known physical or mental limitations of an otherwise qualified applicant or employee who has a disability. However, the word *reasonable* qualifies this situation. The employer does not have to comply if the accommodation would cause undue hardship to the employer. The requirement to provide reasonable accommodation is a key component of ADA.

State and Municipal Hiring Practices

In looking for information on state hiring practices, you may find a disclaimer on a state employment site that the state is an equal opportunity employer. A state may also have an affirmative action policy that directs its hiring managers in state departments and agencies to make all efforts to hire people with disabilities. Even if you can't find such a statement or policy, ADA requires nondiscrimination in the hiring of people with disabilities. The same is true for county, city, town, village, and special district employers.